My PC stuff!

Fill in the following vital information about your computer.

Make & Model: _____

Network name (if any): _____

Microprocessor: _____

RAM: _____ MB

Hard drive capacity: _ _____ MB/GB

Graphics: _____

Serial number: _____

Drive A is my first floppy drive!

Drive A is a: 3¹/₂-inch   5¹/₄-inch

Drive A is on: Top   Bottom

Drive B is my second floppy drive!

Drive B is a: 3¹/₂-inch   5¹/₄-inch

Drive B is on: Top   Bottom

I have no drive B!

Drive C is my hard drive!

I have other drives in my computer.

Drive D is a: Hard drive   CD-ROM   _____

Drive ___ is a: Hard drive   CD-ROM   _____

Drive ___ is a: Hard drive   CD-ROM   _____

Here are other drives I use on the network!

Drive letter   Network PC   Pathname

Drive ___ is on: _____ _____

Drive ___ is on: _____ _____

What plugs into what?

Circle the following items as they apply to your PC.

My modem is on: COM1 COM2 COM3 COM4

My modem speed is: 14.4K 28.8K 33.6K 56K

My printer plugs into: LPT1 LPT2 LPT3

Important numbers

Fill in the following information for your PC hardware.

My dealer: _____ _____

My sales rep's name and extension:

_____ _____

My dealer tech support line:

_____

Operating system tech support:

_____

Fill in the following information for your software. Write in the application name first, and then the tech support number.

Application: _____

Tech Support: _____

Application: _____

Tech Support: _____

Application: _____

Tech Support: _____

...For Dummies: Bestselling Book Series

PCs For Dummies®, 6th Edition

Cheat Sheet

Stuff you have to write down anyway

Windows login/network ID: _____

CompuServe account number: _____

Prodigy account name: _____

AOL login ID: _____

Internet address: _____

Internet Service Provider's phone number: _____

Helpful hints for using your PC

Always quit Windows properly. Choose Sh<u>u</u>tdown from the Start menu; press Ctrl+Esc, U. Click OK. Never just turn your PC off.

Click on the Start button to pop-up the main Start menu. You can also press the Ctrl+Esc key combination.

Start any program in your PC by using the <u>P</u>rograms submenu on the main Start menu.

The desktop is the background you look at in Windows, the thing icons and windows float on.

The taskbar along the bottom of the screen contains buttons, one for each program or window that is running on the desktop.

☒ Close any window or quit any program by clicking on its little X close button.

Use My Computer to familiarize yourself with disk drives, folders, and icons — the way Windows shows you the information inside your computer.

The Help key! Your keyboard lacks a proper Help key, but Windows uses F1 as the Help key. To drive this point home, clip out the little Help key cap to the left and paste it over your keyboard's F1 key. There. Now you have an official *PCs For Dummies* Help key.

...For Dummies: Bestselling Book Series for Beginners

TM

References for the Rest of Us!®

BESTSELLING BOOK SERIES FROM IDG

Are you intimidated and confused by computers? Do you find that traditional manuals are overloaded with technical details you'll never use? Do your friends and family always call you to fix simple problems on their PCs? Then the *...For Dummies*® computer book series from IDG Books Worldwide is for you.

...For Dummies books are written for those frustrated computer users who know they aren't really dumb but find that PC hardware, software, and indeed the unique vocabulary of computing make them feel helpless. *...For Dummies* books use a lighthearted approach, a down-to-earth style, and even cartoons and humorous icons to diffuse computer novices' fears and build their confidence. Lighthearted but not lightweight, these books are a perfect survival guide for anyone forced to use a computer.

"I like my copy so much I told friends; now they bought copies."

— Irene C., Orwell, Ohio

"Quick, concise, nontechnical, and humorous."

— Jay A., Elburn, Illinois

"Thanks, I needed this book. Now I can sleep at night."

— Robin F., British Columbia, Canada

Already, millions of satisfied readers agree. They have made *...For Dummies* books the #1 introductory level computer book series and have written asking for more. So, if you're looking for the most fun and easy way to learn about computers, look to *...For Dummies* books to give you a helping hand.

TM

IDG BOOKS WORLDWIDE

8/98

PCs FOR DUMMIES®
6TH EDITION

by Dan Gookin

IDG Books Worldwide, Inc.
An International Data Group Company

Foster City, CA ♦ Chicago, IL ♦ Indianapolis, IN ♦ New York, NY

PCs For Dummies,® 6th Edition

Published by
IDG Books Worldwide, Inc.
An International Data Group Company
919 E. Hillsdale Blvd.
Suite 400
Foster City, CA 94404
www.idgbooks.com (IDG Books Worldwide Web site)
www.dummies.com (Dummies Press Web site)

Library of Congress Catalog Card No.: 98-87442

ISBN: 0-7645-0435-5

Printed in the United States of America

10 9 8 7 6 5 4 3 2 1

6B/SR/QZ/ZY/IN

Distributed in the United States by IDG Books Worldwide, Inc.

Distributed by Macmillan Canada for Canada; by Transworld Publishers Limited in the United Kingdom; by IDG Norge Books for Norway; by IDG Sweden Books for Sweden; by Woodslane Pty. Ltd. for Australia; by Woodslane (NZ) Ltd. for New Zealand; by Addison Wesley Longman Singapore Pte Ltd. for Singapore, Malaysia, Thailand, Indonesia and Korea; by Norma Comunicaciones S.A. for Colombia; by Intersoft for South Africa; by International Thomson Publishing for Germany, Austria and Switzerland; by Toppan Company Ltd. for Japan; by Distribuidora Cuspide for Argentina; by Livraria Cultura for Brazil; by Ediciencia S.A. for Ecuador; by Ediciones ZETA S.C.R. Ltda. for Peru; by WS Computer Publishing Corporation, Inc., for the Philippines; by Unalis Corporation for Taiwan; by Contemporanea de Ediciones for Venezuela; by Computer Book & Magazine Store for Puerto Rico; by Express Computer Distributors for the Caribbean and West Indies. Authorized Sales Agent: Anthony Rudkin Associates for the Middle East and North Africa.

For general information on IDG Books Worldwide's books in the U.S., please call our Consumer Customer Service department at 800-762-2974. For reseller information, including discounts and premium sales, please call our Reseller Customer Service department at 800-434-3422.

For information on where to purchase IDG Books Worldwide's books outside the U.S., please contact our International Sales department at 650-655-3200 or fax 650-655-3297.

For information on foreign language translations, please contact our Foreign & Subsidiary Rights department at 650-655-3021 or fax 650-655-3281.

For sales inquiries and special prices for bulk quantities, please contact our Sales department at 650-655-3200 or write to the address above.

For information on using IDG Books Worldwide's books in the classroom or for ordering examination copies, please contact our Educational Sales department at 800-434-2086 or fax 317-596-5499.

For press review copies, author interviews, or other publicity information, please contact our Public Relations department at 650-655-3000 or fax 650-655-3299.

For authorization to photocopy items for corporate, personal, or educational use, please contact Copyright Clearance Center, 222 Rosewood Drive, Danvers, MA 01923, or fax 978-750-4470.

is a trademark under exclusive license to IDG Books Worldwide, Inc., from International Data Group, Inc.

About the Author

Dan Gookin got started with computers back in the post vacuum tube age of computing: 1982. His first intention was to buy a computer to replace his aged and constantly breaking typewriter. Working as slave labor in a restaurant, however, Gookin was unable to afford the full "word processor" setup and settled on a computer that had a monitor, a keyboard, and little else. Soon his writing career was under way with several submissions to fiction magazines and lots of rejections.

The big break came in 1984, when he began writing about computers. Applying his flair for fiction with a self-taught knowledge of computers, Gookin was able to demystify the subject and explain technology in a relaxed and understandable voice. He even dared to add humor, which eventually won him a column in a local computer magazine.

Eventually Gookin's talents came to roost as a ghostwriter at a computer book publishing house. That was followed by an editing position at a San Diego computer magazine. During this time, he also regularly participated on a radio talk show about computers. In addition, Gookin kept writing books about computers, some of which became minor bestsellers.

In 1990, Gookin came to IDG Books Worldwide with a proposal. From that initial meeting unfolded an idea for an outrageous book: a long overdue and original idea for the computer book for the rest of us. What became *DOS For Dummies* blossomed into an international bestseller with hundreds of thousands of copies in print and many translations.

Today, Gookin still considers himself a writer and computer "guru" whose job it is to remind everyone that computers are not to be taken too seriously. His approach to computers is light and humorous yet very informative. He knows the complex beasts are important and can help people become productive and successful. Gookin mixes his knowledge of computers with a unique, dry sense of humor that keeps everyone informed — and awake. His favorite quote is "Computers are a notoriously dull subject, but that doesn't mean I have to write about them that way."

Gookin's titles for IDG Books include *Word 97 For Windows For Dummies, C For Dummies, Buying a Computer For Dummies,* and the *Illustrated Computer Dictionary For Dummies.* All told, he's written more than 50 books about computers, some of which he's written more than once. Gookin holds a degree in communications from the University of California, San Diego, and lives with his wife and four boys in the hinterlands of Idaho.

Dan can be contacted via e-mail at dang@idgbooks.com.

ABOUT IDG BOOKS WORLDWIDE

Welcome to the world of IDG Books Worldwide.

IDG Books Worldwide, Inc., is a subsidiary of International Data Group, the world's largest publisher of computer-related information and the leading global provider of information services on information technology. IDG was founded more than 25 years ago and now employs more than 8,500 people worldwide. IDG publishes more than 275 computer publications in over 75 countries (see listing below). More than 90 million people read one or more IDG publications each month.

Launched in 1990, IDG Books Worldwide is today the #1 publisher of best-selling computer books in the United States. We are proud to have received eight awards from the Computer Press Association in recognition of editorial excellence and three from *Computer Currents'* First Annual Readers' Choice Awards. Our best-selling ...*For Dummies*® series has more than 50 million copies in print with translations in 38 languages. IDG Books Worldwide, through a joint venture with IDG's Hi-Tech Beijing, became the first U.S. publisher to publish a computer book in the People's Republic of China. In record time, IDG Books Worldwide has become the first choice for millions of readers around the world who want to learn how to better manage their businesses.

Our mission is simple: Every one of our books is designed to bring extra value and skill-building instructions to the reader. Our books are written by experts who understand and care about our readers. The knowledge base of our editorial staff comes from years of experience in publishing, education, and journalism — experience we use to produce books for the '90s. In short, we care about books, so we attract the best people. We devote special attention to details such as audience, interior design, use of icons, and illustrations. And because we use an efficient process of authoring, editing, and desktop publishing our books electronically, we can spend more time ensuring superior content and spend less time on the technicalities of making books.

You can count on our commitment to deliver high-quality books at competitive prices on topics you want to read about. At IDG Books Worldwide, we continue in the IDG tradition of delivering quality for more than 25 years. You'll find no better book on a subject than one from IDG Books Worldwide.

John Kilcullen
CEO
IDG Books Worldwide, Inc.

Steven Berkowitz
President and Publisher
IDG Books Worldwide, Inc.

Eighth Annual Computer Press Awards ≥1992

Ninth Annual Computer Press Awards ≥1993

Tenth Annual Computer Press Awards ≥1994

Eleventh Annual Computer Press Awards ≥1995

IDG Books Worldwide, Inc., is a subsidiary of International Data Group, the world's largest publisher of computer-related information and the leading global provider of information services on information technology. International Data Group publishes over 275 computer publications in over 75 countries. More than 90 million people read one or more International Data Group publications each month. International Data Group's publications include: **ARGENTINA:** Buyer's Guide, Computerworld Argentina, PC World Argentina; **AUSTRALIA:** Australian Macworld, Australian PC World, Australian Reseller News, Computerworld, IT Casebook, Network World, Publish, Webmaster; **AUSTRIA:** Computerwelt Osterreich, Networks Austria, PC Tip Austria; **BANGLADESH:** PC World Bangladesh; **BELARUS:** PC World Belarus; **BELGIUM:** Data News; **BRAZIL:** Annuário de Informática, Computerworld, Connections, Macworld, PC Player, PC World, Publish, Reseller News, Supergamepower; **BULGARIA:** Computerworld Bulgaria, Network World Bulgaria, PC & MacWorld Bulgaria; **CANADA:** CIO Canada, Client/Server World, ComputerWorld Canada, InfoWorld Canada, NetworkWorld Canada, WebWorld; **CHILE:** Computerworld Chile, PC World Chile; **COLOMBIA:** Computerworld Colombia, PC World Colombia; **COSTA RICA:** PC World Centro America; **THE CZECH AND SLOVAK REPUBLICS:** Computerworld Czechoslovakia, Macworld Czech Republic, PC World Czechoslovakia; **DENMARK:** Communications World Danmark, Computerworld Danmark, Macworld Danmark, PC World Danmark, Techworld Denmark; **DOMINICAN REPUBLIC:** PC World Republica Dominicana; **ECUADOR:** PC World Ecuador; **EGYPT:** Computerworld Middle East, PC World Middle East; **EL SALVADOR:** PC World Centro America; **FINLAND:** MikroPC, Tietoverkko, Tietoviikko; **FRANCE:** Distributique, Hebdo, Info PC, Le Monde Informatique, Macworld, Reseaux & Telecoms, WebMaster France; **GERMANY:** Computer Partner, Computerwoche, Computerwoche Extra, Computerwoche FOCUS, Global Online, Macwelt, PC Welt; **GREECE:** Amiga Computing, GamePro Greece, Multimedia World; **GUATEMALA:** PC World Centro America; **HONDURAS:** PC World Centro America; **HONG KONG:** Computerworld Hong Kong, PC World Hong Kong, Publish in Asia; **HUNGARY:** ABCD CD-ROM, Computerworld Szamitastechnika, Internetto online Magazine, PC World Hungary, PC-X Magazin Hungary; **ICELAND:** Tolvuheimur PC World Island; **INDIA:** Information Communications World, Information Systems Computerworld, PC World India, Publish in Asia; **INDONESIA:** InfoKomputer PC World, Komputek Computerworld, Publish in Asia; **IRELAND:** ComputerScope, PC Live!; **ISRAEL:** Macworld Israel, People & Computers/Computerworld; **ITALY:** Computerworld Italia, Macworld Italia, Networking Italia, PC World Italia; **JAPAN:** DTP World, Macworld Japan, Nikkei Personal Computing, OS/2 World Japan, SunWorld Japan, Windows NT World, Windows World Japan; **KENYA:** PC World East African; **KOREA:** Hi-Tech Information, Macworld Korea, PC World Korea; **MACEDONIA:** PC World Macedonia; **MALAYSIA:** Computerworld Malaysia, PC World Malaysia, Publish in Asia; **MALTA:** PC World Malta; **MEXICO:** Computerworld Mexico, PC World Mexico; **MYANMAR:** PC World Myanmar; **NETHERLANDS:** Computer! Totaal, LAN Internetworking Magazine, LAN World Buyers Guide, Macworld Netherlands, Net, WebWereld, WebWorld; **NEW ZEALAND:** Absolute Beginners Guide and Plain & Simple Series, Computer Buyer, Computer Industry Directory, Computerworld New Zealand, MTB, Network World, PC World New Zealand; **NICARAGUA:** PC World Centro America; **NORWAY:** Computerworld Norge, CW Rapport, Datamagasinet, Financial Rapport, Kursguide Norge, Macworld Norge, Multimediaworld Norge, PC World Ekspress Norge, PC World Nettverk, PC World Norge, PC World ProduktGuide Norge; **PAKISTAN:** Computerworld Pakistan; **PANAMA:** PC World Panama; **PEOPLE'S REPUBLIC OF CHINA:** China Computer Users, China Computerworld, China InfoWorld, China Telecom World Weekly, Computer & Communication, Electronic Design China, Electronics Today, Electronics Weekly, Game Software, PC World China, Popular Computer Week, Software Weekly, Software World, Telecom World; **PERU:** Computerworld Peru, PC World Profesional Peru, PC World SoHo Peru; **PHILIPPINES:** Click!, Computerworld Philippines, PC World Philippines, Publish in Asia; **POLAND:** Computerworld Poland, Computerworld Special Report Poland, Cyber, Macworld Poland, Networld Poland, PC World Komputer; **PORTUGAL:** Cerebro/PC World, Computerworld/Correio Informático, Dealer World Portugal, Mac*In/PC*In Portugal, Multimedia World; **PUERTO RICO:** PC World Puerto Rico; **ROMANIA:** Computerworld Romania, PC World Romania, Telecom Romania; **RUSSIA:** Computerworld Russia, Mir PK, Publish, Seti; **SINGAPORE:** Computerworld Singapore, PC World Singapore, Publish in Asia; **SLOVENIA:** Monitor; **SOUTH AFRICA:** Computing SA, Network World SA, Software World SA; **SPAIN:** Communicaciones World España, Computerworld España, Dealer World España, Macworld España, PC World España; **SRI LANKA:** Infolink PC World; **SWEDEN:** CAP&Design, Computer Sweden, Corporate Computing Sweden, Internetworld Sweden, it.branschen, Macworld Sweden, MaxiData Sweden, MikroDatorn, Natverk & Kommunikation, PC World Sweden, PCaktiv, Windows World Sweden; **SWITZERLAND:** Computerworld Schweiz, Macworld Schweiz, PCtip; **TAIWAN:** Computerworld Taiwan, Macworld Taiwan, NEW ViSiON/Publish, PC World Taiwan; **THAILAND:** Publish in Asia, Thai Computerworld; **TURKEY:** Computerworld Turkiye, Macworld Turkiye, Network World Turkiye, PC World Turkiye; **UKRAINE:** Computerworld Kiev, Multimedia World Ukraine, PC World Ukraine; **UNITED KINGDOM:** Acorn User UK, Amiga Action UK, Amiga Computing UK, Apple Talk UK, Computing, Macworld, Parents and Computers UK, PC Advisor, PC Home, PSX Pro, The WEB; **UNITED STATES:** Cable in the Classroom, CIO Magazine, Computerworld, DOS World, Federal Computer Week, GamePro Magazine, InfoWorld, I-Way, Macworld, Network World, PC Games, PC World, Publish, Video Event, THE WEB Magazine, and WebMaster; online webzines: JavaWorld, NetscapeWorld, and SunWorld Online; **URUGUAY:** InfoWorld Uruguay; **VENEZUELA:** Computerworld Venezuela, PC World Venezuela; and **VIETNAM:** PC World Vietnam. 5/7/98

Author's Acknowledgments

I would like to express my thanks and appreciation to Andy Rathbone, for his contributions to earlier editions of this book.

Thanks to Maryann Yoshimoto, for her medical assistance with the text.

Thanks also to the many readers who write in with questions, which prompts me to write a better and better book each time. Cheers!

Publisher's Acknowledgments

We're proud of this book; please register your comments through our IDG Books Worldwide Online Registration Form located at http://my2cents.dummies.com.

Some of the people who helped bring this book to market include the following:

Acquisitions, Editorial, and Media Development

Project Editor: Rebecca Whitney

Acquisitions Editor: Mike Kelly

Editors: Kathy Cox, Jennifer Ehrlich, Wendy Hatch, Elizabeth Kuball, Paula Lowell, Darren Meiss, Rowena Rappaport, Linda Stark

Technical Editor: Mary Bednarek

Editorial Manager: Mary Corder

Editorial Assistant: Paul Kuzmic

Production

Project Coordinator: Valery Bourke

Layout and Graphics: Lou Boudreau, Linda M. Boyer, J. Tyler Connor, Maridee V. Ennis, Angela F. Hunckler, Jane E. Martin, Drew R. Moore, Anna Rohrer, Brent Savage, Janet Seib, Deirdre Smith, Ian Smith, Kate Snell, Michael A. Sullivan

Proofreaders: Christine Berman, Kelli Botta, Michelle Croninger, Rachel Garvey, Robert Springer, Nancy Price, Rebecca Senninger, Janet M. Withers

Indexer: Sherry Massey

Special Help: Leah Cameron, Constance Carlisle, Suzanne Thomas

---

General and Administrative

IDG Books Worldwide, Inc.: John Kilcullen, CEO; Steven Berkowitz, President and Publisher

IDG Books Technology Publishing: Brenda McLaughlin, Senior Vice President and Group Publisher

Dummies Technology Press and Dummies Editorial: Diane Graves Steele, Vice President and Associate Publisher; Mary Bednarek, Director of Acquisitions and Product Development; Kristin A. Cocks, Editorial Director

Dummies Trade Press: Kathleen A. Welton, Vice President and Publisher; Kevin Thornton, Acquisitions Manager

IDG Books Production for Dummies Press: Michael R. Britton, Vice President of Production and Creative Services; Cindy L. Phipps, Manager of Project Coordination, Production Proofreading, and Indexing; Kathie S. Schutte, Supervisor of Page Layout; Shelley Lea, Supervisor of Graphics and Design; Debbie J. Gates, Production Systems Specialist; Robert Springer, Supervisor of Proofreading; Debbie Stailey, Special Projects Coordinator; Tony Augsburger, Supervisor of Reprints and Bluelines

Dummies Packaging and Book Design: Robin Seaman, Creative Director; Jocelyn Kelaita, Product Packaging Coordinator; Kavish + Kavish, Cover Design

◆

The publisher would like to give special thanks to Patrick J. McGovern, without whom this book would not have been possible.

◆

Contents at a Glance

Cartoons at a Glance

By Rich Tennant

Fax: 978-546-7747 • E-mail: the5wave@tiac.net

Table of Contents

Introduction

Welcome to *PCs For Dummies,* 6th Edition, fully updated to cover Windows 98 and all of tomorrow's technology today.

This book answers the question "How does a computer turn a smart person like you into a dummy?" Computers are useful, yes. And a fair number of people — heaven help them — fall in love with computers. But the rest of us are left sitting dumb and numb in front of the box. It's not that using a computer is beyond the range of our IQs; it's that no one has ever bothered to sit down and explain things in human terms. Until now.

This book talks about using a computer in friendly, human — and often irreverent — terms. Nothing is sacred here. Electronics can be praised by others. This book focuses on you and your needs. In this book, you'll discover everything you need to know about your computer without painful jargon or the prerequisite master's degree in engineering. And you'll have fun.

About This Book

This book is designed so that you can pick it up at any point and start reading — like a reference. It has 33 chapters. Each chapter covers a specific aspect of the computer — turning it on, using a printer, using software, kicking it, and so on. Each chapter is divided into self-contained nuggets of information — sections — all relating to the major theme of the chapter. Sample sections you may find:

- ✔ Your Basic Hardware (A Nerd's-Eye View)
- ✔ "The Manual Tells Me to Boot My Computer: Where Do I Kick It?"
- ✔ Learning Which Buttons You Can Ignore
- ✔ "My Taskbar Is Gone!"
- ✔ General Commands for All Reasons
- ✔ Exiting a Program
- ✔ Turning Off the Computer

You don't have to memorize anything in this book. Nothing about a computer is memorable. Each section is designed so that you can read the information quickly, digest what you've read, and then put down the book and get on with using the computer. If anything technical crops up, you'll be alerted to its presence so that you can cleanly avoid it.

How to Use This Book

This book works like a reference. Start with the topic you want more information about; look for it in the Table of Contents or in the Index. Turn to the area of interest and read the information you need. Then, with the information in your head, you can quickly close the book and freely perform whatever task you need — without learning anything else.

Of course, if you want to read additional information about the topic or find out something else, you can check many of the cross-references used throughout this book or just continue reading.

Whenever a message or information on the screen is described, it looks like this:

```
This is a message on-screen.
```

If you have to type something, it looks like this:

```
Type me
```

You type the text **Type me** as shown here. You're told when and whether to press the Enter key.

Windows menu commands are shown like this:

Choose File⇨Exit.

This line means to select the File menu and choose the Exit command. You can use your computer's mouse, or you can press the Alt key and then the underlined keys, F and then X in the preceding example.

Key combinations you may have to type are shown like this:

Ctrl+S

This line means to press and hold the Ctrl (control) key, type an S, and then release the Ctrl key. It works just like pressing Shift+S on the keyboard produces the uppercase S key. Same deal, different shift key.

What You Don't Need to Read

A lot of technical information is involved with using a computer. To better insulate you from that type of material, I've enclosed it in sidebars that are clearly marked as technical information. You don't have to read that stuff. Often, it's just a complex explanation of information already discussed in the chapter. Reading that information will only teach you something substantial about your computer, which is not the goal here.

And Just Who Are You?

I am going to make some admittedly foolish assumptions about you: You have a computer, and you use it somehow to do something. You use a PC (or are planning on it) and will be using Windows as your PC's operating system or main program.

This book has been updated to cover all the basic information about Windows 98, with a bunch of Windows 95 stuff thrown in just because I'm a nice person. If information relates to a specific version of Windows, I'll name the version (98, 95, or 3.11). Otherwise, when I use the term "Windows," it applies to both Windows 95 and Windows 98.

How This Book Is Organized

This book has eight major parts, each of which is divided into several chapters. Each chapter covers a major topic and is divided into sections, which address issues or concerns about the topic. That's how this book is organized, although how you read it is up to you. Pick a topic, a chapter, a section — whatever — and just start reading. Any related information is cross-referenced in the text.

Icons Used in This Book

This icon alerts you to needless technical information — drivel added because I just feel like explaining something totally unnecessary (a hard habit to break). Feel free to skip over anything tagged with this little picture.

This icon usually indicates helpful advice or an insight that makes using the computer interesting. For example, when you're pouring acid over your computer, be sure to wear a protective apron, gloves, and goggles.

Ummm, I forgot what this one means.

This icon indicates that you need to be careful with the information presented; usually, it's a reminder for you not to do something.

Where to Go from Here

With this book in hand, you're now ready to go out and conquer your PC. Start by looking through the Table of Contents or the Index. Find a topic, turn to the page indicated, and you're ready to go. Also, feel free to write in this book, fill in the blanks, dog-ear the pages, and do anything that would make a librarian blanch. Enjoy.

Part I
Introducing the PC
(If You Don't Yet
Own One)

In this part . . .

*I*t's entirely possible to be a successful, bright, and charming person and yet not know a thing about how to use a computer. Don't let them fool you! The truth is, no higher education is required, no math is necessary, and you definitely don't need to master the thing. Those who feel the desire will. The rest of us can just use the beast and quickly turn it off when we're done. No problem.

This part of the book will get you up to speed on some very basic computer concepts, even if you don't have a computer or are just setting out to buy one. Or maybe you just bought a shotgun and need to know what to shoot at. Whatever the case, this part of the book is just for you.

Chapter 1

Say Hello to Mr. Computer

*W*ho ever said that computers are easy to use? They can be fun. They can be aggravating. They can be enlightening. And they can most certainly be intimidating, which is where all the *dummy* stuff comes about. It's just too bad that computers don't pop out of the box, shake your hand, and give you a big hug. If that were true, this book wouldn't be necessary.

In a way, computers are like babies. They come packaged with great potential and, with the right care and handling, will achieve wondrous things and make you very proud. Like babies, computers require you to get to know them, to learn their moods and which buttons to push. It's a mutual relationship — and one that, fortunately, doesn't involve any drooling or diapers to change.

It's Just Another Electronic Gadget

A computer is that thing on your desk that looks like a TV set illegally parked by a typewriter. Call it whatever you like; it's basically a computer. But, because you may also have a computer on your wrist, in your car, or in the toaster, a more specific term is required: What you have on your desk is really a *PC,* a *p*ersonal computer.

✔ Computers are essentially calculators with a lot more buttons and a larger display. They organize. They help you work with words and numbers. They can educate and entertain.

✔ Computers are not evil. They harbor no sinister intelligence. In fact, when you get to know them, they're rather dumb.

✔ Computers have the potential to be very friendly. Because you can read information on-screen, many computers give you a list of options, provide suggestions, or tell you what to do next. The microwave oven can't do that. Or maybe it can but refuses to.

✔ Computers don't flash 12:00 after a power outage.

✔ Perhaps the most important thing to remember about a computer is that *you* are in the driver's seat. You tell the computer exactly what to do, and it does it. The problem is that a computer obeys your instructions no matter what — even when you tell it to do something goofy. The art of dealing with a computer is a precise one.

✔ Please refrain from whacking your electronics.

What is a computer?

Computers defy description. Unlike other tools that have definite purposes, a computer can do a number of different things, solving an infinite number of problems for an infinite number of people. Just about anything that can be done with words, numbers, information, or communication can be done with a computer.

In a way, a computer is just another electronic gadget. Unlike the toaster and your car's carburetor, which are programmed to do only one thing, a personal computer can be *programmed* to do a number of interesting tasks. It's up to you to tell the computer what you want it to do.

✔ The computer is the chameleon of electronic devices. Your phone can be used only as a phone, your VCR only records and plays videos, and your microwave oven can only zap things (food, mostly). But a computer's potential is limitless.

✔ Computers get the job done by using *software*. The software tells the computer what to do.

✔ No, you never have to learn programming to use a computer. Someone else does the programming, and then you buy the program (the software) to get your work done.

✔ Your job, as computer operator, is to tell the software what to do, which then tells the computer what to do.

✔ Only on cheesy sci-fi shows does the computer ever tell *you* what to do.

✔ You can always *verbally* tell the computer what to do with itself. This happens millions of times a day, by programmers and nonprogrammers alike.

✔ Software is only half of the computer equation. The other side is *hardware,* which is covered in the following section.

✔ Computers can't clean up the house; they lack eyeballs and arms and legs. What you need if you want your house cleaned is a *robot,* which scientists haven't yet perfected for domestic use. When they do, buy *Robots For Dummies.*

What is not a computer?

Theatre. Real estate. Most livestock. Durable goods. Books and music. Fine art. The Hair Club for Men. Sushi. Inflatable stuff. Anything with a knob. Cat litter. False teeth. Everything in the Potpourri category on *Jeopardy!* Dolphin-safe tuna. Anything with grease on it. Anyone who's been on Larry King's show. Larry King himself. Larry King's dog.

What then is a PC?

PC means *personal computer.* It's the name IBM gave to its first personal computer, the IBM PC. That one computer was the Model T of all computers. Even though it was made in 1981, many of its design elements are included in today's models — much to the frustration of PC owners and manufacturers everywhere!

Some history you don't have to read

Not long ago, people referred to personal computers as *microcomputers.* This term came from *microprocessor,* the computer's main chip. The big "I want to control the world and foul up your phone bill" computers were called *mainframes.* Smaller, corporate- and college-size computers (which only fouled up paychecks or grades) were called *minicomputers.*

According to the geeks who ran the mainframes and minicomputers, *micro*computers were hobbyists' playthings — toys. However, the features available on the personal computer — the microcomputer — that you can have on your desk today exceed many of the features of the early mainframes. So there.

- ✔ The term *clone,* and later *compatible,* was once used to describe any computer that used IBM PC-like hardware and could run PC software. Those terms are rarely used today because the standard PC has become more generic. In fact, computers are now sold based on which type of operating system they support; see the section "The operating system (Or "Who's in charge here?")," later in this chapter.

- ✔ The only personal computer that's not a PC is the Macintosh. Its owners prefer to call it a *Mac* rather than a PC, even though the Macintosh is a personal computer.

- ✔ By the way, this book doesn't cover the Macintosh. If that type of computer is more to your liking, rush out and buy *Macs For Dummies,* 6th Edition (published by IDG Books Worldwide, Inc.), by my pal, Computer Magician to the Stars, David Pogue.

- ✔ In addition to the Macintosh, several other variations on the personal computer exist. See Chapter 31 for my derogatory opinions.

- ✔ The original PC wasn't created to start a dynasty, even though it did. Had its designers known how successful it would be, things may have been different (meaning *worse!*).

Hardware and Software

Computers have two parts: hardware and software.

Hardware is the physical part of a computer, anything you can touch. Hardware is nothing by itself but potential. It needs software to tell it what to do. In a way, hardware is like a car without a driver or a symphony orchestra without music (some orchestras are better that way, but I digress).

Software is the brains of a computer. It tells the hardware what to do and how to work. Without the software directing things, the hardware would just sit around and look formidable. You must have software to make a computer go. In fact, software determines your computer's personality.

- ✔ Computer hardware isn't anything you find in your local TrueValue store. With a computer, the hardware is the physical part — the stuff you can touch, feel in your hand, drop on the floor, lug through an airport, or toss out a window.

- ✔ Computer software is the brains of the operation — the instructions that tell the computer what to do, how to act, or when to lose your monthly report.

✔ Computer software is more important than computer hardware. The software tells the hardware what to do.

✔ Although computer software comes on disks (CDs or floppy disks), the *disks* aren't the software. Software is stored on disks just as music is stored on cassettes and CDs.

✔ Without the proper software, your computer is a seriously heavy paperweight.

Your Basic Hardware (A Nerd's-Eye View)

Figure 1-1 shows what a typical computer system looks like. I've flagged the most basic computer things you should identify and know about. They're just the basics. The rest of this book goes into the details.

Monitor: This TV set-like thing typically perches on top of the *console*. The glass part of the monitor is the *screen,* which is where the computer displays information or offers you insults or rude suggestions. Monitors are covered in detail in Chapter 13.

Console: The main computer box is called the *system unit* by geeky types. It contains your computer's guts on the inside, plus a lot of interesting gizmos on the outside. See the section "Stuff on the console," later in this chapter, for information about the greeblies pasted on the console.

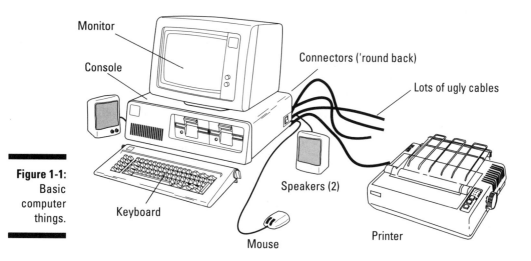

Figure 1-1:
Basic
computer
things.

Keyboard: It's the thing you type on. La-de-da. Chapter 15 cusses and discusses the computer keyboard.

Mouse: It's not a fuzzy little rodent, but rather a computer mouse. These things are especially helpful in using all that graphical software out there. By the way, the mouse is pointing the wrong way in the figure. I did that so that you can see the two mouse buttons. See Chapter 14 for information about proper mouse orientation and button info.

Speakers: Most PCs can beep and squawk through their own speaker. To augment that noise, most computers now sold include a special sound card (that *multimedia* thing). Along with the sound card comes an additional set of stereo speakers, which most people plunk down on each side of the monitor. Pay more money, and you can even get a subwoofer to sit under the desk. Now *that* will scare the neighbors.

Printer: It's where you get the computer's output: the printed stuff, also called *hard copy.* Sashay off to Chapter 16 to increase your PC printer knowledge.

Connectors: Behind your computer are a bunch of holes, each of which is named Jack. Into these *jacks* you plug various peripherals and other devices the computer controls — such as the printer, as shown in Figure 1-1. Some parts of Chapter 11 are devoted to the various PC connectors on a computer's rump.

Lots of ugly cables: One thing they never show you — not in any computer manual and especially not in advertisements — is the ganglia of cables that live behind each and every computer. What a mess! These cables are required in order to plug things into the wall and into each other. No shampoo conditioner on earth can clean up those tangles.

- These parts of the computer are all important. Make sure that you know where the console, keyboard, disk drive, monitor, and printer are in your own system. If the printer isn't present, it's probably a network printer sitting in some other room.

- Part IV of this book covers computer hardware in detail.

- A computer really exists in two places. Most of the computer lives inside the console. Everything else, all the stuff connected to the console, is called *peripherals.* See Chapter 18 for more information about peripherals.

Stuff on the console (front)

The console is the most important part of your computer. It's the main thing, the Big Box. Every part of your computer system either lives inside the console or plugs into it. Figure 1-2 shows what a typical PC console may look like. I've flagged the more interesting places to visit, although they may appear in a different location than shown in the figure.

CD-ROM or DVD drive: This high-capacity disc looks exactly like a musical CD, although it contains computer information. Chapter 7 covers how you use and abuse CD-ROM and DVD drives and discs.

Future expansion: It's usually a blank spot on the front of your computer that enables you to add even more junk later. Such a space may already be taken on the computer, filled with such goodies as a tape backup unit, ZIP drive, another CD-ROM drive, another hard drive, or a mystery grab-bag assortment of other computer things many folks enthusiastically spend their hard-earned money on.

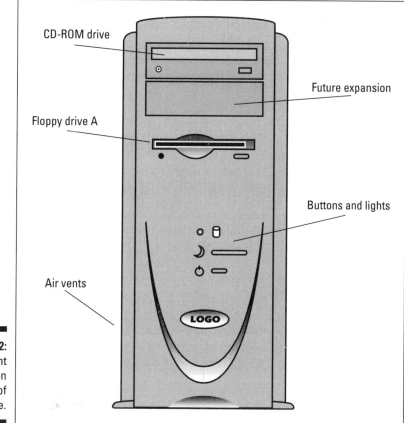

Figure 1-2:
Important
doodads on
the front of
the console.

Floppy drive: This slot eats floppy disks. Most PCs sold in the past few years come with only one floppy drive, dubbed drive A. Older PCs may have two floppy drives, and some very old models may even have the wider $5^1/_4$-inch type. Part III of this book uses several chapters to discuss all the whatnots of disks and drives. It's a big spinnin' deal.

Air vents: Okay, this one isn't truly important, but most consoles sport some type of air vent on the front. Don't block the air vents! The thing has gotta breathe.

Buttons and lights: Most of the computer's buttons are on the keyboard. A few of the more important ones are on the console, and these buttons on fancier PCs are accompanied by many impressive tiny lights. These buttons and lights include the following:

   On-off button: The PC's main power button, the one you use to turn the darn thing on. The on-off button is usually accompanied by a light, although computers make enough racket that you can usually hear when they're turned on.

   Reset button: Allows you to restart the computer without going through the bother of turning it off and then on again. Chapter 4 explains why anyone in his right mind would want to do that.

   Sleep button: A feature on some newer PCs and most laptops. Pressing this button causes your PC to go into a coma, suspending all activity without turning the computer off. Read all about this trick in Chapter 4.

   Hard drive light: Flashes when the hard drive is working. Because the hard drive lives inside the console, this light is your reassurance that it's alive and happy and doing its job.

Older PCs may sport two additional features on the front side of the console. Typically, these doodads are for decoration only; their original function was important only to certain computers in the mid-1980s:

Turbo button: This button, if you have it, does nothing. It's a holdover from the early days of the PC when the computer ran in two modes: very slow and as fast as it could. Obviously, most people would opt to run their computers fast because that's what they paid for. The slow setting is rarely, if ever, used. A small light accompanies the Turbo button.

Keyboard lock: For about ten years, between 1984 and 1994, most PCs came with a tiny key and lock. You used the key to lock the keyboard; when the keyboard was locked, the computer ignored what you typed. Some locks even prevented you from opening the computer's case and getting inside. Mostly, these locks were for show, which is why the fad faded out several years ago.

✔ The console isn't the only part of your computer system that sports an on-off switch. Your PC's monitor, printer, and modem (and almost everything else) also have their own on-off switch. See Chapter 4 for more information about turning everything on.

✔ The on-off symbol shown above may indicate the Reset button on some computers. Check with your computer manual to be sure.

✔ Try not to block the air vents on the front of the console. If you do, the computer may literally suffocate. (Actually, it gets too hot.)

✔ Look in Chapter 11 for information about the horrors that lurk on the console's ugly backside.

✔ If your computer does have a lock and key, don't count on using it for security purposes: I have several computers in the office from different manufacturers, and the same key works with all the locks.

✔ Hard drive lights can be red or green or yellow, and the light flickers when the hard drive is in use. Don't let it freak you out! It's not an alarm; the hard drive is just doing its job. (Personally, I find the green type of hard drive light most comforting — reminds me of Christmas.)

Stuff on the console (back)

As computer designers strive to make their product prettier, they've moved many of the important connections and doodads to the PC's rump. Figure 1-3 shows you where some of the doodads are located and what they connect to. Your computer probably will have most of the items shown in the figure, although they'll probably be in a different location on the PC's backside.

Power connector: This thing is where the PC plugs into a cord that plugs into the wall.

 Keyboard connector: The keyboard plugs into this little hole. On some very old PCs, the hole is much larger.

 Mouse connector: It's generally the same size and shape as the keyboard connector, although this hole has a mouse icon nearby to let you know that the mouse plugs in there.

 USB port: Plug snazzy USB devices into these Certs-size slots. More about what can be plugged into a USB port can be found in Chapter 11.

 Serial, or COM, ports: Most PCs have two of these, labeled COM1 and COM2. It's where an external modem or sometimes a mouse is plugged in. New PCs have 9-pin serial ports, and older PCs may have 25-pin ports.

Printer port: The PC's printer plugs into this connector.

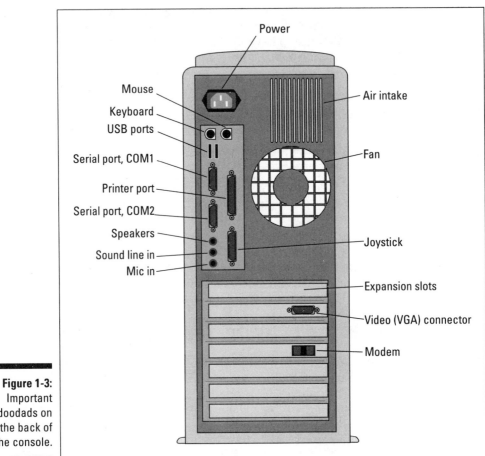

Figure 1-3:
Important
doodads on
the back of
the console.

Joystick port: This port is used mainly for scientific applications.

Monitor connector: Your PC's monitor plugs into this hole. Sometimes the hole is on an expansion slot and is unlabeled. If so, you can tell what the monitor connector is because it has 15 little holes in it — more than the serial port, which is the same size and has only 9 holes.

Speaker/sound-out jack: It's where you plug in your PC's external speakers, or where you would hook up the PC to a sound system. (The USB port can also be used for external speakers.)

Line-in jack: This jack is where you plug in your stereo or VCR to the PC for capturing sound.

Microphone jack: The computer's microphone plugs into this hole.

In addition to the ports, jacks, and holes on the back of the console are expansion slots. They're the backsides of various expansion cards you plug into your PC. Some expansion slots have connectors for other PC goodies as well.

The good news? All this stuff is connected only once. Then your PC's butt faces the wall for the rest of its life, and you never have to look at it again.

"So where is my A drive?"

The A drive is your computer's first floppy drive. It's the only floppy drive if you have one, and it's typically the *top* floppy drive if you have two.

Then again, it could be the *bottom* floppy drive.

To find out which floppy drive is which, watch them when your PC starts up. The first floppy drive, drive A, has a light on it that lights up for a few moments after the PC starts. Immediately write *Drive A* on that drive by using an indelible marker, or use a label maker to create a label for the drive.

The Cheat Sheet inside the front cover of this book includes space for you to jot down your drive A location. That way, you always remember it.

✔ Your first hard drive is always drive C. If you have a second hard drive, it's drive D.

✔ Chapter 7 describes all this disk-drive-lettering nonsense in crystal-clear detail.

✍ ♏ ☐ ○ ♋ •♦ ♐ ♒ ♓ ☐ ♑ ● ⬜ ♍ ☐ (Become a master of hieroglyphics)

Along with all the lights and switches, the typical computer console sports a whole Nile full of symbols. No one ever tells you what they are because they're supposedly international symbols (and even aliens from space would be able to discern their functions without consulting an intergalactic dictionary). In any event, I've listed them all for you in Figure 1-4 in case you stumble over one you cannot recognize and an alien from space isn't handy.

✔ Forget seeing On or Off on a computer switch. To be more politically correct, computers use a bar for On and a circle for Off (as shown in Figure 1-4). You can remember which is which by keeping in mind that a circle is an O and the word *off* stars with the letter *O*. (Then again, so does *on*. Just don't think about it.)

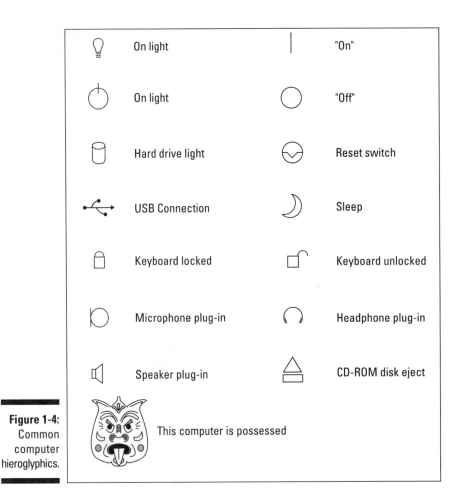

♀	On light	│	"On"
⏻	On light	○	"Off"
⛁	Hard drive light	⊝	Reset switch
⟜⟶	USB Connection	☾	Sleep
🔒	Keyboard locked	🔓	Keyboard unlocked
🎤	Microphone plug-in	🎧	Headphone plug-in
🔊	Speaker plug-in	⏏	CD-ROM disk eject

This computer is possessed

Figure 1-4:
Common
computer
hieroglyphics.

✔ To drive this confusing point home: Most PCs now have a dual On-Off switch with *both* symbols on it. Press once to turn on, and press again to turn off.

✔ Most consoles have a little light that lets you know that the computer is on. This little light is accompanied by a special symbol. In Figure 1-4, three "the computer is on" symbols are shown. What? Would it be that difficult to beat the word *On* into a foreigner's brains? In any event, when the computer is on, it makes noise. That's a definite way to know.

Variations on the typical computer theme

Not all computers look like the image shown in Figure 1-1. In fact, that's an old IBM PC shown there. Today's models are loosely based on the later IBM AT design, which is being replaced by anything slab-like that looks sleek and has blinking lights — two of the highest status symbols a personal computer can attain. Here are some other terms used to describe various PC modes and models:

Desktop: A typical PC configuration with a slab-like console and a monitor holding everything down like a $500 paperweight.

Desktop (small footprint): A PC's *footprint* is the amount of desk space it uses. A small footprint desktop model is just tinier than the full-size desktop model. Of course, in the end it makes no difference: The amount of clutter you have always expands to fill available desk space.

Laptops: A specialty type of computer that folds into a handy lightweight package, ideal for toting around. Laptop PCs work just like their desktop brethren; any exceptions are noted throughout this book.

Towers: Essentially a console standing on its side, making it tall, like a tower. These PCs have more room inside for expansion. They typically sit on the floor, and the monitor and keyboard are on top of the desk. Preferred by power users.

Minitowers: A small, squat version of the tower PC designed for people who work near airports where height restrictions are in effect. Seriously, you can put a minitower on top of your desk, typically next to the monitor and keyboard. A typical minitower is illustrated in Figure 1-2.

Tiffany Towers: Actually the name of a stripper and has nothing to do with computers.

Also see Chapter 31, which presents a list of ten things that may or may not be a PC.

Your Basic Software

Computer software doesn't get the credit it deserves for running your computer. That's probably why it's overpriced. In any event, you need the software to make your hardware go.

The operating system (or "Who's in charge here?")

The most important piece of software is the *operating system*. It's the computer's number-one program — the head honcho, the big cheese, Mr. In Charge, Fearless Leader, da King.

The operating system rules the computer's roost, controlling all the individual pieces and making sure that everything gets along well. It's the actual brains of the operation, telling the nitwitted hardware what to do next. The operating system also controls applications software (see the following section). Each of those programs must bend a knee and take a loyalty oath to the operating system.

- ✔ The computer's most important piece of software is the operating system.

- ✔ The operating system typically comes with the computer when you buy it. You never need to add a second operating system, although operating systems do get updated and improved from time to time. See Chapter 20 for information about upgrading the operating system.

- ✔ It used to be, in the olden days (about 1986), that you bought a program for a specific type of computer. The software store had sections for IBM, Apple, and Commodore. Now you buy software for a specific operating system: Windows, Linux, or Macintosh.

- ✔ For the PC, the most popular operating system used to be DOS. Now it's Windows. Although other popular operating systems exist, Windows is pretty much king of the heap. Bill Gates knows this fact every time he gets his monthly bank statement.

- ✔ Chapter 5 chitty-chats about Windows.

Other types of programs

The operating system is merely in charge of the computer. By itself, an operating system doesn't really do anything for you. Instead, to get work done, you need an application program. *Application programs* are the programs that do the work. They include word processors, spreadsheets, and databases. Whatever it is you do on your computer, it's being done by an application program.

Other types of programs include utilities and games and educational and programming software. Other categories might exist, but I'm too lazy right now to think of them.

- ✔ Part V of this book covers computer software.

- ✔ *Internet browsers* are programs you run on your PC to "browse" through the millions of pages that make up the World Wide Web. See Part VI for more Internet stuff.

- ✔ *Utilities* are programs that carry out special tasks, typically enhancing the capabilities of the operating system.

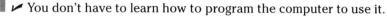

✔ Games. Well. What more can I say?

✔ Educational software doesn't mean only programs to teach Tommy to count. I heartily recommend typing-tutor software to teach you to be a better typist at the computer. I've even used musical software to train my ear so that I can be a better musician. (Hasn't helped much.)

✔ You don't have to learn how to program the computer to use it.

Even so, if you *really* want to tell your computer what to do with itself, consider picking up a programming package. One of the easiest to learn is Microsoft Visual Basic. One of the most popular is the C language. Appropriate *...For Dummies* books on these topics are available (from IDG Books Worldwide, Inc.) if you truly want to be a master of the dopey machine before you.

One Final, Consoling Word of Advice

The last thing you should be concerned about is that your PC — your personal computer — will blow up. It'll never happen. No sparks. No flash. No boom.

In many science fiction movies, computers blow up and spew fire and rocks. Irwin Allen did that in all his 1960s TV shows. Even *Star Trek*'s Mr. Spock was fond of pointing at some alien computer and uttering, in his calm Vulcan way, "Push this button, and the entire planet will become molten rubble." But in reality, it won't happen. Computers are just too dull. Sorry.

Chapter 2
Helpful Hints on PC Setup

● ●

In This Chapter

▶ Opening the boxes and unpacking everything

▶ Finding a place for your PC

▶ Setting up the console

▶ Connecting cables

▶ Setting up the monitor

▶ Setting up the printer

▶ Examining surge protectors

▶ Dealing with hardware and software

● ●

*N*othing can be more satisfying than opening up something new. Computer marketing types even have a name for it: the "out of box" experience. It almost sounds religious.

"Yes, Doctor, I had an out-of-box experience. For a moment, I saw our old bread machine. And then the water heater that blew up last year. It told me that I had to go back . . . go back to assemble my PC."

Sheesh.

Setting up a computer is a task about as endearing as wiring together a VCR and television so that you can watch cable and record HBO at the same time. No one looks forward to it. Fortunately, it's something you need to do only once, or else you can just pay someone else to do it for you.

Opening the Big Boxes and Unpacking Everything

Setting up a computer starts with opening big boxes — typically, two to three. Start by locating a packing list, which should be attached to the outside of one of the boxes. Make sure that everything is present and accounted for and that you have everything you paid for.

 ✔ Sometimes packing lists come separately, or you may have an invoice. Either way, make sure that you have all the boxes you need.

 ✔ If you got your computer through the mail, check to be sure that all the pieces have arrived together. The same rule applies if your computer arrived at your office from the computer or MIS department. If not, contact the delivery people and threaten them with baby-sitting a 2-year-old.

 ✔ Always keep the phone numbers of your dealer and computer manufacturer handy. (Space is provided on the Cheat Sheet in the front of this book.) Also, look out for special support numbers; some manufacturers offer a 24-hour, toll-free support number. Write them numbers down!

Where will Mr. Computer live?

Before you unpack anything, find a home for your computer. Clear off your desk or tabletop, allowing enough room to set down the computer and keyboard. Remember that your computer will have an octopus of cables and peripherals around it. Make room for all that stuff, too.

 ✔ Computers need room to breathe. Don't put your computer in a closet, box, recessed vault, grotto, or other cave-like place with poor ventilation.

 ✔ Don't put your computer by a sunny window because that heats up the computer and gives it anxiety.

 ✔ If you can sit on the table, it can support the computer. Don't put the PC on a wobbly table or anything you wouldn't sit on yourself (like the cat).

Open 'em up!

To open your computer boxes, take the same approach any kid takes at a birthday party: The biggest box must contain the best stuff, so start unpacking the biggest box first.

The big box probably contains the monitor because big monitors are all the current rage. After that, the next-biggest box contains the computer console, keyboard, mouse, documentation, and a bunch of other bits and pieces. You may have even more boxes containing the manuals, the keyboard, and extra goodies.

If you bought a printer, it comes in its own box.

And, of course, all the software you bought comes in more boxes. (The computer industry is a gold mine for the cardboard box industry.)

- If a box says "open me first," do that.
- The console is most likely the first thing you'll set up (unless you see an "open first" box). The console is the least mobile of the units you unpack, so setting it up first gives you a good starting base.
- Say, is that the AT&T building or the box it came in?
- Some boxes have opening instructions. I kid you not! My huge monitor had to be opened on top and then turned upside down so that I could lift the box off of the monitor. Remember that gravity is your friend.
- Wait until you've connected some cables to your console before you squat the monitor on top (or on a sturdy surface, if you have a tower).
- Is there a separate keyboard box? Sometimes a third (or fourth) box is included with your computer — in addition to any software and manuals you may get. This box may contain the keyboard, the mouse, other interesting hardware, or just the manuals that attempt to tell you all about your computer.

- Also, be on the lookout for boxes within boxes! Don't toss out any box until you've examined it thoroughly for anything you may need.
- The section "Setting up the printer," later in this chapter, goes into detail about setting up your printer for the first time.
- If you bought any printer paper, cables, and so on, set them aside with the printer.
- Chapter 16 provides additional information about setting up your computer printer to work with your software.
- All the boxes have numbers on them, usually product numbers. Add them up! If the total is greater than 10,000, phone your dealer. You've just won a prize!
- I'm kidding, of course.

Box-opening etiquette

Be careful when you're opening any box. The "grab and rip" approach can be dangerous because those massive ugly staples used to close the box can fling off and give you an unwanted body piercing. (It's fashionable in parts of Silicon Valley to have a large staple through the eyebrow.)

The same holds true with using a box knife; use a small blade because you don't want to slice through or into anything electronic — or fleshy, for that matter.

Remove any packing material, such as nonbiodegradable foam or polystyrene. Lift the console from the box, and carefully set it on a tabletop. If any piece of equipment comes in a plastic bag, remove the bag.

Watch as the millions of tiny foam peanuts fall all over the floor. If you're unlucky, it's a wood floor and static electricity will energize each foam peanut. They're alive! You'll never get rid of them. Note how some scamper off to reside under the credenza.

"Should I toss out the boxes?"

Computers are shipped with a lot of packing material, plastic bags, twist ties, rubber bands, nylons, and Hershey bars. You can throw out everything that you think is trash. Or, to be good to the environment, you can recycle everything. However, if the computer ends up being a lemon, you may need to ship it back in the original containers or risk losing your warranty.

My best advice is to save all the boxes and packing foam for at least a month, which should give you time to see whether the computer needs to be returned. After that, feel free to toss out the boxes.

I keep all my computer boxes and the packing material (except for the annoying foam peanuts). Heck, I have boxes from 1984. The reason? When I move — although it's not that often — I prefer to pack the computers in their original boxes. Many moving companies won't insure your computers unless they're in the original packing material with the original foam peanuts and Hershey bars, so I never toss out my computer boxes. That's why God invented attics, anyway.

Putting It Together

Assembling a computer is something better left to a technical person. Remind your office computer gurus that they should be assembling your office system. At home, invite your computer-knowledgeable friends over to see your new PC. Don't tell them that it's sitting on the floor suffocating in a bag. Surprise them. Computer people are often delighted to assemble a PC. It's like delivering a calf but without the slosh.

If you're stuck and have to assemble your own PC, here's what you need:

✔ A medium-size Phillips or standard screwdriver (I don't know which — get both).

✔ A tiny, flat-head screwdriver — one designed for teensy-tiny screws.

✔ About an hour of your time.

✔ Plenty of patience.

✔ You probably don't need two screwdrivers, but gather up a few anyway. It looks impressive.

✔ Keep pets and small children at a distance when you set up your PC. If you keep a cold beverage handy, put it in a safe place, where spilling it won't be a problem (like in another time zone).

✔ You may also need a flashlight to see behind your computer after it's set up.

Setting up the console (the boxy thing)

Start by setting the console where you want it. The pretty side, usually containing the company label and computer model name and number, goes toward you. Remove the console from its plastic bag, if you haven't already done so.

✔ Don't block the front of the console with the keyboard or books or disks or a box of Kleenex. Remember that you still need access to the front of the console to turn it on, swap disks, and stare at the pretty glowing lights when you're bored.

✔ The console is the first thing you set up, seeing as how everything else plugs into it.

✔ For now, give yourself some working room behind the console. You need to weasel your way back there to attach some wires and cables. After that's done, you can shove the console to its final resting position.

✔ If you have a tower-model PC, the console sits flat on the floor, usually under a desk. Pull it out and away from the desk for now so that you can connect the cables described later in this section.

✔ The PC's disk drives may contain paper or plastic doohickeys, which are lovingly called tongue depressors. If you find them, remove them and toss them out. They're needed only for shipping. (See Chapter 7 for steps on removing something from your floppy drive.)

✔ Note that some manuals refer to the console as the *system unit*.

Where do it go, George?

You should see a picture of your assembled PC somewhere, either in its setup manuals or on the box. That should help. If not, gander back at Figure 1-1, which is an IBM PC circa 1981, although it still shows you sort of where everything goes. The following figure shows various cables you plug into the back of a typical PC. These figures show generalities; your computer may be slightly different.

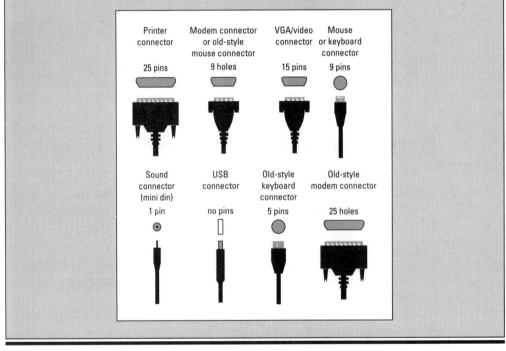

Connecting cables to the console

The *console* is the main computer unit. As such, its duty is to have as many unsightly cables as possible hanging from it. These cables connect around back, where they're most inconvenient to access.

You connect several, if not all, of these cables to the console:

- ✔ Power cord
- ✔ Keyboard cable
- ✔ Mouse cable
- ✔ Monitor cable
- ✔ External speaker cables
- ✔ Microphone cable
- ✔ Printer cable
- ✔ Network cable
- ✔ Modem (phone) cable
- ✔ Jumper cables
- ✔ Transatlantic cable
- ✔ George Washington Cable

General notes on connecting cables

Flat cable connectors typically have a long side and a short side, like the dolabriform pictured in the margin. To remember which side is up, I say "The cable is smiling," or "The cable is frowning." That helps me remember how to plug the thing in, and it's also a sign that, for an adult, I watch too much *Sesame Street*.

The nerds call those things *D-shell connectors*. The connector does look like a D, a really dorky one.

Before connecting a keyboard cable or similar round connector, look into the hole. Make sure that the pins in the cable are all lined up with the tiny holes inside the hole. The smaller, round connectors have notches on one side of the hole, and the cable needs to be lined up.

Don't plug anything into the console while the computer is turned on. You won't get electrocuted (although I'm not certain), but you may damage either the computer or the thing you're plugging in. Always wait until the computer is turned off before plugging in your keyboard cable.

The only exception to this rule is the USB port. You can plug anything into a USB port at any time, and the computer doesn't mind.

Some connectors look alike. But they have subtle differences. Refer to the figure in the sidebar "Where do it go, George?" earlier in this chapter, for cable identification tips. Note that some connectors have holes and others have pins. Some computers even have their connectors labeled, either with words or symbols (which means that you paid more). Table 2-1 shows what some of the words mean and what could possibly plug into them.

A connector or hole with pins is technically a *male* connector. A connector or hole with tiny holes the pins plug into is a *female* connector. I draw a complete blank on why this is so.

Table 2-1	Things You May Plug Cables Into
Whatzit	*What Plugs into Whatzit*
COM1	Plug your mouse into this hole if the connector fits; otherwise, you can plug a modem in here.
COM2	This hole is typically used for outboard motors, er, modems.
LPT1	Printer plugs in here.
LPT2	If you're greedy, your second printer plugs in here. Plug only a second printer in here; don't plug your first printer into an LPT2, LPT3, or anything else.
MOUSE	Mouse must plug in here.
MONITOR	Plug the monitor into this hole.
KYBD	Keyboard goes here (or any other combination of the letters in KEYBOARD).
S-VIDEO	An S-video cable, which connects to a TV set, VCR, or laser disc, goes here.
USB	The non-business end of a USB device plugs into the USB connector's Certs-size slot.
MIC	Microphone.
LINE IN	Stereo (not the microphone).
SPEAKERS	Must be the speakers in here.

Setting up the monitor

Set the monitor on top of the console. Or set it to the side, depending on whether you have enough desk space. Of course, if you have a tower PC, which goes under your desk (or in a nearby tower), the monitor just sits atop your desk. Nothing criminal in that.

- ✔ Do not set a 19-inch or larger monitor on top of a desktop PC unit. The heavy monitor may crush the console, which is designed to support lighter-weight monitors only.

- ✔ Sony JumboTron monitors require an additional power hookup for proper voltage. Contact your electrical company.

- ✔ If there isn't enough cable to put the keyboard and monitor to one side of the console, you can buy extension cables at your favorite computer store.

- ✔ Chapter 13 provides more information about monitors, including how to work the various knobs.

- ✔ Some monitors come with a tilt-and-swivel base, which enables you to move the monitor to various orientations, albeit stiffly. This type of base is also an option you can buy for the monitor if it's not already built in.

- ✔ As with the console, the monitor needs to breathe. Don't set anything on top of the monitor or cover its wee tiny air vents in any way.

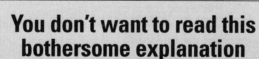

You don't want to read this bothersome explanation

Most of today's computers are sold with a *SuperVGA* graphics system. That fancy term describes how the monitor's and computer's insides are trained to produce some of the most impressive computer graphics in the world (Earth). On that type of system, the video cable has 15 wires in it. Likewise, the connector on the console has 15 holes. To deceive you, another connector of the same size appears on the back of many consoles. But that connector has only 9 holes.

The 9-hole connector is a *serial port,* to which you may connect a mouse, a modem, or some other interesting gizmo. It's not where you plug in the monitor. The monitor plugs into a 15-hole connector.

The monitor has two cables. One goes into the console, which is how the computer displays information on-screen. Call that cable the *video cable.* The second cable is plugged into a wall socket. Call that one the *power cable.* Plug them both in now. Do it simultaneously, using both arms. (Just kidding.)

Setting up the printer

The printer is a device separate and unique from the computer. In a way, it's like a separate computer, one designed just to smear ink all over paper.

Setting up a PC printer is a snap. The hard part comes later, when you must force your software to recognize and control the printer. (I've put that off until Chapter 16, which is buried in the middle of this book, where no one can find it.)

You set up the printer similarly to the way you set up everything else. Take it out of the box, unpack it, and then set it where you want it. Put the printer near the computer — the nearer, the better — although it doesn't need to be too close.

✔ Keeping the printer at arm's length can come in handy.

✔ Be sure to look inside the printer box for manuals, font cartridges, and other stuff the printer needs.

✔ Printers don't come with cables — for a reason. Not every printer is hooked up to an IBM type of computer. Therefore, you have to buy a printer cable separately. (It doesn't have to be any particular brand, just a cable for a PC-to-printer connection.)

✔ Laser printers require *toner cartridges,* which you must purchase separately. Other types of printers usually come with their own ribbons, inkwells, carbon paper, octopi, and so on.

Printer pieces' parts

Printers come in many pieces. You have the printer itself, the ribbon or toner cartridge, and the thing that holds the paper. An instruction sheet that comes with the printer explains what goes where. Find that sheet and heed its instructions.

Basic printer setup requires yanking a few shipping items from the printer's insides, installing the ribbon and toner cartridge, setting up the paper-feeding mechanism or paper tray, adding any font cards, and plugging in the cables.

✔ Si la feuille du mode d'emploi a l'air français, c'est peut-être parce que c'est écrit en français. La plupart des modes d'emploi ont des directives en plusieurs langues. Il faut chercher la version en anglais.

✔ If the instruction sheet reads like it's written in French, it probably is. Most instruction sheets list instructions in several languages. Look for the English version.

✔ Laser printers require a detailed internal setup, which means that you yank out several plastic doohickeys, peel tape, and apply salve to the printer's aching foot pads. Other types of printers may require similar removal of parts. Those parts hold the printer's insides inside during shipment. You don't need to keep them; freely toss them out (even if you plan on moving the printer later).

✔ If you purchased extra memory for your printer, install it before you turn the printer on. Or, better still, have your dealer install it for you.

✔ If you have a font cartridge, it goes into the special font slot hidden somewhere on the printer. An instruction sheet should tell you where it goes. Make sure that the printer is turned off when you plug in the font cartridge.

Connecting the printer cables

Printers have two required cables: the power cable, which plugs into a wall socket, and the printer cable, which plugs into the computer. (Congress passed a law ten years ago requiring that every computing device have, at minimum, two cables.)

The printer cable should already be connected to the PC's console, as described earlier in this chapter. The other end of that cable plugs into the printer. This is the fun part. The connector is big and has two clips on it. There's no way to plug it in wrong, and little guesswork is involved in figuring out where to put it.

✔ The majority of printers plug into the computer's printer port. Aren't you glad that makes sense? A few, however, plug into the PC's serial port.

✔ If your printer has both printer port and serial port options, use the printer port one. You'll thank me later.

✔ You don't need to use the printer right away. I recommend that you get to know the PC first. Then worry about the printer.

Trivial printer cable information

Your printer can be a maximum of 20 feet from your PC. That's the longest a printer cable can be before information is lost. Cables longer than 20 feet just can't carry the signal from the computer, and nothing (or random information) is printed.

A typical printer cable is six feet long — good enough for setting the printer nearby but not necessarily next to the computer. Longer cables are available, and you can always daisy-chain cables. But keep in mind the 20-foot limit.

Oodles of printer tips

Here are some handy computer printer tips you don't have to commit to memory (they're repeated in Chapter 16 anyway, for good measure):

✔ Printers need paper. Laser printers can print on any copy machine paper, but they also accept letterhead and plain typewriter paper.

✔ Avoid using bond paper in a laser printer. Bond paper may have dust or powder on it, and that stuff clogs up the printer. Also avoid erasable typing paper.

✔ Ink printers can use a special type of glossy paper that soaks up the ink well, producing very nice printed copy. Even more expensive paper is available that makes the printed output look photographic.

✔ Some printers can use fanfold paper. It comes with dozens (or hundreds) of sheets connected together. Detachable dots on the sides of the paper enable it to be pulled or pushed through the printer. Insert the paper by using the dots and guides. Some printers automatically line up the paper and are ready to print when you turn them on.

✔ You don't need to have the same printer model as your computer. For example, any model of printer — not just an IBM printer — works with an IBM computer (although IBM salesnoids may claim differently).

✔ You don't need to have the printer turned on unless you're printing something. Leaving some printers turned on wastes lots of electricity. That makes for a big electrical bill when you're not printing anything.

✔ Some newer laser printers are "environmentally friendly." They go quite like a submarine, barely sipping any power until you need them. Then they surface, chow down the power, print, and return to silent mode until you need them again. Sneaky.

✔ The printer does not print unless it's *online*, or *selected*. A button on the printer somewhere enables you to activate the printer, bringing it online or making it selected. No, it's not enough just to turn on the printer.

Most of today's computers are sold with a "smart" printer port. If your printer takes advantage of the smart printer port, ensure that you buy a smart printer cable. Some cheaper printer cables lack the smart feature (which is merely a few extra lines of data).

What about Those Surge Protectors?

Computers make you realize something about modern living: There aren't enough power sockets to plug in everything.

A standard computer requires two power sockets: one for the console and another for the monitor. Extra devices, modems, scanners, printers, expensive gadgets with impressive lights, and so on, all require their own power sockets. As usual, there are right and wrong ways to deal with this situation.

The wrong ways:

- Never use an extension cord to meet your power needs. People trip over extension cords and routinely unplug them.

- Don't use any power splitters or those octopus-like things that turn one socket into three. Computers need grounded sockets, which must have three prongs in them.

- Don't lick the plug before you stick it into the wall.

The right ways:

- Buy a power strip. This device plugs into a single socket and contains as many as six additional sockets. Everything associated with the PC — even the lamp on your desk — can plug into the power strip. You can turn on the whole shebang with your toe through the hole in your sock if that pleases you.

- Buy one of those PowerMeister things. It usually sits below the monitor and has a row of switches: for the computer, monitor, printer, and other items. A single master switch enables you to turn on everything at once.

- Always plug a laser printer into its own socket — never into a power strip or an uninterruptible power supply (see the nearby sidebar "Excuse me, I'm an *uninterruptible* power supply").

TIP

Excuse me, I'm an *uninterruptible* power supply

An *uninterruptible power supply,* or UPS (not the shipping company), is a handy device every PC owner should have. It's not a power strip. Typical UPS units are about the size of a small car battery (hint, hint) and have two, often more, power receptacles on them. You can plug your console and monitor into those receptacles.

What the UPS does — in addition to guarding against spikes, surges, and other nasty power things — is keep your PC running when the power goes off. Not for a long time (mine lasts about 5 minutes), but long enough to let you

save your document, quit Windows, and turn off your PC nicely. That way, you never lose information because of a power outage.

By the way, you don't need to plug *everything* into a UPS. Printers, no way! You can print when the power comes back on. The same goes for scanners, modems, and other fancy devices; use them later. And destroy those dreams of computing for hours during a blackout, being the envy of the block, and so on: When the power goes out, save your work and turn off the PC.

What's Next?

With the computer all set up and ready to roll, you're probably tempted to turn it on. But, wait. You should look for a few things before you steamroll ahead:

- ✔ Find any manuals that came with your computer. Look for the ones that contain directions and troubleshooting help. Keep these manuals handy.

- ✔ Always retain the manuals that came with your computer plus any software manuals. Keep any disks and their software manuals together.

- ✔ You can throw away most of the little scraps of paper. Don't throw away anything that has a phone number on it until you've written the number down elsewhere.

- ✔ Mail in your registration or warranty card. Make a note of the computer's serial number, and file it away as well. In an office situation, you should keep track of all your equipment's serial numbers.

- ✔ Make sure that you have legitimate copies of your software. For example, you should have Windows on your PC's hard disk and a copy of the proper manual. If you don't have a manual, or if you have only photocopied pages, your dealer has sold you a bootlegged version of the software. Do the right thing: Rush to the software store and buy a copy of Windows for your computer. (Don't worry about reporting the dealer; he will pay in the long run.)

You may skip this stuff on surge protectors, but only if you're foolish

A special type of power strip is the *surge protector,* which has protection against power surges and other nasty electrical things that can fry a computer. But *caveat emptor* here: There are varying degrees of surge protectors.

The simplest form of electronic protection is the *line filter.* It sifts out noise from power lines and other offending appliances (like the blender), giving you cleaner power. Surge protectors are more expensive. They protect against power surges, which happen when the electricity company puts out a greater amount of juice over a long period. Spike protection is the highest and most expensive type of protection. A *spike* is a single, high-voltage charge — usually caused by a lightning strike. Only special spike protectors can guard against them, sacrificing themselves and saving your computer's life. (It's kind of religious.)

How serious is all this? Not very. Unless the power in your area is highly unstable and lightning strikes often, don't worry. A power strip with a noise filter, however, is a good investment.

Dealing with software

You may have purchased some software with your computer. If so, great. However, leave all those boxes alone for now. One mistake many beginners make is overwhelming themselves with computer software. Although it's okay to buy lots of software (and if you haven't, you'll probably buy more later), it's counterproductive to use it all right away.

- ✔ Your computer's operating system (Windows) is the most important piece of software you have. Learn how to use it first.

- ✔ See Chapter 5 for more information about what an operating system is.

- ✔ If you have anything you must do — a priority project, for example — set the software you need aside from the rest of the stuff. For example, if learning how to use Quicken, Word, or PageMaker is your top priority, set out the software and get ready to learn and use it first. Everything else can wait.

- ✔ Remember that no job can be done immediately. No matter how annoying your boss is, you must learn to use software before you can be productive with it. Give yourself at least two weeks before you squeeze something brilliant from a computer.

- ✔ Part V of this book covers software in a general sense.

Dealing with other hardware

You may have purchased other hardware goodies, each waiting for setup. Put them on hold for now. Later chapters go into detail about using devices like a mouse, modem, fax, and scanner. The idea here is not to overwhelm you with too much computer stuff right away. Learning about what you have already set up will take time enough.

- ✔ Hardware is added to a computer either internally or externally.

- ✔ Installing internal hardware requires some type of computer nerd. True, you can do it yourself. Many books and magazine articles go into the details, if you want to bother with installing internal hardware. My advice is to force someone else to do it.

- ✔ External hardware requires a power cable and some type of cable to connect it with the PC. A few devices don't use a power cable (they run on your brain waves). Also, you need special software to run the external hardware; a scanner requires scanning software, and a modem requires communications software. These and even more baffling concepts are covered in Part IV of this book.

Chapter 3

Compuspiel (The PC Jargon Roundup)

· ·

· ·

*Y*ou know you're a computer owner when . . . you refer to your spouse as a *peripheral*. Or maybe you call your son's building a Lincoln Logs structure a *child process*. You say that your boss has no *CPU*. Or maybe your mother-in-law is all *output* and no *input*.

Computer terms fill the indexes of boring manuals and pop up in the conversations of computer geeks. Now that you have a PC, you'll start using the terms, too — just like sick people who speak in medical terms they wouldn't have known weeks ago: lacerated basal phalanx for a severed toe, thrombophlebitis for a blood clot in the leg, spasmodic torticollis for a stiff neck, and on and on. Only now you can do it, too — and have nothing seriously wrong with you.

Words and Phrases for $100, Alex

There aren't just computer words you need to learn when you have a computer. No, you need to learn the compuspiel. Certain phrases are heard over and over. They sound meaningless, unless you've taken the following crash course, à la *Jeopardy!*.

The category is Computer Words and Phrases. You are the contestant. Be sure to ring in before your competitors (Alfred Einstein and Bill Gates), or else you'll lose valuable cash and prizes. Good luck.

And the answer is. . . .

A: It appears on the display, the monitor. It can be text or graphics, or anything else the computer is displaying.

Q: What is "on the screen"?

So when your co-worker tells you that this month's report is "up on the screen," don't look on top of your monitor. Very good. Now the $200 answer:

A: I've just listed all the files in a folder.

Q: What is "to pull a directory"?

The old term for *folder* used to be *directory*. Occasionally someone uses the term *directory,* as in "pull a directory of drive A" when he means to list files. The $300 answer:

A: This is something I've created on my computer and have just printed.

Q: What is "hard copy"?

A *hard copy* is simply a printout of something you created on the computer. The $400 answer:

A: Do this when you want to mark all text as a block or choose a group of icons.

Q: What is "select"?

To mark something as a group, you select it. You do this with the mouse, either by dragging the mouse over text or icons or by clicking each item individually. The final, $500 answer:

A: This file contains last-minute information about a product, corrections to the manual, or additional information you should read.

Q: What is a "read-me file"?

Various software programs are shipped with files named README. Opening those files displays information about the software, which can sometimes be useful.

Congratulations — you've won the round!

Acronym Asylum

Computers have probably added more acronyms to the human vocabulary than the U.S. government has. The following sample contains a few you may or may not encounter.

ASCII

ASCII is an acronym, but that's not important. What is important is how you pronounce it. ASCII is pronounced "ask-ee" (similar to "nasty"). It is not pronounced "ask-2."

ASCII is typically used to describe something that's text-only. For example, an ASCII file contains pure text, numbers, and common punctuation symbols. It doesn't contain italics, fancy headlines, or pictures of clowns.

- Most word processors and other programs permit you to save a file in an ASCII, or plain text, format. Because ASCII means that the text is stripped down to its bare essentials, an ASCII file can be read by most other programs and computers.

- Windows typically refers to the ASCII format as a "text document" or "text-only."

- Why not save all data files in ASCII format? Because ASCII is too limiting. Word processors stick their own, special codes into ASCII files to simplify formatting and other chores. Plus, ASCII applies to only text and numbers. It's useless for graphics and similar information.

- ASCII stands for the American Standard Code for Information Interchange. It's a set of numbers (0 through 127), each of which is assigned to a letter of the alphabet (both upper- and lowercase), the numerals 0 through 9, punctuation symbols, other weird characters, and 32 special control codes that represent keys on the keyboard, such as Enter, Backspace, Tab, and Esc, and aren't you bored now?

DVD

The next-generation CD-ROM drive is the *DVD*. It stands for Digital Versatile Disc, which can store lots more information than a mere mortal CD.

To use a DVD disc, which looks just like a CD, you need a special DVD drive, which looks just like a CD-ROM drive. Many new computers offer this drive as an option, and it'll probably be standard in the future.

DVD drives can read older CDs, no problem. For more information about the whole DVD fiasco, see Chapter 7.

Where did ASCII come from?

In the mid-1960s, programmer types created ASCII to be a universal language, like Esperanto, but with a big-business-size marketing budget. The programmers decided to limit the number of ASCII characters to 128. At the time, it was a good-size number (huge, in fact); most computers at the time could efficiently handle values of 128. (Today's PCs deal with 256-size values on up.)

The idea was that any ASCII-compatible computer could exchange files and information with other ASCII-compatible computers, even if the two computers came from different home planets. This idea still works today. You can take an ASCII file from an IBM type of computer and magically beam it into a Macintosh, and the file still looks more or less the same. (Nothing is perfect, however, and the result always requires additional work. Don't get your hopes up.)

GUI

GUI is yet another computer acronym. It's pronounced "gooey," as in "ooey GUI, rich and chewy." *GUI* stands for Graphical User Interface and means that you control the computer through pictures and symbols on the computer's screen. This process is the opposite of typing text commands at a DOS prompt. Supposedly, it's easier, but the jury's still out.

- Where did the term GUI come from? Who knows. Read the mountains of legal paperwork, or take a software attorney to lunch.
- You need a computer mouse to make a GUI work right.
- After you pronounce GUI as "gooey" a few times, you'll be able to stifle the urge to giggle. That urge returns when you pronounce the plural, "gooeys."

RAM (memory)

RAM and *memory* are two interchangeable terms. They both refer to temporary storage inside a computer. Regardless of whatever the term is technically, you should know that the more RAM or memory the computer has, the more it can do. More RAM is better than less RAM, and a Dodge RAM beats the pants off a Ford truck any day of the week.

✔ More memory means that you can do more than you can with less memory.

✔ Replace the word *memory* with *money* in the preceding item, and read the sentence again.

✔ *RAM* stands for Random Access Memory. Specifically, it refers to the type of chip inside the computer where information is stored.

✔ Reader SL from Hemet, California, writes to say, "Undoubtedly, you are a computer expert, but . . . a Ford truck does slam a Ram anytime, regardless of day, week, month, or year." He even includes a *USA Today* clipping about truck sales to drive the point home. Well, SL, that may be true, but it just doesn't make for a clever punch line to end the section, so between you and me (and I drive a Dakota), let's say that Dodge is better. And the war is on.

USB

The USB is the Universal Serial Bus, a new slot in the back of most newer computers into which you can plug a variety of interesting devices. The nifty thing about the USB, and why you'll read more about it, is that it requires no effort on your behalf to install, for example, a new keyboard, modem, speakers, scanner, videocamera, or a variety of interesting devices. I blah-blah-blah on this topic at length in Chapter 11.

WWW

In computer lingo, WWW is not the name of a wrestling foundation, nor is it the pattern on Charlie Brown's shirt. WWW is an acronym for World Wide Web, which is sometimes just called "the Web." It's a fun and popular way to access information stored on the Internet. This book bores you with that subject in Part VI.

Ugly Hardware Terms

Unbeknownst to most people, the terms *doojobbie, thingamabob,* and *whatzis* are heavily copyrighted by various secretive international groups. When it came time to give various names to certain doodads (also copyrighted) on a computer, scientists were at a loss. So they made up names. This section is merely a sample.

CD-ROM

A *CD-ROM* is the same thing as a music CD, except that it stores computer information instead. Whereas you can get maybe 12 or 18 songs on a music CD, though, computer CDs can store entire encyclopedias of information. Because of that, most computer software comes on a CD-ROM disc, which computer users refer to as "CD," just like the music CDs.

The ROM part of CD-ROM stands for Read-Only Memory. The CD-ROM drive only reads CDs. To write information to a CD, you need a special disc drive called a CD-R or CD-RW, which are techy things this book may or may not cover later.

Disk

Information — no, let me start over: Data is stored on a disk inside your computer. *Disks* store stuff long-term. Computer memory stores stuff short-term. If you want to keep the stuff you create, you save it to disk.

Disks come in many varieties: floppy, hard, CD-ROM, slipped, and brake. Whatever. Just remember that whenever someone implores you to "save to disk," he means to put your stuff — your data — safely away for later use or abuse.

Function keys (also known as F-keys)

Your keyboard has various zones and areas, just like various neighborhoods around big cities. It has alphanumeric, numeric, cursor, and function neighborhoods. (It has empty spaces, too, just like around Indianapolis.)

Some of the keys in the top row on your keyboard are labeled F1 through F12. These are your keyboard's *function keys.* They're called that because they have no standard purpose, not like the P key, which produces some form of P when you press it (unless you're eating potato chips and a crumb lodges under the key).

The IBM designers left open the purpose of each function key, so whichever program you're using may do something different with these keys. In Windows, however, the F1 key always displays help information. It's the only key that's the same, though; other programs may use F2 through F12 for something entirely weird.

Macintosh

The very first computer with personality was the Macintosh. Your PC, it doesn't have personality. It's a serious business machine. Apple, which makes the Macintosh, spends millions each year trying to convince the general public that its computer is for business. Yeah. Right.

Seriously, the Macintosh is just a different computer. It has a GUI, like Windows, plus a bunch of fun and interesting software. It's not as popular, though, and therefore isn't as widely supported as your PC.

- ✔ Macintosh people call their computers Macs rather than PCs.
- ✔ Because Mac people paid much more for their computers, they take it really personally when you attack them — even when you're more than justified and the facts stack up like the pancakes at an IHOP.

Network

A *network* is two or more computers connected by some type of network hose and special network software that allows all the machines to stop working at one time.

Seriously, networked computers can share information. They can all use one printer, for example. They can all access files and programs from common hard drives, and employees can send messages back and forth asking each other where to have lunch that day.

Here are three ways to tell whether you're on a network:

1. Your co-workers and you can share a printer, files, or messages without getting out of your chairs.
2. You must log in or log out when you're using the computer.
3. When the server stops working, *everyone* in the office screams.

- ✔ If you don't have a network, forget about them.
- ✔ If you're in an office where two computers share a single printer and you have this thing called an A-B switch connecting them, what you really need is a network.
- ✔ See Chapter 10 for more networking information, if you dare.

Ugly Software Terms

Software isn't immune from ugly terminology. In fact, people close to computers forget how utterly strange the terms are. Desktop? Data? Windows? How could such innocent words, well understood by most little kids, be twisted into something that drives the typical adult batty? This section confirms it with a few of the more offensive, yet common, software terms.

Data

If you need to use the words *information* or *stuff* and you have a computer, you say *data* instead.

The only major cultural crime committed here is pronouncing *data* incorrectly. It's "DAY-ta." Say it like someone from the Northeast would say *waiter,* but with a *d* rather than a *w.*

Do not pronounce *data* as "dadda." Your dadda is married to your momma.

Desktop

Desktop is a fancy term for the screen background when you use Windows. On the desktop, you find icons and windows, which you can use to interact with the computer. The idea originated from making the computer work like your real-life desktop: It had paper, a telephone, a Rolodex, and other handy items. How that bold idea degenerated into graphical icons and windows is anyone's guess.

Documents

Documents are special types of files created by word processors. Documents are written things — stuff you can print and send to people: memos, letters, chapters from a book, reports, essays, mail you'll later regret you sent, and so on. Anything a word processor produces is a document kind of file.

- Non-word-processing software may refer to the files it creates as documents. It just sounds more professional than data file or "that thing I did in CorelDRAW!"
- Spreadsheets create worksheets, which may also be called documents.
- A *file* is the name of a chunk of data saved to disk. Files are covered in an upcoming section, unless you're reading this chapter backward.

DOS prompt

In Windows, the *DOS prompt* is the name of the program that used to be your PC's operating system. Now it's relegated to being yet another window on the screen, a text-based way to control the computer and run old, decrepit DOS programs.

The DOS prompt itself consists of the strange and confusing characters you see at the beginning of each line while you're working with DOS. It's the computer's way of prompting you to tell it what to do.

The DOS prompt usually looks like this:

```
C:\>
```

- ✔ You type commands at the DOS prompt to make the computer do something useful.

- ✔ The letter in the prompt usually tells you which disk drive you're raiding.

- ✔ This book rarely touches the subject of DOS. For that information, I recommend checking out the all-time bestseller *DOS For Dummies,* 3rd Edition, or, if you're using Windows 95 or later, check out *DOS For Dummies, Windows 95 Edition,* both of which were written by me and are available from IDG Books Überwelt.

Files

A *file* is a collection of information (hey: *data*) stored by the computer. There are different types of files, each storing different types of stuff.

Program files contain instructions for the computer to do something useful, like balance a checkbook.

Data files contain the stuff you create, like a letter to Miss Manners or a picture of your office falling into a bubbling pit of molten lead.

Text (hey: *ASCII*) files contain plain ol' boring text.

- ✔ They didn't have to call them files. They could have called them packets or cubbies or containers or reticules. But they called them files (probably because computers are used mostly in offices).

- ✔ Files are ethereal. You can't pick up and hold a file. You can hold the disk that contains the file (or files). And you can print a file and then hold the sheaf of papers. But you can't touch a file. In a way, they're like angels.

✔ The name given to a file is referred to as the *filename*.

✔ You must come up with your own names for the files you create. If a program refuses to accept your creative filename, you're probably in or treading dangerously close to the Forbidden Filenames Zone. Turn to Chapter 9 quickly, before the beating of the drums reaches a fever pitch.

✔ Approximately 7,000 files can dance on the head of a light pen.

Folders

Files are stored on disk in special places called *folders* — just like in the real world, which could be their inspiration. Well, either that or an origami class.

Folders are used for organization. After all, a disk can contain hundreds, if not thousands, of files. If you don't stuff related files into different folders, you essentially re-create the bureaucracy from Hell: too much information and a bunch of deadbeats unwilling to help you find anything. Typically, this situation is undesirable.

The nifty thing about folders is that Windows displays icons for them that actually look like folders. You open the folders to see files and even more folders. Chapter 8 goes into how it works.

In days of yore, folders were known by another name: directories (or subdirectories). You may still read or hear this term. Mentally replace it with *folder,* and you'll be okay.

Icon

Father Murphy would certainly freak if you told him that you were *clicking on icons,* yet that's just what you do on a computer running a GUI. (See the "GUI" section, earlier in this chapter.)

Computer geeks needed a name for the symbols in a GUI. Those symbols often represent something greater, so they called them *icons.*

✔ These icons have nothing to do with the icons you may see hanging in a Greek Orthodox church. (There's a big difference between Greeks and geeks.)

✔ In case you really don't know: Icons are pictures of the saints. They typically hang in churches, although I have an icon of Saint Jude on my computer.

✔ Saint Jude is the patron saint of those who believe their situation to be hopeless.

Kilobyte and megabyte and gigabyte

Bytes are confusing, but they don't have to be. A *byte* is merely computer-speak for a storage place that holds only one character. The term *kilo* means 1,000, so one *kilobyte* is roughly 1,000 bytes, about 1,000 characters, or a little less than half a page of text or a county Shriners' convention.

The term *mega* means 1 million, or 1,000,000. One *megabyte* is 1,000 kilo-bytes, so it's about 1,000,000 characters or somewhere close to 500 pages or an Idaho full of Shriners.

The term *giga* means one billion, or 1,000,000,000. That's 1,000 megabytes and half a Sagan ("billions and billions").

- ✔ Kilobyte is commonly abbreviated as K.
- ✔ Megabyte is commonly abbreviated as MB.
- ✔ Gigabyte is commonly abbreviated as GB.

Multimedia

Treat *multimedia* as nothing more than a buzzword. Simply put, a multimedia PC is one with sound, a CD-ROM drive, and enough graphics sizzle to play television-like videos on the screen. Nearly every PC sold today is set up that way, so it's really not a descriptive term anymore (though it's still used).

Read this stuff only if you want to be precise

Okay, confession time. One kilobyte does not equal 1,000 bytes or characters. It's really 1,024 bytes. The extra 24 bytes are a tax levied by Congress. Seriously, 1,024 is the number 2 raised to the 10th power — 2^{10}. Computers just love the number 2, and 1,024 is the closest power of 2 to 1,000. It's okay for us humans to think that 1K equals 1,000. The extra change does, however, add up over time.

Likewise, 1MB equals 1,048,576 bytes, not an even million. One megabyte is actually 1,024K, which means that 1,024 multiplied by 1,024 gives you one mega of bytes. This stuff, like the concept of a billion dollars, is all trivial.

Multitasking

To *multitask* is to do more than one thing at a time. For example, when you're on the phone, cooking dinner, looking at the TV, and fending off a small child, you're multitasking; you're doing four — or more — things at one time. Computers can do that with no problem and without losing track of the conversation, burning dinner, or putting food in baby's ear.

Multitasking is really a job for a computer's *operating system* (see that section later in this chapter). All computer hardware can multitask; it takes software to make it do so.

Multitasking doesn't seem obvious or even useful to many first-time PC users. The reason is simple: You're only one person, and you have only one set of eyes and hands. Your computer has only one keyboard and one monitor. What's the point of trying to do several things at one time?

Ah, the secret: A lot of the time you spend using the computer is spent waiting. You wait for the database to sort. You wait for a graphics image to redraw itself; you wait for the computer to copy a file. With multitasking, all this stuff can happen *while you're doing something else.* That's the beauty of it.

✔ With a multitasking computer, you can move on and do something else while the computer toils at some task by itself.

✔ When you're not working on a particular program, it's said to be in the *background,* which is similar to putting something on the back burner. It continues to cook, but you don't need to pay attention to it.

✔ Whatever you're working on in a multitasking environment is said to be in the *foreground.* It's just like putting something on a front burner, where it can bubble over and melt on your shoe.

✔ Windows is a multitasking operating system. You can find more information about it in Chapter 5.

Opening a program or file

"Hey, Vern! Give me a can opener and some vice grips. Let's open that Excel file on your PC."

Uh, not exactly. *To open* in compuspiel means to transfer something from disk to the computer's memory; to *run* a program means to open a file on disk to work with it.

- ✔ You open data files by using special Open commands in your program. For example, in Windows, you open files to load them into memory.

- ✔ You also open program files to run them. See the section "Run, execute, launch," later in this chapter.

- ✔ The old term for opening a file was *load*.

    The following expressions mean exactly the same thing as "open a program":

    - Execute a program

    - Run a program

    - Start a program

    - Load up a program

    - Boot up a program

    - Launch a program

Operating system

An *operating system* is software that controls your computer. It's the main piece of software. The head honcho. The big cheese. The software all other software bows to. Major kowtow to the operating system.

Both your PC's hardware and software must be controlled by an operating system. The most popular flavor of operating system is Windows. It once was DOS. And then there's something called OS/2, which tried to kill off both DOS and Windows. The story is very soap opera-ish. Here's a quick who's who.

DOS (where the *OS* stands for *operating system*) is the granddaddy of them all. It's old, cryptic, text-oriented, slow, and limited, with the added plus that they don't make it anymore. (Well, Microsoft doesn't make it, but IBM still does. Sorta.)

Windows used to be a DOS program. Now, however, Microsoft has decided that Windows should wing it alone as an operating system. It's less cryptic than DOS, tries to be fun to use, and ends up being about as manageable as a 40-pound carry-on bag in a commuter plane (but it's pretty).

Windows 95? 98? See the section "Windows," later in this chapter.

OS/2 (where the *OS* stands for *operating system*) was designed by Microsoft and IBM to replace DOS. Then Microsoft got mad at IBM and decided that Windows would replace DOS. Whatever. IBM decided that OS/2 was still good, so the company pushes it to this day. It has a great deal of virtue but a relatively small following.

- ✔ This book concentrates on Windows, specifically Windows 98 but also Windows 95 (they're similar). If you haven't yet upgraded, you will! Not that I'm nuts about the latest version of Windows, but when an 800-pound gorilla wants you to eat a dirt clod, you eat it (if you gather my drift).

- ✔ Some feel-good types refer to the operating system as the *operating environment.* I prefer "system" rather than "environment." It's easier to say while chewing gum.

Quit, exit, close

Just as programs can be started up, they can be turned off. You don't do so by flipping the computer's power switch, however, no matter how tempting this idea may be. Instead, you must find the way the program meant for you to quit.

The manual helps. If you have one, look in the index for the word *exit.* Or, if you have a computer guru nearby, you can slowly wave the manual high above your head.

- ✔ Nearly all Windows programs quit by using the last command on the first menu, which is typically the File⇨Exit command.

- ✔ When the program leaves the screen, it returns you to Windows.

- ✔ Remember to save your work before exiting a program.

- ✔ Part of the joy of Windows is that you don't really have to quit a program when you're done. You can instead *minimize* it, or shrink it down to unobtrusiveness. That temporarily gets it out of the way so that you can do something else. (I cover this topic in Chapter 6.)

The following phrases all describe leaving a program:

- • Exiting a program
- • Quitting a program
- • Getting out of a program
- • Returning to Windows
- • Closing the program's window
- • Bag this junk, and let's get a pizza

Run, execute, launch

Running a program means working with it so that you can do something useful. You can run 1-2-3, you can execute 1-2-3, and you can launch 1-2-3. These three confusing terms refer to the same thing.

- You run a program by starting it in Windows. You do this by double-clicking the mouse on the program's icon or by plucking the program's name from the pop-up Start menu.

- *Run* is the most common term, although some manual writers say *execute* because the thought of putting 1-2-3 before a firing squad is so emotionally satisfying.

Save

Saving is the process of telling the computer to transfer the information you just created to a disk for storage and safekeeping. Therefore, "save your data" has nothing to do with religious conviction.

- When you save something to disk, you can reload it later to work on it again. If you don't save, you have to re-create your stuff all over again from scratch.

- If you don't tell the computer to save your work, it doesn't do so automatically.

- Actually, Quicken does save your work automatically. It's the only program I know of that does so without any effort on your behalf.

- After you learn how to save your work, try to save it every five minutes or so. Some programs even offer an automatic-save feature that automatically saves your work every few minutes or just after the power goes out.

Start button

"Click the Start button" may sound like some insider's lingo, a 1990s equivalent of "You bet your sweet bippy." This phrase seems odd only until you notice that Windows has a button named *Start* on the screen. By clicking that button, you can direct Windows to do any number of interesting or useful things. In fact, you may even see the Start button in Microsoft advertisements. It's big on starting things. And because the keyboard is already too full of buttons, the company put its Start button up on the screen.

✔ Actually, some keyboards do have a Start button. The new Microsoft keyboards include a special Windows button that performs the same function as the Start button on the screen. These earth people are clever, no?

✔ See Chapter 15 for more info about weird buttons on the keyboard.

Taskbar

Along the bottom of the Windows screen (the desktop), lurks a bar — like a handlebar you would hang on to if the floor suddenly dropped from beneath you and an ugly pit of molten lava appeared. In Windows, you use the taskbar to control various programs and windows that appear on the screen. It's part of "multitasking madness," which this book goes into in Chapter 6. Also, the taskbar is where the Start button lurks.

Version

Software changes. Bugs are ironed out, things are improved, and new features are added. To keep track of changes, software developers slap version numbers on their software.

The first version of a program is known as Version 1.0, pronounced "version one-point-oh." A minor improvement makes it Version 1.1 ("one-point-one"). A major improvement starts all over again with 2.0 ("two-point-oh").

A version number helps you keep track of how old or recent your software is. The number is especially important with your operating system. For example, some programs do not run on the older version of Windows, Version 3.0 ("three-point-oh"). Some programs run on only Version 3.1 ("three-point-one"). Some run only on Windows 95, which is actually a fancy name for Windows 4.0 ("four-point-oh").

✔ Windows 98 is actually Windows Version 4.1. Strange, but true.

✔ The software version number is usually listed on the box, although with some programs you have to tell the program to display that information.

✔ Most people avoid the point-oh version of software: 1.0, 2.0, 3.0, and so on. Major release numbers typically have bugs and other problems that aren't fixed until the 1.1, 2.1, or 3.1 release.

✔ Because people have become wise to version numbers, some companies don't use them anymore. Witness: Microsoft Word 97. That product should really be called Word 8.0. It's really only Word 4.0 because they skipped numbers 3 through 6. Ah, logic.

Window

A *window* (which is not the same thing as Windows) is a graphical area on the screen that contains an application or document or displays information. You can move the window around, close it, shrink it, and do a number of other interesting things, some of which I cover in Chapter 5.

✔ Things appear on the screen (actually, on the *desktop*) in windows. That's probably why they call the operating system Windows.

✔ A definite difference exists between lowercase windows and uppercase Windows: The latter is the name of the operating system. (Just keep reading.)

Windows

The current and most popular operating system for the PC is *Windows,* lovingly cobbled together by Microsoft. Windows was designed to replace the ugly and nonintuitive DOS prompt with a beautiful and nonintuitive graphical user interface (see the "GUI"section, near the beginning of this chapter).

The operating system is called Windows because it fills the screen with overlapping windows — box-like areas containing their own programs or other information. The graphics also represent what you create more accurately than does the boring DOS text screen. For example, you can type a document in your word processor and see it on the screen pretty much the same way as it prints.

✔ Windows, with an initial capital letter, refers to the Windows operating system. The lowercase version, windows, refers to the box-like areas on-screen.

✔ Windows 95 is really Windows Version 4.0.

✔ Windows 98 is the current version of Windows, which should really be Windows Version 5.0, but it's actually Version 4.1. Like anyone is paying attention to this. . . .

✔ A special jumbo version of Windows, Windows NT, works for big companies with big computers and big networks and big dollars.

✔ Windows wasn't inspired by the Macintosh. Nope. No way. And Microsoft has lots of lawyers on retainer who will make you agree.

Ugly Internet Terms

Way back in the late 1960s, the U.S. government wanted to develop a huge computer network, one without any specific location so that it would survive a nuclear attack. The network was originally called ARPAnet, used primarily by military types but also by researchers at university and government installations. The descendant of that computer network is now called the Internet, and it can barely survive an attack by legions of 14-year-olds armed with a computer, a modem, and America Online software.

Seriously, the *Internet* is not a single computer or even software. It's a bunch of computers all over the world that send, receive, and store information. You use specialized software to access that information, which can be fun and useful or dreary and maddening. It all depends. See Part VI for the lowdown. Until then, bask in the following terms from heck.

Browse

Browsing is the time-consuming act of reading information on the Internet, specifically the World Wide Web. To browse, you need software called a *Web browser*. What you do with the browser is visit various Web pages on the Internet and consume information.

E-mail

Electronic mail is fun, and it's the number-one reason most people are on the Internet. You can send messages nearly instantaneously to just about anyone else in the world who has an Internet e-mail account. This subject is covered in extreme depth in Chapter 25.

E-mail attachment

Sending messages just isn't enough. With e-mail on the Internet, you can also send files. This feature can be the source of excitement and woe for many; receiving a file doesn't necessarily mean that your computer can read it. Because of that, I have a whole chapter devoted to understanding e-mail attachments (see Chapter 25).

Favorites

When you visit on the Web some place you like, you can drop a bookmark there. The *bookmark* is a reminder of where you've been — like a bookmark in a book. Your browser then keeps a list of bookmarks available so that you can revisit your favorite Internet Web pages.

Alas, the title of this section is "Favorites." That's because Microsoft calls a Web page bookmark a "favorite" and not a bookmark. Every other Web browser in the world calls them bookmarks. But to Microsoft, they're "favorites," so get used to the confusion now.

Link

A *link* is an underlined bit of text on a Web page, usually shown in a different color from other text. Clicking the link with your mouse takes you to a Web page with related information. That's how the World Wide Web works: Millions of links interconnect just about every Web page in the world.

Web page

A *Web page* is a document on the Internet, one that contains text and graphics, which is viewed by using a Web browser. Millions and millions of Web pages exist, each containing information or trivia to please minds both complex and simple. Part VI of this book covers the whole caboodle with a minimum of fuss.

Terms Too Ugly to List Elsewhere

I hate 'em. Here they are:

Default

A horrid word, usually associated with a mortgage, *default* really means, "Here's what happens when you don't do anything." In a way, it's what happens when you don't pay your mortgage. On a computer, it's what happens when you don't make any choices and blindly obey the computer's suggestion.

I hate the word *default*. Computer nerds and manuals use it thusly:

```
The Print Very Tiny Text option is on by default.
```

or

```
The default colors are red with a green background.
```

This message means that, if the computer were to have its way, it would make these selections, thinking that everything would be aesthetically pleasing to you.

- ✔ I prefer using the term "favorite" rather than "default." It works for me.
- ✔ If you ever want to choose the default option, just press the Enter key.
- ✔ Basically, the default option or choice is the option that works best for 99 percent of the people using the program. So, if you just press the Enter key rather than fiddle around, the program automatically makes the right choice — supposedly.
- ✔ The default option is similar to the "any key" option in that neither of them appears on the keyboard.
- ✔ Default can also mean "standard option" or "what to select when you don't have a clue." For example, small children pinch each other by default.

Directory

This ugly, nasty, pre-Windows term is used by DOS and UNIX people to describe a folder. Why couldn't they just use "folder"? It's the same thing. The worst part is that you see this term bandied about like everyone knows what it is, especially its rude variant: root directory. That just means the main folder on a disk. Yuck.

Driver

A *driver* is a special piece of software that introduces a strange piece of hardware to your computer system. Specifically, the driver introduces the hardware to your PC's operating system, which means that the operating system, your PC's hardware, you, your software — okay, the whole gang can now — access that hardware.

DRIVER: Hello! This is Norville. He's your new scanner!

OPERATING SYSTEM: Okay. Everyone, meet Norville.

EVERYONE: Hello, Norville!

ADOBE PHOTOSHOP: Hi Norville! I'm a graphics package, and I can now use you to scan in graphical images.

NORVILLE: It's nice to be wanted.

You personally will never have to mess with drivers. However, your software and various manuals will refer to them. *Driver* is just one of those annoying terms that crop up. Try not to think of a chauffeur, and you'll do okay.

Key combination

A *key combination* is two or more keys pressed at one time. You do this all the time when you press Shift+S to get a capital S. The computer keyboard has three shift keys: Shift, Alt, and Ctrl. Pressing any of those keys in combination with other keys is called a key combination.

- ✔ Pressing your forehead against the keyboard is called exhaustion.
- ✔ Chapter 15 discusses using your keyboard.

Login (or log-in or logon or log-on)

When the prisoner (you) identifies himself to the warden (the computer), he does so by logging in. It's yet another case where one word — *log,* which normally means a dead tree — is perverted into both a noun and a verb by evil computer scientists.

As a noun, *login* is your ID when you present yourself to the computer. You type your name or a code and then a password to confirm that you are who you say you are. That process is *logging in.* You can replace "on" for "in" to mean the same thing: Use your logon and you're logging on, for example. Weird.

Toggle

In compuspiel, when something is a *toggle,* it means that it has two settings, one of which is on and the other is off. If you activate the toggle, it switches from one setting to the other, like a toggle switch. I suppose that's where they got the term. Anyway, don't boggle over toggle.

- ✔ Toggle switches are confusing because you use one switch or button to do two things. I'll let you wait in eager anticipation for your first encounter with one.

Part II
Using Your PC
(If You Already
Own One)

"ALRIGHT, STEADY EVERYONE. MARGO, GO OVER TO TOM'S PC AND PRESS 'ESCAPE',...VERY CAREFULLY."

In this part . . .

No one frets over using a TV. It has two knobs (or it did at one time): the on-off-volume knob and the channel changer. Push-button phones? No problem: Punch in the number and it rings on the other end. No Enter key. No setup. And microwave ovens? How about that "Popcorn" button, eh?

No wonder computers can be such a pain in the neck. Too many buttons! No dials! Nothing that says, "Pay attention to me and ignore everything else."

The chapters in this part of the book are designed to familiarize you with the computer — how to turn it on and get it to do something. Truly, that's the only stuff you need to know. Everything else is for show.

Chapter 4

The Big Red Switch

*S*hould turning something on or off be complicated? Of course not. Then again, a computer isn't known for being the most logical of devices. Heck, you would think that the computer would have several On and Off switches just to make it tough on you. But no.

The truth is that there's just one Big Red Switch that makes the PC stop or go. Of course, the switch isn't that big. And it's often not red. What's more of an issue is when and how to throw the switch and all the stuff that happens in between. That's what makes you pull your hair out in clumps or chant a mantra while clutching your New Age power crystal in one hand and flipping the power switch with the other.

Well, fret no more. This chapter covers the basics of turning a computer on and what happens just after that and then doesn't neglect the important stuff about turning the computer off. A lot of things happen as Mr. PC begins his sunshiny day. Oh — and this is definitely worth $6 of this book's cover price — this chapter tells you the lowdown on whether you can let your computer run all day and all night without ever turning it off. (Yes, it can be done.)

Turning the Computer On

Turning a computer on is as easy as reaching for that big red switch and flipping it to the On position. Some computers may have their big red switch in front, and some have the switch on the side. Still other computers may even paint their big red switch brown or fawn white, or it may be one of those push-button jobbies.

✔ In keeping with the international flavor of computing, computer companies have done away with the illogical, Western-culture-dominated habit of putting the words *on* and *off* on their On-Off switches. To be more politically correct, the PC's switch uses a bar for On and a circle for Off (go back and see Figure 1-3 in Chapter 1 to refresh your own memory banks).

✔ If you can't see the screen, wait awhile. If nothing appears, turn the monitor on.

✔ If the computer doesn't turn on, check to see whether it's plugged in. If it still doesn't turn on, refer to Chapter 26.

✔ Two nerdy terms for turning on a computer: Power-on and power-up.

✔ If the computer does something unexpected or if you notice that it's being especially unfriendly, first panic. Then turn to Part VII of this book to figure out what went wrong.

✔ Make sure that a disk isn't in drive A when you start your computer. If a disk is in floppy disk drive A, the computer doesn't start from the hard drive like it's supposed to. Keep drive A empty. (Some people keep a disk in drive A because it looks cool; don't be a fool. Just say no to disks in drive A when you boot your computer.)

✔ See Chapter 7 for more information about drive A.

Technical stuff to ignore

Your computer has many plug-inable items attached to it. Each one of them has its own On/Off switch. There's no specific order to follow when you turn any equipment on or off, although an old adage is "Turn the computer box on last." Or was it first? I don't remember.

One way to save yourself the hassle is to buy a power strip or one of the fancier computer power-control-center devices. You plug everything into it and then turn on the whole shebang with one switch.

"The manual tells me to boot my computer: Where do I kick it?"

Oh, don't be silly. Booting a computer has nothing to do with kicking it. Instead, *booting* simply refers to turning on a computer. To *boot a computer* means to turn it on. Rebooting a computer is the same as pressing the Reset button. It's all weird nerd talk.

Look! Up on the screen!

Heavenly choirs rejoice! Windows is here! Whether you're using Windows 95 or Windows 98, you see a colorful display on the screen, proudly announcing your PC's operating system.

Of course, you don't see Windows right away. First comes some text, a copyright notice, and some numbers and odd instructions. Whatever. After that, the PC goes graphical. You may see more bits of text fly by, like the closing credits of a movie (but don't bother looking for the dolly grip or best boy).

- ✔ Lots of chaos occurs as Windows loads. Don't fret over any of it.

- ✔ Some monitors may display text as Windows starts up, or even before your computer is turned on. My Hitachi monitor, for example, tells me "Invalid Sync" whenever it's on and the computer is off. Your monitor may also display various numbers and values as it changes video modes. It's nothing to concern yourself with; just enjoy the show.

- ✔ Starting the computer with the Big Red Switch is the mechanical part. What you're starting up is the computer hardware, which is nothing other than a lot of heavy, cold, and calculating electronic junk the cat likes to sleep on. Eventually, your computer's software brings the computer to life, allowing it to do something. With Windows 98 (and Windows 95 before it), you see the "Windows in the clouds" scene, which is meant only to entertain you while Windows seemingly takes several weeks to get out of bed.

- ✔ If your computer was shut down "improperly" (a power outage occurred or some doofus just flipped the switch), you may see a message asking you to press any key to run the ScanDisk program. Do so. If ScanDisk finds any errors, fix them by pressing the Enter key. You do not need an "undo disk," so select the Skip Undo option; press the right-arrow key and then Enter.

- ✔ See the section "Turning the Computer Off," later in this chapter, for information about how to properly turn off your computer.

Don't mess with system passwords

Some PCs have the capability to have a system password. I don't recommend using it. The password sounds nifty: A prompt appears right after you turn on your computer, preventing unauthorized access from anyone who doesn't know the password. If you forget your password, you're seriously screwed. Often, you have to call the manufacturer (and wait on hold forever) to get the secret instructions for removing the password. It can be painful.

My advice: Don't bother with system passwords.

You can set your password by accessing your PC's setup program, typically by pressing either the F1 or F2 key right when your PC starts up. The Setup program controls various technical aspects of your PC and is definitely not the place you want to wander around while innocent or intoxicated. If you've already been brave (or foolish) enough to set a password for your PC, remove it.

More information about your PC's setup program is in Chapter 11.

"My computer says 'Non-system disk.' What gives?"

It happens a lot, even to Bill Gates!

```
Non-system disk or disk error
Replace and strike any key when ready
```

Remove the floppy disk from drive A and press the Enter key. Your computer then starts up normally.

The reason you see the message is that you or someone else has left a floppy disk in your PC's drive A. The computer has tried to start itself up by using software on that disk and — whaddya know? — no software is on that disk! The software (your PC's operating system) is really on your PC's hard drive, which can't be loaded until you remove that dern floppy disk from drive A and whack the Enter key.

And just who the heck are you?

Windows seems pretty easy to get into; it's doing all the work! If your PC is shackled to a network, however, you'll be forced to show some ID before getting into the good stuff. Apparently, you can't buy liquor or drive a computer without proper identification.

The Enter Network Password dialog box, as shown in Figure 4-1, is the way Windows gently asks, "Just who the heck are you?" You type your special username, press the Tab key, and then type your password. Click the OK button, and Windows lets you in.

Figure 4-1:
Windows
meekly
asks for a
password.

Enter Network Password	? X

Enter your network password for Microsoft Networking.

OK

Cancel

User name: Finster McGillicutty

Password: |

If you type the wrong password, security alarms sound, a metal gate drops over you and your PC, the hounds are released, and Windows dutifully erases the hard drive lest security be breached.

Just kidding! If you goof up, you get a second shot. If you goof up again, Windows lets you in anyway.

- ✔ Windows probably already knows your username and displays it proudly for you, as shown in Figure 4-1. Your job is merely to enter the proper password.

- ✔ Press the Tab key to move between the User Name and Password text boxes.

- ✔ Telling the network who you are is technically called *logging in.* It has nothing to do with timber.

- ✔ Chapter 10 discusses computer networking, if you want to go nuts about it.

- ✔ If this whole password/login stuff annoys you, just press the Esc key on the keyboard to bypass the timid security.

- ✔ If they guarded the crown jewels as feebly as Windows guards its network, we would all be wearing funny, expensive hats.

It's about time this operating system showed up

After a time, and then times and half a time, Windows presents itself on the screen in all its graphical goodness and glory, as shown in Figure 4-2. What you see is the desktop, Windows' main screen, or home plate, if you will. Windows is finally ready for you to use. Time to get to work.

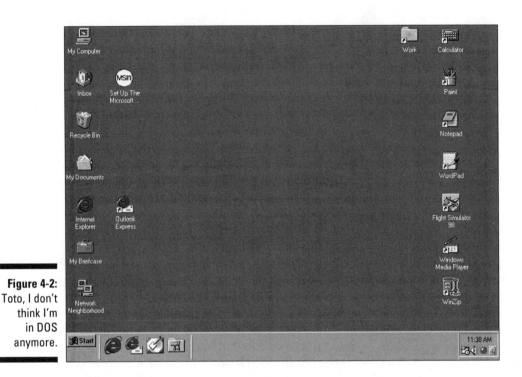

Figure 4-2:
Toto, I don't
think I'm
in DOS
anymore.

✔ Between the time you type your password and Windows finally displays the desktop, other messages or windows may be displayed on the screen. Some of them disappear, and others require you to click an OK or Cancel button to rid yourself of them. (See Chapter 14, which talks about using the mouse, if the point-and-click stuff seems strange to you.)

✔ Chapters 5 and 6 offer more information about Windows and getting to work.

✔ Windows really does take awhile to show up on the screen, so don't be discouraged; rumor has it that Samuel Beckett was working on *Waiting for Windot* before he died. [1]

Getting Your Work Done

Between turning your computer on and off, you should do something. Get work done. Do it now.

[1]This is a literary reference. Beckett wrote *Waiting for Godot* ("gah-doh"), who never shows up.

Turning the Computer Off

Sure, turning a computer off is easy: Just flip the big red switch. The power goes "dink," the fan softly warbles away, and the hard drive spins to a low hum and then stops. Unfortunately, that's just not polite enough for your computer. It's rude. Windows insists that you shut down properly; if you don't, it gets really, really sore.

Before you can feel the satisfaction of flipping that big red switch, heed these steps to properly furl Windows' sails:

1. Pop up the Start menu.

If you can see the Start button on the taskbar (see the bottom-left corner of Figure 4-2), click that button by using your mouse.

The best and most reliable way to make the Start menu appear is to press the Ctrl+Esc key combination. It works every time, whether you can see the Start button or not.

2. Choose the Sh<u>u</u>t Down menu item.

Click it with the mouse or press the U key because you can't yodel without the U sound.

The Shut Down Windows dialog box appears, as shown in Figure 4-3, filled with even more options for shutting down your PC.

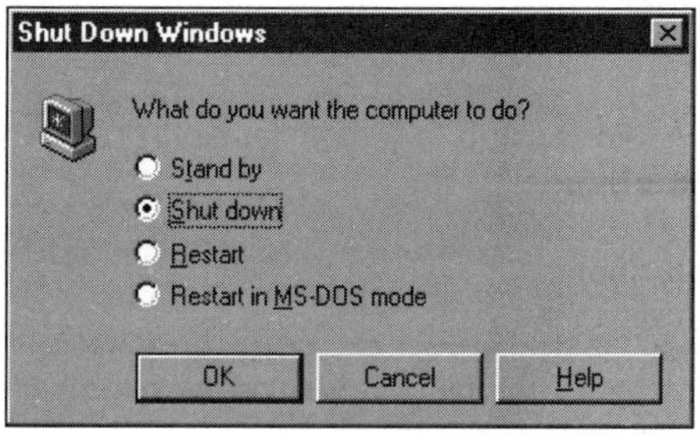

Figure 4-3:
This dialog
box is
Windows'
exit door.

> **Shut Down Windows**   ☒
>
> What do you want the computer to do?
>
> ○ Stand by
> ● Shut down
> ○ Restart
> ○ Restart in MS-DOS mode
>
> [OK]   [Cancel]   [Help]

3. Click the OK button.

Ignore the options! The proper one you want, Shut down (or Shut down the computer), is already selected for you.

4. Windows is outta here!

Bye-bye.

- If you haven't saved any information in any programs, you're told about it. Go ahead and save everything.

- If you've been running some older DOS programs, the whole operation stops. You must quit your DOS programs *before* you shut down Windows. (It's a sibling rivalry thing.) Refer to your DOS program's manual or a proper *...For Dummies* book near you.

Eventually, after more disk commotion than seems necessary, you see a screen that tells you, and I quote, "It's now safe to turn off your computer." Look, Ma, no sparks!

5. Flip the big red switch off.

Click. You're done.

Some PCs may actually shut themselves off automatically. If so, you don't need to do Step 5. You may still have to switch off your monitor, printer, and other devices around the PC.

✔ Yes, you shut down by first pressing the Start button. Such logic.

✔ The Stand By option in Figure 4-3 appears only if you have a computer capable of sleeping. See the section "Placing Your PC in Suspended Animation," later in this chapter.

✔ Another option for shutting down a computer is to log in as a different user. This item appears in the Shut Down Windows dialog box in Windows 95 and as a separate menu item on the Start menu in Windows 98. Choose that option if you're one of several people using the same PC and you want to keep Mr. Computer on for someone else to use.

✔ Never turn off a computer when you're in the middle of something. Always quit your programs, and then shut down Windows properly. The only time you can safely turn off your PC is when the screen tells you that it's *safe* to do so. An exception is when your computer has gone totally AWOL. When that happens, refer to Part VII of this book.

✔ If you're familiar with DOS (where you could shut down the computer at any time), be wary of seeing that friendly C:\> on the screen and thinking, "Golly, it's okay to shut down the computer now." Not so with Windows! You must first *quit* DOS, which you do by typing the EXIT command:

```
C> EXIT
```

This command makes your DOS prompt vanish, and, lo, you're back in Windows.

✔ If Windows detects any unsaved programs as it quits, it asks you to save them. For DOS programs, Windows begs you to save them and actually refuses to quit: Go ahead and save your DOS stuff; then quit your DOS programs; then repeat the steps in this section before you flip the big red switch.

✔ It's a good idea to wait at least 30 to 40 seconds before turning the computer on again. That gives the computer's hard drives time to slow down and stop. (Basically, it's just a bad idea to flip the PC's power switch rapidly from On to Off to On again.)

✔ If possible, try not to turn a computer off more than three times a day. My advice is to leave the machine on all day and, if you really want to turn it off, turn it off only at night. However, there is one school of thought that recommends leaving the computer on all the time. If that's your cup of java, see the next section.

"I Want to Leave My Computer Off All the Time"

Hey, I'm with you.

"I Want to Leave My Computer On All the Time"

The great debate rages: Should you leave your computer on all the time? Anyone who knows anything will tell you "Yes." Leave your computer on all the time, 24 hours a day, 7 days a week, and 14 days a week on the planet Mars. The only time you should turn a system off is when it will be unused for longer than a weekend.

Computers like being on all the time. You leave your refrigerator on all night or when you're away on trips, so why not your PC? It doesn't increase your electrical bill much, either.

Whatever you do with your PC, it's always a good idea to turn its monitor off when you're away. Some monitors can sleep just like PCs, but if they don't, turning them off can save some electricity.

The reason for leaving your computer on, if you care to know

Lots of interesting reasons exist for why you should leave your computer on all the time. One is that the initial process of turning a computer on is a tremendous jolt to the system. Computer folks often say that you subtract one day from a computer's life every time you switch the system off and then on. But who knows?

The truth is that leaving the computer on all the time keeps the temperature inside the box even. When you turn a system off, its electrical components cool. Turn the PC on again, and its components heat right back up. (The system's fan keeps them from getting too hot.) That temperature change from turning the system off and on causes the damage. After awhile, the solder joints become brittle, and they crack. That's when real problems occur. By leaving your PC on all the time — or just by minimizing the number of times you turn it off and on — you can prolong its life.

An opposing school of thought claims that, although the preceding information is true, leaving a computer on all the time wears down the bearings in the hard drive and causes the cooling fan to poop out prematurely. So be nice to your hard drive's packed bearings and turn your PC off once a day.

Ack! You just can't win. (I leave all my computers on all the time, if you care to know.)

✔ A screen-dimming program *(screen saver)* can *blank out* the monitor after your PC has been idle a specific length of time. You can find a Windows screen saver in the Control Panel. From the Start menu, choose Settings➪Control Panel and then double-click the Display icon with the mouse. Click the Screen Saver tab and do whatever is necessary there, which I don't have time to explain here.

✔ If you do leave your computer on all the time, don't put it under a dust cover. The dust cover gives the computer its very own greenhouse effect and brings the temperatures inside the system way past the sweltering point, like in a sweaty Southern courtroom drama.

Placing Your PC in Suspended Animation

As an alternative to leaving your PC on all the time, you may consider giving it a coma instead. It isn't anything evil, and your PC doesn't have an out-of-body experience while it's down. The true purpose of giving your PC a coma — or putting it in suspended animation — is to save energy.

To suspend your PC rather than shut it down, follow these steps:

1. Pop up the Start menu.

Click the Start button on the taskbar, or press the Ctrl+Esc key combination.

2a. Choose the Suspend menu item.

This item appears in Windows 95. Click it with the mouse or press the N key because this is the *N.*

In Windows 98, the Suspend menu item appears in the Shut Down Windows dialog box as Stand By:.

2b. Alternatively, choose the Shut Down menu item, and then click Stand By **in the Shut Down Windows dialog box. Click OK.**

If you don't see either command, your PC cannot be suspended (only some newer models can).

3. Watch as your PC sleeps.

Fwoot! (The sound you hear may vary.) Your PC looks like it has just switched off, but it's not off. It's almost better than off.

✔ Most newer PCs and all laptop computers have *suspend mode.* Activating it shifts your PC into low gear: The monitor goes blank, and everything inside the box whirs down to low-power mode. Although the computer is still on, it looks like it's off. In laptops, suspend mode saves power over the long haul.

✔ You don't have to save your work before you use the Suspend command — although it's still a good idea to always save your work whenever you're leaving your PC.

✔ To reanimate your computer, you merely touch a key or move the mouse. Everything snaps back to the way it was.

✔ On a laptop, you enter suspend mode by closing the lid with the power on, activating a keyboard command, or choosing the proper command from the Start menu.

✔ Some desktop PCs have a sleep button on the console, which lets you instantly suspend the computer. The button typically has a moon icon on it or nearby. Pressing that button instantly suspends the computer. Press the button again to wake it back up.

✔ The advantage of using the Suspend command rather than shutting down is that your PC pops back to life faster than if you had turned it all the way off. Not only that, but it also saves power and makes the spotted owl happy.

Resetting Your PC

Resetting your computer is a way to turn it off and on again without having to actually do that (and it's healthier for the PC than kicking the power cord out of the wall, despite the satisfying feeling that gives you). When you *reset,* you're restarting the computer while it's on.

You can reset in three ways, two of which I don't recommend.

First not-recommended way: If your computer has a reset switch, you can push it. Ka-chinka! The computer stops whatever it's doing (or not doing) and starts all over again.

Second not-recommended way: Press the Ctrl, Alt, and Delete keys at the same time. You have to do that twice in a row in Windows because it doesn't like for you to press Ctrl+Alt+Delete, the reasons for which I get into in the following section.

Do not use either of the two preceding techniques. Instead, try the suggestions in the following section first.

- ✔ Ctrl+Alt+Delete is known as the three-finger salute, or Control-Alt-Delete.

- ✔ Ctrl+Alt+Delete is also called the *Vulcan nerve pinch* because your fingers are arched in a manner similar to Mr. Spock's when he rendered the bad guys unconscious.

- ✔ A reset is often called a *warm boot.* It's like a cold boot that has been sitting in front of the furnace all night.

- ✔ As with turning a computer off, you shouldn't reset while the disk drive light is on or while you're in an application (except when the program has flown south). Above all, do not reset to quit an application. Always quit your programs properly and wait until Windows tells you that it's safe before you turn off your computer.

- ✔ Remember to remove any floppy disks from drive A before resetting. If you leave a disk in there, the computer tries to start itself from that disk.

The proper way to reset in Windows

Windows just doesn't let you press Ctrl+Alt+Delete to reset. The reason is probably that it's a bad idea to reset in the middle of something — and Windows is always in the middle of something. So rather than use a reset command, Windows uses Ctrl+Alt+Delete to kill off programs that run amok.

If you press Ctrl+Alt+Delete in Windows, you see a Close Program dialog box, like the one shown in Figure 4-4. Because it's best not to mess with this dialog box, click the Cancel button or press the Esc key.

Figure 4-4:
The Close
Program
dialog box
in Windows.

Close Program	? X
Starfleet [not responding]
My Computer
The American Heritage Dictionary
Explorer
Csinsm32
Csusem32
Systray
Optmod
Hidbman
Runner

WARNING: Pressing CTRL+ALT+DEL again will restart your computer. You will lose unsaved information in all programs that are running.

[End Task] [Shut Down] [Cancel]

✔ Don't press Ctrl+Alt+Delete in Windows unless you want to kill off a program. If you want to kill off a program, see the section in Chapter 27 about killing off a program run amok.

✔ If you really want to reset in Windows, you need to use the Shut Down command, as described in the section "Turning the Computer Off," earlier in this chapter. In Step 2 in the Shut Down dialog box, choose the Restart or Restart the computer option.

✔ In the old version of Windows (before Windows 95), Ctrl+Alt+Delete also killed off a program, but only the program you were using. This process was confusing for everyone, which is a good reason not to use Ctrl+Alt+Delete in the older version of Windows.

When to reset

Now the question arises: When should you reset? Obviously, whenever you're panicked. I reset only if the keyboard is totally locked up, and the program seems to have gone to the mall for some Mrs. Fields' cookies and a soda. (Sometimes Ctrl+Alt+Delete doesn't work in these situations, so if you don't have a big reset button, you have to turn the computer off, wait, and then turn it on again.)

The only other time you really need to reset is just to start over. For example, I was experimenting with a program that made my keyboard click every time I pressed a key. I had no obvious way to turn off this annoying pestilence, so I reset.

Chapter 5

The Operating System (Or "It Does Windows!")

*T*he PC's original operating system was DOS. But DOS was ugly, and everyone complained about it, so Microsoft gave us Windows, which is pretty, and everyone complains about it. Still, your PC needs an operating system, and Windows is probably the one you're stuck with. I know that because I've seen Bill Gates's planner, and it says, in Step 9 in the section on taking over the world, "Get everyone to use Windows."

This book specifically covers Windows 98, the latest PC operating system. Even so, because Windows 98 is only a minor update from the preceding version, Windows 95, almost all the information applies to both versions. The following tidbits of text help get you oriented to your PC's operating system, whether you have it or not, whether you like it or not.

"Why the Heck Do I Need an Operating System?"

I've always figured that operating systems were unnecessary. In fact, the first thing I did when I got my first DOS computer was type ERASE DOS, just to see what would happen.

Nothing happened.

Well, I got a `File not found` error. Luckily for me, DOS didn't get erased.

Windows, like DOS, is an operating system. An operating system is necessary to run your computer. It's the software that controls everything — all the hardware. Additionally, your PC's operating system is what dishes up applications programs for you — serving them to you like a waiter in a restaurant. You choose Word Processing from a menu, and the operating system runs that program. Simple. Maybe even fun.

- ✔ Your primary duty with Windows is to tell it to run your software. I cover this task in Chapter 6.

- ✔ As your secondary duty, you use Windows to manage the many files and documents you create. That's another aspect of an operating system: organizing all your computer junk and storing it properly on the hard drive. Chapter 8 covers this subject.

- ✔ Your tertiary (meaning *third*) duty in Windows is to run your computer. It's the geeky aspect, the thing that drives too many people over the edge. Might be covered in this book. Might not. I haven't made up my mind.

Windows, Your PC's Real Brain

The main program in charge of your PC is Windows. Ideally (which means that it could never happen in real life), a computer's operating system should be quiet and efficient, never getting in the way and carrying out your instructions like a dutiful and grateful servant.

In reality, Windows is a rude little kid. It behaves like an arrogant teenager who's handsome and fun but who won't tell you where he has hidden your car keys or your wallet unless you play poker with him. In other words, with Windows in charge of your PC, you must play the game by Windows rules.

Where is the desktop?

Windows works graphically. It shows you graphical images, or *icons,* representing everything inside your computer. These graphics are all pasted on a background called the *desktop.* In Figure 5-1, the desktop has the famous Windows clouds background.

You control everything by using your computer's mouse. The mouse controls the pointer on the desktop, which looks like an arrow-shaped UFO in Figure 5-1. You use the mouse and its pointer to point at things, grab them, drag them around, punch 'em, scratch 'em till they bleed, and other mouse-y things like that.

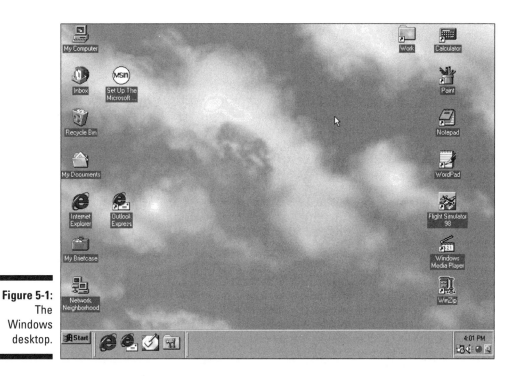

Figure 5-1:
The
Windows
desktop.

Oh, you can also use the keyboard, although graphical operating systems such as Windows love mice more than they love keyboards.

- The *desktop* is merely the background on which Windows shows you its stuff — like an old sheet you hang from the wall to bore your neighbors with your Cayman Islands vacation slide show.

- The little pictures are called *icons*.

- Figure 5-1 shows what Windows may look like. On your computer, it looks different (probably because your computer doesn't like you).

- Refer to the end of Chapter 14 for more information about using a mouse, including all those mouse activities and their associated terms.

- Using your keyboard is covered somewhat in Chapter 15.

Between labors, Hercules did not go to the taskbar

That gunboat-gray strip along the bottom of the desktop is called the *taskbar*. It's the Windows main control center.

On the left end of the taskbar is the Start button. Yes, that's where you start programs in Windows. You can also shut down Windows by using the Start button. Start. Stop. Microsoft can't make up its mind.

On the right end of the taskbar is the *system tray.* I like to call it the loud time because it typically looks like a speaker shouting out the time of day. Other items may show up on the system tray (refer to Figure 5-1, for example). If you don't have a sound system in your PC, the speaker doesn't show up. If you're computing on the international date line, the time doesn't show up either.

From time to time, buttons appear in the middle of the taskbar. Each button represents a window or program you have floating open on the desktop. Or it can represent a program you've put away or *minimized,* which I cover in Chapter 6. All this means something, which I probably get into later.

The taskbar can also be home to various toolbars in Windows 98. For example, Figure 5-1 shows the Quick Launch bar just this side of the Start button. That toolbar contains buttons that let you quickly start programs, and it may or may not appear on-screen, depending on the number of sunspots this month.

✔ You can point the mouse at the various items on the system tray to get more information or to control them. Clicking the items usually does something, depending on what and how you click. For example, double-click the time, and you can set the computer's clock (it's covered in Chapter 11).

✔ The taskbar can float on any edge of the desktop; use your mouse to drag the taskbar to the top, left, or right sides of the screen. (Point the mouse at a blank part of the taskbar to drag it.) Most folks leave it on the bottom, which is where this book assumes that it lies.

The almighty Start button

Everything in Windows starts with the Start button, conveniently located on the left side of the taskbar. The Start button controls a pop-up menu (and submenus galore!), on which you find various commands and programs.

To pop up the Start menu, click its button by using your mouse. Click.

TECHNICAL STUFF

"My taskbar is gone!"

The taskbar tends to wander. It can not only go up, down, left, and right, but also get fatter and skinnier. Sometimes it can get so skinny that you can't see it anymore. All you see is a thin, gray line at the bottom of the screen. That can drive you batty.

That thin, gray line is still the taskbar. It's just that someone has shrunk it to Lilliputian size. To make the line thicker, hover the mouse pointer over the taskbar's edge. The mouse pointer changes to a this-way-or-that-way arrow. Then drag the taskbar to a nicer, plumper size. You can even use this trick to make the taskbar fatter when it's crowded with too many buttons.

Another way the taskbar can disappear is if you tell it to hide. This vanishing act is done in the Taskbar Properties dialog box: Right-click your mouse on the taskbar and choose Properties from the pop-up shortcut menu. In the Taskbar Properties dialog box, make sure that the Auto Hide option doesn't have a check mark by it (click the box next to Auto Hide to remove the check mark). Click the OK button to go on your merry way.

If you've really lost the taskbar, try this set of keystrokes: Press Ctrl+Esc, Alt+Enter, and S, and then press the up-arrow key a few times to see the taskbar. Press the Esc key when the taskbar is fully visible.

Remember: You can always get at the Start button by pressing Ctrl+Esc. This keystroke works whether the taskbar is visible or has been sent by Houdini to some other realm.

If you would rather use your keyboard, press the Ctrl+Esc key combination. This action is guaranteed to work, popping up the Start button's menu even when you can't otherwise see the Start button.

Some newfangled keyboards sport a Windows key (two of them, actually). The key cap has the Windows flag logo, and the key sits just outside the Alt key on either side of the spacebar. Pressing that key also pops up the Start menu.

There. That's it for the Start button discussion in this chapter. For more information, see the section in Chapter 6 about starting a program in Windows.

The My Computer and Explorer Programs

The second chore of an operating system is to work with the files, documents, and other junk stored on your computer. Two programs tackle this job: My Computer and Explorer.

It's My Computer

My Computer has Macintosh written all over it. It's a program that displays information in your computer as pretty little icons, each of them grouped into folders.

My Computer

You start My Computer by double-clicking the little My Computer icon in the upper-left corner of the desktop. This effort displays a list of goodies inside your computer, primarily your disk drives, as shown in Figure 5-2.

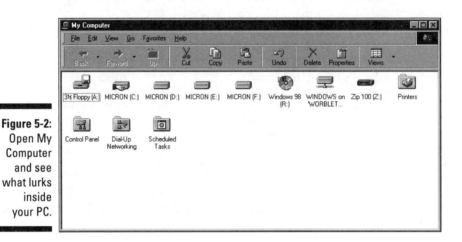

Figure 5-2:
Open My
Computer
and see
what lurks
inside
your PC.

If you point at and double-click one of your system's disk drives, such as drive C:, it opens to reveal a window full of folders and icons, as shown in Figure 5-3. The icons represent files on your system. You can open folders (by double-clicking) to display another window chock-full of more files and folders. It can get insane!

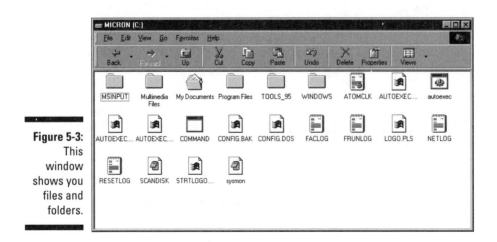

Figure 5-3:
This
window
shows you
files and
folders.

✔ You double-click an icon to open it. Double-clicking some icons runs (opens) programs. For folders, the double-click opens the folder, revealing its contents.

✔ Icons represent files on your computer, which can be files you create, program files, or other files that sprout from certain fungi.

✔ Folders are simply storage places for more icons and files.

✔ See the section "Closing a window," later in this chapter, for information about closing windows opened in My Computer.

The disk explorer

Explorer (which is called Windows Explorer, although I use the term *Explorer*) works just like My Computer, except that Explorer displays information in a different way. (Microsoft just couldn't make up its mind here: "Which way should we have people see files on their computers? Hey! Why not two utterly different and confusing ways?")

Start Explorer by clicking the Start button and choosing Programs⇨ Windows Explorer from the menu.

Unlike My Computer, Explorer has only one window, as shown in Figure 5-4. The disk drives and folders on your computer appear on the left side of the window; files and folders appear on the right.

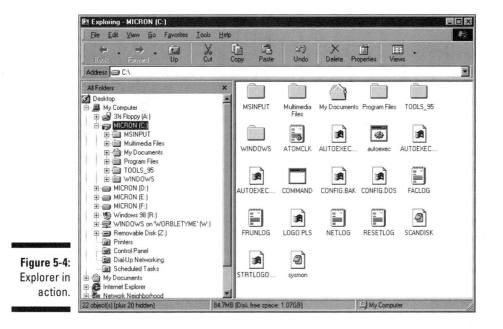

Figure 5-4: Explorer in action.

Okay. Enough of Explorer. Choose File⇨Close to quit the program because there's no sense in wasting screen real estate with something so ugly.

- ✔ Computer nerds prefer Explorer. I recommend using My Computer first, until you get used to it. Then use Explorer, which can be quicker.

- ✔ A quick way to start Explorer is to press the Windows and E keys together — like pressing Shift+E to get a capital E (for Explorer), but use the fancy Windows key rather than Shift.

- ✔ I discuss the My Computer and Explorer programs in more detail in Part III of this book.

- ✔ Windows sports another explorer, Internet Explorer. It's covered in Part VI of this book.

The Geeks Tweak at the Control Panel

The third chore Windows accomplishes is serving as kindergarten teacher for all your computer's innards and peripherals. Those devices are controlled, coddled, and contained by using the Control Panel.

The *Control Panel* is a folder you can open just about anywhere in Windows. You can start it from the Start menu by choosing Settings⇨Control Panel. Or you can double-click the folder that appears in the main My Computer window (refer to the preceding section). Either way, the Control Panel window with all its pretty icons appears, similar to what's shown in Figure 5-5.

Figure 5-5:
The Control Panel.

Each of the icons in the Control Panel represents some aspect of your computer, something to control. By opening an icon, you see a window with more information, more controls, more chaos.

My advice: Leave this one to the experts.

Close the Control Panel window by choosing File⇨Close from the menu.

 ✔ Open an icon in the Control Panel by double-clicking.

 ✔ I have no idea what most of the things in the Control Panel do. In fact, they frighten me.

 ✔ Various chapters in Part IV of this book have you mess with parts of the Control Panel. Mostly, you leave it alone.

 ✔ The number of items you see in the Control Panel varies. You may find some items in your PC's Control Panel that aren't shown in Figure 5-5 and find some items in Figure 5-5 that aren't in your Control Panel.

Using Gizmos in Windows

Windows is a virtual FAO Schwarz of fun things to play with, stuff to drive you crazy, and interesting toys over which you waste colossal amounts of time. It has tiny buttons you push with the mouse, graphics that slide and stretch, things to poke, and stuff that drops down. In other words, *gizmos* are on the screen, most of which control the way the windows look and how programs in Windows operate.

Changing a window's size

Your windows can be just about any size, from filling the entire screen to too small to be useful and everything in between.

To make a window fill the entire screen — which is where it's most useful — click the *Maximize* button in the window's upper-right corner. (This step changes the button's full window-image thing to an overlapping window-image thing. Click that button again to restore the window to its original size.)

To turn a window into a mere button on the taskbar, click the *Minimize* button in the upper-right corner of a window. This action shoves the window out of the way, shrinking it to a button on the taskbar — but it isn't the same as quitting. To restore the taskbar button to a window, click the button.

When a window isn't full-screen or an icon, you can change its size by grabbing an edge with the mouse: Hover the mouse over one side of the window or a corner, press and hold the left mouse button, and drag the window in or out to a new size. Release the mouse button to snap the window into place.

- Enlarging a window to full-screen size is called *maximizing*.

- Shrinking a window into an icon is called *minimizing*.

- Positioning a window "just so" on the screen and then having Windows move it for no reason is called *frustrating*.

- If you use your imagination, the Maximize button looks like a full-screen window and the Minimize button looks like a button on the taskbar. Then again, if you use your imagination, Windows looks like a bright, sunny day with green grass and birds chirping in the meadow.

Moving a window around

Windows puts its windows wherever Windows wants. To move a window to a new position, drag the window by its title bar (the topmost strip on the window, typically above the menu bar). This action is akin to the cliché of a caveman dragging his woman around by her hair. That never really happened, of course, not after the women started carrying their own clubs, anyway.

- By the way, you cannot move a window around when it's maximized (filling the screen). Refer to the preceding section to find out how to maximize a window.

- By the way (Part 2), you cannot move Uncle Buster around when he's maximized after a holiday meal. It's the same concept Microsoft borrowed for maximized windows.

Scrolling about

Often, what you're looking at in a window is larger than the window. For example, if a tanned, svelte, and bikini-clad Claudia Schiffer (or Mel Gibson, for the ladies) walked by a tiny window in your wall, you would be able to see only a small part of her bronzed form. If you could move the window up and down the wall, you could see more of her, but only the same size as the window at a time. That's how scrolling works.

To facilitate scrolling a window around, one or two scroll bars are used. The *scroll bar* is a long, skinny thing, with an arrow at either end and an elevator-like box in the middle, as shown here, in the left margin. You use the arrows and elevator to move the window's image up and down or left and right, revealing more of the total picture.

Accessing a menu

All the commands and whatnot of the Windows application are included on a handy — and always visible — menu bar. It's usually at the top of a window, right below the title bar and down the street from Tom's Bar.

Each word on the menu bar — File and Edit, for example — is a menu title. It represents a drop-down menu, which contains commands related to the title. For example, the File menu contains Save, Open, New, Close, and other commands related to files.

To access these commands, click the menu title with the mouse. The menu drops down. Then choose a menu item or command. If you don't like what you see, click the menu title again to make the menu go away or choose another menu.

  ✔ You can access the menus by using your keyboard, if you like. Press either the Alt or F10 key. This action highlights the first menu on the menu bar. To choose a menu or item on a menu, press the underlined letter, such as F for File. The letters to press are underlined in this book, just as they are in Windows.

  ✔ In this book, the format File⇨Close is used to represent menu choices. To access that command on the menu, you press Alt,F,C.

  ✔ To choose the File⇨Close command, you can also press Alt+F (the Alt and F keys together, and then release both keys) and then C.

  ✔ Oh, bother. Just use your mouse. Point. Click. Click. Sheesh.

Closing a window

Closing a program's window is the same as quitting the program; you make it disappear. The most common way to close a window is to click the X button in the upper-right corner of the window.

Another striking way to close a window — striking because it's obvious — is to choose the Exit or Close command from the File menu. This action also quits the program you're running.

  ✔ You can't quit Windows by closing a window, which is how it worked in the old version of Windows. Instead, use the Shutdown command on the main Start menu. See the section "Turning the Computer Off," in Chapter 4, for more information.

Gizmos in a Dialog Box

When it comes to making choices, Windows displays a specialized type of window called a dialog box. A *dialog box* contains gadgets and gizmos you click and slide and type in, all of which control something or set certain optional options. Clicking an OK button sends your choices off to Windows for proper digestion.

If all that sounds complicated, consider the old DOS-prompt way of doing things:

```
C> FORMAT A: /S /U /F:144 /V:DOODYDISK
```

That's a real, honest-to-goodness DOS command. In Windows, a dialog box lets you do something similar but in a graphical way. Figure 5-6, in fact, shows you how the same command looks.

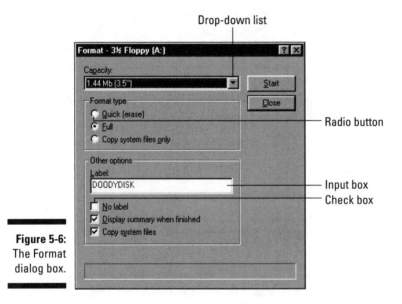

Figure 5-6:
The Format
dialog box.

All the doojobbies shown in Figure 5-6 are manipulated with the mouse. What they do isn't important right now. What the doojobbies are called *is* important. All the following definitions refer to Figure 5-6:

Drop-down list: Under the word *Capacity* is a drop-down list. You drop down the list by clicking the down-pointing arrow button to the right of the list. This action displays a list of choices, one of which you point at and click with the mouse. If the list is long, it has a scroll bar to one side, which you can use to scroll through the long list.

Radio button: The round buttons in a dialog box are radio buttons. They're grouped together into families, such as the three shown in Figure 5-6. Like in an old car radio, only one of the buttons at a time can be punched. To punch a button, click it once with the mouse. A round dot fills the one button that is *on.*

Input box: Any box or area you can type in is an input box. In Figure 5-6, it's the box under the word *Label.*

Check box: The square buttons in a dialog box are check boxes. Unlike with radio buttons, you can click the mouse in as many or all of the check boxes as necessary. A check mark appears in the box if an option is on. To remove the check mark and turn the option off, click the mouse in the box again.

After you've made your selections, you typically click an OK button. (In Figure 5-6, the OK button is called Start.) If you don't like your choices, click Close.

To get help, click the question mark button in the dialog box's upper-right corner. This action changes the mouse pointer into the combo arrow-pointer question mark thing. When that happens, point and click any part of the dialog box to see a pop-up cartoon bubble supposedly offering help. Click the mouse to make the cartoon bubble go away.

✔ Pressing the Enter key in a dialog box is the same as clicking the OK button with your mouse.

✔ Pressing the Esc (escape) key on your keyboard is the same as clicking the Cancel button in a dialog box.

✔ You can press the F1 key to get help with whichever part of the dialog box you're messing with.

✔ Some dialog boxes feature an *Apply* button. It works like an OK button, except that it enables you to see your changes without closing the dialog box. If you like the changes, you can then click OK. Or, if the changes stink, you can reset them or click the Cancel button. See? Microsoft is being nice here. Make a note of it on your calendar.

✔ If more than one input box appears in a dialog box, press the Tab key to move between them. Don't press the Enter key because that's the same as clicking the OK button and telling Windows that you're done with the dialog box.

✔ Another type of list, similar to the drop-down list and not shown in Figure 5-6, is a *scrolling list.* It works the same as the drop-down list, except that the list is always visible inside the dialog box.

✔ If you like a mental challenge, you can use your keyboard to work a dialog box. Look for the underlined letter in each part of the dialog box (such as *p* in `Capacity` in Figure 5-6). Press the Alt key plus that key, and it's the same as choosing that command with a mouse.

How to Properly Beg for Help

Windows has an incredible Help system, and all Windows-specific programs share it. You always activate Help by pressing the F1 key. From there, you're shown the help *engine* that enables you to look up topics, search for topics, or see related items, all by properly using your mouse. The help engine is divided into three panels: Contents, Index, and Search (or Find in Windows 95). Here are some hints:

- ✔ The Contents panel shows you information just like the yechy manual, with chapters and pages and text written by Ph.D.s for Ph.D.s.

- ✔ The Index panel is the most useful. Click the word Index to see that panel, and then type your topic, such as **Shortcut**, in the box at the top of the panel. In the bottom part of the panel, click a subtopic, and then click the Display button to read all about it.

- ✔ Ignore the Search panel.

- ✔ Most of the helpful information is displayed as a list of steps or tips.

- ✔ You can click the gray squares to see more information about related topics.

- ✔ To get general Windows help, choose Help from the main Start menu.

- ✔ You can click the underlined text (with a dotted underline) to see a pop-up window defining the term.

The help engine is its own program. When you're done using Help, remember to quit: Click the X close button in the upper-left corner of the window.

General Windows Advice

Use your mouse. If you don't have a mouse, you can still use Windows — but not as elegantly. Ack, who am I kidding? You need a mouse to use Windows!

Have someone organize your Start menu items for you. Ask this person to put your most popular programs on the desktop as *shortcut icons.* Offer a jar of mixed nuts (less than 50 percent peanuts, lightly salted) as a bribe.

Keep in mind that Windows can run several programs at a time. Look at the buttons on the taskbar to see whether a program is already running before starting a second copy. (Yes, you can run several copies of a program under Windows, although you probably need to run only one.)

Always quit Windows properly. Never just turn your PC off or punch the Reset button. Review the steps in Chapter 4 for properly shutting down Windows if you've forgotten how.

Chapter 6

Getting Your Work Done

• •

In This Chapter

▶ Starting a program

▶ Making your program's window fill the screen

▶ Switching programs

▶ Cutting, copying, and pasting

▶ Using common Windows program commands

▶ Quitting your program

• •

*E*ver notice that people in soap operas don't do any work? Sure, they all have jobs. You may see them "at work." But no one really works. They talk. They whisper about James breaking up with Linda because Eva is leaving the convent. They wonder whether Alex really has an evil twin. They fear Harry, who walks around with an egg carton and is under investigation for stealing tissue samples from the eye clinic. And they giggle about Wilma, who claims to be pregnant with an alien space baby and keeps complaining that the grocery store doesn't stock any size 9 Huggies.

For you, life is more routine (except for the reading of Uncle Cedric's will, which even *America's Funniest Home Videos* believed to be staged). Eventually, the time comes to get something done. That's what you bought all that software for: to get your work done.

Starting a Program in Windows

Oh, you can sit and spin in Windows all day without getting anything of value done. Me? I do it all the time. To get working, you need to start a program. You use the Start button and the annoying menu that pops (actually, *slips*) up. Here are the steps:

1. Pop up the Start menu.

Click the mouse on the taskbar's Start button. Up pops the menu. Pressing the Ctrl+Esc key combination does the same thing.

2. Choose Programs.

Click the word *Programs,* and you see the slippery Programs submenu appear, such as the one shown in Figure 6-1.

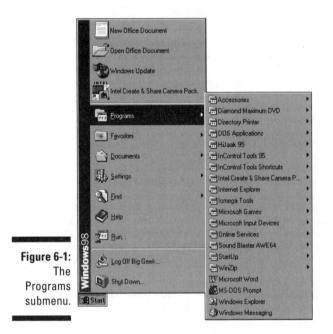

Figure 6-1: The Programs submenu.

3. Pluck out your program from those listed on the submenu.

For example, in Figure 6-1 you would point and click the words *Microsoft Word* to start that program.

If your program doesn't appear on the list, try one of the other submenus listed; Accessories, Internet Explorer, Microsoft Office, and others contain even more programs. Yes, and you even see sub-sub-submenus (and on and on) with even more programs.

You gots programs comin' outta yer ears!

4. Your program starts; the Start menu goes away.

✔ At times, the program you want to start may appear right on top of the main Start menu. If so, point and click, and the program starts up.

✔ The menus are rather slippery. They pop up and disappear as your mouse roves over them. Be careful! It can be aggravating if either you're a sloppy mouse mover or your mouse is too sensitive.

✔ Quickly start any recently worked-on stuff by using the Documents submenu: Pop up the Start menu and click Documents. Look for your document on the list. If it's there, click it to start it. If it's not there, you can take the day off and watch your favorite soap.

Starting your program from an icon on the desktop

A quick way to start a program without playing slip-and-slide with the Start menu is to find the program's icon floating on the desktop. This method works for any icon on the desktop, whether it represents a program or a file you created, such as your database listing the times weird Harry shows up at the eyeball clinic.

To place an icon of your favorite program on the desktop, fire up the Explorer or My Computer program. Locate your program (here's the technical part) in its proper folder or wherever it's stashed.

You can refer to the section in Chapter 9 about finding wayward files and programs if you need help.

Now, the cinchy part: Using the *right* mouse button, drag the icon from the Explorer or My Computer window out to the desktop. Remember to use the right button, not the button you normally press. When you release the right button (pointing at the desktop), a pop-up shortcut menu appears. Choose the item Create Shortcut(s) Here. Lo, the shortcut is created on the desktop, available for easy access.

Using the Quick Launch bar

Windows 98 sports many, many toolbars you can slap down on top of the taskbar. Although most of them are a joke, one that's really handy is the Quick Launch bar.

To see the Quick Launch bar displayed, right-click the taskbar and choose Toolbars⇨Quick Launch from the pop-up menu.

You can add new icons to the Quick Launch bar by dragging them there from a My Computer window or from Windows Explorer — similar to the way icons are dragged to the desktop, as described in the preceding section.

The beauty of the Quick Launch bar is that the icons that appear there need only one click to start. Put all your very, very most favorite programs on the Quick Launch bar for easy access.

✔ Windows 95 does not have a Quick Launch bar.

✔ To see the Quick Launch bar displayed with large icons, right-click the Quick Launch bar (on the left side, where the vertical bar is) and choose View➪Large from the pop-up menu.

✔ Try to put only a handful of icons on the Quick Launch bar. The way I see it, *everything* should be on the Start menu, and only the programs you use all the time should have a spot on the Quick Launch bar. On my PC, I put only four icons there.

Maximizing Your Work

This section has nothing to do with self-help. Instead, you may find it useful to maximize your program's window after it starts. Some programs start in full-screen mode right off. Other programs start as only a measly window on the screen. Blech! Who needs that?

To make your program's window fill the screen — and get every dollar per pixel you paid for that monitor — click the window's Maximize button (the middle button in the upper-right corner, or see the image in the margin).

✔ Some windows can't be maximized. Some games, for example, have a fixed window size you can't change. Don't be greedy.

✔ If you have a humongous monitor, you may opt to run your programs without switching them to full-screen.

✔ If you're working with several programs, you may want to arrange their windows on-screen so that each is visible. To do that, right-click the mouse on a blank part of the taskbar, or right-click the time (on the right side of the taskbar). From the menu that pops up, choose either Tile Horizontally or Tile Vertically to arrange your windows on-screen.

Switching from One Program to Another (Without Quitting)

In Windows, you can run several programs at one time. Imagine the productivity boost! Dream of getting two things done at once! Then realize the chaos. Fortunately, you don't really run several programs at a time as much as you can switch between two or more at a time without having to stop and restart, stop and restart, over and over.

Although Windows can run more than one program at a time, as a human —
and I assume that you are — you can work on only the program whose
window is up in front or on top o' the pile or filling the entire screen. To
switch to another program, you have several options:

The quick way: The quickest way to switch programs is to grab the mouse
and click in another program's window, as long as that window is visible.
Clicking in a window brings that window to the top of the pile.

The quick way if you can't see the window: Look for a button on the
taskbar corresponding to the window you want. Click that button. Thwooop!
The window stands before you, eager to please.

 The shove-aside way: Minimize the current window, shrinking it to a button
on the taskbar. This action doesn't quit the program; it just shoves it aside,
enabling you to access whatever other windows lie behind it. You accomplish the minimization process by clicking the Minimize button in the upper-
right corner of the window (see the image in the margin).

Non-mousey ways: If you run out of mouse methods for switching programs,
try one of the two keyboard methods. They're awful to remember, although
I'm fond of the Alt+Tab key combination approach.

  ✔ **Alt+Tab:** Press the Alt and Tab keys at the same time — but hold down
    the Alt key and release the Tab key. This action summons a little picture
    box in the center of the screen that displays icons for your windows
    and programs. Keep holding down the Alt key and tap the Tab key until
    the icon representing your program or window is in the box. Release
    the Alt key.

  ✔ **Alt+Esc:** Press the Alt and Esc keys at the same time. This action
    switches you to the next program you have active (in the order in
    which you use the programs). You may have to press Alt+Esc a few
    times to find the program or window you want.

  ✔ To switch to another window, click it.

  ✔ You can use two key combinations to switch to another window or
    program: Alt+Esc or Alt+Tab.

Minimizing a window by clicking the Minimize button in the upper-right
corner of the window does not quit that application. Instead, the program
shrinks to icon size at the bottom of the screen. Double-click that icon if you
want to access the program's window.

General Commands for All Reasons

Windows programs all do things in similar ways. One of those ways is to use common commands. It enables you to easily understand how to use new Windows applications because everything is done in kind of the same way. Another advantage is that you can cut or copy and paste information between two different applications. Ah, yes, more productivity boosting, thanks to Chairman Bill.

Copy

To copy something in Windows, select it with the mouse: Drag the mouse over some text, click a picture or an icon with the mouse, or drag the mouse around the object. This action highlights the text, picture, or icon, which means that it has been *selected* and is ready for copying.

After selecting the whatever, choose Edit➪Copy. This step puts a copy of the whatever into the secret Windows storage place, the *Clipboard,* from whence it can be pasted (see the "Paste" section, later in this chapter).

The quick-key shortcut for this step is Ctrl+C. That's easy to remember because *C* means copy.

- ✔ After your text or picture is copied, it can then be pasted. You can paste it into the same program or switch to another program for pasting.

- ✔ When you copy something, it's put in the Clipboard in Windows. Unfortunately, the Clipboard holds only one thing at a time. Whenever you copy or cut, the new item replaces whatever was already in the Clipboard. (This type of Clipboard doesn't seem handy, but Microsoft would like for me to remind you here of all the time you're saving in Windows.)

Cut

Cutting something in Windows is just like copying: You select a picture or some text or an icon and then choose the Edit➪Cut menu command. Unlike with Copy, however, the picture or text you cut is copied to the Clipboard and then deleted from your application.

The quick-key shortcut for this trick is Ctrl+X. You can remember it because when you cut something, you "X it out." (I know, I'm pushing it here, but the Ctrl+C key combination is already taken.)

Paste

The Paste command is used to take text, a picture, or an icon stored in the Clipboard and slap it down into the current application. You can paste a picture into text or text into a picture, and icons can go just about anywhere. Ah, the miracle of Windows.

To paste, choose the Edit⇨Paste command. Or you can press Ctrl+V, the Paste key, from the keyboard. The V must stand for vwapp! or voom! or Vomica or something.

✔ You can paste text or a picture from the Clipboard back into the current application, or you can switch to another application for pasting.

✔ You can paste material cut or copied from any Windows application into another Windows application.

✔ You cannot paste graphics into a program that cannot accept graphics. Likewise, you cannot paste text into a program that works only with graphics.

✔ You may be wondering, "Why didn't they just make Ctrl+P the Paste shortcut key?" Alas, Ctrl+P is the Print command's shortcut key.

Undo

The powers at Microsoft have graced sloppy Windows users (meaning all of us) with the blessed Undo command. This command undoes whatever stupid thing you just did.

To undo, choose Edit⇨Undo from the menu. Undo just happens to be the first item on the list. How convenient. The key command is Ctrl+Z; the Z means, "Zap that mistake back to Seattle!"

✔ Undo undoes just about anything you can do: "unchange" edits, replace cut graphics, and fix up a bad marriage, for example.

✔ If you look at your keyboard (and you shouldn't, if you're a touch-typist), you see that the Z, X, C, and V keys are all together on the left side of the bottom row, as shown in Figure 6-2. Hey! Those are the common Windows shortcut keys. That may explain why the letters don't make much sense.

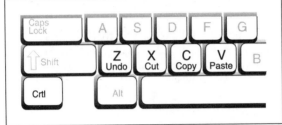

Figure 6-2:
The Undo,
Cut, Copy,
and Paste
keys on
your
keyboard.

Save

After you've etched your brilliance into silicon and the phosphor on the screen glows warmly in your eyes, you need to save your work to disk. Not only does the computer keep your stuff nice and tidy on disk, but you can also open it up later to work on it again.

Saving is done by using the File⇨Save command. This step summons the Save dialog box, which you then use to save your work to disk. (The Save dialog box is presented officially in Chapter 8.)

The Save shortcut key is the logical Ctrl+S key combination.

- Always save your work. I save my stuff every five minutes or so.

- Save! Save! Save! Remember that.

- Jesus saves.

- The first time you save something to disk, you must give it a name and tell Windows where to put it (which you can read about in Chapter 8, so don't think that I'm being crude here). After that, you just use the Save command to continue to save the file to disk; you don't have to give it a name again. Just save!

- A variation of the Save command is Save As. This command works like Save, although it allows you to give the file a new name when you save it. That keeps the original version intact.

Open

After something has been saved on disk, you retrieve it by using the Open command. This command lets you find your stuff on disk and open it up like a present on your birthday. Your stuff then appears in the program's window, ready for you to do something with it.

To open something on disk, choose the File⇨Open command or use the handy Ctrl+O keyboard shortcut. This command displays the Open dialog box, where you use the various controls and whatnots to grab your file from the disk.

  ✔ Chapter 8 covers the Open dialog box in corpulent depth.

  ✔ Some programs may use the Load command rather than Open. Load is typically the earmark of an outdated DOS program, souped-up to run on Windows.

Print

The Print command takes your lovely work that you see on-screen and causes something similar-looking to spew forth from the printer.

To print, use the File⇨Print command. It displays the Print dialog box, which has a bunch of hocus-pocus in it, so you usually click the OK button, and your something then prints. The keyboard shortcut for the Print command is Ctrl+P. Easy 'nuff.

  ✔ Make sure that the printer is on, has paper, and is ready to print before you try to print something.

  ✔ Chapter 16 covers the details of printing something.

Quit (or Exit or Close)

When you're done working, quit your program and wander off to do something else. This command is perhaps the best one of any Windows program.

To quit, choose the File⇨Exit command. Alas, some programs may not have a File menu, let alone an Exit command. If so, the last command (at the bottom) of the first menu typically does the trick.

The keyboard combination to quit any Windows program, and to close any window, is bizarre: Alt+F4. It's just too strange to think up anything clever to say about it.

  ✔ If your application doesn't have a File⇨Exit command, you can quit by clicking the program window's X button in the upper-right corner.

  ✔ Sometimes the command is File⇨Close.

  ✔ You don't have to quit. If you're working on something and want to put it aside for later, you can minimize the program. See the section, "Switching from One Program to Another (Without Quitting)," earlier in this chapter, for the details.

Part III
Disks, Drives, Files, and Whatnot

The 5th Wave   By Rich Tennant

"Put down, 'Causes foot damage'."

In this part . . .

Little did they know in 776 B.C., when the first Olympic games were held, that the sport of tossing the discus was a portent of mankind's future. Soon, respectable people in business clothing would be tossing various disks around, some in joy, most in frustration. Even though today's disks are used to store information, there are a lot of similarities to the ancient Greek games — minus nudity, for the most part.

The chapters in this part of the book deal with disks. Actually, the true topic is information as it's stored on computer disks. That disk could be a floppy disk, hard disk, CD, or some network disk on an alien computer. It really shouldn't be that frustrating, but if you do throw a tantrum and toss a few heavy objects, you're bound to please the Olympian gods.

Chapter 7
All about Disks and Drives

● ●

In This Chapter

▶ Using disk drives

▶ How different types of disk drives work

▶ Disk drives and drive letters

▶ All about floppy disks

▶ Identifying a rogue disk

▶ Write-protecting floppy disks

▶ Formatting disks

▶ All about CD-ROM and DVD drives

▶ Discovering ZIP drive disks and other strange disks

● ●

I believe that my first love affair with a computer was with the disk drive. Back then (long, long ago), I used a cassette tape rather than a disk drive for storage. So I fell madly for my first 180K, 5¹/₄-inch floppy drive. I swooned deeply the first time I got to use a whopping 5MB hard drive at work (it was bigger than two cinder blocks side by side). It's easy to imagine how anyone can love a hard drive after dealing with a 3-foot-high stack of floppy disks for several years.

Oh, please. Don't let me get misty on you. Disk drives are important to your PC because that's where the computer's operating system, your software, and all the lovely data you create resides. This chapter is about disks and drives and all the madness that comes with them. It's a hefty chapter, so grab yourself a treat and a beverage before you start reading.

"Why Does My PC Need Disk Drives?"

Computers use disks for long-term storage. They're a supplement to your computer's memory, which provides short-term storage. The longer-term storage provided by your disk drives means that you can keep the stuff you create.

In a computer, all information you create and all the programs you run must work in RAM. Unfortunately, RAM is temporary. Turn off Mr. Computer, and everything in memory goes *poof!* To supplement that storage, the information you create is saved to disk, where it sticks around even when the power is off.

✔ You use disks to store information long-term. The information, or *files*, can then be opened later for another peek, a re-edit, to show to friends, or just because.

✔ Chapter 12 discusses computer memory, or RAM.

✔ Some bozos refer to disk storage as *memory*. Forget that they said so! Disk "memory" is long-term storage. Don't confuse it with computer memory.

✔ Like memory (RAM), disk storage is measured in bytes, mostly *megabytes* and *gigabytes*. See Chapter 12 for more information about what these terms measure.

✔ Your computer can't use the information directly on a disk. Instead, it copies the information to its memory. From there, the computer can manipulate the data, send it to the printer, or occasionally lose it. Because the computer is working with only a copy of the data, the original data is still safe on the disk.

✔ Never worry if the file on disk is larger than your PC's memory. For example, you may have a 15MB graphics image but only 8MB of RAM in your computer. Don't sweat it! If the computer can't open the file, it lets you know. Most of the time, however, it surprises you by reading it anyway. Amazing devices, those computers.

Different Types of Disk Drives for Different Needs

Computers can store small amounts of information on little floppy disks and large amounts of information on massive hard disks. It would be simple if those were the only two types of disks in the world, but they aren't.

Before getting into it, you should know two things about disk drives:

✔ A disk drive is a device that reads a disk. The information is stored on the disk, similar to the way a movie is stored on a videocassette.

✔ Computer disks are hardware. The information stored on them is software, just as your videocassette of *The Ten Commandments* isn't the movie itself; the movie is recorded on the cassette. (The movie is like software, and the cassette is hardware.)

Floppy drives. A floppy drive eats floppy disks, which typically store 1.4MB of information. That's enough to make backup copies of your documents for transportation between two computers, although that's about it. About ten years ago, all PC software came on floppy disks. Today the CD-ROM disc is used instead.

Hard drives. The PC's main long-term storage device is the hard drive. The hard drive's disk stores gigabytes of information, more than enough for Windows, your software, and all the data you can create. Unlike with floppy disks, you cannot remove a hard disk. But that's usually not a problem because you have other ways of getting files from a hard disk to another computer.

CD-ROM drives. A CD-ROM drive eats CD-ROM discs, which look just like music CDs. Computer CDs can store many megabytes of information, and most new computer software comes on a CD.

The only drawback to a CD is that you cannot write information to one. The RO in CD-ROM means Read-Only. That's typically not a problem, though, because most people don't have a need to write that much information to a disc all at one time.

ZIP drives. A special type of disk drive on many computers sold today is the ZIP drive. ZIP drives eat ZIP disks, which work much like floppy disks, although they can store 100MB of information — more than 75 floppy disks at about half the cost.

ZIP drives are not standard equipment on most PCs, although they're optional with most systems and can be added to any existing PC. You can get either an external or internal ZIP drive added to your computer. Their advantage is that they can store lots of information and can move it between two computers more easily than fumbling with a stack of floppy disks.

Specialty drives. Many, many different types of disk drives are available, depending on your long-term storage needs. In addition to the more popular types just mentioned, you can also find recordable CD-R drives, CD-RW drives, MO drives, and a host of removable hard drives and tape drives. It's enough to drive you batty.

- The drive is the device that reads the disk.

- The disk is the thing that contains the data — the media inside the drive.

- The terms hard disk and hard drive are often used interchangeably, although incorrectly so.

- IBM, always proving that it's different, calls the hard drive a *fixed disk*. No, it does not mean that the disk was once broken. (It's fixed, as in immovable.)

- ✔ ZIP drives are not related to the ZIP file format, which is used to compress files downloaded from the Internet or from other users. See Chapter 25 for more information about ZIP files.

- ✔ ZIP disks are expensive, typically $15 or more for a single disk when you buy them in bulk.

- ✔ The ZIP drive's big brother is the JAZ drive, which can store 1GB of information or more on a single disk.

- ✔ To record your own CD-ROM CDs, you need a CD-R drive. It's a specialty device not usually offered as a basic PC option. Although anyone can add and use a CD-R, it's really designed for specific applications, such as archiving lots of data or creating software or information for mass distribution.

- ✔ The CD-RW drive is a readable/writable CD-ROM drive. Again, as with CD-R drives, they're specialty devices destined for specific applications.

- ✔ More information about CD-ROM drives and the newer DVD drives can be found later in this chapter.

- ✔ MO drives are Magneto-Optical drives, which swallow a small, 3-inch CD-like disk. MO drives can read and write to their MO disks just like a floppy drive reads and writes to a floppy disk, although the disks can store a larger amount of information.

Know Thy Disk Drives

All the disk drives in your computer have names. Rather than let you assign the name, which would be confusing, Microsoft decided to name every disk drive in your computer after a famous letter of the alphabet, from A through Z.

Drives from A (skipping B) to C

The first disk drive on every computer is drive A. That's the floppy drive.

The second disk drive on every computer is drive C. That's the hard drive.

See? Doesn't this all make sense?

The CD-ROM drive is usually drive D. . . .

Oh? Drive B? Well, drive B is reserved for the second floppy drive, if you have one. (You probably don't.)

Back in the early days, PCs were sold without hard drives. The "deluxe" model IBM PC sported two floppy drives, A and B. Most PCs sold in the early 1980s came that way.

When the first hard drive came along, they named it drive C. Most PCs are now sold with one floppy drive and one hard drive. Drive B is remembered only because it isn't there. (If this makes sense to you, you're going to *love* computers!)

> ✔ People pronounce A: as "A-colon," as in:
>
> **Alex Trebek:** People use this to digest food.
>
> **You:** A colon.
>
> **Alex:** I'm sorry, you must phrase that response in the form of a question.

Drive D, anyone?

The first hard drive in your computer (the disk drive you use most often) is named drive C. If you have a second hard drive, it's drive D. That's because your PC's operating system gives letters to its favorite drives before naming any other drive in the system.

In Figure 7-1, you see my test computer with a whopping four hard drives: C, D, E, and F. Each hard drive in the system is given a name or letter higher than the previous hard drives. That's how it works.

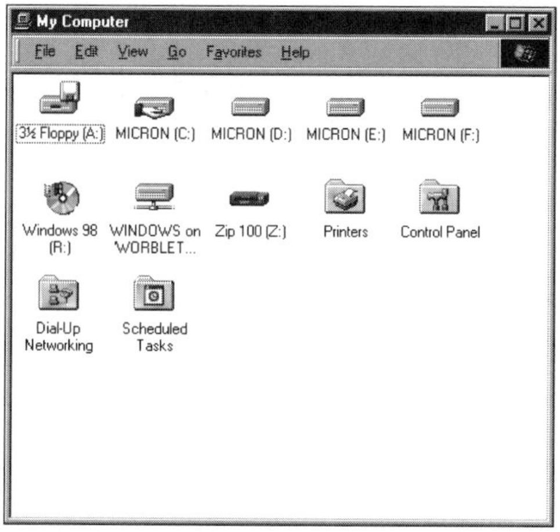

Figure 7-1:
Several
hard drives
visible in
the My
Computer
window.

Your computer may have only a drive C hard drive. Or you might have a drive D too. If so, great! It just means that you have more room to store your stuff.

- Don't neglect your hard drive D (or E or F)! That's just more storage for your stuff. There's nothing wrong with installing software or saving your stuff to another hard drive.

- On my computers, I typically install games on drive D. I have no reason for it, other than it forces me to use drive D.

- The computer names drives historically: Floppy drives came first for the PC, so they're named first (A and B). Then came hard drives, named C and up. Then came other drives, which are given letters after the last hard drive letter (see the following section).

- Sometimes your PC manufacturer installs a very large hard drive. Because of some oddball limitations I don't want to get into, the large hard drive is *partitioned* into smaller drives (don't ask why). For example, the PC in Figure 7-1 has one large hard drive that was partitioned into drives C, D, E, and F. Newer computers don't have this problem; the entire hard drive is all drive C.

Naming other drives

After your last hard drive, which could be drive C or D or whatever, Windows gives names to every other type of disk drive in your system, all the way up to drive Z if necessary.

Your PC's CD-ROM is typically given the next drive letter after the last hard drive. For years, it was drive D on most computers. However, because hard drives have become larger and are usually split *(partitioned)* into drives C and D, the CD-ROM drive could have any letter.

After the CD-ROM drive, your PC may give names to any other type of drive in your system. For example, you may have a ZIP drive. If so, your PC's disk drives may be named like this:

Drive A: Floppy drive

Drive C: Hard drive

Drive D: 'Nother hard drive

Drive E: CD-ROM drive

Drive F: ZIP drive

Other types of drives are available too, each of which uses the next-highest letter of the alphabet. For example, if your PC is on a network, you might have drive G as a network disk drive. It can get nuts.

My advice is to fill in this book's Cheat Sheet with the names and locations of your computer's disk drives and their letters. If you have a label maker, label your removable drives: Put A on drive A, E (or whatever) on your CD-ROM drive, and F on your ZIP drive (if you have one), and so on.

✔ Knowing your system's disk drives helps with some software installation programs. For example, they may ask you to type your CD-ROM drive's letter.

✔ Don't always depend on a PC's CD-ROM drive to have the same drive letter on every computer!

✔ Notice in Figure 7-1 that the CD-ROM drive and ZIP drive on my PC don't follow the standard letter-naming routines. The CD-ROM is drive R, and the ZIP disk is drive Z. You can change the drive letters of your PC's CD-ROM, ZIP drive, or any removable disk if you follow certain secretive steps.

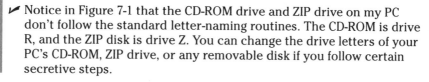

And now, the tricky part: Using the letter as a name

To every disk drive there is a name, and that name is a letter of the alphabet. Yet, although you have an A drive and a C drive, Windows doesn't see them that way. Nope, Windows adds a colon to the drive letter. Only when the letter is followed by a colon does Windows know that you're talking about a disk drive. So:

Drive A is known as A: to Windows.

Drive C is known as C: to Windows.

This strategy works for all your disk drives, from D: through Z:. You pronounce their names as "A colon," "C colon," and on up.

You can even see the colon name specified in Figure 7-1, although it's enclosed in parentheses on-screen.

Floppy Disk Cavalcade!

The standard PC model sold today comes with a single floppy drive. All computers — even the Macintosh — use the same style of floppy drive. There's no confusion.

In addition to having the same style floppy drive, everyone also buys the same type of floppy disk. You have no decision to make and no hell to go through, like in the old days (see the following sidebar, "Antiquated disk formats of yore").

Technically, the floppy disk is a $3\frac{1}{2}$-inch, high-density diskette. The diskette may also be referred to as "IBM formatted" or "DS, HD." It's all the same type of disk, the only one you can buy in most places.

Figure 7-2 shows what a typical $3\frac{1}{2}$-inch floppy disk looks like.

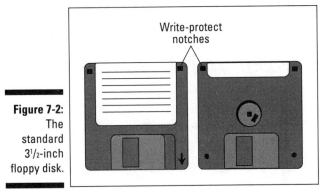

Figure 7-2:
The standard $3\frac{1}{2}$-inch floppy disk.

✔ It's tempting to use these disks as beverage coasters. Don't. Moisture can seep underneath the sliding metal thing and freak out the disk inside.

✔ Nothing is wrong with buying discount disks in bulk. I just did and saved a bundle.

✔ Pay a little extra and buy preformatted disks. Look for a box that says "IBM Formatted" or "Formatted for IBM and Compatibles." This effort saves you some time later because unformatted disks must be formatted before you can use them. (I cover the subject of formatting later in this chapter, in the section "Formatting a floppy disk.")

✔ No, the "IBM" on the label of a preformatted box of disks does not mean that they're only for IBM-brand computers. If you have a PC, you can use an IBM disk.

✔ Most 3¹/₂-inch disks come in little plastic sleeves. You can throw away the sleeves.

✔ Australia: Best scuba diving in the world!

Hmmm, I wonder what's on this disk?

Ever pick up a disk and wonder silently, "Where the heck did this disk come from?" If you do that a lot, I have one maxim for you: Label your floppy disks!

Every box of disks — even the cheapies — comes with several sticky labels. Here's how you use them:

1. **Write information on the sticky label by using a pen.**

   Describe the disk's contents, or give it a general name: Files for Home or Backup Stuff or Emergency Disk or — you get the idea.

2. **Peel the label off and gently apply it to the disk.**

   (Make your own sound effects here.)

Antiquated disk formats of yore

Once upon a time . . . floppy disks were *really* floppy. They were 8-inch pizzas (although square) that had serious flop to them. No PC on earth ever came with an 8-inch disk drive (think about how big that would be!), although in the early days, you could add one as an external option.

After the 8-inch pizza came the 5¹/₄-inch disk, called the mini-floppy by old-timers. These disks are now as out of style as the gavotte, although some computers may still sport a 5¹/₂-inch disk drive for compatibility with older PCs.

The original 5¹/₄-inch disk was improved in two ways. First, computer scientists in white lab coats improved the disk's storage capability, allowing twice as much information to be put on a single disk. Those newer disks were called *double-density* (DD), and the original disks became *single-density* (SD).

Eventually, the scientists figured out that you could write on *both* sides of the disk, so you had single-sided (SS) and double-sided (DS) disks. Then a final improvement was made, packing even more information on a high-density (HD) disk. This situation explains the hieroglyph on today's floppy disks: DS, HD, which stands for a double-sided, high-density disk.

There. That's easy. With all your floppy disks labeled, you never worry about what's on them. And you'll be able to find commonly used disks more quickly.

- ✔ You can always tell what's on a disk by opening it up and looking. No — put that screwdriver away! Instead, use the My Computer program: Open My Computer, and then double-click the floppy drive containing the disk in question, such as floppy drive A. That action displays the disk's contents in a window on the screen.

- ✔ Label disks right after you format them. That way, all formatted disks have labels. If you find a disk without a label, that tells you that it's probably unformatted.

- ✔ Don't use sticky notes as disk labels. They fall off when you're not looking and can sometimes get stuck inside your disk drives.

Write-protecting a floppy disk

You can protect floppy disks in such a way as to prevent yourself or anyone else from modifying or deleting anything on the disk.

To *write-protect* a $3^1/_2$-inch disk, locate the little sliding tile on the lower-left side of the disk as you slide it into the drive. If the tile covers the hole, the disk can be written to. If you slide the tile off the hole (so that you can see through it), the disk is write-protected (see Figure 7-2).

When a disk is write-protected, you cannot alter, modify, change, or delete anything on that disk. You cannot accidentally reformat it. You can read from the disk and copy files from it. But changing the disk's contents — forget it!

Floppy disk do's and donuts

Disks store information in the form of magnetic impulses. That means if you bring a disk close to a magnet, you copy new, random magnetic impulses over your important data. Don't use the Schwan guy's refrigerator magnet to stick a floppy to the refrigerator!

- ✔ Keep your floppy disks away from magnets, including telephone handsets, speakers on radios and TV sets, executive-style paper-clip holders, desk fans, photocopiers, 1.21-gigawatt power amplifiers, and the planet Jupiter.

✔ Don't set books or heavy items on top of disks. The pressure can push dust granules into the disk.

✔ Avoid extreme temperatures. Don't leave a disk sitting on the dash of your car or even on a window sill. And, even if the novel thought occurs to you, don't store your disks in the freezer.

✔ Don't touch the disk surface; touch only its protective cover. Don't spray WD-40 inside, even if the disk makes a noise as it spins. (Your disk drive is probably making the noise, anyway. Keep the WD-40 out of there, too.)

✔ Never remove a disk from a floppy drive when the drive light is on. Wait.

✔ Never remove a disk from a floppy drive while you're using (or "logged to") that drive. Wait until you've saved all your files before removing the floppy disk. Also close the floppy disk's window before you yank it out.

✔ When you're mailing a disk, don't use a floppy disk mailer from the drugstore. Don't fold the disk in half and mail it in a standard-size envelope. Instead, buy a photo mailer, which is the same as a floppy disk mailer but doesn't cost as much.

Formatting a floppy disk

All floppy disks must be formatted. Unless you were smart enough to buy preformatted floppy disks, you have to format them at some point. A disk must be formatted before you can use it.

If the disk isn't formatted and you try to access it, Windows spits up an ugly error message, similar to the one shown in Figure 7-3. If that happens, click the Yes button and get ready for formatting.

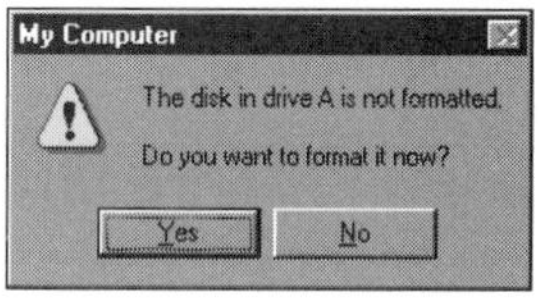

Figure 7-3:
The "disk is unformatted" error message in Windows.

My Computer

The disk in drive A is not formatted.

Do you want to format it now?

[Yes]   [No]

Stick an unformatted disk in drive A (or B). Make sure that the disk is the proper size and type for that floppy drive. Then follow these steps:

1. **Open the My Computer icon.**

   Double-click the My Computer icon, sitting all by itself in the upper-left corner of the screen. This step displays a list of disk drives in your computer, plus some oddball folders (see Figure 7-1).

2. **Stick an unformatted disk into drive A.**

   Or use drive B. Or the disk can already be in the drive.

   Make sure that the disk is unformatted or is an older disk you don't mind utterly erasing. The process of formatting a disk removes any information already on that disk. That's something you don't want to find out accidentally later.

3. **Select drive A.**

   Point the mouse at drive A's icon and click once. This step highlights that disk drive, selecting it for action.

4. **Choose File⇨Format from the menu.**

   The Format dialog box appears (see Figure 7-4).

Figure 7-4: The Format dialog box.

Format - 3½ Floppy (A:)
Capacity:
1.44 Mb (3.5")
Format type
⦿ Quick (erase)
○ Full
○ Copy system files only
Other options
Label:
☐ No label
☑ Display summary when finished
☐ Copy system files

Buttons: Start, Close

5. **Click the Start button.**

   Ignore those dialog box options! Point at the Start button and click the mouse.

The formatting process takes a minute or longer, so count the holes in the ceiling tiles for a while. When Windows finishes formatting . . . nothing happens. Well, you may see a summary screen. Press Esc to close the dialog box, and you're ready to use the disk.

✔ The floppy drives in the My Computer window have little floppy disks on their shoulders.

✔ If your PC sports a B floppy drive, you can format the disks in it by using the preceding steps.

✔ MO drives are formatted by using the same steps as just described.

✔ ZIP disks are formatted in a similar method as floppy disks, although you choose the special ZIP-disk format option from the pop-up menu. And, yes, it's okay to format ZIP disks. In fact, you can delete any files that Iomega (the manufacturer) puts on the ZIP disks. As long as your ZIP drive is properly installed and working, you don't need those files.

✔ Be sure to format a new disk or one that doesn't contain anything you want to keep. Reformatting completely erases a disk, so be careful what you stick in the drive.

✔ After the disk is formatted, slap a label on it. You can use one of the sticky labels that came with the disk. Be sure to write on the label *before* you slap it on the disk.

Never, under any circumstances, format a hard drive. It's next to impossible to do in Windows, but don't even make the attempt. Formatting a hard drive is something they do at the factory. Trained technicians, often wearing white lab coats and caps and carrying clipboards and wearing laminated badges that have bad photos on them, do the formatting.

CD-ROM Drives (Or, When a Disk Is a Disc)

CD-ROM drives eat special CD-ROM discs, which I call CDs, or computer CDs. The computer CDs look exactly like music CDs, although they store megabytes and megabytes of computer information. The CD-ROM drive can access that information, making it available to you just like it was on a hard disk or floppy.

✔ The RO in CD-ROM means Read-Only. You can only read information from a CD-ROM disc. You cannot add new information to the disc or erase or change information already on the disc.

✔ Some CD-ROM discs can be written to. They're known as CD-R drives for CD *recordable* or sometimes CD-RW for *read-write*. They behave just like normal computer CDs, although you have to run special programs to write information to them.

Inserting a computer CD into a CD-ROM drive

Computer CDs go into CD-ROM drives in one of three ways: slide-in, tray, or caddy.

The first way (my favorite) is just to slide the CD into the CD-ROM drive, similar to the way some car CD players work. Pushing the CD into the slot causes some gremlin inside the drive to eventually grab the CD and suck it in all the way. Amazing.

The second way to put a CD in the drive is by setting it into a sliding tray that pops out of the CD-ROM drive like a little kid sticking out his tongue. Press the CD-ROM drive's eject button to pop-out the tray (often called a "drink holder" in many computer joke punch lines). Drop the CD into the tray, label up. Gently nudge the tray back into the computer. The tray should slide back in the rest of the way on its own.

The third way to slip a computer CD into a CD-ROM drive — my least favorite way — is to use the *caddy* or container. The disc goes into the container label up, so you can see the label through the container's clear cover. Close the container and then shove it into the drive. I'm not a fan of this type of drive because putting the CD-ROM in the caddy is an extra step that I'd rather not do.

When the disc is in the drive, you use it just like any other disk in your computer.

✔ If you have the caddy-type of CD-ROM drive, it behooves you to go out and buy a whole bunch of extra caddies. That way, you can keep all your CD-ROM discs in their own caddies, which saves you time when you need to swap them in the CD-ROM drive.

✔ If you don't have the caddy-type of CD-ROM drive, you might want to go out and buy some extra "jewel cases" in which to store your computer CDs.

Ejecting a computer CD

Follow these steps to eject a computer CD from the CD-ROM drive:

1. **Locate the CD-ROM drive icon by using the My Computer program.**

   Open the My Computer icon on the Windows desktop by double-clicking it with the mouse. A window appears, showing you all the disc drives in your computer, plus a few token folders.

Wambooli
(D:)

2. **Point the mouse at the CD-ROM drive icon.**

   A sample of what the icon looks like appears in the margin.

3. **Click the mouse's right button.**

   This step displays the shortcut menu for the CD-ROM drive, as shown in Figure 7-5.

Figure 7-5:
A CD-ROM
drive's
shortcut
menu.

Open
Explore
Find...
Backup
AutoPlay
Sharing...
Add to Zip
Eject
Create Shortcut
Properties

4. **Choose Eject from the menu.**

   Point at the word *Eject* with your mouse and click.

   The disc spits out of the CD-ROM drive.

   ✔ These steps also work for ZIP disks, MO disks, and certain other types of removable disks — but not floppy disks.

   ✔ Oh, and you can always eject a CD by pushing the manual eject button on the CD-ROM drive. Note that some model CD-ROM drives require you to press two buttons simultaneously to eject.

I am the future! I be DVD

DVD is the Next Big Thing as far as computer disk drives are concerned. If your PC doesn't have a DVD drive now, your next PC probably will. Though they're now sold as options, I predict that the computer of the future will have a DVD drive rather than a CD-ROM drive.

DVD is an acronym for Digital Versatile Disk. The drives look just like CD-ROM drives, although they have the DVD logo on them, plus a special DVD light that flashes when a DVD disk is being read.

Although the DVD disks look just like computer CDs, they're capable of storing more than 4GB of information (compared to 600MB for a typical computer CD). Some future versions of DVD disks are rumored to be able to hold more than 17GB of information (barely enough for Excel 2010, most likely).

And now, the bad news: Not much DVD software is available, although plenty is in the works. Sure, movie CDs are available. In fact, DVD's other acronym spells out as Digital *Video* Disk, designed to eventually replace the VCR in most homes. For my PC and its DVD player, the only DVD disks I have are movies. A DVD player that comes with Windows 98 lets me view the movies, though it's not conducive to getting work done.

Chapter 8

Organizing Your Files

*W*ant to know a secret? Computers can be much easier to deal with if you organize your files in folders. Sounds simple, right? Yet you would think that creating and using a folder is as painful as a root canal. People run away from organizing their hard disks like extras in a monster movie. You may as well say "contracting boils" rather than "creating a folder." Sheesh.

This chapter tries, in as painless a way as possible, to give you the best possible pointers for organizing stuff on your PC. I promise not to waggle my finger or call anyone a loser for not using folders. Just read along, smile, follow a few steps, and you too will soon enjoy the benefits of having an organized hard drive.

"Why Should I Bother Organizing My Hard Drive?"

The truth is, you don't have to organize your hard drive. Heck, you could use your computer for months and never create or bother with a folder. But problems would crop up quickly:

✔ Without folders, files just go anywhere. Although you may be able to find them, you probably won't.

✔ Different programs stick their files in different folders. Who knows where your stuff is?

✔ Ever pull your hair out over finding a lost file? It's probably because you didn't care much about folders when you created and saved the file.

✔ With folders, your files can be neatly tucked into areas with similar files. You can organize your stuff by project, by type of file, or however you see fit.

The true problem is that Windows, honestly, doesn't give a hoot whether you use folders. If you do, you'll be organized and can always find your stuff. If you don't, working on the computer takes longer, but everything still works.

Personally, I'd rather be organized and keep those clumps of hair that look *great* on my head.

Building Towns on the Wild Hard Disk Frontier (Or "What Is a Folder?")

A *folder* is a storage place for files in your computer, on the hard drive specifically. Folders keep files together — like a private resort on your hard disk. All the files in that one folder are all in one, handy place.

Folders can hold, in addition to files, more folders. It's just another level of organization. For example, you can have a folder named Finances and in that folder have other folders, one for 1998, one for 1999, and on up until the day you die.

✔ Whether you use your files or not, Windows always puts them in folders on disk. When you save something in Windows, you're really placing it in a specific folder somewhere on your hard drive.

✔ Folders contain files, just like folders in a filing cabinet contain files. Golly, what an analogy.

✔ In the olden days, folders were known as *directories,* or often the prepositional *subdirectories.* I would have no need to bring this up, except that some dorky program (including Windows) always refers to a directory-this or that-subdirectory. Directory, folder — same thing.

Names and places

A folder is a folder is a folder. Some folders have special names. To witness this and get familiar with the oddball naming methods Windows uses, take a gander at your PC's monitor. (Turn your computer on because this demonstration works only when the thing is on.)

The desktop: The thing you stare at when Windows is up and running is called the *desktop*. You may have to close some windows and minimize some programs to see the whole thing. That's the topmost level of organization on your computer. What does it mean? Absolutely nothing.

- ✔ The desktop is merely the screen you see when you use Windows.

- ✔ Any icons pasted to the desktop, such as Network Neighborhood, Microsoft Network, Briefcase, or whatever you've put there, are considered part of the desktop.

- ✔ The desktop level is just the topmost level of organization in Windows. It has nothing to do with whether you're a good person.

My Computer: The next level of organization is your computer, represented by the My Computer icon in the upper-left corner of the desktop.

Open the My Computer icon by double-clicking it with your mouse. A window appears, showing you all the disk drives in your computer, plus two guest folders: Control Panel and Printers.

- ✔ The My Computer icon shows you what's "in" your computer. Because this chapter deals with disk storage, what it shows you is primarily your disk drives: floppy drives, hard drives, CD-ROMs, and whatever else you have available for storing files.

- ✔ The Control Panel folder is a gizmo that enables you to tweak and fiddle with various parts of your computer. It has nothing to do with disk storage or organizing files.

- ✔ Ditto for the Printers folder. That's a container for all the printers attached to your computer (see Chapter 16).

- ✔ The Scheduled Tasks folder lists automated programs, such as a disk cleanup tool that runs on a weekly basis. This folder isn't in Windows 95.

- ✔ You may also find the Dial-Up Networking folder in the main My Computer window. This folder is covered in Part VI of this book.

The root folder: Every disk has at least one folder. That one folder — the main folder — is called the *root folder*. Like a tree (and this isn't a dog joke), all other folders on your hard drive branch out from that main, root folder.

✔ The root folder does not have a cutesy icon associated with it. In fact, if the root folder looks like anything, it looks like the disk drive. At least that's how My Computer and the Explorer programs display it.

✔ When you open a disk drive in My Computer or in Explorer, the files and folders you see are all stored in the root folder.

✔ The root folder may also be called the *root directory.* This term is merely a throwback to the old days of DOS (which is a throwback to the days of UNIX, which King Herod used).

The My Documents folder: A special folder in Windows 98 is the My Documents folder. It's the place where most programs in Windows first attempt to save any new documents you create. That makes so much sense that it makes you wonder why we had to wait through six versions of DOS and four versions of Windows before Microsoft came up with the concept.

✔ If you're using Windows 95, you may or may not have a My Documents folder. (You have it if you've installed Microsoft Office.) If you don't have the My Documents folder, you can create it.

✔ All your new documents should be created in the My Documents folder.

✔ Yes, you'll be creating more folders inside the My Documents folder to keep things *organized.*

✔ In the United Kingdom, you'll keep things *organised* instead.

Regular old folders: These folders on your hard drive contain files and maybe even other folders.

✔ Ideally, the folder's name should give you some hint about its contents.

✔ A few special folders, such as Control Panel and Printers, don't truly contain files and stuff you store on a hard drive. You can spot these folders easily because they don't look like the plain yellow folder shown in the margin. Don't mess with 'em.

The tree structure

The whole mess of folders and files is organized into something the computer nerds call the *tree structure.* The folders all start at the root, branching out to more folders and folders, and eventually you end up with files, kind of like the leaves on a tree. There are no aphids in this simile.

Why bother with the tree structure? Because it keeps your files organized. To see how it all works, follow this brief tutorial (which isn't really a tutorial because *...For Dummies* books traditionally don't have tutorials in them, Q.E.D.).

1. Fire up the Explorer program.

Explorer is much better suited for hopping between folders than is My Computer. To start Explorer from the Start menu, choose Programs⇨Windows Explorer.

If your keyboard has a Windows key on it, you can start Explorer by pressing the Windows key and the E key together. This keystroke combo is known as Win+E ("winnie") in professional circles.

Explorer appears on-screen, looking something like Figure 8-1.

✔ If you don't see the Explorer toolbar, choose View⇨Toolbars⇨Standard Buttons. You may also want to choose Address Bar and Text Labels from the Toolbars submenu.

✔ Figure 8-1 shows Explorer as Windows 98 shows it, which looks much like the Internet Explorer program. In Windows 95, Explorer looks subtly different, although it still works the same. Choose View⇨Toolbar from the menu in Windows 95 to see the toolbar.

✔ Adjust the size of the Explorer window, if necessary, to see all of the toolbar.

✔ The Explorer window is divided into two parts, or panels. On the left is the tree structure — showing the way your hard drive is organized from the desktop down to the lowliest folder. On the right are the contents of whatever you have highlighted on the left.

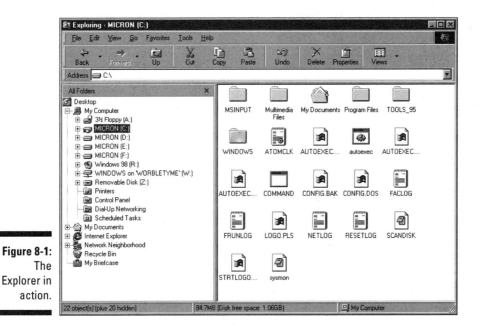

Figure 8-1:
The Explorer in action.

2. Scroll to the top of the left panel.

If you can't see the Desktop displayed in the left panel, use the scroll bar (the up-and-down one in the middle) to scroll to the top of the window. The first thing you should see is the Desktop item.

Beneath the Desktop, you find My Computer.

Beneath My Computer, you find all the disk drives in your computer, plus the two weirdo folders.

3. Look in drive C.

In the left panel, click your computer's drive C.

Drive C may have a name and then a drive letter, such as

```
MICRON (C:)
```

Or it may just have the drive letter and colon in parentheses:

```
(C:)
```

Either way, click the drive's name to display its contents in Explorer's right panel.

✔ What you're looking at in the right panel, the contents of drive C, is actually the root folder. This concept is explained earlier in this chapter.

✔ The Views button on the far right side of the Explorer toolbar in Windows 98 lets you see files and icons displayed in four different ways. If you have oodles of time to waste, click the button once to see the different views. Click again to see another view.

✔ Windows 95 has four buttons to the right of the Explorer toolbar. Clicking each button displays the files in a different view.

✔ My favorite Explorer view is Large Icons view, as shown in Figure 8-1.

✔ Some folks like Large Icons view. It's similar to what My Computer shows you.

✔ Nerds just love Details view, which looks like DOS, except in a fancy font.

✔ Don't ask me why they put the drive letter (and colon) in parentheses. I would have figured that the colon was confusing enough. But, no, not for Microsoft, I suppose.

✔ Drive C is your computer's first hard drive. Refer to Chapter 7 to discover why that's not drive A and to discover other miscellaneous hard-drive trivia.

4. Open your drive C.

Click the little plus sign (+) by that drive. (If you see a minus sign by the drive, no need to click; the drive is already open.)

Opening drive C by clicking the plus sign shows all drive C's folders in the panel on the left side of Explorer.

✔ Explorer's left panel shows you your computer's tree structure: the disks and folders. The right panel shows you the contents.

✔ A plus sign appears next to a drive or folder when it's closed. You click the plus sign to open the drive or folder.

✔ A minus sign appears next to a drive or folder when it's already open.

✔ If you're familiar with working an outline program on a computer, you can see that the Explorer tree structure works in a similar way. If you're not familiar with an outline program, just nod your head in silent agreement.

5. Look in the Windows folder.

Scroll down through the left panel until you see the Windows folder. Click the folder's name to see its contents displayed in the right panel.

You may have to use the middle scroll bar to scroll the left panel down far enough to find the Windows folder.

If you see a warning about modifying files in the Windows folder, choose View⇨as Web Page from the menu. That should disable the warnings.

6. Look in the Media folder.

Using the *right* panel only, locate the Media folder. You may have to use the scroll bar (or scroll bars) to find the folder. When you do, click the Media folder with the mouse. This step opens it and displays its contents in the right panel.

✔ Opening a folder in the right panel works just like it does in My Computer. It's a very un-Explorer thing to do, so don't let your computer guru know that you've tried it.

✔ You may not have a Media folder in your Windows folder. If not, open some other folder that looks interesting. Don't take all day.

✔ Notice how the Media folder's icon in the Explorer's *left* panel is open a bit? That's how you can tell which folder you're looking in. Also, a caption may be visible above the right panel that says Contents of 'Media.' Big hint, there.

7. Use the Go to a Different Folder drop-down thing to return to the root folder.

Click your mouse on the arrow next to the Go to a Different Folder drop-down thing, dropping down the list. Use the scroll bar (if necessary) to scroll up and find the root level, which is listed as drive C (see Step 3). Click that item. Figure 8-2 shows an example.

Figure 8-2: Zooming back to the root with the Go to a Different Folder drop-down thing.

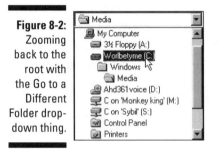

This action takes you directly to the root folder — or to any other folder above the one you're in. It's a speedy way to move from one folder to another (which is the point of this whole exercise).

If you just want to hop up one folder, use the Up One Level button on the toolbar.

Crawling down through the depths of your system's tree structure is involved but not that painful. This task becomes necessary when you create lots of important folders for your stuff.

No, this isn't like spelunking.

Folder Calisthenics

Folders aren't mold. They don't happen with the proper moisture, heat conditions, or proximity to Seattle.

You must make an effort to create folders on your hard drive!

You must make an effort to use folders on your hard drive!

You must believe me when I tell you that it isn't that hard!

Enough finger wagging.

Where to put your folders

Folders can live anywhere on your hard drive. Therefore, you can put them anywhere. There are no rules and no speed limit, kind of like driving in Montana in the daytime.

✔ Sure, you can create all your folders in the *root folder* (or *root directory*), the first list of files and folders you see on a hard drive. But that isn't being organized. Besides, Windows places a limit on the number of folders you can have in the root. Better create 'em somewhere else.

✔ The best place to put your new folders is in the handy My Documents folder. That's why it's there — for your documents. It also makes backing up your files easier because they're all in one folder.

✔ By putting folders into categories, you can arrange your work nicely. For example, I have a folder named Graphics located inside the My Documents folder. Inside the Graphics folder are folders organized into various image categories. It's one example of how a well-named and organized folder can help you quickly find your stuff.

✔ Even more organization: Inside the My Documents folder, you should create more folders like categories. I have general folders named Graphics, Video, Work, Finances, and even one called Stuff.

My Finances folder has folders for various years. For example, inside the 1997 folder, you would find everything in that year about my finances, in case you ever want to sue me.

The beauty of this scheme is that whenever I need a financial file, I know to look in the Finances folder and then in the proper year. Then I can find the file I need.

I organize my correspondence the same way: The My Documents folder contains the Letters folder that contains folders for personal, work, and miscellaneous stuff. (Those folders are named Personal, Work, and Misc.) Inside each folder are other folders that further organize things.

✔ See? Aren't I organized? You can be, too, if you create and organize your folders in Windows.

A brief exercise in creating a folder

Creating a folder is easy. Deciding where to create it is the hard part. As an example, the following steps create a folder named Stuff in the My Documents folder on drive C:

1. Open the My Documents folder on the desktop.

Double-click the My Documents icon on the Windows desktop. This step opens a window detailing all the documents in your computer.

If you don't have a My Documents icon on the desktop (as is probably the case in Windows 95), do this instead: Open the My Computer icon, open drive C, and then open the My Documents folder. If you don't have a My Documents folder, create one after following this tutorial.

2. Choose File⇨New⇨Folder.

This step places a new folder in the window, looking something like the icon in the margin. (It may look different, depending on which view you've chosen from the View menu.)

Ta-da! There's your new folder.

3. Give the folder a name other than the silly New Folder.

Type a new name. Be clever. Remember that this folder will contain files and possibly other folders, all of which should relate somehow to the folder's name. For this tutorial, type the nondescript name **Stuff**.

- Use the Backspace key to back up and erase if you make a mistake.

- See Chapter 9 for information about naming files. The same rules apply when you're naming a folder.

4. Press Enter to lock in the name.

5. Do something with the folder. Create more folders; cut and paste some files in there — you get the idea.

Double-click the folder's icon to open it. A blank window is displayed because it's a new folder and has no contents.

Now you can create more folders or copy and paste files and folders into the new folder.

See? Wasn't that easy?

- You can always create a new folder and move files there. Go on an organizational frenzy!

- Chapter 9 covers copying and pasting files.

- If you've just created the Stuff folder and have no use for it, kill it off! See the section "Removing a folder," just a few paragraphs beyond this very spot.

Making a shortcut to your folder on the desktop

Some folders are just so darn handy that you want to keep them on the desktop, where you can always get at them. To do so, you shouldn't copy the folder; that would eat up too much disk space. Instead, just create a shortcut — like the shortcut path Peter Rabbit used to get into Mr. MacGregor's garden.

To create a shortcut folder on the desktop, first locate the folder you want to use. You can do this in the Explorer or My Computer program. Make it a popular folder. For example, I'm working on a book named *PCs For Dummies,* so I'll create a shortcut to my PCs For Dummies folder right there on the desktop. How handy.

Click the mouse once on the folder to select it. The folder appears in a darker color, telling the world that it's selected.

Choose the Edit⇨Copy command from the menu. The folder is copied, sorta.

Point the mouse at the desktop and click the *right* mouse button — a right-click. Up pops a shortcut menu, similar to the one you see in Figure 8-3. Choose the Paste Shortcut command from the list. *Voilà* — a shortcut to your folder lives on the desktop.

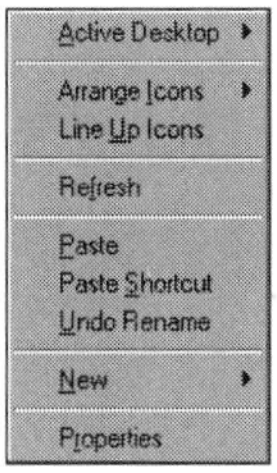

Figure 8-3:
The
desktop's
pop-up
menu.

Active Desktop ▶
Arrange Icons ▶
Line Up Icons
Refresh
Paste
Paste Shortcut
Undo Rename
New ▶
Properties

- ✔ Shortcuts are used just like the real McCoy. Double-click them to open and see the files and folders inside.

- ✔ The desktop shortcut menu for Windows 95 contains fewer items than shown in Figure 8-3. The Paste Shortcut command still works the same, however.

- ✔ The advantage of shortcuts is that you can put them anywhere, giving you easy access to your files without copying them all over blazes.

- ✔ See Chapter 9 for more information about shortcuts if the subject is driving you bonkers.

Removing a folder

Find the folder you want to trash by using either the Explorer or My Computer programs. Drag that folder across the desktop and drop it in the Recycle Bin icon.

Fwoosh! It's gone.

- ✔ Death to the folder!

- ✔ A warning box may appear, telling you that you're about to delete a folder and only bad people do that and don't you want to change your mind? Click Yes to trash it.

- ✔ If you can see the toolbar, you can click the Delete button to zap a folder.

- ✔ You can also use the Undo command to immediately undelete a folder. This command works only *immediately after* the folder is deleted, so be timely. You can either choose Edit⇨Undo Delete, press Ctrl+Z, or click the Undo button on the toolbar.

- ✔ Deleting a folder kills off everything in that folder — files, folders, and all the files and folders in those folders. Egads! It's mass carnage! Be careful with this one, lest you have to confess to some hard drive war-crimes tribunal.

- ✔ It's possible to rescue anything Windows deletes. Chapter 9 covers this topic.

Using the Open Dialog Box

One time that folders come into play is when you use the Open command to go out to a disk and fetch up a file. You must know in which folder you put something, plus how to find that folder on the disk. You do all this by working the Open dialog box, which is a standard feature in all Windows application programs.

Figure 8-4 shows a typical Open dialog box. Here is how you would work it to find a file for opening on disk:

1. **Look for your file. If it's there, open it.**

   In the big list in the center of the dialog box is a buncha file icons. If you find your file there, double-click it to open. That file then appears, ready for tweaking in your favorite program.

   You may need to use the left-right scroll bar at the bottom of the list to see more files.

2. **If your file can't be found, switch disk drives.**

   Use the Look In drop-down list at the top of the dialog box. Click the down arrow to the right of the list to display it. Then pluck out a disk drive from the list, such as drive C, to start looking there.

Open

Look in: 🗁 My Documents

☐ Audio	🗀 Video	📄 Envelopes
☐ Font Stowage	🗀 Work	📄 GHOST
☐ Graphics	📄 Airline food	📄 Letter to Be
☐ Great American Novel	📄 All My Fonts	📄 Letter to my
☐ Personal	📄 bed	📄 my trip
☐ Temporary	📄 Declaration of Independence	📄 Nasty Fax

File name: _____   [Open]

Files of type: Word for Windows (*.doc) ▾   [Cancel]

Figure 8-4: The typical Open dialog box.

The contents of the big list in the center of the dialog box change to show you the files on drive C (in the *root folder*).

If you find your file, open it!

3. **Open up a folder for further looking.**

If you can't find your file, look for a folder in the big list. Double-click the folder to open it, and look in there for the file.

Keep opening folders to find the one you want. (If your hard drive is organized and your folders cleverly named, it should be a snap.)

If you find your file, open it!

If you want to go back up to the preceding folder, click the handy Up One Level button (shown in the margin).

TECHNICAL STUFF

Sneaky information about the Open and Save dialog boxes

Both the Open and Save dialog boxes display a list of files, just like the Explorer or My Computer windows. That's obvious. What often isn't obvious is that the list of files works exactly like the list of files displayed in the Explorer or My Computer windows.

For example, you can rename a folder or file displayed in an Open or Save As dialog box. You can right-click a file and copy it or cut it. You can open a file by double-clicking it. Just about anything you can do with files in Windows can be done in that wee, tiny Open or Save As dialog box. Weird, huh?

✔ At the bottom of the dialog box is a drop-down list titled Files of Type. It can help you narrow the types of files displayed in the Open dialog box's big list. For example, in Figure 8-4, only files of the Word for Windows (*.doc) type are displayed in the big list. Another option is All Files, which displays every type of file available.

✔ Some Open dialog boxes are more complex than the one shown in Figure 8-4. For example, the Open dialog box in Microsoft Word is a doozy. It still works the same; it just has more annoying options to ignore.

✔ The Desktop button (fourth from the right in Figure 8-4) appears only with Windows 98; the button doesn't appear in the Open dialog box if you're using Windows 95.

✔ The Browse dialog box is similar to the Open dialog box. It appears whenever you click a Browse button to go hunt down a file for Windows.

✔ You can also open a file by clicking it once and then clicking the Open button. I find that if you're going to click it once, you may as well click it twice and forget the Open button.

✔ If you're nerdy, you can type the file's full pathname (if you know it) in the File name box. It's a very DOS-y thing to do. Cover your mouse's eyes if you try it (you don't want to shame him).

Using the Save Dialog Box

The Save dialog box is the most important dialog box you'll ever use in Windows. It's the key to organization. If you use it properly and take advantage of the unique folders you've created, you can *always* find your stuff on disk. Misuse the Save dialog box and, heck, the bad guys will take over the Wild West, and Miss Millie and the orphans will go hungry — maybe even die. You wouldn't want that on your conscience, would ya?

You summon the Save dialog box by using the File⇨Save command. (I know that it says "Save As" in Figure 8-5, but it's still what you see when you first save a file — so there.) Here's how you go about working it:

1. **Most important: Make sure that you're in the proper folder.**

   The Save dialog box initially puts your document in the My Documents folder, which is handy because any other folder or subfolder you want is probably right close.

Figure 8-5:
The typical
Save
dialog box.

The folder's name is listed in the Save In drop-down list. In Figure 8-5, it's My Documents. If that isn't what you want, move on to Step 2.

If the folder is okay, skip to Step 4.

2. **Hunt for the folder in which you want to save your stuff.**

   Click the down arrow on the right side of the Save In drop-down list (at the top of the dialog box). This step displays another drop-down list. In the list, click the proper disk drive on which you want to save your file; for example, drive C.

   Notice that the contents of the big list in the center of the dialog box change to show you the files in the root folder on drive C.

   I don't recommend saving your file in the root folder; it's not kosher.

3. **Open a folder.**

   Locate the folder in which you want to save your stuff, or the folder that contains the folder (and so on). For example, open your Work folder or the My Documents folder.

   As you open various folders, the contents of the file list in the center of the dialog box change.

   When you find the folder you want — the perfect folder for your stuff — move on to the next step. Otherwise, keep opening folders.

4. **Type a name for the saved file.**

   In the File Name input box, type a name. It's the name for your saved file, the name you should be able to recognize later and say (out loud), "Say! That's my file. The one I want. I am so happy I saved it with a short, clever name that tells me exactly what's in the file. Oh, joy."

   See Chapter 9 for more information about naming files. Basically, you can name a file anything you want, although being brief and sticking to letters and numbers are best.

   If you give the file an unacceptable name, you can't save it. Windows is fussy about filenames.

5. Click the Save button.

Click! This last, official act saves the file to disk, with a proper name and in a proper folder.

If the Save button appears to be broken, you probably typed an improper filename. Try giving the file a new name (refer to Step 4).

After you save your stuff once, the File⇨Save command simply resaves it to disk without your having to give it another name and work the Save dialog box.

You can choose the Save As command again to see the Save As dialog box (again). This step allows you to save something you're working on with a new name, in a new location, or as a different type of file.

As with the Open dialog box, some Save dialog boxes are more complex than the one shown in Figure 8-5. The same business goes on; they just have more things to get in the way.

What the Heck Is a Pathname?

A *pathname* is geekspeak for the longest possible filename you can imagine. It's used to pinpoint a file's location on a certain disk drive and in a certain folder. Long. Technical. Complex. It's a wonder that anyone has to deal with these things.

As an example, consider the file named Red Blocks.bmp. This file typically lives in the Windows folder on drive C. Therefore, its full, ugly pathname is

```
C:\WINDOWS\RED BLOCKS.BMP
```

It reads this way:

C:	It's on drive C.
\WINDOWS	It's in the Windows folder.
RED BLOCKS.BMP	The filename.

Therefore, the pathname tells you right where the file is. Suppose that you're told to go out and hunt down the file represented by this pathname:

```
C:\My Documents\Personal\Letters\Family\Zack.doc
```

You look on drive C, open the My Documents folder, open the Personal folder, open Letters, open Family, and then look for the file named Zack.doc.

✔ The backslash is used as a separator in a pathname. It separates the drive letter from the first folder, all the folders in between, and the last folder name from the filename.

✔ A double backslash (\\ ) at the beginning of a pathname means that you've discovered something on a network hard drive. Run for cover! (See Chapter 10 for more information about computer networks.)

✔ Don't confuse the backslash (\ ) with the slash character (/). Windows uses the backslash for some backward reason.

✔ See Chapter 9 for more information about filenames.

✔ A full pathname usually includes the *filename extension* — the period and last three characters of the filename. You may have directed Windows to withhold that information from you, not displaying it in My Computer or the Explorer. Even so, you *need* that information for a pathname. See? It is technical.

The terrible thing about pathnames is that you often have to make them up yourself. For example, some program may say, "Enter the pathname to your file," in which case it's up to *you* to figure everything out.

Chapter 9
Messin' with Files

. . . .

In This Chapter

▶ Naming a file

▶ Discovering what not to name a file

▶ Renaming a file

▶ Selecting file icons

▶ Moving files (cut and paste)

▶ Copying files (copy and paste)

▶ Making a file shortcut

▶ Deleting files

▶ Undeleting files

▶ Dragging files with the mouse

▶ Finding files

. . . .

*F*iles are chunks of stuff stored on your PC's disk drives. When you create something, you save it to disk as a file. To work on it again, you open that file. Easy enough.

The hard part comes with controlling the files. Like a kindergarten teacher with a room full of unruly 5-year-olds, it's your job to make sure that the files don't get out of hand. Fortunately, Windows lets you organize the files; just like in kindergarten, you can cut and paste, putting them where they belong. And you can give them new names and even kill them off — all without offending anyone's sense of moral justice.

✔ Windows displays files as icons. The *icon* is really the picture you see, either on the desktop or in the My Computer or Explorer programs. The file is what lives on disk.

✔ Everything on disk is a *file*. Some files are *programs,* and some files are *documents* or stuff you create.

File-Naming Rules and Regulations

If there's one thing mankind is good at, it's giving things names. Find a new bug — you get to name it. Discover a comet, and you can slap it with a new name; scientists exploring the cosmos give stars and features on planets new names every day. Even back when God showed Adam all the animals (Genesis 1:19, 20), he gave them all clever names. Adam didn't say, "There's a dog! There's another dog! That's a dog, too!" That leads me to believe that Adam was definitely more than 3 years old at the time. But I digress.

When you create something on your PC and save it to disk, you should give it a proper name. That name is attached to the stuff you created as a file. You see the file (as an icon) in the My Computer and Explorer programs and whenever you use an Open or Browse dialog box. That's how computers keep your stuff organized.

✔ The file's name reminds you of what's in the file, of what it's all about (just like naming the dog Downstoppit tells everyone what the dog is all about).

✔ All the rules for naming files in the following sections also apply to naming folders.

✔ See Chapter 8 for more information about the Open dialog box.

✔ I realize that not everyone accepts the idea that Adam sat down one spring day to name all the beasts that creepeth and crawleth. But you gotta figure that someone did it sometime.

File-naming tips

Keep the following notions in mind when you name any file:

Be brief. Keep the filename brief yet descriptive, like in the following examples:

```
Stocks
Outline
House plans
Vacation Itinerary
Plot to overthrow Finland
```

Use only letters, numbers, and spaces. Filenames can contain just about any key you press on the keyboard. Even so, it's best to stick with letters, numbers, and spaces.

- ✔ Technically, you can give a file a 255-character-long name. Don't.

- ✔ If you give a file too long a name, it's easier to make a single typo and confuse Windows when you try to open the file.

- ✔ Another long filename snafu: The rows of files listed in the Open or Save dialog box get farther and farther apart if a long filename is in the list. Shorter filenames mean shorter columns in a list.

- ✔ Also, if you give a file a long, long name, only the first part of that long filename appears below the icon.

- ✔ Upper- and lowercase don't matter to a computer. Although it's proper to capitalize Finland, for example, a computer matches that to `finland`, `Finland`, `FINLAND`, or any combination of upper- and lowercase letters.

Don't name a file this way

Windows gets mad if you use any of these characters to name a file:

```
* / : < > ? \ |
```

Nothing bad happens if you attempt to use these characters; Windows just refuses to save the file or change its name. (A warning dialog box may glow in your face if you make the attempt.)

- ✔ Each of these symbols holds a special meaning to Windows (or DOS). Using them in a filename confuses Windows to the point of becoming verklempt.

- ✔ Although you can use any number of periods in a filename, you cannot name a file with all periods. I know that it's strange, and I'm probably the only one on the planet to have tried it, but it still won't work.

Renaming a file

If you think that the name you just gave a file is stupid, you can easily change it:

1. **Locate the file.**

   Use the My Computer or Explorer program to find your program, or it may be stuck right on the desktop.

2. **Select the file.**

   When you find the file, click it once with the mouse. This step selects the file, highlighting it on-screen.

What the heck is a filename extension?

The last part of a filename is typically a period followed by one to three characters. Known as the *filename extension,* it's used by Windows to identify the type of file. For example, a .BMP extension tags a Paint graphics image, and .DOC indicates a document created by WordPad.

You never have to type these extensions when you name or rename a file. In fact, you shouldn't. Windows *needs* that information — that filename extension — or else it screws up when you try to open the file for editing.

A way around the filename extension dilemma in Windows 98 is to choose View⇨Folder Options from the Explorer or My Computer program's menu. This command displays the Folder Options dialog box. Click the View panel. Make sure that a check mark is next to the option Hide Files Extensions for Known File Types. This step effectively turns off the display of filename extensions so that you never have to bother with them.

Click OK to exit the Folder Options dialog box.

3. Press the F2 key.

F2 is the shortcut key for the Rename command. You can also choose File⇨Rename from the menu.

A file can be renamed in mousey ways, but because you type the new name at the keyboard, pressing the F2 key is a natural.

4. Type a new name.

Press the Backspace key to back up and erase if you need to.

Notice that the text for the old name is selected. If you're familiar with using the Windows text-editing keys, you can use them to edit the old name. (See the section in Chapter 15 about common Windows editing keys for more information.)

5. Press the Enter key.

This step locks in the new name.

- ✔ You can press the Esc key at any time before pressing Enter to undo the damage and return to the file's original name.

- ✔ Windows doesn't let you rename a file with the name of an existing file.

- ✔ You must give a file a name. You cannot name a file nothing.

- ✔ You cannot rename a group of files all at once. Rename files one at a time.

✔ You can also rename a file by right-clicking it with a mouse and choosing Rename from the shortcut menu. Or you can click the file's icon once and choose <u>F</u>ile➪Rena<u>m</u>e from the menu. Because you're typing anyway, isn't the F2 key faster?

Files Hither, Thither, and Yon

Files just don't stand still. You always find yourself moving them, copying them, and killing them off. If you don't do that, your hard drive gets all junky and, out of embarrassment, you're forced to turn off the computer when friends come over.

Messing with files is done primarily in the My Computer or Explorer programs. My Computer is friendlier and makes more sense if you're just starting out. After a time, you may prefer Explorer because it doesn't litter the screen with windows, one for every folder.

Selecting one or more files

Before you can mess with any file, it must be selected. Like log rolling, it can be done individually or in groups.

To select a single file, locate it in My Computer or Explorer. Click it once with the mouse. This step selects the file, which appears highlighted (blue, possibly) on-screen. The file is now ready for action.

Selecting a group of files can be done in a number of ways. The easiest way is to press and hold down the Ctrl (control) key on your keyboard. Then click all the files you want selected as a group, one after the other. This method is known as _control+clicking_ files.

If you're looking at files by using Icon view, you can lasso a group of them by using the mouse. Drag the mouse over the files: Start in the upper-left corner above the files; then drag down and to the right to create a rectangle surrounding the file icons you want to select, as shown in Figure 9-1. Release the mouse button, and all the files you've lassoed are selected as a group.

✔ To select a group of files, press and hold the Ctrl key as you click each one.

✔ To select all the files in a folder, choose <u>E</u>dit➪Select <u>A</u>ll. The handy keyboard shortcut key for this procedure is Ctrl+A.

✔ To unselect a file from a group, just Ctrl+click it again.

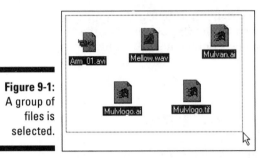

Figure 9-1:
A group of
files is
selected.

Cutting and pasting (moving files)

In the old days, you didn't cut and paste a file — you *moved* it. In Windows, where everything is like kindergarten anyway, you cut and paste. To cut and paste (move) a file, follow these steps:

1. Locate the file you want to move.

Hunker down in the Explorer or My Computer program, looking for the file or files you want to move.

2. Select it.

Click the file once to select it. Or you can select a group of files, by using the techniques described earlier in this chapter.

3. Choose Edit⇨Cut.

The file appears dimmed in the window. It means that it has been *cut* and is ready to be pasted. Nothing is wrong; keep moving on with the next step.

4. Open the folder where you want the file pasted.

Again, use the Explorer or My Computer program to hunt down the proper destination folder.

5. Choose Edit⇨Paste.

The file is deeply moved.

✔ Don't eat the paste.

✔ You can also cut and paste folders; however, it's a Big Deal because you're also cutting and pasting the folder's contents — which can be massive. Don't do this casually; cut and paste a folder only when you're up for major disk reorganization.

Copying and pasting (copying files)

Copying and pasting a file works just like cutting and pasting, with two differences.

The original file isn't deleted. When you're done copying and pasting, you have two identical copies of the file: the original and the copy.

The second difference is that you use the Edit➪Copy command rather than Edit➪Cut. See the preceding section for the steps and details.

Oftentimes, you don't really need to copy a file anywhere on your hard drive. Instead, create a shortcut to that file. See the section "Creating shortcuts," later in this chapter.

Copying a file to a floppy disk

A simple way to copy one or more files to a floppy disk is to use the Send To command. It's cinchy.

1. **Locate the file you want to copy to your floppy.**

   Use My Computer or Explorer for this step.

2. **Select the file.**

   Click the file or press the Ctrl key and Ctrl+click a group of files.

3. **Make sure that a formatted floppy disk is ready for the file in drive A.**

   See Chapter 7 for more information about floppy disks, formatting them, and sticking one in drive A.

4. **Choose File➪Send To➪3 ¹/₂ Floppy (A).**

   The file is copied.

   ✔ Using the Send To command is not the only way to copy (or cut) a file to a floppy disk. You can also copy and paste or cut and paste the file, just as you would to any other disk in your computer.

   ✔ You can also copy or cut files from a floppy disk to your hard drive. The process works the same way no matter which type of disk you're working with (although the special Send To command is set up to copy files to a floppy disk).

Creating shortcuts

A shortcut is a 99 percent fat-free copy of a file. It enables you to see and access the file from anywhere on your system but without the extra baggage required to copy the file all over creation. For example, you can drop a shortcut to WordPerfect on the desktop, where you can always get to it — much quicker than by using the Start menu.

Making a shortcut is a cinch: Just follow the same steps for copying a file as detailed in the previous sections about cutting, copying, and pasting files. The only exception is that you choose Edit⇨Paste Shortcut from the menu rather than the standard Paste command.

To paste a shortcut on the desktop, point the mouse at the desktop and click the right mouse button. Up pops a shortcut menu, from which you can choose the Paste Shortcut command.

Shortcut to Work Folder

✔ Shortcut icons have a little arrow in a white box nestled in their lower-left corner (see the figure in the margin). This icon tells you that the file is a shortcut and not the real McCoy.

✔ You can make shortcuts for popular folders and stick them on the desktop for easy access.

✔ You can open shortcuts just like any other icon: Double-click to open that document, run an application, or open a folder.

✔ Have no fear when you're deleting shortcuts; removing that icon does not remove the original file.

✔ Windows gives each shortcut a name, starting with `Shortcut to` and ending with the original filename. You can use the techniques described earlier in this chapter to rename the shortcut to something saner.

Deleting files

Unlike credit cards and driver's licenses, files don't simply expire. You must make an effort to rid yourself of old or temporary files you don't need. Otherwise, files collect like lint balls outside a dryer vent.

To kill a file, select it and choose File⇨Delete. This process doesn't truly remove the file; it merely moves the thing over to the Recycle Bin. From there, you can easily undelete the file later.

If you want a sensitive file utterly crushed, click it once with the mouse and press Shift+Delete. Windows displays a warning dialog box, explaining that the file will be utterly crushed (or something to that effect). Click Yes to zap it off to eternity.

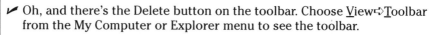

 ✔ You can also delete files by pressing the Delete key.

✔ Oh, and there's the Delete button on the toolbar. Choose <u>V</u>iew⟹<u>T</u>oolbar from the My Computer or Explorer menu to see the toolbar.

✔ You can delete folders like you do files; just keep in mind that you delete the folder's contents — which can be dozens of icons, files, folders, jewelry, small children, and food for the homeless. Better be careful with that one.

 ✔ Never delete any file in the Windows folder or any of the folders in the Windows folder.

✔ Never delete any file in the root folder of a hard drive.

✔ In fact, never delete any file unless you created it yourself.

 ✔ Don't delete programs! Instead, you can use a special tool in the Windows Control Panel for removing old applications you no longer need. See Chapter 20 for more information.

Undeleting files

Because you probably want your file back in a hurry, here it goes:

1. **Open the Recycle Bin on the desktop.**

 Double-click the Recycle Bin icon. It looks like a little trash can, as pictured in the margin.

If you have the Plus! package installed, you may have changed the Recycle Bin icon to resemble something else. I don't know what, so I can't tell you exactly here.

Figure 9-2 shows the Recycle Bin window open on my computer. I've chosen the <u>V</u>iew⟹<u>D</u>etails command because it allows me to sort the files in a specific order and to see other nerdy information.

2. **Select the file you want recovered.**

Click the file to resurrect it.

Choose <u>V</u>iew⟹Arrange <u>I</u>cons⟹by <u>D</u>elete Date from the menu to display files in the order they were deleted (by date). That way, it's cinchy to find any recently departed files you may want back.

3. **Choose <u>F</u>ile⟹<u>R</u>estore.**

The file is magically removed from the Recycle Bin and restored to the folder and disk from which it was so brutally seized.

4. **Close the Recycle Bin window.**

Click the window's X (close) button in the upper-right corner.

✔ There is no time limit on when you can restore files; they're available in the Recycle Bin for quite some time.

✔ Even so: Don't let the convenience of the Recycle Bin lead you down the path of sloppiness. Never delete a file unless you're certain that you want it gone, gone, gone.

Flush!

The Recycle Bin can eat up a lot of your PC's disk space, what with storing all those zombie files and whatnot. In fact, my Recycle Bin (as shown in Figure 9-2) contains 14.9MB worth of junk! That's three times larger than my first PC hard drive!

If you need more disk space, you can *empty* the Recycle Bin. Choose File⇨ Empty Recycle Bin from the Recycle Bin's menu. Emptying the Recycle Bin permanently zaps all those files; after doing so, you won't be able to recover anything. Be careful!

Working with Files Can Be a Drag

It's possible to cut, copy, and paste your files without having to choose any menu items. You simply grab the files you want to tweak and then move or copy them with the mouse.

The only drawback to this approach is that you must have *two* or more folders open on your desktop at one time to make it work. As an example, Figure 9-3 shows two windows representing two folders.

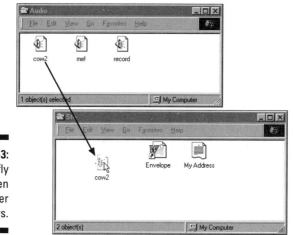

Figure 9-3:
Files fly
between
two folder
windows.

Moving files: To move a file from one folder to another, drag it with the mouse from one window to another, which is sort of shown in the figure (envision the dragging action in your head). The mouse is dragging the file COW2 from the Audio folder into the Sto folder.

Copying files: To copy a file from one folder's window to another, press and hold the Ctrl key, and drag the file. This process is known as a *control-drag.*

- ✔ Files are *moved* when you drag them from one folder to another on the same hard drive.

- ✔ Files are *copied* when you drag them from one disk drive to another.

- ✔ Windows automatically moves files when you drag them between two folders on the same disk drive.

- ✔ Windows automatically copies files when you drag them from one disk to another; you have no need to press the Ctrl key in this situation.

- ✔ To move a file from one disk to another, press and hold the Shift key before you click the file to drag it.

The cinchy way to copy and move files

Copying. Moving. Dragging. Control-dragging. It's a mess! The way I remember the difference between copying and moving files is not to memorize the techniques. Instead, I use the right mouse button to drag any file or group of files I want moved, copied, or shortcutted.

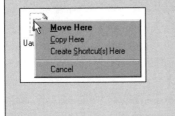

When you drag file icons around by using the right mouse button and then release the right mouse button, a pop-up menu appears. That menu has four items on it:

- ✔ Move Here

- ✔ Copy Here

- ✔ Create Shortcut(s) Here

- ✔ Cancel

Choose one of those options to move, copy, or paste a shortcut of the file (or files) you're dragging.

Finding Wayward Files (And Programs)

Files come and go. You may never find that one file you're looking for — especially if you're an unorganized person. Or maybe you saved your files in a panic during an earthquake. No finger wagging here; instead, follow these steps to locate any wayward file:

To summon the Find dialog box in the Explorer program window, choose Tools⇨Find⇨Files or Folders. In My Computer, choose File⇨Find.

If you have the Windows key on your keyboard, press Win+F to display the Find dialog box, no matter what else you're doing in Windows.

The Find dialog box is shown in Figure 9-4. By working the various controls there, you can hunt down just about any file or folder anywhere in your computer — even if it fell out of a hole in the back and lay tangled in your cable vines.

This section tells you how to work the Find dialog box to find whatever files you're looking for. In all cases, when the search is done, you see one of two results:

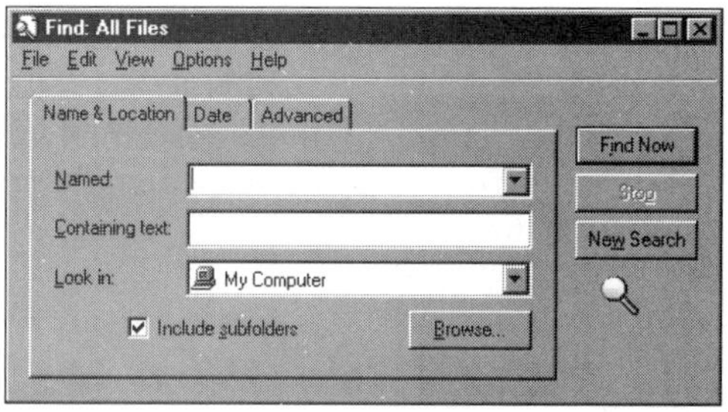

Figure 9-4:
The Find
dialog box.

✔ **No dice.** If no files are found, you see the message 0 file(s) found at the bottom of the Find dialog box. The file list will be empty. Weep bitterly and gnash your teeth.

✔ **Eureka!** When files are found, they're listed in the Find dialog box's file list. Figure 9-5 shows files that were found on the hard drive. Whew!

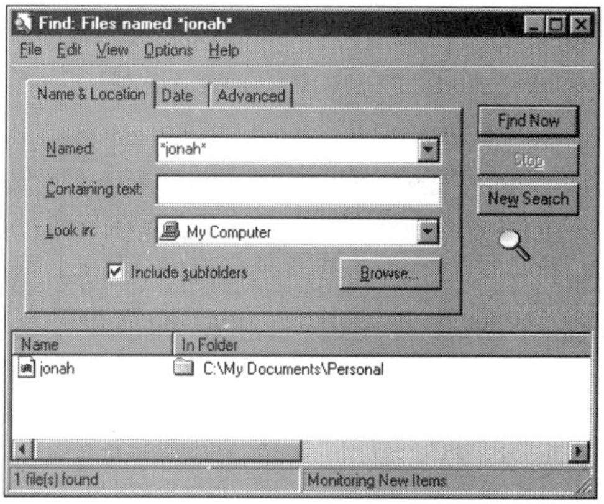

Figure 9-5:
There be
files here!

After the files have been found, you can do one of three things with them:

✔ Double-click the file in the file list to open it, to run that program or edit that file.

✔ Drag the file out on the desktop, where you can more easily access it, or drag it into the folder you thought it should be in.

✔ Simply look in the file list's In Folder column to see which folder holds that file. In Figure 9-5, the file is found in the Personal folder inside the My Documents folder. And where else would Jonah be?

✔ You can also get to the Find dialog box from the Start menu. Choose Find⇨Files or Folders.

✔ Refer to the section "What is a pathname?" in Chapter 8 for more information about reading the In Folder column in the Find dialog box.

 ✔ You can mix and match the searching methods described in this section. The more you can tell Windows about the file, the more easily it can find just the one you're looking for.

"Quick! Hurry! I want to find a lost file!"

Summon the Find dialog box. Click the Name & Location tab to bring that panel in front (as shown back in Figure 9-4).

1. **Type your filename in the <u>N</u>amed input box.**

2. **From the <u>L</u>ook In drop-down list, choose your main hard drive, C.**

   Or, if you know that the file is on another disk drive in your system, choose it instead. (Or just choose one after the other.)

3. **Make sure that the Include <u>S</u>ubfolders box has a check mark in it.**

   If not, click the mouse in that box.

4. **Click the F<u>i</u>nd Now button.**

   Any matching files found are displayed in the list at the bottom of the dialog box.

 ✔ If you don't know the exact name but know only part of a filename, use asterisks to fill in the parts you don't know. For example, I have various graphics files of my son Jonah on disk. To find them all, I had Windows search by using this pattern:

```
*JONAH*
```

 ✔ The results of that search are shown back in Figure 9-5. The asterisks match all characters before and after JONAH. If I knew that the file started with JONAH, I could type

```
JONAH*
```

 ✔ The asterisk matches any or all of the characters at the end of the filename. The same holds true for the beginning:

```
*JONAH
```

 ✔ The asterisk matches all characters that come before JONAH in a filename.

"Where the heck is my program?"

Finding programs works just like finding files. Follow the steps in the preceding section, and type your program name for the filename.

If you don't know the program name, click the mouse on the Advanced tab of the Find dialog box. That step brings the Advanced panel forward. In the Of Type drop-down list, select the Application item. Click the Find Now button. The Find dialog box lists all the programs on your computer. All of them. Your program is somewhere in the list. Use the scroll bars to locate it.

"I forgot the name of the file, but I know that it contains the word 'execrable'!"

Follow these steps:

1. **Bring up the Advanced panel in the Find dialog box.**

   Click the mouse on the Advanced tab to bring the Advanced panel forward if it isn't already.

2. **Make sure that All Files and Folders is selected in the Of <u>T</u>ype drop-down list.**

   If it isn't, choose that item: Click the mouse on the down arrow to the right of the drop-down list. Pluck out All Files and Folders from the list. (It should be the first item.)

   You can save a little time if you know which program created the document you want to find. For example, if you know that it's a Word document, you can choose Microsoft Word Document from the drop-down list.

3. **Bring up the Name & Location panel.**

   This step moves you back to the main panel, where you should see the Containing Text input box.

4. **Type the text you want to search for.**

   Enter the smallest tidbit of text that you suppose would exactly match text in that one file you're looking for, such as

   ```
   execrable
   ```

   Don't add a period at the end.

5. **Click the F<u>i</u>nd Now button.**

   Hopefully, the file list shows you what you want. If not, you can try again with another word.

✔ My wife recently used this method to find our brother-in-law's résumé on our computer. She typed his last name. Of the many documents that were found, one named Document turned out to be the right one. Moral: Name your résumé documents Résumé, not Document.

"I forgot the file's name, but I know that it's a spreadsheet!"

Although searching by file type displays a ton of files, it's a better way to find a file than scouting through *every* file on your hard drive. Here you go:

1. Summon the Advanced panel in the Find dialog box.

Click the Advanced tab. This step brings forward the Advanced panel.

2. Choose the file type from the Of Type drop-down list.

For example, click Microsoft Excel Worksheet in the list. If the file is of another type, choose that proper type from the list.

3. Click the Find Now button.

I guarantee that a bunch of files will be displayed. Your job is to search through the list to find the exact one you want. Good luck!

If you need to be more precise, you can better search for the file if you know the exact date on which it was created or last saved to disk. I cover this trick in the following section.

"All I know is that I created it last Tuesday!"

To find a file created on a specific date, try these steps:

1. Bring up the Date panel in the Find dialog box.

Click the mouse on the Date tab to bring that panel forward in the Find dialog box.

2. Click the button next to Find All Files.

This action allows you to choose one of the three options in the drop-down list: Modified, Created or Last Accessed. Because the file you want was created last Tuesday (see the title of this section), choose Created.

3a. If you know that the file was created in the past month, choose the During the Previous X Month(s) button.

Use the up or down buttons to change the number of months; 1 for one month, 6 for six months, and so on. This process is perhaps the least accurate and most time-consuming way to find a file by its date; lots of files will be listed.

3b. If you know that the file was created just a few days ago, click the During the Previous X Day(s) button.

Use the up or down buttons to enter the number of days back to search. For example, if today is Thursday and you think that you created the file sometime this week, enter **4** in the box. This method is more exact than searching by month but not as precise as knowing the exact date.

3c. If you kind of know the date when the file was created, click the Between X and X button.

Enter the proper dates in the boxes, earliest date first. Or, if you know that the file was created on November 1, 1998, type **11/1/98** in both boxes. Better still, type **10/31/98** in the first box and **11/2/98** in the second.

4. Click the Find Now button.

Windows lists a batch of files for you to scour. Why so many? Because it listed all the files created on the dates you specified. That could potentially be a hoard.

✔ Combining this searching technique with the others typically narrows the file list to the ones you want.

✔ Refer to Chapter 8 for excellent methods for storing files in folders so that you never lose anything again.

Chapter 10
Ode to the Network Slave

● ●

In This Chapter

▶ Exploring how networks share resources

▶ Logging in to your network

▶ Using the Network Neighborhood

▶ Accessing a network disk drive or folder

▶ Making a network drive part of My Computer

▶ Sharing your disk drives on the network

▶ Dealing with network crashes

● ●

*B*ack when the earth was new, there were these humongous computers called *mainframes*. They lived in air-conditioned glass rooms and drew more power than Las Vegas on a moonless night. Spindly, tanless men in lab coats ran the computers. They scoffed at and belittled the sorry users of their computers, who were shackled to the mainframe by means of a cable and who worked on a *dumb terminal* — a computer without a brain. Little did they know that the Personal Computer Revolution was coming. Soon, users would all have their own personal computers. The era of computer independence would be born.

The mainframe computer still exists, but filling the space of its vacuum tubes are computer networks, in which you take a formerly independent computer and wire it together with other personal computers. Two or more computers shackled to each other — with maybe a printer tossed in between them — is a *network*. You can add more computers, printers — even mainframes and orbiting satellites. It boggles the mind.

The concept of a network and how it works is way beyond the realm of *PCs For Dummies*. You have to look elsewhere for the techy, plug-this-in stuff. If you're a sole computer user sitting at home in your den, you can read this chapter for extra bonus points, redeemable for valuable cash prizes. Otherwise, everyone at the office or anyone who has heard about *the network* should glance at a few of the sections in this chapter.

- ✔ A *node* is a computer on the network. If your computer is on a network, it's a node.

- ✔ This chapter covers only the measly peer-to-peer networking that comes with Windows. Windows NT? Novell networking? Banyan vines? Go somewhere else.

- ✔ The dawn of the computer era closely reflects Greek mythology. Before computers existed, chaos — in the form of a slide rule — reigned. Then came the Titans, the mainframes. Then a combined form of Apple and IBM became Zeus, establishing the reign of the Olympians, the personal computers.

Can't We All Just Get Along?

Computers foster a lust for sharing information. Not just a lust — a necessity. The screen satisfies this necessity by showing you the results of your labors. The printer is another extension, providing you with valuable hard copy. The hard copy — okay, *paper* — can be shared with a number of users, although the information is still locked up electronically inside the PC.

One day, someone noticed how silly it was to make hard copy and then have another computer user retype all that information. After all, the information was in the computer. Why couldn't he just "beam" it back and forth between computers? That's what most of them did, in two ways: by sharing disks between two computers and by connecting the computers by using special cables.

- ✔ Sharing disks between PCs isn't a hassle. Most information is shared and distributed from one computer to another via the handy floppy disk. (ZIP disks are also filling this function, albeit slowly.)

- ✔ Sharing disks between different types of computers — Macintoshes and PCs, for example — is possible but not easy. Those two systems use different disk formats. A PC cannot read a Macintosh disk, nor can it understand what's on that disk.

- ✔ Any two computers equipped with serial ports can be connected together with a *null-modem cable* so that they can exchange information. The different systems can also talk over phone lines by using a modem. The null-modem cable is simply a more direct route, usually intended for two computers sitting in the same room.

- ✔ See Chapter 17 for additional information about modems. Null modems are pondered in the nearby sidebar "Extra-boring information about the infamous null-modem cable."

Extra-boring information about the infamous null-modem cable

Nothing causes more headaches than dealing with the null-modem cable or its evil twin, the null-modem adapter. So stop sending me all those questions and listen up.

A *null-modem cable* is a special sort of serial cable. It's also called a *twisted pair*. It's designed so that a cable between two computers' serial ports has the talk-listen wires switched: talk-to-listen, listen-to-talk. Otherwise, the computers would have their talk-to-talk lines and listen-to-listen lines connected, and it would be too much like the United Nations to get anything accomplished. The null-modem adapter is simply a small box that swaps the wires for a standard serial cable.

After both computers are hooked together comes the tricky part. Both systems must run special communications software, and they require tedious configuring and liters of sweat to get everything right. Even then, you can exchange only basic text files (ASCII) between the two separate systems. This process is really something more for bored nerds to tinker with than for real humans such as you and me to worry about.

If you really need to send files between two computers, or between a desktop PC and a laptop model, you can buy software to do it. Some software even comes with special cables to make the job easier.

The 29¢ Overview of Everything a Network Is All About

Caution: Do not attempt to drive or operate any heavy machinery while reading the following information.

Computers have networks; so does your television. Computers have programs; so does your television. Computers can use that black cable — with the pokey wire in the middle — just like cable television. In a way, a computer network is very similar to something you would pick up on your television but far, far more productive.

Up front, I'm happy to tell you that networks, networking, and connectivity (a big, ugly IBM word meaning "plug this into the cat and watch it jump!") is a job best left up to Those In Charge. No one enjoys working with networks. Sane people pay undernourished compuphiles millions of dollars a year to create and maintain networks, so your knowledge about them needs to be only minimal. Here's the good stuff:

✔ Networks are about three things: exchanging files, sharing resources, and running common programs.

- *Exchanging files* means that you can send and receive files from other people on the network without having to leave your computer. Either the files come waddling down the network cable, or you pick them up from a central drop-off point. The idea is that you can get information from another computer without someone having to hand you a floppy disk.

- *Sharing resources* refers to common hardware that several computers can use on the network. For example, the printer down the hall may be *on* the network. You can print on it, and so can Bob in accounting or Phyllis or that new person they hired in marketing that everyone assumes is having an affair with the boss. Certain hard drives may be *on* the network. You can copy your files to there or from there.

- *Running common programs* refers to applications kept on other computers. With some types of networks, you can access another computer and run a program on that computer — all through a little wire hanging out the back of your PC. That works, but it slows down the other computer immensely. Instead, a big computer is often dedicated as the file server. Its task is to act as a huge disk drive to hold programs for everyone else to use.

✔ Networks are often called *LANs*. LAN is an acronym for Local Area Network.

"What Is Client/Server Computing?"

I haven't the foggiest idea.

Logging In to the Network

Before you use a network, you must log in. You do that when you first start Windows. You're presented with a dialog box that tells you to log in to the network.

Actually, the box never says "login" or "log in." But that's what it would have said had Microsoft not wanted Windows to be so darn friendly. It says User name instead. Two words. Much friendlier.

You log in by typing in your username, which is usually some appalling contraction of your first and last names, and then by pressing the Tab key and typing your secret password, which is probably written on a sticky note pasted to your monitor. Figure 10-1 shows the Windows login dialog box, which you may see every time you start Windows.

- ✓ After you log in, you can use the network.

- ✓ Even so, if you don't want to log in, press the Esc key when you see the login dialog box, and you can still use the network.

- ✓ If you press Esc to skip merrily over the Enter Network Password dialog box, you cannot access other network resources. It's like being bad in school: You can't play with the other kids until you play nice with your own computer.

- ✓ If you have a password, don't write it down! Commit it to memory, lest your files slip into enemy hands.

- ✓ If you have access to the Internet, you'll probably use a different username and password, as well as a whole different method to access Internet e-mail and the World Wide Web (see Part VI of this book).

- ✓ After you've logged in, you can access the network printer and various drives on the network. Using the drives and printers is covered in the following few sections of this chapter.

Figure 10-1:
That
annoying
login
dialog box.

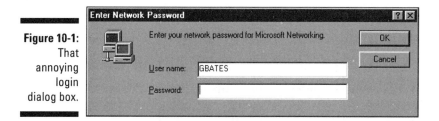

Doing Net Things

A *networked PC* means that you can do networky things. Primarily, you can use other printers and disk drives on the network. If you find files on those disk drives, you might be able to steal them or run programs. Any folder named Financial Data on any network computer is fair game. It's a Silicon Valley law.

A loverly stroll through the Network Neighborhood

 If you have a networked Windows computer, you can find on the desktop an icon named Network Neighborhood. That's your key to all the computers and printers on the network. The icon is depicted in the margin.

You can fish for things in the Network Neighborhood in two ways. The first way is stupid, so I don't talk about it here. The second, and obvious, way is to open the Network Neighborhood icon by double-clicking it. This action displays a window detailing all the computers on your network, similar to Figure 10-2.

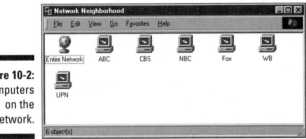

Figure 10-2:
Computers
on the
network.

Not every computer on the network shares everything. For example, the computer named CBS in Figure 10-2 doesn't share anything — no disk drives or printers. The computer named Fox, however, shares a few things.

You can see what a computer shares by opening that computer's icon; double-click it in the Network Neighborhood folder. Figure 10-3 shows how Windows displays the things the Fox computer shares.

- ✔ Folders in a computer's window are up for grabs.

- ✔ In Figure 10-3, the folder named Drive C represents all folders on hard drive C.

- ✔ You can access files in those folders by opening them — just as you would on your computer.

- ✔ Printers in a computer's folder, as shown in Figure 10-3, indicate that your computer can access and use that network printer for printing. To make it so, double-click the printer's icon to set things up. (It's a long, step-by-step process you probably want someone else to do.)

- ✔ The Network Neighborhood is safe enough for you to go outside at night.

✔ The off-chance exists that the Network Neighborhood icon may appear even if your PC isn't connected to a network. It happens if your computer dealer used a network to install and configure your PC or, in some cases, when you set up your PC for the Internet.

✔ You can change the view in the Network Neighborhood window just as you can in any Explorer or My Computer window: Choose a new view from the View menu. Figure 10-2 shows what you see after choosing the View➪Large Icons command.

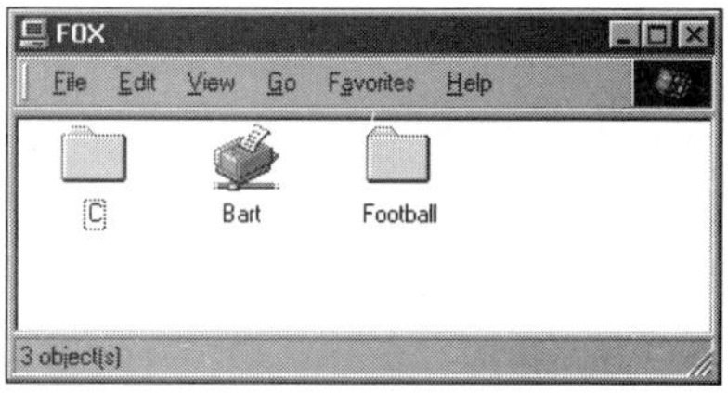

Figure 10-3:
Items available for sharing on a network computer.

Using a network disk drive or folder

The basic job of the network is to keep you from walking somewhere else in your office with a floppy disk. Exchanging disks in that manner is referred to as *sneaker net* by computer wieners. Sneaker net. Get it? The network consists of walking disks back and forth. Ah, such jocularity.

To move a file to another computer on the network, you must access a network drive, which is a hard drive (or a floppy drive) on any computer other than your own. You can fish out the file on that drive by using the Network Neighborhood. A better way is to always have that drive present on your computer. It lives in the My Computer window as a so-called network drive.

Figure 10-4 shows the My Computer window. In it, you see two network disk drives, labeled M and S. They're disk drives on other computers on the network; M represents drive C on the computer named Monkey King, and S represents drive C on the computer named Koby. These hard drives can be used like any other hard drives, although they live elsewhere in the Network Neighborhood.

To add a network drive to your My Computer window, follow these steps:

1. **Search for the network drive you want to add.**

   Open the Network Neighborhood icon and search various computers on your network, looking for an available drive. (Refer to the section "A loverly stroll through the Network Neighborhood," earlier in this chapter, for more information about probing the Network Neighborhood.)

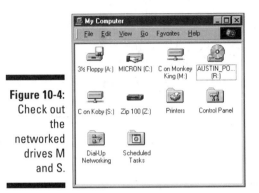

Figure 10-4:
Check out
the
networked
drives M
and S.

For example, you may open the ABC computer and find that its hard drive C is up and available for sharing.

You can also open up any network drive to look for a specific folder you may want to have handy.

2. **Right-click the network drive (or folder) you want to add to the My Computer window.**

   Point the mouse at the folder you want to add and click the right mouse button. A pop-up shortcut menu appears.

3. **Choose <u>M</u>ap Network Drive.**

   The Map Network Drive dialog box appears, as shown in Figure 10-5. Don't panic. I've never seen the word *map* used that way either.

Figure 10-5:
The Map
Network
Drive
dialog box.

4. **Choose a drive letter for the networked drive.**

   You can give the network drive any available drive letter on your computer (but not the letters *A*, *B*, or *C*, which the PC is selfish about). If you have a hard drive C and a CD-ROM drive D, you can assign the networked drive any letter from E through Z — whatever's available.

   I try to give network drives a letter to remember them by. So Neody in my office is shared as drive N on other computers.

Choose the drive letter from the drop-down list, or just press that letter key on your keyboard.

The drive letter you assign is personal to your computer. It does not affect any other computer on the network.

5. Do you always want to use the network drive?

If you want this network connection made every time you start your computer, click in the box next to `Reconnect at logon`. This step puts a check mark in the box, meaning that Windows always gives you that network drive in the My Computer window when your PC starts. Nifty, eh?

6. Click OK.

Click. The networked drive is now as easy to use as any disk drive on your PC. Ah, the joys of networking.

✔ Network drives appear as disk drive icons, but with a little pipe beneath them (refer to Figure 10-4).

✔ You can even network with older Windows computers, although it works differently on those systems.

✔ Novell networks? I haven't a clue. That's why they pay the Novell guys so much money.

Disconnecting a network drive

If you no longer want to connect to a drive on the network, you need to disconnect. This process works just like hanging up the phone; the connection isn't there anymore, although the other disk drive is still fine and up for grabs on the network. (It doesn't delete the other drive, just like hanging up the phone on your friends doesn't kill them.)

Disconnect any folder by selecting that folder; click its icon once with the mouse. Choose File➪Disconnect. The folder is history.

"I Wanna Share My Drives and Folders on the Network!"

Surrendering your vital computer parts to the network is a snap. Of course, you may not want to do that, depending on what you keep on your computer. Some security is involved, but not much.

To make your disk drives or any folder up for grabs on the network, follow these steps:

1. **Select the disk drive or folder you want to share.**

   You do this step in My Computer or Explorer. Click once on the disk drive or folder. This action highlights the icon, displaying it in a horrid shade of blue.

2. **Choose File⇨Sharing.**

   The disk drive or folder's Properties dialog box appears, similar to what you see in Figure 10-6. Make sure that the Sharing panel is forward; click that tab if it is not.

3. **Click the Shared As button.**

   This step puts a dot in that item's radio button, activating the rest of the dialog box. Next come fill-in-the-blanks.

4. **Type a name for your shared drive.**

   The input box next to Share Name typically contains the disk drive letter or folder name. You can leave it blank or be creative with something a wee bit more descriptive.

   Don't press the Enter key yet!

5. **Ah, forget typing a comment in the Comment box.**

6. Choose an access level.

Your hard drive has three levels of access, each of them listed under Access Type:

- **Read Only** means that others can only look at the stuff on your hard drive. They can't erase anything, change anything, or add new files.

- **Full** means that others can do anything on your hard drive that you can — including erase every file and rename your vital system documents.

- **Depends on Password** allows other people either Read-Only or Full Access depending on which password they type. You set the passwords in the two input boxes at the bottom of the dialog box.

My advice: Choose Read-Only access. If you trust your coworkers, choose Full. I don't mess with passwords because I forget them anyway. (All my computers share the same password: *none*.)

7. Click OK.

Your disk drive or folder is now shared. It works the same on your system but is available to others via the Network Neighborhood on their computers.

✔ When you share something, its icon grows a little serving hand.

✔ A *server* is a serving dish, typically silver with a domed lid. A *servant* is a person who serves you something. A waiter or waitress is a person who serves you food in a restaurant. "Servers" don't serve you food, and servants don't get tipped.

✔ Sharing your printer works similarly to sharing a disk drive or folder. The printers attached to your PC are shown in the Printers folder, which lurks in the My Computer main window. Aside from sharing the printer, you also have to make sure that other computers on the network are properly configured to use that printer before they can print anything. See? Major pain. Let someone else do it.

Down Goes the Network, Glub, Glub, Glub

Networks crash more than teenagers. It doesn't mean that using a network is unstable business. Instead, you run into problems because too many things that barely work don't work well together. Eventually, one puff of air brings the whole house of cards tumbling down.

- ✔ When you suspect network trouble, yelp for help. Never try to fix the problem on your own (which is a safe assumption).

- ✔ When a network computer goes down, you can still use your PC; you just can't access any files or printers that were on the network.

- ✔ Never unplug the network connections on the back of your PC when the network is on.

- ✔ *Crash* is the technical term for when a computer stops working. Nothing actually crunches or smashes. In fact, a typical crash is more like an ice age: Everything suddenly stops, frozen in its tracks, and when the experts thaw it all out, they find a mammoth chewing on buttercups.

- ✔ General troubleshooting and "Oh, dear Lord, help me!" advice is offered in Part VII of this book.

Part IV
The Non-Nerd's Guide to Computer Hardware

The 5th Wave   By Rich Tennant

"WHOA, HOLD THE PHONE! IT SAYS, 'THE ELECTRICITY COMING OUT OF A SURGE PROTECTOR IS GENERALLY CLEANER AND SAFER THAN THAT GOING INTO ONE, UNLESS—<u>UN-LESSS</u>— YOU ARE STANDING IN A BUCKET OF WATER.'"

In this part . . .

Bud was awful proud when he learned that his computer geek son, Melvin, was into hardware. But after touring the local TrueValue store, Bud learned the truth: Melvin's hardware was *computer* hardware. It had no cordless drills, jigsaws, or routers. Nope, Melvin's was a world of CPUs, EPROMs, cables, and techy stuff.

You just can't use a computer without encountering hardware. And you need to know the terminology so that when the manual says, "Plug this into your mouse port," you don't incite the ire of PETA. This part of the book describes the various hardware goodies associated with a PC, the terms you encounter, and how everything fits into the Big Picture.

Chapter 11

Just Your Basic Computer Guts

● ●

In This Chapter

▶ A quick tour of the motherboard

▶ Getting to know the microprocessor

▶ Finding out which microprocessor your PC has

▶ Understanding the BIOS

▶ All about printer ports, serial ports, and USB ports

▶ Setting the date and time

▶ Understanding expansion slots

▶ The power supply goes "POOF!"

● ●

*B*eneath its smooth, cream-colored case, your computer is a mess. Yes, it's a veritable sushi bar of interesting pieces, flecks, and chunks of technology. Tossed into this electronics salad are various components whose names you may encounter from time to time. There's the *motherboard, microprocessor, BIOS, ports, power supplies,* and *expansion slots.* This isn't anything you'd see — or even touch — but it's stuff you may want to understand. After all, you paid for it.

A major item inside your PC that's not covered in this chapter is memory. See Chapter 12 for a discussion of that.

The Mother of All Boards

The motherboard is the main piece of circuitry inside your PC. Like the downtown of a big city, it's where everything happens.

A more technical description, if you care

The motherboard is a piece of fiberglass, usually dark green because computer scientists are a macho bunch and pink or powder blue is definitely out. Chips and whatnot are soldered to the motherboard and then connected by tiny copper wires, or *traces*, which look like little roads all over the motherboard. This is how the various chips, resistors, and capacitors chat with each other.

Electricity is supplied to everything via a thin, metal sheet sandwiched in the middle of the motherboard itself. Somehow, through the miracle of electronics, everything works and the result is a working computer. Of course, to make it practical, you need a power supply, monitor, keyboard, disk drives, and yaddi yaddi yaddi.

The motherboard is important because the most important things inside your PC cling to it. In fact, for the most part, the console is simply a housing for the motherboard. (Disk drives used to be separate on some early systems.) You can find the following electronic goodies on the motherboard; there's no need to memorize this list:

- ✔ The microprocessor — the computer's main chip
- ✔ The computer's memory
- ✔ Expansion slots and the special expansion cards that plug into them
- ✔ Special chips called ROM chips
- ✔ The BIOS
- ✔ Other support circuitry
- ✔ Sharp, pointy things

Although the motherboard contains a lot of items, it's essentially one unit and is referred to as such. Just like the mall has many stores but everyone calls it *the mall*.

- ✔ IBM calls the motherboard in its computers the *planar* board. Ugh.
- ✔ You can add or remove only two things on the motherboard: extra memory and expansion cards (which plug into the expansion slots). This chore, referred to as *upgrading*, is best left to the gurus.
- ✔ Oh, some motherboards allow you to remove and add a microprocessor. I recommend against it, however. I tell why later.

The Microprocessor

At the core of every computer is the *microprocessor.* That's the computer's main chip. No, it's not the computer's *brain.* (Software is the brain.) Instead, the microprocessor acts like a tiny, fast calculator. It just adds and subtracts (and does the tango and the jitterbug).

The microprocessor itself deals with other elements in the computer. Primarily, these elements provide either *input* or *output,* which compu-jockeys call *I/O.*

Input is information flowing into the microprocessor.

Output is information the microprocessor generates and spits out.

Pretty much the whole computer obsesses over this input and output stuff.

- ✔ The main chip inside the computer is the *microprocessor,* which is essentially a tiny calculator with a BIG price tag.

- ✔ The microprocessor is also called the CPU, which stands for Central Processing Unit. Military types like the term.

- ✔ When your jaw is tired, you can refer to the microprocessor as the *processor.*

- ✔ Outwardly the microprocessor resembles a large, flat, after-dinner mint — with 200 legs.

- ✔ You measure a computer's power by its microprocessor, so it would be nice if microprocessors were given powerful names, like Hercules or Samson or Sir Percival. Unfortunately, they're named after powerful numbers, like 80386, 486, and Pentium.

- ✔ In addition to the Pentium name are variations on a theme. (I guess Sextium was too risqué for them.) You can find the Pentium II and Pentium Pro as well as the Pentium MMX. Other chip names you might hear about are Celeron, AMD, and Cyrix.

- ✔ Eight more processor names, and we'll have a pantheon!

- ✔ In addition to the numbers assigned to them, microprocessors are also gauged by how fast they can think. This value is given in *megahertz,* abbreviated MHz. The bigger the MHz value, the faster the microprocessor, which is about all you need to know.

- ✔ Input for the microprocessor comes from several places in the computer: the computer's memory, disk drives, keyboard, mouse, modem, and on and on.

- ✔ The microprocessor sends its output to the computer's memory, disk drives, screen, printer, modem, and on and on.

✔ I have to say "on and on" in this book because the publisher doesn't like the term "etc." (which is Latin for "on and on").

✔ Software coordinates all this Input/Output chaos for you. It's like a harried assistant at a day-care center when the kids are all high on Pixie Stix.

"Okay, wise guy, so which microprocessor lives in my PC?"

Who knows which microprocessor lurks in the heart of your PC? Better get a big wrench. Better still, right-click the mouse on the My Computer icon in the upper-left corner of the desktop. This action brings up a shortcut menu for your computer. Choose the last item, Properties. The System Properties dialog box is displayed, looking something like Figure 11-1.

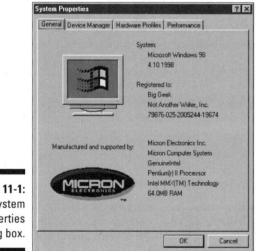

Figure 11-1:
The System
Properties
dialog box.

Details! Details! The first panel in the System Properties dialog box (General) contains information about Windows, you, and your computer. It says what type of microprocessor lives in your PC and the total amount of memory (RAM) your system has.

✔ In Figure 11-1, the computer has a Pentium II microprocessor and 64MB of memory.

✔ The (r) after the Pentium in the dialog box is supposed to be ®, the registered trademark thingy. It doesn't mean that you pronounce the microprocessor's name as "pentiumer."

✔ If you have a 486 system, your microprocessor's number appears where you see Pentium Pro(r) in Figure 11-1. For a 486 microprocessor, it would probably just say 80486. This number is the microprocessor you have in your PC, not some secret code.

✔ Figure 11-1 also boasts that the computer was manufactured by Micron Electronics, Inc. I am not an employee of Micron; I bought my computer from them. (It's an Idaho thing.) Your computer manufacturer may have its name displayed there as well. Ain't no way to get rid of it, either.

✔ Refer to Chapter 14 for more information on right-clicking the mouse. You do that a lot in Windows.

Family matters (or "We're all named after famous license plates")

Microprocessors run around in families. The 386 family of microprocessors really started it all. Then came the 486, which was followed by the Pentium. Yeah, it should have been the 586, but they couldn't copyright that number so they made up the word *Pentium* instead.

What should be the 686 is called the *Pentium Pro*. And then there are the Pentium MMX and Pentium II systems, which provide more instructions for computer games and multimedia. The 786? *Pentium Pro Pro* maybe?

By the way, the MMX doesn't stand for anything. Internally, Intel refers to it as "MMX Technology," which is trademarked. It can't trademark just MMX though, especially if it claims that it stands for something like Multimedia Extensions or Multimedia Instruction set or Math Matrix Extensions or anything else.

Table 11-1 lists the popular numbers assigned to microprocessors, along with other technical drivel associated with them. For your amusement, I even include the ancient microprocessors of the proto-PCs in the list.

What about bugs in the Pentium?

About a year after the first Pentium microprocessor came out, someone on the Internet discovered a problem the Pentium had with doing certain division problems. When two particular numbers were divided, the Pentium produced a result that wasn't quite accurate. Oh, for Mrs. Jones's tenth grade geometry class, it would have been okay. But for sending people to Mars, it would have been a tad too big of a boo-boo.

Intel quickly (well, maybe not that quickly) admitted to the mistake and offered replacement Pentiums. Then it fixed the problem, and all the

Pentiums that now roll out of the factory do much better in math. And Intel's stock doubled and split, and there was happiness throughout the land. Now there's nothing more to worry about.

Table 11-1   Microprocessor Number Quiz (Extra Credit Only)

Microprocessor	*Relative Power (Bits)*	*Type of PC and Observations*
8088	8/16	Early PCs, the PC XT, and some laptops. This type was a veritable slug.
8086	16/16	The 8086 was faster than the 8088, but more expensive.
80286	16/16	AT types of PCs and compatibles and some laptops. This microprocessor first appeared in the IBM PC AT.
80386	32/32	The father of the X86 family of computers.
80386SX (386SX)	16/32	Laptops and inexpensive systems.
80486	32/32	Also called the i486 or the 486DX.
80486SX	32/32	A cheaper version of the full-blown 80486.
80486DX2	32/32	A slightly cheaper and faster alternative to the normal 486DX.
80486DX4	32/32	An even faster 486DX chip.
586/Pentium	32/64	It's easier to trademark a trendy name than a number.
Pentium Pro	32/64	Super-dooper Pentium.
Pentium MMX	32/64	A Pentium with extra power to give computer games and graphics more umph.
Pentium II	32/64	More dooper and sooper than a Pentium Pro. Also comes in MMX varieties.
Celeron	32/64	A cheapy version of the Pentium for "home" computers. It lacks some of the Pentium II's beef.

The "and later" syndrome

You may be thrown the following common curve ball: "This software works only with 80386 *and later* microprocessors." It's the "and later" part that gets you. How do you know what is later than an 80386, especially if you don't have a copy of the venerated *Byte* magazine PC Microprocessor Time Line in front of you? The following should help:

- ✔ Earliest: 8088, 8086, V20, and V30

- ✔ Middle ages: 80286

- ✔ Latest: 80386, 386SX, and so on

- ✔ Extremely tardy: 80486, 486SX

- ✔ Absentee: Pentium

- ✔ Deceased: Pentium Pro

The latest microprocessors are at the bottom of the list. They can run any and all software written for microprocessors listed above them.

- ✔ Some descriptions may say "greater" rather than "later." Later refers to the point in history when the microprocessor was introduced. Greater is like James the Greater in the Bible. He was bigger and more powerful than James the Lesser, who was rumored to be an accountant.

- ✔ If the software requires MMX or a Pentium II, you need to have that type of microprocessor. I cover this subject in the next section.

- ✔ Any software that claims to work on a "Pentium" microprocessor works on any PC with any flavor Pentium, including the cheapo Celeron processor.

- ✔ All microprocessors are said to be *backward compatible*. That means that software written for an earlier microprocessor works on a later model.

What's the MMX deal?

A few years back, the boy and girls at Intel dreamt up the Pentium MMX microprocessor. It was just like a regular Pentium, but the new processor contains extra instructions that optimize computer video, sound, and other aspects of games and multimedia software. That may not seem like much, but with those types of applications, any type of improvement in speed is a great help.

The downside to the MMX miracle is that you must run software specifically written for the Pentium MMX before any of the nifty stuff happens. So, although a Pentium MMX is better than a plain old Pentium, you get the most from it only when you run software that's designed to exploit the full potential of the MMX part of the Pentium processor.

- ✔ All Pentium II microprocessors also sport the MMX feature.

- ✔ I actually experienced MMX envy just last month when I installed a game on my old Pentium Pro system. The game chastised me for not having MMX and said that it would deliberately run slower and cause my little man to die more often because of my error, so I quickly uninstalled the game and reinstalled it on my Pentium II system. Whew!

Upgrading your microprocessor

Just about every PC sold today has a special doojobbie on the motherboard that allows you to replace your PC's microprocessor. You just lift out the old, pokey one and replace it with a faster, newer one. Simple. Elegant. And expensive!

In my travels, I know of few people who actually upgrade their microprocessors. Only if you made the wrong microprocessor decision when you first bought your PC is it necessary. Normally, after two or three years (when a newer, faster microprocessor becomes available), it just makes more sense to go out and buy a whole new computer. After all, other things would need updating inside the PC as well: the hard drive, ports, and other technology.

Why not replace everything at once?

- ✔ If you really want to replace your microprocessor, have someone else do it for you. Often the places that sell the upgrades include installation with the microprocessor price.

- ✔ Remember that PC manufacturers and dealers buy their microprocessors in bulk. Their new computers are sometimes cheaper than an upgrade.

The BIOS

In addition to a microprocessor and memory, your computer needs some instructions to tell it what to do. Those instructions are written on a special ROM chip called the *BIOS,* which stands for something unimportant but is pronounced "bye-oss."

The job of the BIOS is communication. It allows the microprocessor to control — or talk with — other parts of your computer, such as the screen, the printer, the keyboard, and so on. Those instructions were written by the people who built your computer and are permanently etched on the BIOS chip (or chips) soldered onto the motherboard.

- ✔ Refer to the next chapter for information on what a ROM chip is.

- ✔ The BIOS is what starts your computer. In fact, you probably see the BIOS copyright message every time your computer warms up.

- ✔ The operating system (Windows) is the true program that controls your PC. It tells the microprocessor what to do, controls the disk drives, manages your files, organizes information, and communicates with the BIOS to get things done.

- ✔ In addition to the main BIOS, your computer may have other BIOSs. For example, the video BIOS controls your system's graphics display, the hard drive BIOS controls the hard disk, and so on. Your network adapter may have its own BIOS. Normally, when you see the term BIOS by itself, it refers to the PC's main BIOS.

- ✔ Okay, BIOS stands for Basic Input/Output System. Are you happy now?

What Are Ports?

The term *port* (also called a *jack* in some circles) refers to a hole in the back of the computer, or a festive dessert wine. You can plug in any one of a variety of external devices with which the computer can communicate through a port.

Most new PCs sold today have four ports worthy of looking into:

- ✔ The printer port (usually a parallel port)
- ✔ The serial port
- ✔ The joystick port
- ✔ The USB port

Each of these ports has a variety of different devices that can plug into them. This section describes them in detail and all the miraculous things that can be done with them.

- ✔ The first IBM PC didn't come with any ports. You had to add a printer port or serial port by using a special expansion card.

✔ Actually, the printer port on the first IBM PC came with the video card. (I had to say that here, not that it will win you the bonus round in *Jeopardy!* or anything.)

✔ Traditionally, since about 1984 or so, most PCs have come with two serial ports and one printer port.

✔ Since about 1993 or so, most PCs have also come with a joystick port.

✔ The USB (Universal Serial Bus) port is a new addition to most PCs sold in the late 1990s. Its power and versatility will eventually let it replace most of the other ports on a PC. Just you wait and see.

✔ Most PCs also have a mouse port and keyboard port. However, the mouse and keyboard are usually the only things plugged into those holes, so their worthiness and stature next to the more versatile ports mentioned here is questionable.

✔ Another popular type of port is the SCSI port, though it tends to be a technical thing. See the section "SCSI ports (say 'scuzzy')," later in this chapter.

Printer ports

Mysteriously enough, the printer port is where you plug in your printer. The printer cable has one connector that plugs into the printer and a second that plugs into the computer. Both connectors are different, so it's impossible to plug a printer cable in backward.

✔ For more information on printers, refer to Chapter 16.

✔ Printer ports are also called *parallel ports* or, to old-time nerds, they're known as Centronics ports. People who refer to ports in this manner should be slapped.

✔ Other devices can be connected to a printer port, although typically the only one you have is the printer. Examples of other devices that connect to a printer port are ZIP drives, voice synthesizers, network connections, external hard drives, extra keyboards, tape backup units, and choo-choo train sets.

Surreal ports

The serial port is far more versatile than the printer port; it supports a variety of interesting items, which is why it's generically called a serial port rather than a this-or-that port.

You can often plug the following items into a serial port: a modem, serial printer, mouse, or just about anything that requires two-way communications. Most computers come with two serial ports.

✔ A serial port can also be called a modem port.

✔ Serial ports are also called RS-232 ports. No, that's not a Radio Shack part number. Instead, it refers to Recommended Standard 232, which I assume is the 232nd standard The Committee came up with that year. Busy guys.

✔ You can plug a computer mouse into a serial port. In that case, the mouse is called a serial mouse. The mouse can also be plugged into its own port, called — shockingly enough — a mouse port. (Refer to your local pet store for more information on mice, or turn to Chapter 14.)

✔ Other uses for serial ports are to plug in scanners and digital cameras.

SCSI ports (say "scuzzy")

A special Superman-type of serial port is the SCSI port, with the SCSI being pronounced *scuzzy*. I'm not making that up. What does it stand for? Who cares! It's just a special type of fast serial port. The beauty of a SCSI port is that you can plug a gaggle of things into it. Here are just a few of the items to stick onto a SCSI port:

✔ Hard drives, from one to six of them

✔ A scanner

✔ A tape backup drive

✔ A CD-ROM drive

✔ A removable hard drive or magneto-optical drive

Oh, I could name more, but that's the basic bones.

Definitely skip over this stuff

Serial ports are complex in that you must configure them. Printer ports are set up to work in a specific manner and require no configuration. But with a serial port, you must configure both the port on your computer as well as the device with which you're communicating.

You need to configure four items on a serial port: the speed at which the port operates; the data word format, or the size of the bytes

you're sending; the number of stop bits; and the parity. This is a real hassle only when you need to connect a serial printer — and they don't even make those anymore, so I don't discuss it here.

Your communications software messes with this technical serial port information. That subject is put way off until Chapter 17.

There are two drawbacks to the SCSI port. First, it must be added to your computer on an expansion card (though you can have your computer built with a SCSI card preinstalled by the manufacturer). Second, all SCSI devices must be configured, which can be a pain.

Every SCSI device must have its own unique ID number. That isn't a problem, because you can set the ID number by using a handy gizmo on the back of every SCSI device. What *is* a pain is that the last SCSI device must be *terminated*. That's doesn't mean "killed." It means there's just another hassle to deal with.

My advice: You probably don't need a SCSI port on your PC. In fact, I bought one only because I wanted to use a special gizmo that required a SCSI port. Call me eccentric.

Joystick ports

Believe it or not, but one of the first expansion options for the original IBM PC was a joystick port. IBM didn't call it that. No, it called it the A-to-D port, for Analog-to-Digital. That sounds very scientific, doesn't it? But the truth is, the hole was designed for plugging in a joystick.

In addition to a joystick, you can plug a MIDI musical instrument into the joystick (A-to-D) port. You plug a special gadget into the joystick port and then plug the 5-pin MIDI cable into the gadget. Most MIDI keyboard starter kits come with this gadget (which has a real name, but I'm too lazy to look it up).

Also, if you're a closet Mr. Science type, you can use the joystick port for "scientific applications." For example, I have an anemometer (one of those wind-things) that mounts on the roof of my office and connects to the PC via the joystick port. That way, I can tell whether the wind is blowing, even without looking at the trees outside.

USB ports

The USB port is poised to take over the world. Unlike other ports on a PC, the USB is smart. When you plug in a USB device, Windows 98 instantly recognizes it and configures the device for you. You don't even need to reset the PC. Amazing.

For example, I bought one of those monitor-top videocameras for my PC. After plugging the thing into the USB port (with the computer on), Windows instantly recognized the camera, installed the proper software, and let me use it right away. (I still had to install the camera software, but the whole process was a heck of a lot easier than unscrewing the case.)

Someday you may own a PC that has a USB keyboard, joystick, scanner, mouse, modem, monitor, and electroshock-therapy unit. With USB, it's plug in and go. (Heck, even the Macintosh has a USB port.)

- ✔ USB stands for Universal Serial Bus. It's a modified type of serial port.
- ✔ The USB port has the USB symbol located nearby (see the margin).
- ✔ You can plug in USB devices as you need them. If you have a scanner and joystick hooked up, unplug one and plug in your PC's camera instead. There is no penalty or glitch when this happens.
- ✔ The USB is not a total solution. The port's speed is too slow to make it possible for external disk drives to be connected. This problem may be solved in the future, however.

It Knows the Date and Time!

Most computers come with an internal clock. Tick-tock. The clock is battery operated, which enables it to keep track of the time, day or night, whether or not the PC is plugged in. To check the current time, gander at the far-right side of the Windows taskbar. Living on the system tray is the current time.

- ✔ If you point the mouse at the time, Windows displays the current date and time in a long format. This is shown in Figure 11-2.
- ✔ If you don't see the time, click the Start button to pop up its menu and choose Settings➪Taskbar & Start Menu. In the Taskbar Properties dialog box, Taskbar Options panel, look for the check box on the bottom titled Show Clock. Click the mouse on that check box to put a check mark there. Click the OK button, and Windows shows you the time on the taskbar.
- ✔ The format for the date and time varies depending on how your computer is set up. Windows displays a date and time format based on your country or region. This book assumes the typical (and I agree, backward) U.S. method of listing the date.
- ✔ Who cares if the computer knows what day it is? Well, because your files are time- — and date- — stamped, you can figure things out, like which is a later version of two similar files or two files with the same name on different disks.

Figure 11-2:
The current
date and
time (more
or less).

Saturday,March 20,1999
9:41 PM

"My PC's clock is off"

When it comes to keeping time, computers use a geologic clock. Well, maybe it's not that bad, but computers do seem to lose track of the time a few weeks or so. Why? Who knows! But the time can always be reset, which is nice.

To set or change the date and time on your PC, double-click the mouse on the time on the taskbar: Point the mouse at the time on the right end of the taskbar and double-click. Click-click. This step displays the Date/Time Properties dialog box, as shown in Figure 11-3. Manipulate the controls in the Date/Time Properties dialog box to change or set the date or time. Click OK when you're done.

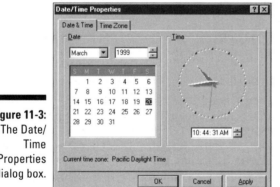

Figure 11-3:
The Date/
Time
Properties
dialog box.

✔ To set a new month, pluck the proper month from the drop-down list.

✔ To set a new year, type the year in the year box, or click the up and down arrows with the mouse to change the year.

✔ Pick a new day of the month by clicking on that number with the mouse.

✔ Set the clock by typing a new value for hours, minutes, or seconds. Double-click the mouse on the hours, minutes, or seconds displayed, and then type a new value.

- ✔ To set a.m. or p.m., double-click to select either item and then click the down or up arrow to change it.

- ✔ a.m. means morning or before noon. p.m. means afternoon and evening (up to midnight).

- ✔ Midnight is 12:00 a.m.

- ✔ To set the time, type the new time. For example, type **10:00** if it's 9:58 or so. Then when the time lady (or whoever) says that it's 10 o'clock, click on the Apply button in the Date/Time Properties dialog box. That sets the time instantly.

- ✔ Few people bother setting the seconds on their PC clocks. I mean, why do it if the thing will be off a few minutes every week anyway?

What causes the clock to go screwy?

PC clocks go nuts for several reasons, most of which would require a degree in either electronics or witchcraft to fully understand. The most down-to-earth reason your PC's clock gets lost is that your computer's software interrupts it. You know — like those moments when you try to type at the keyboard and nothing happens. The same deal goes with the clock: Some programs are so busy that they don't let anything else go on in the computer, including letting the clock tick. Sad, rude, but true.

- ✔ Some computer activities may interrupt the clock, such as a lot of disk access. They cannot be avoided; they're just a part of computer life.

- ✔ Don't be too quick to blame the PC's internal battery for your clock woes. True, a battery does maintain the clock, which keeps the time even when the PC is off. But when the battery goes, the clock goes as well. It's not a gradual thing.

- ✔ If your PC has a Suspend feature, that can screw up the clock. This feature is found mostly on laptops, but a few newer desktops also support the Suspend command. See Chapter 4 for information on Suspend. And know that when you use it, you may be messing with your PC's clock.

Expansion Slots

On the back of the motherboard, near the rear of the computer, in the low-rent district, you find several long, thin slots. These are *expansion slots,* into which you can plug special *expansion cards.* The idea is that you can expand your system by adding options not included with the basic PC.

- Your PC can have from 3 to 12 expansion slots. The average is 5. Or 8. It depends on how big your console is. Tower computer models have the most expansion slots; small-footprint models have the fewest.

- Some El Cheapo PCs — often called "home" machines — lack expansion slots. They cannot be upgraded! Hey, maybe that's why it was the cheapest model at Computer City, no?

- Although it's possible for anyone to plug in a card and expand a computer system, it's a job best left to those willing to risk both life and machine. (No, it's not life-threatening — at least if the PC is unplugged first — but it is complicated.)

- The salespeople never tell you this one: Most expansion cards come squirming with cables, which makes the seemingly sleek motherboard look more like an electronic pasta dish. Some cables are threaded inside the PC; others are left hanging limply out the back. It's the cables that make the upgrading and installation process so difficult.

- Expansion cards are sometimes referred to as *daughterboards*. Cute, huh? But explain this: The expansion slot is also referred to as the *bus*. Computers. . . .

- After you add a new expansion card, you need to tell Windows about it. On a good day (sunshine, hot coffee, birds chirping, like that), Windows recognizes and automatically configures the new hardware when you restart your PC. Otherwise, you need to open the Control Panel and start the Add New Hardware icon. The details of this process are far too boring to list here.

TECHNICAL STUFF

I wouldn't read this expansion slot stuff if I were you

There are different systems for expansion slots and cards in a PC. The most common is the ISA, which stands for Industry Standard Architecture. Many inexpensive PC expansion options come on ISA cards: sound options, some low-end video cards, and network cards. ISA cards are being phased out in favor of PCI cards.

Beyond ISA is the PCI standard. It's the faster of the two, so most of the high-end stuff plugs into a PCI slot: network cards, high-end video, DVD cards, SCSI cards — just about everything, in fact.

Why these different slot systems? Because the ISA isn't as technically advanced as some users require. And it's slow. Today's systems use the faster PCI slots for super-dooper video graphics, slippery-fast hard drives, and smokin' network interfaces. Everything else used to plug into the dopey old ISA slots. Pretty soon, everything will be PCI.

The Power Supply (Sometimes It Goes POOF!)

The final mystery item in the box is the *power supply,* which, much to your relief, doesn't go poof! Hardly at all. The power supply does three things: It brings in power from the wall socket, it supplies power to the motherboard and disk drives, and it contains the on/off switch.

✔ The power supply makes most of the noise when your PC runs. It contains a fan that regulates the temperature inside the console, keeping everything nice and cool. (Electronic components get hot when electricity races through them — just like you would! This heat has the ugly consequence of making them misbehave, which is why cooling is needed.)

✔ Power supplies are rated in watts. The more stuff your computer has — the more disk drives, memory, expansion cards, and so on — the greater the number of watts the power supply should provide. The typical PC has a power supply rated at 150 or 200 watts. More powerful systems may require a power supply of 220 or 250 watts.

✔ Boom! If lightning strikes or something deleterious comes marching down the power line, your power supply will blow. Don't panic. It's designed to pop and smolder. This effect in no way damages the rest of your computer. You just need to buy a new power supply and have someone replace it. Everything else in your system should survive the disaster (which is how the power supply is designed, fortunately).

✔ One way to help your power supply — and your computer — from potentially going poof (even in a lightning strike) is to invest in a surge protector or UPS. See Chapter 2.

Chapter 12

Memory (RAM-a-Lama Ding-Dong)

• •

In This Chapter

▶ Understanding PC memory

▶ Memory questions and answers

▶ Adding memory to your computer

▶ The lowdown on kilobytes and megabytes

• •

Do you know whether you have enough memory? How could you remember something like that? No matter how old people get, we never run out of memory. It's a limitless resource, although remembering certain dates seems to elude various male members of the species. Too bad it's not the same for your computer, where memory is gobbled up quicker than a stray Milky Way bar at a fat camp.

Memory, or Random-Access Memory (RAM), is a storage place in a computer, just like disk space. Unlike disk storage, memory is the only place inside the computer where the real work gets done. Obviously, the more memory you have, the more work you can do. Not only that, but having more memory also means that the computer is capable of grander tasks, such as working with graphics, animation, sound, and music — and your PC remembers everyone it meets without ever having to look twice at a name tag.

What Is Memory?

All computers need memory. That's where the work gets done. The microprocessor is capable of storing information inside itself, but only so much. It needs extra memory just like humans need notepads and libraries.

For example, when you create a document with your word processor, each character you type is placed in a specific location in memory. After the character is there, the microprocessor doesn't need to access it again unless you're editing, searching or replacing, or doing something active to the text.

After something is created in memory — a document, spreadsheet, or graphic — it's saved to disk. Your disk drives provide long-term storage for information. Then, when you need to access the information again, you open it back into memory from disk. After the information is there, the microprocessor can again work over the information.

The only nasty thing about memory is that it's volatile. When you turn off the power, the contents of memory go *poof!* This is okay if you've saved to disk, but if you haven't, everything is lost. Even resetting your computer zaps the contents of memory. Always save (if you can) before you reset or turn off your PC.

- The more memory you have, the better. With more memory, you can work on larger documents and spreadsheets, enjoy applications that use graphics and sound, and boast about it to your friends.

- All computers have a limited amount of memory, which means that some day you may run short. When that happens, you see an error message shouting, "Out of memory!" Don't panic. The computer can handle the situation. You can add more memory to your system if you want. Consult your favorite computer guru.

- One of the sure signs that your PC needs more memory: It slows to a crawl. I have a laptop with only (only!) 8MB of memory. Under Windows 98, that's just not enough and, although my computer gets work done, I spend a lot of time waiting for it to catch up. (I think I'll steal a few memory chips from my wife's laptop. Shhh! Don't tell!)

- Turning off the power makes the *contents* of memory go bye-bye. It doesn't destroy the memory chips themselves.

- When you open something on disk, the computer copies that information from disk into the computer's memory. Only in memory can that information be examined or changed. When you save information back to disk, the computer copies it from memory to the disk.

- The term *RAM* is used interchangeably with the word *memory*. They're the same thing. (In fact, RAM stands for Random-Access Memory, in case you've been working any crossword puzzles lately.)

- Memory is a component of the motherboard, sitting very close to the microprocessor. Memory exists as a series of tiny chips called RAM chips. The RAM chips typically come as groups soldered together on a thin strip of fiberglass. The whole gang is referred to as a single in-line memory module (SIMM).

- You can add more memory to the computer by plugging in more RAM chips (or SIMMs), either on the motherboard itself or via some cutesy memory expansion card. Again, leave this job to the pros.

Common memory questions

How much memory do I need?

Your brain has all the storage you need for a lifetime.

No, I mean how much memory does my computer need?

The amount of memory your PC needs depends on two things. The first, and most important, is the memory requirement of your software. Some programs, such as spreadsheets and graphics applications, require lots of memory. For example, Adobe Photoshop (a graphics package) says — right on the box — that it needs 16MB of RAM. Yowie!

The second and more limiting factor is cost. Memory costs money. It's not as expensive as it was back in the old stone-tablet days of computing, but it still costs a lot. The 16MB of memory that Adobe Photoshop wants to use could cost you about $40 or less. (That's almost $2,850 in dog dollars!) That's cheap compared with the $500 16MB would have cost you three years ago; heck, I paid $500 for 16*K* of RAM in 1983!

Generally speaking, all computers should have at least 16MB of RAM. Older models may have less, but to run today's software you need at least 16MB, preferably 32MB or 64MB or more.

Can I add more memory to my PC?

Yes. You do this typically because your applications need more memory. The programs just won't run (or will run sluggishly) without more memory.

See the section "Adding more memory to your PC" later in this chapter.

Can I lose computer memory?

No. Your computer has only a finite amount of memory, but it cannot be "lost" to anything. Programs use memory when you run them. For example, when you run WordPerfect, it eats up a specific amount of memory. But when you quit WordPerfect, all that memory is made available to the next program. While a program runs, it "grabs" memory for its own uses. When the program is done, it reluctantly lets the memory go.

What about copying programs?

Copying a program or file uses some memory, but don't confuse disk "memory" with computer memory or RAM. You can copy a huge file from one disk to another without worrying about running out of memory. The operating system (Windows) handles the details. (You may run out of disk space, but that's another problem.)

Computer memory can never be "destroyed." Even after a huge program runs or you copy a very large file, your system still has the same amount of RAM it had before.

Disk "memory" is just storage space on disk. It's possible to store on your hard drive a program that's huge in size — hundreds of megabytes — more than could possibly fit in memory. How does that work? Some say it's voodoo. Others say it's because Windows loads only a small portion of the file into memory (RAM) at a time. Who knows what the truth really is?

How much memory is in my PC right now?

This information may be a mystery to you but isn't a secret to your computer. How much memory lives inside the beast can be seen by displaying the System Properties dialog box. The amount of memory (shown as RAM) is displayed right beneath the type of microprocessor that lives in your PC.

> ✔ To display the System Properties dialog box, refer to the section "Okay, wise guy, so which microprocessor lives in my PC?" in Chapter 11.
>
> ✔ Figure 11-1 shows you what the System Properties dialog box looks like.
>
> ✔ Refer to the section "Measuring Memory," later in this chapter, for more information on what a megabyte (MB) is.

Adding more memory to your PC

No electronic equivalent of Geritol is available for your computer. If you think that your PC has tired RAM or maybe it didn't have enough memory in the first place, you can always add more.

Adding memory to your computer is Lego-block simple. The only difference is that the typical Lego block set — the cool Space Station or Rescue Helicopter set, for example, costs less than $20. Your computer, on the other hand, may cost one hundred times that much. This 100 is not something to be taken lightly.

Upgrading memory involves five complex and boring steps:

1. **Figure out how much memory you need to add.**

   For example, if you have 8MB in your system, you probably need another 8MB to give yourself the full power of Windows. If you have the bucks, you can upgrade to 32MB or even 64MB — or even 128MB. More! More! More!

2. **Figure out how much memory you can install.**

   This step is technical. It involves knowing how memory is added to your computer and in what increments. You should simply tell the shop or your favorite technical guru how much you think you need, and he'll tell you how much you can have.

3. **Buy something.**

   In this case, you buy the memory chips or you buy the expansion card into which the memory chips are installed.

4. **Pay someone else to plug in the chips and do the upgrade.**

   Oh, you can do it yourself, but I'd pay someone else to do it.

5. **Gloat.**

   After you have the memory, brag to your friends about it. Heck, it used to be impressive to say that you had 640K of RAM. Then came the "I have 4 megabytes of memory in my 386" round of impressiveness. Today? Anything less than 128 megabytes and your kids will roll their eyes at you.

✔ PC memory usually comes in given sizes: 4MB, 8MB, 16MB, and then in multiples of 16MB after that. Yeah, you get oddball sizes, but just about everything can be divided evenly by 2.

✔ Another shocker: You might think that moving from 16MB to 64MB in your system requires that you buy 48MB of memory chips. Wrong! It may mean that you have to buy the full 64MB and then toss out your original 16MB. It all has to do with how memory fits in a PC, which is something even the gods themselves don't fully understand.

✔ If you want to try upgrading memory yourself, go ahead. Plenty of easy books on the subject of upgrading memory are available, as well as how-to articles in some of the popular magazines. I still recommend having someone else do it, however.

✔ More information on memory terms is covered throughout the first part of this chapter.

Boring technical details on the differences between RAM and ROM

RAM stands for Random-Access Memory. It refers to memory that the microprocessor can read from and write to. When you create something in memory, it's done in RAM. *RAM* is memory and vice versa.

ROM stands for Read-Only Memory. The microprocessor can read from ROM, but it cannot write to it or modify it. ROM is permanent. Often, ROM chips contain special instructions for the computer — important stuff that will never change. Because that information is stored on a memory chip, the microprocessor can access it. The instructions are always there because they are unerasable.

Measuring Memory

Many interesting terms orbit the planet memory. The most basic of these terms refer to the quantity of memory (see Table 12-1).

Table 12-1		Memory Quantities	
Term	*Abbr*	*About*	*Actual*
Byte		1 byte	1 byte
Kilobyte	K or KB	1,000 bytes	1,024 bytes
Megabyte	M or MB	1,000,000 bytes	1,048,576 bytes
Gigabyte	G or GB	1,000,000,000 bytes	1,073,741,824 bytes
Terabyte	T or TB	1,000,000,000,000 bytes	1,099,511,627,776 bytes

Memory is measured by the byte. Think of a byte as a single character, a letter in the middle of a word. For example, the word *spatula* is seven bytes long and would require seven bytes of computer memory storage.

A half-page of text is about 1,000 bytes. To make that a handy figure to know, computer nerds refer to 1,000 bytes as a *kilobyte,* or one K or KB.

The term *megabyte* refers to 1,000K, or one million bytes. The abbreviation MB (or M) indicates megabyte, so 8MB means eight megabytes of memory.

Further than the megabyte is the *gigabyte.* As you can guess, it's one billion bytes, or about 1,000 megabytes. A *terabyte* is one trillion bytes, or enough RAM to dim the lights when you start the PC. Other trivia:

✔ Bytes are composed of eight bits. The word *bit* is a contraction of *binary digit*. *Binary* is base two, or a counting system where only ones and zeros are used. Computers count in binary, and we group their bits into clusters of eight for convenient consumption as bytes.

✔ The term *giga* is actually Greek, and it means giant.

✔ The term *tera* is also Greek. It means monster!

✔ You have no reason to worry about how much ROM (Read-Only Memory) is in your computer.

✔ A specific location in memory is called an *address*.

✔ Some hardware states that it sits at a specific memory address in your computer. This address is often given as a *hexadecimal* (base 16) number, which often doesn't look like a number at all (that is, C800 or A400). What does that mean? Who knows? But the numbers are important to the person you pay to install and set up your hardware.

And just what the heck is "extended memory?"

Back in the old days, several dozen terms were used to describe memory in a PC: conventional memory, DOS memory, upper memory, high memory, HMA memory, expanded memory, DMPI memory, extended memory, and on and on.

The only memory term you see used anymore is *extended memory.* All the memory in your PC is extended memory, which is a holdover term from the ancient days when memory terms were important.

What does this stuff mean to you?

If you see software which says that it requires "16MB of extended memory," just know that they simply mean 16MB of "memory." All the memory in your PC is extended already.

Chapter 13

The Bonehead's Guide
to PC Monitors

• •

• •

*T*he first thing you notice on any computer is the screen, or what a nerd would call the video display monitor or even a CRT (cathode ray tube). In the old days, the wrong kind of display could really fry your eyeballs. I remember riding the elevator with bug-eyed people desperately searching for Visine. Today's computer screens are easier to look at and can produce much more stunning displays. Visine sales are down considerably.

This chapter is about the video display, computer screen, monitor, or the thing you look at when you use a computer.

Monitors and Graphics 101

While you're staring at the computer's monitor, waiting eternally for Windows, you should know that there really are two things that make up the PC video system: the monitor and the display adapter.

What's a screen dump?

No, a screen dump is not a pile of old monitors somewhere in the desert.

Dump is an ungraceful yet popular computer term meaning "to transfer a lot of information from one place to another." The information is typically unloaded — like from a dump truck — in one ugly batch, not sorted out or made neat or anything.

A *screen dump* is the process of taking the information on your computer screen and sending it off to the printer or to a file. Under DOS, this procedure was done with the magic Print Screen key on the keyboard. In Windows, the Print Screen key does kind of the same thing, but nothing is printed.

In Windows, when you press the Print Screen key, you take a snapshot of the desktop. All that graphical information is saved like a photograph in the Clipboard. You can then paste the information into any program that can swallow graphical images. So even though nothing prints, you still get a dump of what was on the screen.

The *monitor* is the physical, television-like thing you see on top of or near the console. Like a TV, it has various knobs for adjustments similar to those on many TV sets. But that's where the similarity ends. Your computer monitor is not a TV set.

The *display adapter* is an expansion card plugged into the motherboard inside your console. The display adapter contains special circuitry that takes information from your computer and tosses it up on the screen. The display adapter tells the monitor what to display, where to display it, and what colors to use — like an electronic interior designer.

Even though it's tucked away inside your PC, the display adapter is more important than the monitor. It determines how many colors you see and how fancy the graphics are that appear on your monitor. Monitors? They're just dumb.

  ✔ In a way, the PC's monitor is like its mouth. It displays information as a type of visual feedback, enabling you to know what's going on or to see the result of some operation. In that respect, it seems like my PC spends most of its time yawning.

  ✔ You need both a monitor and a display adapter.

  ✔ In some PCs, especially laptops, the display adapter is built into the motherboard.

  ✔ Take another look at Chapter 11 for a review of motherboards and expansion cards.

✔ The term *monitor* refers to the physical device — the monitor that sits on top of or to the side of your console. The terms *screen* and *display* are both used to describe what appears on the monitor's screen — information the computer is showing you.

✔ The display adapter may also be called the display adapter card, video adapter, video hardware, video system, or Phil.

All about Display Adapters (Expansion Cards)

The secretive, internal part of a PC's video system is the display adapter. It's an expansion card that plugs into your PC's motherboard and gives your computer the capability to display lovely text and graphics on the monitor.

Display adapters come in various price ranges and have features for artists, game players, computer designers, and regular Joes like you and me and guys named Joe. Here's the quick round-up:

✔ All display adapters sold today are a superset of the old SuperVGA standard. Other standards and different names and descriptions may exist, but everything is pretty much compatible with all the software out there. Choosing a proper display adapter is more a matter of cost and needs than of compatibility.

✔ Speaking of cost, display adapters cost more if they have more features. The primary feature of display adapters is video memory. Most display adapters should have about 2 or 4MB of video memory. The high-end jobs come with 8MB or more, which means that the card is capable of displaying more colors and higher resolutions.

Do you need more colors and higher resolutions? Only if your software demands it. In most cases, you'll be fine with whatever video adapter your dealer tosses into your PC. However, you can upgrade to another video adapter at any time, swapping out the old one for the new one.

✔ The yardsticks of PC graphics are color and resolution. Color refers to the number of colors that can be displayed at one time; resolution refers to the number of dots ("pixels") that can be displayed vertically and horizontally.

✔ If your PC has a DVD drive, you need a display adapter capable of producing the DVD image on the monitor. The display adapters typically have an S-video out port on them, which lets you connect a TV to the computer for watching things on a larger screen.

✔ Some high-resolution graphics systems are applicable to only certain kinds of software. Computer graphics, CAD, and animation and design are all areas where paying top dollar for your display is worth it. If you're using only basic applications, such as a word processor, you don't need top-dollar displays.

Getting to Know and Love Your Monitor

The monitors sold today are really miraculous things. My first PC monitor had an On-Off switch, a contrast knob, and a brightness knob. My second PC monitor (which was a *color* monitor), had extra knobs for adjusting the color — but they were around back. Today, monitors have so many buttons and knobs that they look like a second keyboard.

Take a gander at your PC's monitor for a second. It probably has a row of tiny buttons along the bottom. If you can't see the buttons, they're probably hidden behind a panel. Figure 13-1 shows what the buttons may look like and what they control.

Figure 13-1:
Icons found
on the
typical PC
monitor.

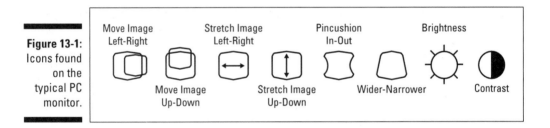

You press one button to adjust one aspect of the monitor. For example, if the image is too far to the right, press the Move Image Left-Right button. Pressing a + or – button on the monitor then moves the image left or right.

✔ Some monitors may even display information on the screen as they're being adjusted. Don't let it freak you out.

✔ By pressing the Left-Right, Up-Down, and then the stretch buttons, you can adjust the monitor's image to fill the screen.

✔ Most monitors also have a Save or Store button, which remembers the settings you've entered, making them permanent.

✔ Your monitor may also display text when it starts (such as "Invalid Sync") or various numbers describing the monitor's frequency. Don't let that bug you; the numbers should disappear momentarily.

TECHNICAL STUFF

Monitor terms to numb your brain

Thinking about all the technical issues surrounding a PC monitor will make you shudder. Do it now: Shudder. Egads! Here are some non-layman terms that describe various parts of a PC monitor.

One final warning: You really don't need to read this sidebar. I'd skip it, if I were you.

Analog: Your PC's monitor is an analog monitor, as are all VGA monitors.

Bandwidth: The speed at which information is sent from the computer (actually, the graphics adapter) to the monitor. The bandwidth is a value, measured in *megahertz* (MHz), and the monitor must be capable of accepting the bandwidth of the graphics adapter. The higher the bandwidth value, the better.

Composite: A type of monitor that's similar to a TV set. Popular in the olden days. Also known as an RGB monitor.

Digital: The newer flat-panel displays are all digital, as were (ironically) older PC monitors.

Dot pitch: Refers to the distance between each dot, or pixel, on the screen (as measured from the center of each pixel). The closer the dots, the better the image is. A dot pitch of 0.28

mm (millimeters) is really good, with smaller values being even better.

Interlacing: A method of tricking the monitor into displaying a picture that is better than it should be able to display. Interlacing takes twice as long to paint the image on-screen by painting only half of it at once. It also makes the picture flicker, which is why a noninterlacing video system is better.

Multiscanning: The capability of a single monitor to switch between multiple analog and digital modes.

Picture tube size: The diagonal measurement of your monitor's picture tube, from corner to corner. Bigger monitors have larger display areas and are more expensive. The 14- to 17-inch monitors are common, but you can buy special monitors up to 21 inches and beyond, given the size of your ego or vision problems.

Scan rate: The rate at which a monitor's electron gun paints the image on the screen. It's measured in kilohertz (kHz), and the higher the value, the better.

Thumbprint: Just threw this one in here to see whether you were paying attention.

How 'bout them new flat-screen displays?

Eventually, your computer will be connected to a flat-panel monitor, similar to the screens used on PC laptops. These monitors not only are lightweight, thin, and beautiful to look at, but they also induce envy in everyone who sees them. The bad news? They're very expensive.

Right now, flat-screen displays are where the $1,000 laser printer was about six years ago. You can take this statement to mean that in about six years, just about every PC will be sold with a flat-screen display rather than a clunky monitor.

✔ Flat-screen displays are digital, which means that they'll require either a special adapter to run from your PC's SuperVGA graphics adapter or a proprietary digital adapter. Rumor has it that eventually a new digital graphics adapter will be developed specifically for the flat-screen displays.

✔ If you want a large-screen monitor, you have to steer away from flat-screen displays. The biggest one I've seen is just under 17 inches. We're still a few years out from the wall-size TV set, I suppose.

Cleaning your monitor

Computer monitors grow dust like a 5 o'clock shadow. And, in addition to the dust, you always find fingerprints and sneeze globs on your screen. Monitors are messy.

To clean your monitor, spray some window cleaner on a soft towel or tissue. Then gently rub the screen. You also can use vinegar if you want your computer to have that tossed salad smell.

Never spray window cleaner directly on the screen. It may dribble down into the monitor and wreak electronic terror.

✔ For cleaning the monitor's housing (the non-screen part), you can use some Formula 409 or Fantastik. Again, spray it on a cloth and wipe the monitor. This method also works for cleaning the PC itself, if you're in a nesting mood.

✔ A fond term for that layer of dust that coats your monitor is *pixel dust*. Ah, computers can be painfully cute at times.

Tweaking the Display in Windows

Aside from messing with the knobs on the front (or the back) for adjusting the brightness and contrast, you can do a number of strange things with the images displayed on your PC's monitor. Windows and its Control Panel handles all this stuff.

In the Control Panel lives an icon you use to tweak your monitor. This section tells you what you can do there. Here's how to open the thing up:

1. Open the Control Panel.

From the Start menu, choose Settings⇨Control Panel. This step displays the Control Panel's main window.

2. Open the Display icon.

Double-click the Display icon. This step conjures up the Display Properties dialog box, similar to, but prettier than, what's shown in Figure 13-2.

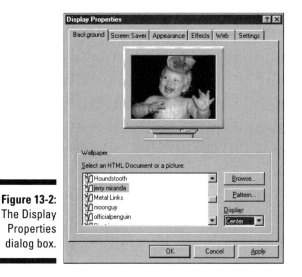

Figure 13-2:
The Display
Properties
dialog box.

3. Mess with the Display Properties dialog box.

You can change the desktop's background, add a screen saver, and change the system colors or screen resolution by using the Display Properties dialog box. The sections that follow outline how it's done.

4. Close the Display Properties dialog box.

When you're done, you can click the OK button to keep your changes or click Cancel to go back to the way things were.

The Display Properties dialog box has several panels: Background, Screen Saver, and Appearance for example. Each panel displays a different set of controls for manipulating one or more aspects of the display. Click on the proper tab to bring that panel forward.

Changing the background (wallpaper)

The background, or wallpaper, is what you see when you look at the desktop. You can see a pattern or a pretty picture or just about anything other than the dingy gray Windows really wants to display.

Summon the Display Properties dialog box, as described in the preceding section. Make sure that the Background panel is forward, as shown in Figure 13-2.

You can put an image up on the desktop in two ways. The first is with a pattern; the second is with a graphical image or wallpaper.

The patterns are listed in the Pattern area of the dialog box. A bunch of them are displayed, each of them equally boring.

The Wallpaper area lists a bunch of graphics files you can apply to the desktop. If the image is large enough, it can cover the entire screen. If it's small, you may want to tile them on the screen, in which case you click in the radio button by the word *Tile* if you have WIndows 95. If you have Windows 98, you choose Tile from a drop-down box.

Whenever you choose a new pattern or wallpaper, it appears in the mini-monitor preview window. It's rather small, so the effect isn't stunning. If you want to see a true preview, click the Apply button.

If you created your own graphics file, you can use it as the wallpaper. First, the graphics must be a bitmapped image or BMP file. GIF files also work, but you have to use the Browse button to locate and select them.

Click OK to keep your new desktop image; click Cancel to forget it.

Adjusting the resolution and colors

Muster the Display Properties dialog box, as explained earlier in this chapter. Click the mouse on the Settings tab to bring that panel forward. What you see looks something like Figure 13-3.

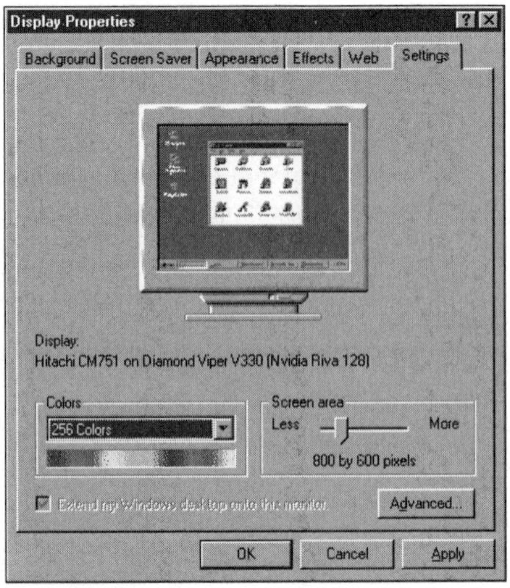

Figure 13-3:
The
Settings
Panel in the
Display
Properties
dialog box.

The Settings panel in the Display Properties dialog box is where you tweak your monitor's color and resolution. You can have only so much of both, and this part of the dialog box lets you see just how much you can get away with.

I don't go through all the details here. Basically, you choose your colors first, from 256 colors on up to 16-bit or 32-bit or whatever it gives you. *Remember:* The resolution changes, depending on the number of colors you choose.

Next, select a resolution. The mini-monitor preview window changes to reflect your choice. If you choose a higher resolution, don't be surprised if the number of colors decreases. These two things are linked, in case you haven't guessed.

If you're fortunate enough to have a 21-inch or larger monitor, run Windows at the 1024-x-768 resolution (at least). This setting displays a ton of information on the screen at once and uses 256 or more colors. You can adjust most of your software (typically through some sort of Zoom command) to display text larger on the screen, making it an even trade-off.

✔ The number of colors and resolution depend on your graphics adapter's capabilities. Don't blame me if it isn't that high.

How Windows games can screw up your monitor's resolution

Games are truly fussy when it comes to your monitor's graphical resolution and the number of colors available. This statement is most true for children's games that run under Windows. For some stubborn reason, they insist on a color setting of exactly 256 colors. If your monitor is set to display more colors, you don't see the game at all (or you see it sporadically). This situation drives parents nuts.

To change the number of colors, follow the steps in the preceding section "Adjusting the resolution and colors." Set the new color value to 256 — even if your monitor is capable of

much more. Only at that setting do you see the game.

Alas, changing your monitor's color remains in effect for not only for the game but also for all of Windows. You can change it back, as described in the preceding section. However, you have to reset everything back to 256 colors the next time you want to play the game. If you find this problem annoying, just take your kids' advice and buy them a nifty new Pentium MMX. "C'mon, Dad! You can put it on your card!"

Adding a screen saver

A long, long time ago, PC monitors were susceptible to something called *phosphor burn-in*. After a time, the same image became *etched* on your screen. Visions of 1-2-3 or WordPerfect would haunt PC users, even with the monitor turned off!

One of the preventive measures against phosphor burn-in was to run a *screen saver* program. That program would blank the monitor. After several minutes of inactivity — no typing or moving the mouse — the screen went blank. Touching the mouse or pressing any key resumed computer operation, but the screen saver saved the monitor from phosphor burn-in.

Fortunately, phosphor burn-in is a thing of the past. Today's monitors are less likely to have an image burned in. Regardless, the screen saver is still with us. It serves more as an amusement than as a tool to prevent monitor damage. In fact, most new PC users figure that a screen saver is just a goofy thing to have.

Bring up the Display Properties dialog box, as discussed earlier in this chapter. Click the Screen Saver tab to bring that panel forward. The dialog box should look something like Figure 13-4.

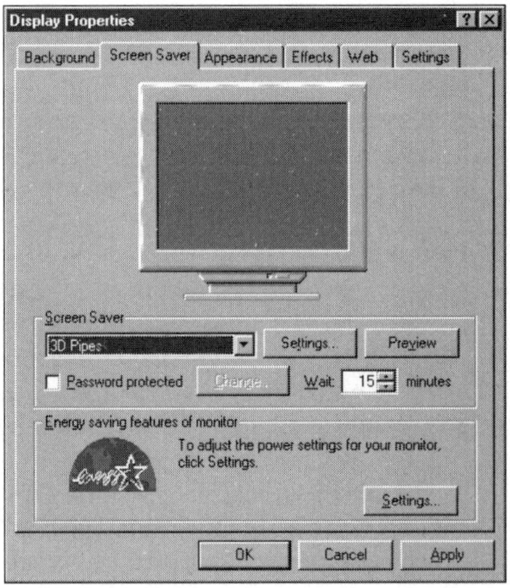

Figure 13-4:
Choose a screen saver here.

Again, this dialog box is messy — but fun to play in — so I don't go into much detail. You choose a screen saver from the Screen Saver drop-down list. Windows offers several.

Click the Settings button to make adjustments for your chosen screen saver.

Click the Preview button to see what the screen saver does. (Move the mouse a tad to turn the screen saver off.)

In the Wait box, enter the number of idle minutes after which you want the screen saver to kick in. For example, in Figure 13-4, the screen is saved after 15 minutes of no keyboard or mouse activity; everything goes blank, and the computer waits for a key to be pressed or the mouse to move.

Don't bother with a password. If you do, Windows doesn't let you back in after the screen saver kicks on. Instead, you have to type a password. Forget the password? You need to reset the computer to get back in.

- ✔ A safe key to press for switching off the screen saver is Ctrl. Unlike other keys on your keyboard, this key won't mess with any application that appears after the screen saver vanishes.

  No, that doesn't switch off the screen saver; it merely hides it so that you can see the desktop again.

- ✔ A cool way to switch off the screen saver is to pound your desk with your fist. That jostles the mouse and deactivates the screen saver.

Dueling Monitors

One of the features Windows 98 boasts is that it supports two or more monitors on one PC. Let me tell you: This boast is nothing new. All PCs can handle two monitors: a color and a monochrome ("black and white"). But where's the glamour in that?

With Windows 98 and the proper hardware installed, your PC can handle two or more monitors. Notice that I said "proper hardware." You can't just go out and buy a second video adapter and have everything work. It must be one of the handful recognized by Windows as dual-monitor happy. When you meet that weird requirement, you can have two (or more) monitors on one PC.

Adjusting the two monitors is handled in the Display Properties dialog box. Right-click the desktop and choose Properties from the shortcut menu. In the Display Properties dialog box, click the Settings tab to bring that panel forward. You see your two monitors displayed, as shown in Figure 13-5.

You can drag the monitor's image inside the dialog box to position them left, right, or on top of each other. The numbers on each monitor correspond to the monitors listed in the drop-down Display list.

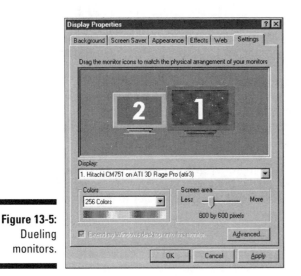

Figure 13-5:
Dueling
monitors.

Now what's the point? Obviously, more monitors give you more screen acreage. You can read e-mail on one monitor and browse the Web on another. Whatever. It's all greed, you know.

- ✔ A file in the Windows folder on drive C is called Display.Txt. Open that file and read the information there about which video adapters are supported for dual monitors.

- ✔ If the second monitor is recognized, Windows displays a text message on it when your PC starts. That's your "Yippee! It worked!" signal that everything's okay.

- ✔ To activate a monitor, click its icon in the Display Properties dialog box. Click Yes if you're asked to enable the monitor.

- ✔ Each monitor can have its own resolution and settings, as shown in Figure 13-5. Just choose the monitor from the Display drop-down list and make the settings that are necessary.

- ✔ The desktop image appears on both monitors.

- ✔ Windows can be dragged from one monitor to the other. It's really kind of neat to see.

- ✔ Games run only on your main monitor (the one that's active when the PC first starts). DOS programs also run on only the main monitor. In the future, some games may take advantage of multiple monitors, but I wouldn't count on it. (It's just too weird.)

- ✔ Maximizing a window enlarges it to fill the entire screen of only one monitor. You can, however, stretch a window across several monitors.

- ✔ The screen saver appears on both monitors, which is nifty. (I haven't yet found a screen saver that works on only one of the monitors.)

Chapter 14

The Joys of Having (And Using) a Mouse

*T*he PC wasn't always a mouse-friendly machine. No, the Macintosh was the computer with the mouse. Computer mice were just too much fun to be associated with serious IBM business machines. Mac users? They were a silly lot, anyway.

Today, it's hard to find any PC that isn't sold with its own mouse. Some mice are fun, like the wacky models Logitech sells. Other mice, like the IBM computer mouse (which has the serious IBM letters etched into its case), are meant strictly for business. Regardless, a mouse is a handy thing to have, especially when you're using a graphically drunk operating system like Windows.

✔ Doug Englebart invented the computer mouse at the Stanford Research Institute in the 1960s. He got only $10,000 for his invention, but in 1997 won the $500,000 Lemelson-MIT Prize for American Innovation.

✔ Rumor has it that Apple founder Steve Jobs didn't even want the first Macintosh model to have a keyboard. Apparently, he believed that everything could be done by using a mouse. (Yeah: "Click 20 times to type an A, 21 times to type a B. . . .")

> ✔ The plural of computer mouse is *mice*. One computer has a mouse. Two computers, they have mice.
>
> ✔ And just why isn't one lice a louse?

A Mouse in Your PC House

A computer mouse is a little plastic rodent running around on your desk. It looks like a bar of soap with a large, rolling ball embedded in its belly. On the top, you find at least two push-buttons. A tail, or cord, runs from the mouse into the back of your PC. Figure 14-1 shows a typical mouse.

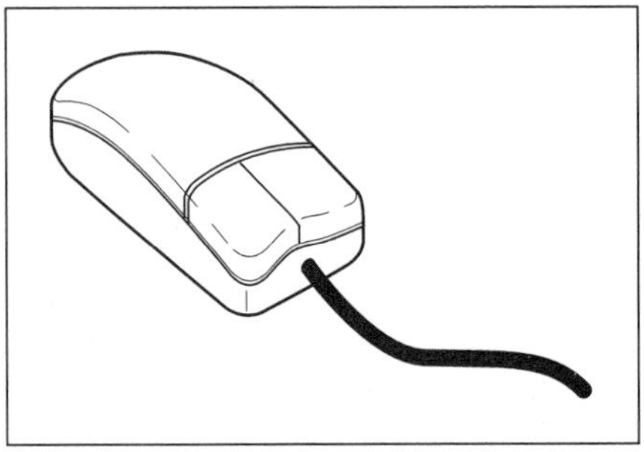

Figure 14-1:
Typical computer mouse.

> ✔ Even though your computer may have come with its own mouse, don't think that you can't buy another model. Refer to the section "Types of Mice," later in this chapter, for some of the varieties.
>
> ✔ You need a mouse to use Windows.

> ✔ You need to designate a special mouse area on your desk and keep it clear of desk debris so that you have room to move the mouse around. An area about the size of this book is typically all you need to roll the mouse around.
>
> ✔ A mouse works best when it's moved across a *mouse pad,* which is a small piece of plastic or rubber that sits on your desk. The mouse pad provides more traction than your slippery desktop, so the mouse's movements are more accurate. (Also, it reminds you to keep that area of your desk clean.)

> ✔ The best mouse pads have a rough surface, which the mouse can really grip. Poorly designed mouse pads are slick and should be avoided. Also, it's a status symbol to have something cool on your mouse pad: your PC's logo, a photo of your favorite movie star, or a fractal pattern. Uncool mouse pads have the names of computer stores on them or pictures of cats.

Types of Mice

There are many species of computer mice. The most common model looks like a bar of soap with two buttons. Some mice have more buttons. I've seen one model that had 52 buttons so that you could actually type with it. (I wonder why the thing never caught on?)

Aside from the standard model are a few variations. Some of the most popular are covered in this section.

The wheel mouse

Although Steve Jobs's vision for the Macintosh may have been fewer buttons, Bill Gates's vision is going in the other direction: More buttons! Microsoft added three buttons to the keyboard to help you use Windows (see Chapter 15) and a new button to it's Microsoft IntelliMouse mouse, which everyone calls the wheel mouse.

The wheel mouse, as shown in Figure 14-2, has an extra button between the two standard buttons. That button is a wheel, which you can spin up or down to scroll a document in those few Windows programs that obey the wheel mouse. Or you can press and hold the wheel button to "pan" the document up or down or left or right.

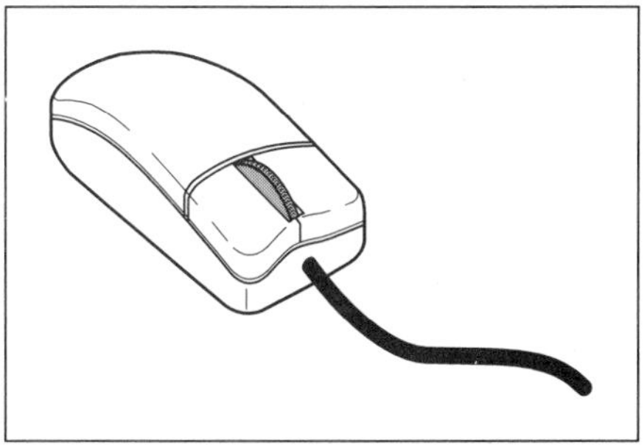

Figure 14-2:
The wheel
mouse that
Microsoft
calls the
IntelliMouse.

After using the IntelliMouse for a while, I can say that I've come to like it. I use the wheel all the time to scroll documents — typically by pressing and holding the wheel button instead of spinning the wheel. It's nifty. And this opinion has nothing to do with the fact that Microsoft gave me the mouse free. Nothing whatsoever.

✔ C'mon Microsoft: Do more buttons truly make the thing easier to use? If more people watched what Microsoft does rather than listen to what Bill Gates says, I think we'd know the truth.

✔ You don't need a wheel mouse.

✔ Only specific applications bother with the wheel. They include all the Microsoft Office 97 programs, plus all of Windows' own programs if you install the wheel mouse disk.

✔ Other than the wheel and the extra scrolling abilities it gives you in some programs, a wheel mouse has no advantage over the standard two-button mouse.

✔ No, the wheel is turned by your finger. You don't have to turn the mouse upside down or slap it with your palm, like the old Atari Football game.

Rolling the trackball: The upside-down mouse

A trackball mouse looks like a regular mouse turned upside down. Rather than roll the mouse around, you use your thumb or index finger to roll the ball itself. Because the whole contraption stays stationary, it doesn't use up nearly as much room and the cord never gets tangled.

Trackballs aren't for everyone. The only crowd that really loves them are the artist types, who prefer the precise movements the trackball gives you. Are you wearing all black? If so, you'll probably love a trackball mouse.

✔ A trackball has buttons, just like a mouse. In fact, your software doesn't know whether you're using a mouse or a trackball.

✔ The buttons are one reason many normal mouse users hate trackballs: You must press the button with your thumb. Egads!

✔ No, you can't just turn your mouse upside down to make it a trackball. You have to buy one.

✔ Trackballs are more expensive than regular mice.

Cordless mice

The latest rage seems to be cordless anything, though I can't see a time in the future when we have cordless toasters. A cordless mouse looks like a regular mouse (okay, it's a little fatter) minus the cord. Instead of using a cord, this mouse sends its signals through the air, using either radio waves or infrared technology or mind waves or something. The mouse of the 21st century has arrived!

The cordless mouse sends its signals to a small receiving unit located somewhere on your desk. The receiving unit then relays the signals down a cord that plugs into the back of your computer.

Mickey Niner to base, Mickey Niner to base! Bogey at three o'clock! Prepare to release mouse button.

Kachinka!

- A radio-controlled cordless mouse usually costs more than an infrared cordless mouse, and both types cost more than their tailed counterparts.

- The receiving unit for a radio-controlled cordless mouse can be anywhere within a six-foot radius of the mouse. The receiving unit for an infrared mouse can be up to six feet away too, but it must be within a direct line of sight. (The radio signal can transmit through objects; the infrared light can't.)

- Both types of cordless mice need batteries. Be sure to keep a spare set around so that you can still work when they fail at a crucial moment.

- Cordless mice are fatter than regular mice, probably to hold the batteries, although it could be genetic.

- If your infrared cordless mouse starts acting strangely, you've probably set something in front of its receiving unit. It's easy to do because that line of sight area will be the only clean spot on your desk.

- This bullet is for JFN of New Brunswick, Rhode Island: No, Fred, you can't use your TV remote control when the infrared mouse fails. And it's not the mouse that keeps changing the channel to *Designing Women.* I'd call the cable company, if I were you.

Know the differences between a mouse and a mousse!

A mouse is either a furry little rodent — like Mickey — or a handy peripheral for your PC. A mousse, on the other hand, is this upper-class dessert that pretends to be pudding. Or it could be something people put on their hair to make it look messed up. Know which is which before you buy.

Connecting the Mouse

Plug the mouse into the mouse hole — the mouse *port* — in the back of your computer. This port is a tiny, round hole, looking similar to a keyboard connector. (They're identical, in fact.) I've even noticed how some consoles have color-coded connectors and holes so that you don't plug the mouse into the keyboard hole (which are really both the same thing, anyway).

If your PC lacks a proper mouse port, the mouse most likely plugs into a serial port, typically COM1 or COM3. It's true for older mice and older computers, and it works only if you have a serial-type mouse.

✔ It's a good idea to turn your computer off before you connect or disconnect the mouse. See Chapter 5 for shutdown instructions.

✔ The mouse may come with its own software, which you install by using the Windows handy install program thingy. See Chapter 20.

✔ Use a serial mouse only if you absolutely have to. The serial port mouse could possibly interfere with your PC's modem. To ensure that it doesn't, plug the mouse into COM1 and ensure that the modem is plugged into COM2.

✔ The tail points *away* from you when you use the mouse. (Oh, I could tell a story here about a former boss, but I won't.)

Using Your Computer Mouse

The computer's mouse controls a pointer or mouse cursor on the screen. When you move the mouse around, rolling it on your desktop, the pointer on the screen moves in a similar manner. Roll the mouse left and the pointer moves left; roll it in circles and the pointer mimics that action; drop the mouse off the table and your computer yells out, "Ouch!" (Just kidding.)

The mouse should have two or more buttons. Your index and middle finger rest on the buttons while the mouse is cradled in the palm of your hand.

There's no need to squeeze the mouse; a gentle grip is all that's necessary.

You press the left, or main, mouse button by using your index finger. Because the button is sensitive, you only have to bend your finger a wee bit to press it. The same thing works for the right button; a small bend in your middle finger makes it click.

You use the button(s) to manipulate various items on the computer screen. It goes like this: You move the mouse, which moves the cursor on the screen over to something interesting. You click the mouse button, and something even more interesting happens.

✔ When you're holding a live mouse, you keep it in your palm, with the palm up. A mechanical mouse is held against the desktop with your palm down; its tail extends away from your hand, heading toward the back of your computer.

✔ Most people hold the mouse in their palm with their thumb against the left edge and their ring finger against the right edge. The index finger and middle finger can then hover over the buttons along the top.

(If these were medieval times, the mouse would be a fist weapon, not a finger weapon.)

✔ Computer nerds grab potato chips with the middle finger and thumb of their right hand. That way, their index finger doesn't get greasy stuff on the mouse button.

✔ Your mouse can be left-handed or right-handed. The mouse is treated as though you're right-handed unless you tell Windows otherwise. See the section "I'm a southpaw, and the buttons are backward!" later in this chapter.

✔ The first time you use a mouse, you want to move it in wild circles on your desk so that you can watch the pointer spiral on the screen. This urge takes a long time to wear off (if it ever does).

✔ When the mouse cord becomes tangled, raise the mouse in your hand and whip it about violently.

✔ When the mouse pointer appears to be stuck on the screen, violently slam the mouse down on the mouse pad a few times.

Point the mouse

When you're told to "point the mouse," it means that you move the mouse on the desktop, which moves the mouse pointer on the screen to point at something interesting (or not).

Try not to pick the mouse up and point it at something like a TV remote control. It just doesn't work that way.

Buttons on the mouse

The mouse has two (or more) push-button switches on its top, the back side where the tail pokes out. Each button makes a clicking noise when you push it. *Click!*

You use the left button most of the time. It's called the *main* mouse button or sometimes, cleverly, the *left* mouse button. If the instructions say to "click the mouse," you push the left button with your index finger.

The right button is used for special purposes, particularly in Windows. Whenever you're directed to use that button, the instructions typically say "click the right mouse button," which is also referred to as a *right-click*.

✔ So as not to confuse you too much, there is no such thing as a *left-click*. It's merely called a *click*.

- If you have a wheel mouse, the wheel button is the center button, which you can also click. At no time in Windows do you need to click the wheel button on anything; most clicking is left or right.

Click the mouse

A *click* is a press of the mouse button.

Often you read "click the mouse on the OK button." This instruction means that a graphic something-or-other is on the screen with the word *OK* on it. Using the mouse, you hover the pointer over the word *OK*. Then, with your index finger, click the mouse button. This action is referred to as *clicking the mouse on something*. (You could roll the mouse around on your forehead and click it there if you like — just make sure that no one's looking.)

- When you push the button on your mouse, it makes a clicking noise. So most programs tell you to "click" your mouse button when they really mean for you to press the mouse button.

- When you're clicking the button, push it down once and release it. Don't hold it down continuously. (Actually, it makes two clicks — one when it's pushed, and another when it's released. Is your hearing that good?)

- Sometimes you may be asked to press a key combination along with clicking the mouse. A popular combo is Ctrl+click, which means to press and hold down the Ctrl (control) key before you click the mouse.

- Watch out! I'm Ctrl+clicking! Stand back!

Double-clicking the mouse

A *double-click* is two rapid clicks in a row. You do that in Windows to open something.

- The time between clicks varies, but it doesn't have to be that quick.

- Try not to move the mouse around between the clicks; both clicks have to be on the same spot.

- Clicking and double-clicking are two different activities. When the manual says to "click," click the mouse's left button once. Double-clicking is clicking the left button twice.

- If you double-click your mouse and nothing happens, you may not be clicking fast enough. Try clicking it as fast as you can. If this speed is too quick for you, it can be adjusted. See the section "Double-clicking doesn't work!" later in this chapter.

Right-clicking the mouse

Most of the time, you click the mouse's left button, referred to simply as a *click*. Whenever you need to click the mouse's right button (the not-the-main button), it's called a *right-click*.

You do a lot of right-clicking in Windows.

Dragging the mouse

To drag something with the mouse, follow these steps:

1. **Point the mouse cursor at the something you want to drag.**

2. **Press and hold the mouse's button.**

   That's the left button. Press and hold the button down — don't click! This action has the effect of picking up whatever the mouse is pointing at on the screen.

   If it's not picking something up, a drag also selects objects by drawing a rubber-band-like rectangle around them.

3. **Move the mouse to a new location.**

   The drag operation is really a *move;* you start at one point on the screen and move (drag) the whatever to another location.

4. **Release the mouse button.**

   Lift your finger off the left mouse button. You're done dragging.

   ✔ A drag has the effect of grabbing something (pressing the button) and then moving it about on the screen (dragging it). When you release the mouse button, you let go of whatever it was you were dragging.

   ✔ You can also drag to select a group of items. In this case, dragging draws a rectangle around the items you want to select.

   ✔ Dragging is used in many drawing and painting programs to create an image on the screen. In this sense, dragging is like pressing a pen tip or paintbrush to paper.

   ✔ Sometimes you may be asked to press a key while dragging, referred to as a Ctrl+drag (control-drag) or Shift+drag or some other key combination. If so, press that key — Ctrl, Shift, Alt, or whatever — *before* you first click the mouse to drag something.

Mouse hygiene: Cleaning your mouse ball

Your desk constantly collects a layer of dust and hair, especially if you have a cat around or a picture of a cat on your mouse pad. If your mouse isn't behaving the way it used to, you may need to clean its ball. It's easy; there's no need for the repair shop or a guy in a van.

Turn the mouse upside down, and you see a little round plate holding the ball in place. Push or twist the plate in the direction of the arrow that says Open. The plate should come off, and the ball rolls out.

Pull out any hair or debris from the mouse-ball hole and brush any stray offal off the ball itself. Put the ball back inside, reattach the plate, and you are on your way.

Try to keep the mouse pad clean as well: Brush it off occasionally to clear away the potato chips, drool, and other detritus that accumulates there.

Right-dragging the mouse

A right-drag is the same as a normal drag. The only difference is that you press the *right* mouse button rather than the left one.

Unless you're otherwise told to do so, all drags are left-drags.

Selecting with the mouse

Selecting is the process of highlighting something, making it the target for whatever plans you have. For example, you select a file you want to copy by first clicking its icon. You can select text by dragging the mouse pointer over the text you want. Graphics are selected by clicking them or dragging a rectangle around the area you want selected.

Selecting is the same as clicking. When the manual says to select that doohickey over there, you move the mouse pointer and click the doohickey. Simple.

To unselect something, such as when you click the wrong thing or change your mind, just click elsewhere, on the desktop, for example. That de-selects whatever object you've clicked, rendering it free to escape.

Tweaking the Mouse

If you ever give your mouse a close examination, you notice that it has no knobs or adjustable screws anywhere. Aside from its buttons, you have no way to fine-tune Mr. Mouse's movements or appearance on the screen (that is, unless you use the handy Mouse icon in the Windows Control Panel).

Lurking in the Control Panel is the Mouse icon, which opens the Mouse Properties dialog box, where you can tweak your mouse. This section describes a few handy things you can do there. Here are the general steps you take to open the Mouse icon for business:

1. **Open the Control Panel.**

   From the Start menu, choose Settings⇨Control Panel. The Control Panel's main window appears.

2. **Open the Mouse icon.**

   Mouse

   Funny how that mouse icon looks like the type of mouse Microsoft is now selling. Oh, whatever. Double-click on the Mouse icon. This action brings forth the Mouse Properties dialog box, as shown in Figure 14-3.

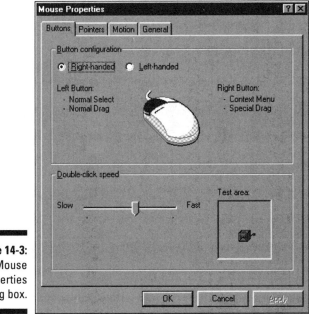

Figure 14-3:
The Mouse
Properties
dialog box.

If you have the Microsoft IntelliMouse (the wheel mouse) installed on your PC, you see a different dialog box, one with even more goodies and things to do than the boring old "I'm a stupid two-button mouse" dialog box. An example is shown in Figure 14-4.

3. **Goof around in the Mouse Properties dialog box.**

   Several subtle things are permissible in the Mouse Properties dialog box. A few of the more popular tasks are discussed in the sections that follow.

4. **Close the dialog box.**

   When you're done messing around, you have two choices: click the OK button to keep your changes, or click Cancel to return to the way things were.

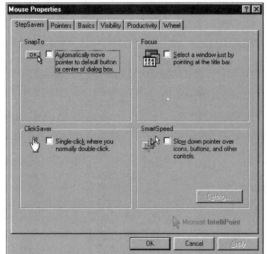

Figure 14-4:
The wheel mouse's Mouse Properties dialog box.

The Mouse Properties dialog box has several panels, each of which controls a different mousey thing. To display a particular panel, click the corresponding tab.

"My mouse pointer moves too slow/fast!"

Especially if you have a large-screen monitor, you may want to adjust the mouse's speed, making it more responsive on your large pixel real estate. Or perhaps you notice that your mouse pad isn't big enough — or too small. In any case, you can set the mouse's response time and speed by using the Mouse Properties dialog box.

Use the instructions for summoning the Mouse Properties dialog box as presented in the preceding section. Click the Motion tab to bring that panel forward. What you see looks something like Figure 14-5.

If you're using a wheel mouse, you need to click the Basics panel, which is shown in Figure 14-6.

The doojobbie in the Pointer Speed area is called a *slider*. Grab it with the mouse, and drag it left to make your mouse slower or less responsive. Drag the slider to the right to make the mouse more responsive.

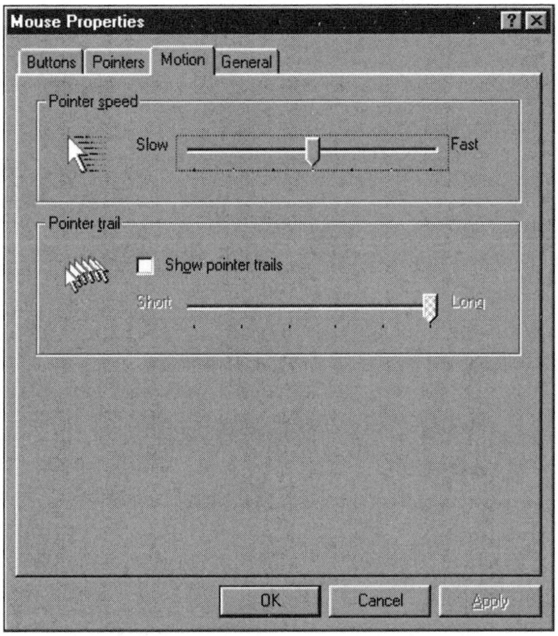

Figure 14-5:
The Mouse
Properties
dialog box,
Motion
panel
forward.

As a test: Drag the slider to the extreme direction, first one side and then the other. Test the mouse along the way by clicking the Apply button. When the pointer gets to a speed and responsiveness that delights you, click OK.

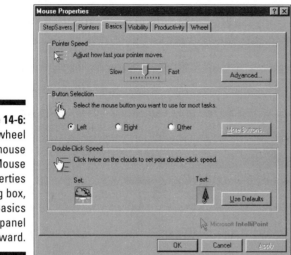

Figure 14-6:
The wheel
mouse
Mouse
Properties
dialog box,
Basics
panel
forward.

"Double-clicking doesn't work!"

If you can't seem to double-click, one of two things is happening: Either
you're moving the mouse pointer a little bit between clicks, or the double-
click *rate* is set too fast for mere human fingers to manage.

Bring forth the Mouse Properties dialog box, as discussed earlier in this
chapter.

For normal, non-wheel mice: Click the Buttons tab to bring that panel
forward. (It should look something like Figure 14-3.)

In the Double-Click Speed area is a slider. Drag the slider to the right to make
double-clicking easier. Drag the slider to the left if you keep accidentally
moving the mouse between clicks.

To test, first click the Apply button. This action resets Windows to your new
mouse specifications. Then double-click the jack-in-the-box in the Test area.
If you double-click the box and the stupid clown pops up, you have a proper
double-click speed set.

If you have the wheel mouse: Click the Basics tab (see Figure 14-6). Double-
click in the Set box (on the clouds) to set your double-click speed. Then test
your speed by clicking the umbrella in the Test box. Keep trying until you
find your speed; both the double-clicks in the Set and Test boxes must
match.

Click OK to close the Mouse Properties dialog box.

"I'd like to change the mouse pointer to something less dignified"

If you click the Pointers tab in the Mouse Properties dialog box, you see gizmos for changing the way the mouse pointer looks. I don't go into much detail here because this stuff is an obnoxious waste of time.

"My buddy has an animated mouse pointer—how do I get one?"

A ton of animated cursors are available in the Microsoft Plus! Package (both Windows 95 and Windows 98 versions). You might also find some in the same places you pick up shareware software: online or through mail-order houses.

Animated cursors are set up in the Pointers tab in the Mouse Properties dialog box. Follow these steps:

1. **Open the Mouse Properties dialog box and gander at the Pointers page (click the Pointers tab as described earlier in this chapter).**

2. **Choose the pointer you want to change.**

   That hourglass pointer sure looks dull.

3. **Click the Browse button.**

   A Browse dialog box opens. See Chapter 8 for more information on the Browse dialog box (which works like an Open dialog box).

   The Browse dialog box should be set to the folder where Windows stores all its mouse pointer things. If not, change to the \Windows\Cursors folder on your C drive.

4. **Click on a new cursor in the dialog box.**

   Some of the cursors are shown as icons. Others are just shown using the dull "I am a file" icon Windows loves so much.

5. **Preview that cursor.**

   After clicking on the cursor, look in the Preview box to see whether it's an animated cursor. Animated cursors move. (Did I need to say that?)

6. **If you don't like the cursor, repeat Steps 4 and 5.**

7. **Click Open.**

   The cursor you chose replaces the one Windows stupidly has suggested on the Pointers page of the Mouse Properties dialog box.

8. **Click OK.**

   Your change is locked in.

If you download animated cursor files or get a disk full of them from a friend, they should be saved in the Cursors folder in the Windows main folder. (The pathname is C:\Windows\Cursors.) That way they show up in the list when you choose a new pointer in the Browse dialog box.

"I'm a southpaw, and the buttons are backward!"

Hey, Lefty, if you just can't stand the idea of using a mouse in the right-hand/ left-brain-dominated world, you can switch things over — even putting the mouse on the nontraditional left-hand side of your PC keyboard. (Oh, brother. . . .)

Summon the Mouse Properties dialog box by using the instructions offered earlier in this chapter. On the Buttons panel, click the Left-handed radio button. This action mentally switches the buttons in Windows' head: The right button takes on left-button tasks and vice-versa.

For the wheel mouse, use the Basics panel (refer to Figure 14-6) rather than the Buttons panel, which you won't be able to find anyway.

✔ This book, and all manuals and computer books, assume that the left mouse button is the main button. *Right-clicks* are clicks of the right mouse button. If you tell Windows to use the left-handed mouse, these buttons are reversed. Keep in mind that your documentation will not reflect that.

✔ There is no setting for ambidextrous people, wise guy!

Mouse Woes

Mice are just the most innocent of things when it comes to terror in your computer. They really can be reliable and trustworthy, but every so often they annoy you by not working properly. The following are some common mouse-related ailments and how to fix them.

The mouse is a slug

Slow mice happen over time. Why? Who knows. Personally, I think that gunk gets inside the mouse and slows it down. Not even removing the mouse ball and cleaning it up helps. It's just gunk.

The solution here is drastic: Buy another mouse. Computer mice typically work well for two to three years. After that, for some reason, they get sluggish and jerky. Rather than pound your mouse into your desktop, just break down and buy a new one. You'll be amazed at how much better it works and how much more calmly you use the PC.

The vanishing mouse

After a terrifically productive session of managing your files, you may suddenly notice that your mouse is gone.

No! Wait, there it is!

But then it's gone again, vanishing in and out like a Cheshire cat. I have no idea why this is so.

The solution: Reset your computer. Refer to Chapter 4.

The stuck mouse

There sits the pointer, dead on the screen. You move the mouse. Nothing. You motivate the mouse with your handy repertoire of nasty epitaphs. Nothing. You slam the mouse into your desktop. Nothing. Nothing. Nothing.

A dead mouse usually means a dead computer. Sure, try to use the keyboard to make something happen: Press Ctrl+Esc to pop up the Start menu — if you can. Chances are that everything is locked up — and I don't know why — and you need to manually reset. It's one of the rare instances when you really must press the PC's Reset button or turn it off and then turn it on again. Refer to Chapter 4.

The terror of mouse droppings

The opposite of the stuck mouse is the stuck mouse pointer. This effect, called "mouse droppings," occurs when a trail of mouse pointers sticks to the screen wherever you move the pointer.

Whenever you see mouse droppings, it usually means one thing: The computer is gaga. One solution takes care of mouse droppings: Reset your PC. Refer to Chapter 4 for the details.

Don't confuse mouse droppings with mouse *trails* where the pointer has shadows that follow it around the screen. You can set this option in the Mouse Properties dialog box. Mouse trails are useful on laptop computers where spotting the mouse isn't obvious. Unlike mouse trails, mouse droppings do not disappear.

Chapter 15

Using and Abusing Your Keyboard

- -

In This Chapter

▶ Understanding the keyboard

▶ Finding important keys

▶ Locating the Any key

▶ Using the special shift keys

▶ Using your keyboard

▶ Using Windows editing keys

▶ Setting up a foreign language keyboard layout

▶ Using a Dvorak keyboard layout

▶ Soothing common keyboard woes

- -

*N*othing beats the full responsiveness of a real keyboard when the keys punch down evenly and are light to the touch, maybe even clicking loudly when you press them. Clackity-clack-clack. A loud, clicky keyboard really makes it sound like you're getting a lot of work done. (If only the mouse made noise. . . .)

> ✔ This chapter deals with everything about your keyboard, save for one key: Print Screen. Because that key has Screen in its name, refer to Chapter 13 (on PC monitors) for information on what it does (see the section, "What's a screen dump?"). Then refer to Chapter 16 for information on actually using the Print Screen key.

Knowest Thy Keyboard

Your keyboard is the direct line of communication between you and the computer. The computer has no ears. You can try yelling. You can wave your arms. But the computer hears nothing unless you type something to it on the keyboard. The typical PC keyboard is shown in Figure 15-1. The nerds call it the *enhanced 101-key keyboard*. Yes, there are 101 keys on it. You can count them yourself, if you have the time.

Function keys

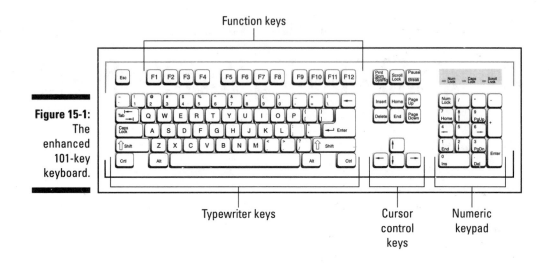

Figure 15-1:
The
enhanced
101-key
keyboard.

Typewriter keys

Cursor
control
keys

Numeric
keypad

✔ Why name a keyboard? Because older PCs used different types of keyboards with different key layouts. Hopefully, all those models are in garages or landfills by now.

✔ Most keyboards sold today have 104 keys: There are three extra "Windows" keys clustered around the spacebar. The later section "What are those weird Windows keys?" goes into detail about those keys.

Basic keyboard layout

Four main areas are mapped out on your PC's keyboard. Refer to Figure 15-1.

Typewriter keys: These keys are the normal-looking light-colored keys in the center of the keyboard. They include letters, numbers, and punctuation.

Function keys: These keys are positioned on the top row of the keyboard. They are labeled F1, F2, F3, and on up to F11 and F12.

Cursor-control keys: Often called *arrow keys,* these four keys move the text cursor in the direction of their arrows. Above them are more cursor control keys — the six pack of Insert, Delete, Home, End, PgUp, and PgDn.

Numeric keypad: Popular among bank tellers with zippy fingers, the numeric keypad contains the calculator-like keys.

- ✔ The numeric keypad has a split personality. Sometimes it's used to generate numbers, other times it duplicates the cursor keys. See the section "The keys of state" later in this chapter for more information on this duplicity.

- ✔ The keys labeled F1, F2, and so on, are called *function keys.*

- ✔ The original PC's keyboard lacked the F11 and F12 keys. This isn't a shame since few programs use those keys anyway.

- ✔ The cursor-control keys are used to move the text cursor around, which typically looks like a blinking toothpick when you type or edit text in Windows. The mouse pointer is often called the cursor, although the cursor keys don't move it around.

- ✔ The PgUp and PgDn keys stand for Page Up and Page Down. The labels on the key caps may be fully spelled out or abbreviated.

- ✔ Insert and Delete are editing keys, often used with the cursor keys.

- ✔ The Print Screen key may also be labeled PrtScr or Print Scrn.

So where is the Any key?

Nothing is more frustrating than hunting down that elusive *Any* key. After all, the screen says, `Press any key to continue`. So where is it?

Any key refers to, literally, any key on your keyboard. But why beat around the bush?: When it says to press the Any key, press the spacebar.

- ✔ If you can't find the spacebar, or you think it's the place where you order drinks on the Starship Enterprise, press the Enter key.

- ✔ So why do they say "Press any key" instead of saying "Press the spacebar to continue"? I guess it's because they want to make things *easy* for you by giving you the whole keyboard to choose from. And if that's really the case, why not just break down and say, "Slap your keyboard a few times with your open palms to continue"?

Where is the Help key?

There is no key labeled Help. There is one on a Macintosh keyboard, but this is *PCs For Dummies*, not *Macs For Dummies*. Mac Dummies are all fun. We're all-business, remember?

Whenever you need help in Windows, whack the F1 key. F1 equals help — no way to commit that to memory. However, I've included a little fake key cap cover on this book's Cheat Sheet. Clip it out and paste it over the F1 key on your keyboard. That way, you have a handy Help key, just like those Macintosh jokers.

Know your ones and zeros

On a typewriter, the lowercase letter L and the number 1 are often the same. In fact, I remember my old Royal upright lacked a 1 key altogether. Unfortunately, on a computer there is a big difference between a one and a little L.

If you're typing 1,001, for example, don't type l,00l by mistake — especially when working with a spreadsheet. The computer will gag.

The same holds true for the uppercase letter O and the number 0. They're different. Use a zero for numbers and a big O for big O things.

On some computer screens, you can tell the difference between zero and O because the zero often has a slash through it, like this: I am a Ø and I am an O. On newer computers, the O just looks like a O.

What are those weird Windows keys?

Most newer PC keyboards sport three new keys: the Windows key, the Shortcut Menu key, and another Windows key. They sit between the Alt and Ctrl keys on either side of the Spacebar (see Figure 15-2).

Figure 15-2:
Those
weird
Windows
keys.

 The Windows key serves the same purpose as pressing Ctrl+Esc; it pops up the Start menu thing. It's also used for a few quick shortcuts: Win+E starts the Windows Explorer; Win+F pops up the Find dialog box; Win+R pops up the Run dialog box; and a few others not worth mentioning.

The Shortcut Menu key displays the shortcut menu for whatever item is currently selected on the screen. This is the same as right-clicking the mouse on something.

I don't know of anyone who swears by these keys, and I've only used them just to see what they do so I could write about it here.

"Must I learn to type to use a computer?"

No one needs to learn to type to use a computer. Plenty of computer users hunt and peck. In fact, most programmers don't know how to type; they sit all hunched over the keyboard and punch in enigmatic computer languages using greasy, garlic-and-herb potato-chip-smeared fingers. But that's not being very productive.

As a bonus to owning a computer, you can have it teach you how to type. The Mavis

Beacon Teaches Typing software package will do just that. Other packages are available, but I personally love the name Mavis Beacon.

Trivia: A computer software developer once halted all development and had his programmers sit down and learn how to touch type. It took two weeks, but afterwards they all got their work done a lot faster and had more time available to break away and play Quake.

The keys of state (or keys to change the keyboard's mood)

Several keys affect the way the keyboard behaves. I call them the keys of state. They are Shift, Caps Lock, Num Lock, and Scroll Lock.

Shift: No surprises here. The Shift key works just like it does on the typewriter. Hold it down to make capital letters. By pressing the Shift key, you also can create the %@#^ characters that come in handy for cussing in comic strips. When you release the Shift key, everything returns to normal, just like a typewriter.

Caps Lock: This key works like holding down the Shift key, but it only produces capital letters; it does not shift the other keys as a typewriter's Shift Lock key would do. (See the sidebar "The Caps Lock key doesn't work exactly like the typewriter's Shift Lock key" for more information.) Press Caps Lock again, and the letters return to their normal lowercase state.

Num Lock: Pressing this key makes the numeric keypad on the right side of the keyboard produce numbers. Press this key again, and you can use the numeric keypad for moving the text cursor around on the screen.

Scroll Lock: This key has no purpose in life. I've seen some old DOS spreadsheet programs use it. When Scroll Lock was pressed, the arrow keys moved the whole spreadsheet around, as opposed to moving a cell highlight. Scroll Lock does little else important or famous.

For math whizzes only
(like any would be reading this book)

Clustered around the numeric keypad, like campers roasting marshmallows around a fire, are various keys to help you work with numbers. Especially if you're dabbling with a spreadsheet or other number-crunching software, you'll find these keys come in handy. Take a look at your keyboard's numeric keypad right now just to reassure yourself.

What? You were expecting a ×_or ÷ key? Forget it! This is a computer. It uses special oddball symbols for mathematical operations:

✔ + is for addition

✔ – is for subtraction

✔ * is for multiplication

✔ / is for division

The only strange symbol here is the asterisk for multiplication. Don't use the little X! It's not the same thing. The / (slash) is okay for division, but don't waste your time hunting for the ÷ symbol. It's not there.

✔ The Caps Lock, Num Lock, and Scroll Lock keys have lights. When the light is on, the key's feature is turned on.

✔ On some computers the Num Lock is already on when the computer starts. Annoying, huh?

✔ When Num Lock is on, the numeric keypad produces numbers. Remember that fact when you use your spreadsheet. Otherwise, those numbers you thought you just typed in actually move the cell highlighter all over creation.

Various and sundry shift-like keys

You produce an uppercase S by pressing Shift+S, though no one needs to say "press Shift+S" because most typewriter-using people know that it works that way. But computer keyboards have two other shift keys to drive you nuts: Alt and Ctrl. Why? The answer is *pure greed*.

Like the Shift key, the Ctrl and Alt keys are never used by themselves. Instead, they give new meaning to a second key.

Alt: The Alt key is used like the Shift key. For example, holding down the Alt key and pressing the F4 key (referred to as "pressing Alt+F4") closes a window on the desktop. You press and hold the Alt key, tap the F4 key, and then release both keys.

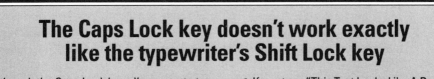

The Caps Lock key doesn't work exactly like the typewriter's Shift Lock key

Although the Caps Lock key allows you to type all-capital letters, it's not just like the typewriter's Shift Lock key. Here are the key [sic] differences:

✔ The Caps Lock key only affects letters; it doesn't affect any other keys.

✔ The Caps Lock key doesn't affect any punctuation marks.

✔ If you type "This Text Looks Like A Ransom Note" and it looks like "tHIS tEXT lOOKS lIKE a rANSOM nOTE," the Caps Lock key is inadvertently turned on. Press it once to turn it off.

✔ If you press the Shift key while Caps Lock is on, the letter keys return to normal. (Shift kind of cancels out Caps Lock.)

Ctrl: The Control key, abbreviated as Ctrl, is also used like the Shift key. In most Windows programs, if you hold down the Ctrl key and press S (press Ctrl+S, in other words), you save something. Likewise, in most programs, you press Ctrl+P to print (and so on for each clever letter of the alphabet).

✔ Even though you may see Ctrl+S or Alt+S with a capital S, this doesn't mean you must type Ctrl+Shift+S or Alt+Shift+S. The S is simply written in uppercase since "Ctrl+s" looks like a typesetting error.

✔ Don't be surprised if these shift keys are used in combination with each other. I've seen Shift+Ctrl+C and Ctrl+Alt. You use Ctrl+Esc to pop up the Start menu. Just remember to press and hold the shift keys first, and then tap the letter key. Release all the keys together.

✔ Some manuals use the term ^Y rather than Ctrl+Y. They mean the same thing: Hold down the Ctrl key, press Y, and release the Ctrl key.

✔ Okay, I lied. With some programs, you do press the Alt key by itself. For example, you can press the Alt key to activate the menu bar in a Windows program. You can also press the Ctrl key by itself to switch off the Windows screen saver.

Enter and Return, the evil twin keys

Nearly all PC computer keyboards have two keys labeled Enter. Both keys work identically, with the second Enter key placed by the numeric keypad to facilitate rapid entry of numbers.

So what is the Return key? Many early computers sported a Return key. Essentially, it's the same thing as the Enter key. (Macintosh keyboards have both an Enter and a Return key.)

I mention the differences here because I just saw a manual the other day that said to "press Return." There is no Return key! Press the Enter key when some dopey manual suggests that you press Return. (Or just go out and buy a Macintosh and press the Return key on that keyboard when the PC manual says "press Return.")

✔ Pressing the Enter key is the same as clicking OK in a dialog box.

✔ In your word processor, only press Enter at the end of a paragraph.

✔ Don't press Enter after filling in a text box inside a dialog box. Use the Tab key to move from text box to text box. This rule also applies when using some database programs; use the Tab key to skip merrily between the fields. La, la, la.

✔ The difference between Enter and Return is only semantic. Enter has its roots in the electronic calculator industry. You pressed Enter to enter numbers or a formula. Return, on the other hand, comes from the electronic typewriter. Pressing Return on a typewriter caused the carriage to return to the left margin. It also advanced the paper one line.

The Tab key

Like on a typewriter, pressing Tab moves the cursor over to the next tab stop, though on some computers pressing Tab causes the computer to produce a can of a refreshing diet beverage.

✔ To confuse matters, the Tab key sometimes isn't labeled Tab. Instead, it has two arrows on it — one pointing left and the other right. Weird stuff.

✔ The computer treats a tab as a single, separate character. When you backspace over a tab in a word processing program, the tab disappears completely in one chunk — not space by space.

✔ One calorie more than water.

✔ Use the Tab key to indent paragraphs; don't press the spacebar five times. You'll thank yourself later when your word processing program doesn't mangle paragraphs. (Or at least it gives your word processor one less way to mangle paragraphs.)

The mystery of the slash and backslash keys

Two slash keys are on your keyboard, and you can easily be confused.

The forward slash (/) leans forward (duh!), like it's falling to the right. This slash is primarily used to denote division, such as 52/13 (52 divided by 13). In English, it's used to divide various words or, most often, as an incorrect replacement for a hyphen.

The backslash (\) leans to the left. This character is used in *pathnames,* which are complex and discussed only near the end of Chapter 8, where no one can find them.

Don't confuse the two! If you do, the computer will become anxious, and it may leave a grease stain on your desktop.

The "Knock it off!" keys

Three "Hey! Stop that!" keys are on your PC's keyboard. Only one of them works in Windows; the other two are holdovers from DOS and don't work in Windows (though feel free to try).

Esc: The Escape key, labeled Esc on most keyboards, is supposed to enable you to escape from your current situation and seek higher ground. For example, if you don't like the dialog box in Windows, press Esc and it's gone. Esc can be a good pinch hitter to try first when something goes awry.

Break: By itself, the Break key does nothing. But when you hold down the Ctrl key and press the Break key (Ctrl+Break), you can often break DOS's fascination with itself and get back to something constructive. This key combination is useless in Windows.

The secret behind the SysRq key

Simply pretend that the SysRq key isn't there. Don't mess with it. Windows doesn't use it. DOS never did.

IBM added the SysRq key to the keyboard many years ago to be used in a future version of DOS. Everyone is still waiting. So, although the SysRq key has kind of a cool name, it never really amounted to anything. Feel free to press it whenever you don't want to do anything. (It's Ctrl+Print Screen on your keyboard.)

Oh: SysRq stands for System Request, in case you were wondering.

Ctrl+C: This key combination was DOS's hand brake. If you ever bother to fire up a DOS prompt window, you can use Ctrl+C to stop DOS from doing just about anything. (If not, try Ctrl+Break.)

 ✔ You may notice that your keyboard has no true Break key. That key is often disguised as the Scroll Lock or Pause key. The word Break may be on the front, below a line, in a different color, or written in Hebrew.

 ✔ Why is the key called Break? Why not call it the Brake key? Wouldn't that make sense? Who wants a computer to break, anyway? Golly.

Don't bother with the Pause key

Honestly, the Pause key doesn't work in Windows. In DOS, it would pause output. So if you were displaying a long file on the screen, you could press the Pause key and everything would stop. After you read a few lines, you could press the Pause key again, and everything would start up again. This process isn't necessary in Windows.

Pause does have a cousin of sorts. The Ctrl+S key combination is also used to freeze information, suspending it as it's displayed on the screen. Even so, about the only time you can use Ctrl+S is when you're online with your modem and some remote system is sending you text. Then it's okay to press Ctrl+S to pause the display. Press Ctrl+Q to get the text started again.

 ✔ I suppose Bill Gates is trying to tell us that there's no stopping Windows.

 ✔ The Pause key may also be labeled Hold on some keyboards.

 ✔ Ctrl+S pauses text.

 ✔ Ctrl+Q resumes text.

Common Windows Editing Keys

Almost any time text is selected in Windows it can be edited. For that task, you need to know only one set of editing keys — the Windows editing keys. These keys are pretty easy to understand — at least compared with the ugly old WordStar cursor key diamond. I shudder at the thought. . . .

Enough shuddering! Table 15-1 lists the key commands used whenever text is selected in Windows.

Table 15-1	Windows Editing Key Commands
Key	**Function**
←	Moves the text cursor left (back) one character
→	Moves the text cursor right (forward) one character
Ctrl+←	Moves the text cursor left one word
Ctrl+→	Moves the text cursor right one word
Home	Moves the text cursor to the start of the line
End	Moves the text cursor to the end of the line
Delete	Deletes current character
Backspace	Deletes preceding character
↑	Moves the text cursor up one line
↓	Moves the text cursor down one line
PgUp	Moves the text cursor up to the preceding page (screen)
PgDn	Moves the text cursor down to the next page (screen)
Ctrl+↑	Moves the text cursor to the preceding paragraph
Ctrl+↓	Moves the text cursor to the next paragraph
Ctrl+Delete	Deletes from the cursor's position to the end of the line

Oui! Oui! Je veux taper en français!

You have a computer in your hands, and it's capable of just about anything. One of its magic tricks is the Chameleon Keyboard. By using the Windows Control Panel, you can tweak Mr. Keyboard into behaving like a keyboard in a downtown Paris café — minus the Marxists.

To type in a different language, follow these steps:

1. Open the Control Panel.

From the handy Start menu, choose Settings⇨Control Panel. This summons the Control Panel's main window.

2. Open the Keyboard icon.

Keyboard

Double-click on the Keyboard icon to open it. The Keyboard Properties dialog box is displayed.

3. Click on the Language **tab to bring that panel forward.**

You'll see the Language panel, as shown in Figure 15-3.

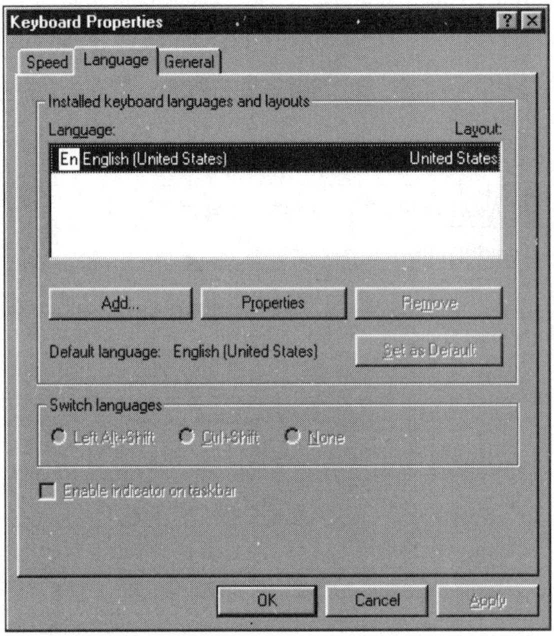

Figure 15-3:
The
Keyboard
Properties
dialog box.

4. Click the Add **button.**

The Add Language dialog box is displayed.

5. Choose your language from the drop-down list.

There are quite a few languages to choose from, including some I've never heard of before. There are *five* variations of French to choose from, *nine* variations of English. No Klingon, though.

Choose your language. Click the OK button.

6. Meanwhile, back in the Keyboard Properties dialog box. . . .

The second language has been added to the list. Pay special attention to the Switch languages area of the dialog box. That area tells you which keys you use to switch between various keyboard languages.

For example, press the Left Alt+Shift keys together to switch from one keyboard language layout to another. Or if you'd rather use the Ctrl+Shift key combination, click on that radio button instead.

7. Close the dialog box.

Click the OK button.

At this time, Windows may beg for its installation disks or CD-ROM disc. You have to put the proper disk into the drive to complete the operation. You may even have to reset the computer.

✔ Alas, these steps merely switch your keyboard over to a different language *layout*. Your words won't magically appear in a foreign tongue.

✔ You can switch between the normal keyboard and the foreign language keyboard by pressing the left Alt and Shift keys together. A small, boring, two-letter indicator in the system tray (on the right side of the taskbar) tells you which keyboard layout is active.

✔ I have no idea where Microsoft is hiding the list of the keyboard layouts. They used to be in the Windows manual, but not anymore. Anyway, the keyboard layouts show you which new, funky keys are where. This is strange if you're just messing around, but if you seriously need to type in another language, it's incredibly handy.

What about Dvorak's Keyboard?

The first typewriters were piano-sized beasts with a few mechanical problems. If anybody typed faster than ten words a minute, the keys jammed.

To slow people down, the designers made the typewriter's keyboard as awkward as possible. They placed the most common keys along the outside edges of the keyboard, forcing a typist's fingers to move as far as possible. All the extra finger work slowed people down; nobody could jam the keys, and the repair people were happy.

✔ This antique key arrangement you have on your keyboard right now in the last moments of the twentieth century, is called *QWERTY* because the Q, W, E, R, T, and Y keys all sit along the top row, from left to right.

✔ No one ever thinks about this, but the keys on your PC's keyboard don't need to be staggered as they are on a typewriter. This is just more fluff to fill your brain.

Then along came Dvorak

By the 1930s, the engineers had the typewriter mechanics down pat. They didn't have to slow anybody down anymore. So a guy named August Dvorak designed a new keyboard layout.

Dvorak's new keyboard layout placed the most-commonly-used keys directly underneath the right hand so that it could do most of the work (see Figure 15-4). The other common keys appeared directly under the left hand's fingers. No more finger stretches!

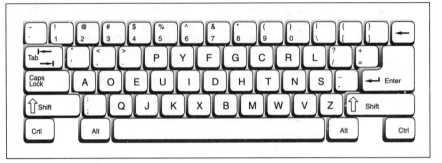

Figure 15-4:
The Dvorak
keyboard
layout.

✔ With Dvorak's layout, people could type much faster and with less finger strain.

✔ No, the Dvorak keyboard doesn't spell DVORAK like the QWERTY keyboard spells QWERTY. And August Dvorak is a cousin of the famous musical composer Antonin Dvořák. Also, nobody knows this, but Alfred Nobel invented plywood as well as dynamite.

✔ Although the general public has given up its 8-tracks for CDs and beta-maxes for VHS, few people want to give up their old keyboard for a new, more efficient layout.

Hey! I want to try this Dvorak thing!

If you're up for it, you can tell Windows to reconfigure your keyboard in the Dvorak layout. In the Language panel of the Keyboard Properties dialog box, (refer to Figure 15-3), find the Language list and click on English. Then click the Properties button. The Language Properties dialog box appears (see Figure 15-5).

Figure 15-5:
The
Language
Properties
dialog box.

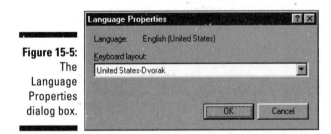

Locate `United States-Dvorak` in the drop-down list. Click `OK` to close the Language Properties dialog box. Then click `OK` to close the Keyboard Properties dialog box. You may be asked to insert your Windows distribution diskettes or CD-ROM disc. Do so.

When the operation is complete, Windows has programmed a new keyboard for you. You have to relearn your typing skills, as well as move around the key caps. Or you can buy a new Dvorak keyboard from a mail-order outfit.

Figure 15-4 shows you the new layout.

- ✔ If you decide to learn the Dvorak keyboard, be sure to learn the QWERTY method, too, or you'll be lost when trying to use keyboards at libraries and offices (or any of the 99 percent of all keyboards you encounter).

- ✔ Unless you buy a Dvorak keyboard, the keys on your PC's keyboard will still resemble QWERTY. You can try prying up the keycaps and re-arranging them ala Figure 15-4. The publisher and myself cannot be held accountable if this doesn't work.

- ✔ Unlike a foreign language keyboard layout, there is no handy key combination to switch between Dvorak and QWERTY. Heck, man, if you're gonna commit, commit.

- ✔ To restore your original keyboard, go through the steps described earlier in this section, but choose `United States` from the list.

- ✔ There is a Mavis Beacon Teaches Typing Dvorak Style. It's included with the regular Mavis Beacon package discussed in the sidebar "Must I learn to type to use a computer?" earlier in this chapter.

The Keyboard Follies

Keyboards aren't without their sticking points — and I don't mean what happens when you spill a cola in there. The following sections mull over some of the more trying times you may have with your PC keyboard.

"My keyboard beeps at me!"

Common problem. Many potential causes and cures.

Reason 1: You can't type anything! Whatever program you're using doesn't want you to type or expects you to be pressing some other key. Remember that in Windows you can only use one window at a time — even if you're looking at another window.

Reason 2: You're typing too fast. The PC's keyboard can only swallow so many keys at once. When its li'l stomach is full, it starts beeping at you until it can digest.

Reason 3: The computer is dead! Refer to Chapter 5 for information on resetting.

Keyboard templates

When trying to remember which key does what, many people put sticky notes on their keyboards. Entrepreneurs, recognizing a new market, created keyboard templates. A *keyboard template* is a piece of cardboard or plastic that fits around the keyboard. The keys stick up snugly from holes cut strategically through the middle.

The template contains a description of each key's function, conveniently placed next to each key.

✔ Because key commands change with each program, you need a different template for each program you use.

✔ No one on this planet ever learned how to use WordPerfect's 48-odd function key combinations without a keyboard template.

✔ Depending on templates can be dangerous, especially when the cleaning crew accidentally throws yours away, leaving you with no clues on how to operate your computer. Make a backup version by using the copy machine and a pair of scissors, and keep it in a safe place.

"Oops! I just spilled java into the keyboard!"

Sooner or later, you'll spill something gross into the keyboard. The grossest liquids are thick or sugary: soft drinks, fruit juice, cheap sherry, or St. Bernard drool (not sugary, but thick). These things can seriously damage the keyboard. Here's what to do:

1. **Pick up the glass or push the St. Bernard out of the way.**

2. **Save your work (if the keyboard is still functional), turn off the computer, and unplug the keyboard.**

3. **Turn the keyboard upside down and give it a few good shakes (away from your co-workers' keyboards, if possible).**

4. **Use a sponge to sop up as much stuff as possible and then just let the keyboard dry out.**

   It usually takes about 24 hours.

✔ Surprisingly enough, the keyboard will probably still work, especially if there wasn't much sugar in the beverage.

✔ Unfortunately, spilling something in a keyboard probably cuts its life expectancy in half. The dried gunk beneath the keys attracts dust and grime, making the keyboard get dirty much more quickly than normal.

✔ If you find the keys stickkkkkking when you try to type, compare the cost of a new keyboard with the cost of having the old one professionally cleaned.

✔ Keyboards are very delicate; if your keyboard doesn't work after taking the above steps, then it's probably dead.

✔ Some companies sell plastic keyboard covers. These covers are custom fitted to the keyboard and work well. Smokers, especially, should consider purchasing one. (A simple sheet of plastic wrap works almost equally well, but research shows that it lasts no longer than a few days.)

"Ouch! My wrists hurt!"

Several years back, the *New England Journal of Medicine* published an article documenting "Space Invaders Wrist," a soreness caused by rapid hand movements at the controls of the Space Invaders arcade game.

Because typists move their fingers at a similarly rapid rate, they're subject to the same muscle soreness. In fact, U.S. Labor Department statistics show that a typist's fingers move farther in an hour than the fingers of every nose-picking commuter driving on the freeways right now.

Because of the strain, many typists suffer from Carpal Tunnel Syndrome (also called RSI, or repetitive stress injury), a soreness caused when muscles rub against each other in a small wrist passage called the Carpal Tunnel (the names Lincoln Tunnel and Holland Tunnel are already copyrighted by the State of New York). Some victims wear expensive, reinforced gloves that, if they don't actually help alleviate the pain, at least draw sympathetic stares from onlookers.

Whether you have carpal tunnel or RSI or your wrists are as limber as rubber tree plants, you may want to consider an *ergonomic* keyboard. That type of keyboard is specially designed at an angle to relieve the stress of typing for long or short periods. Although ergonomic keyboards cost a little more than standard keyboards, they are well worth the investment if you type for long hours — or if you at least want to look like you type for long hours.

✔ A chair's seat and backrest should support a comfortable posture — choose a chair that can be adjusted to your own preference. When your hands are resting on the keyboard, the upper arm and forearm should form a right angle, with the hands extending in a reasonably straight line from the forearm. Your eyes should also be level with the monitor so that your neck doesn't tilt. Figure 15-6 illustrates the correct and incorrect ways to sit at a computer.

✔ Many keyboards come with adjustable legs underneath for positioning the keys to a comfortable angle.

✔ If you can't adjust your desk or keyboard to the right height, buy a chair that can be adjusted up or down, or have your building supervisor install hydraulic lifts in the basement.

✔ Try using a palm or wrist pad. These foam or rubber devices rest in front of the keyboard and support the palms while you're typing.

✔ Hire Mrs. Grimwold, my old piano teacher, to walk around the office and whack people's sagging wrists with a ruler.

Figure 15-6:
How to sit
at a
computer.

Eyes level
with monitor

Wrist level
with keyboard

Correct   Incorrect

Chapter 16

The Printer, the Paper, the Document Maker

• •

• •

*O*ne technology that's really changed over the past dozen years is computer printers. No one makes a big fuss over the advancements, probably because printers lack the flash of a fancy monitor or the thrill of a faster microprocessor. Yet, compared with the pricey clunkers of yesterday, with their horrid "dot matrix" output, a computer printer today is a quiet deal worth screaming over.

This chapter gives you a crash introduction to the glamorous world of computer printers. Well, maybe not glamorous, but you get the idea.

Welcome to Printerland

Forget brand names and all the technical mumblings for a moment. Two major types of printers are popular: *ink* and *laser*. Sounds like a 21st century tattoo parlor, huh? The differences between the two types of printers are basic: the quality of the image and the price.

Ink printers are considered the "low end," even though their quality and sophistication is higher than top-end printers of just a few years ago. Ink printers are primarily color printers, capable of producing near-photographic output, and their price range makes them handy for everyone to have and use.

Laser printers are generally more expensive than ink printers, and a wee bit faster. Most expensive brands can print in color, but for the most part a laser printer remains the workhorse printer for most office environments.

A third type of printer is the impact printer. These printers are rarely found anymore, though the dot matrix and "daisy wheel" impact printers of the 1980s were once the most popular printers sold. Today they're used primarily for printing multipart forms, since their impact mechanism can press through carbon paper.

Impact printers produce lower-quality images and are relatively inexpensive. They are ideal when quality and speed don't count, such as for the home or in the government.

✔ Impact printers are also called *dot matrix* printers. The name refers to the grid of dots used to create the image. On the really cheap printers, this shows up annoyingly well.

✔ An older type of impact printer was the *daisy wheel*. This printer is essentially an electronic typewriter, and it produces similar output — but no graphics. The laser printer has replaced the daisy wheel as the printer of choice in business today.

✔ Popular with laptops a few years back were little *thermal* printers. Like some older-model fax machines, thermal printers print with heat on waxy paper. These printers were replaced by small ink printers just a few years back.

✔ Three important switches on the front of your printer (or on its control panel, wherever that may be) are the On-Line or Select switch, plus the Form Feed and Line Feed switches. The functions of these switches are covered later in this chapter.

The printer produces hard copy. That's anything you do on your computer screen that eventually winds up on paper.

What is PostScript?

A PostScript printer isn't a name-brand printer. It's more like a type of printer. PostScript printers — no matter who makes them — can work with all applications that support the PostScript printing language. This makes them a universal type of printer.

PostScript is actually a printing *language* — like a programming language — that tells the printer exactly what to do, what to print, and how to make it look. The printing language can be very precise, which is why many printers support it and most applications can customize their output for a PostScript printer.

All Apple (Macintosh) laser printers use PostScript (at least the expensive, good ones do). On the PC side, you really need a PostScript printer only if your applications output PostScript documents. In that case, your final hard copy may look better, but since those applications can also print well on a non-PostScript printer, the point is rather moot.

One last thing: PostScript printers are expensive. That's probably why no one buys them, at least not on the PC side of the computer planet.

Examining Your Printer's Control Panel

Every printer has a control panel. The newer models have LCD screens that display lots of text: Printer jammed; I'm out of paper; That's plagiarism; and so on. My first printer had three buttons on it, plus a sliding switch. And some printers have only an on-off and paper-eject button. Whatever, look at your printer's panel now.

First, locate two things on the panel:

- The on-line or select button
- The form feed button

My inkjet printer has only two buttons, on-line and form feed. Your printer may be likewise logically labeled.

Some laser printers may have an on-line button, but no form feed button. In that case, you need to refer to your printer's manual for information on doing a form-feed, which involves choosing a menu item or pressing a combination of keys somehow.

The purpose of the on-line or select button is to tell your printer whether or not to ignore the computer. When the printer is off-line or deselected, the computer can't print. You would take the printer off-line if, for example, you had to un-jam it or if you wanted to eject a page of paper.

Only when the printer is on-line or selected can the computer print.

The form feed button is often necessary to eject a page of paper from the printer. Although I can't think of any specific instances when you'd need to do that, I know I've had to write about it enough that it's not a once-in-a-blue-moon type of activity.

Gutenberg Never Had It This Rough (Setting Up Your Printer)

This is the easy part: To set up your printer, you just plug it into your PC. Simple enough.

First, unpack your printer. This is covered in Chapter 2, so I assume you're coming here from there, otherwise *you're reading the book in the wrong order!*

1. **Start by turning your computer off. Make sure that the printer's off, too.**

2. **Plug one end of the printer cable into the printer port on the back of your PC's console.**

   Specifically, you find a connection called the printer port on the rear of the PC console. It may be labeled as such or dubbed "LPT1." Plug the other end of the cable into the printer. (If you get good at this, you can charge your friends 50 bucks to perform the same feat for them.)

3. **You also need to plug the printer into a grounded wall socket.**

There. You're done with that part. Read on to find out what additional challenges await in this exciting process.

- ✔ The PC's printer port is also called a *parallel port*.

- ✔ There may be more than one printer port on your PC, in which case they're referred to as LPT1, LPT2, or even LPT3.

- ✔ If you have more than one printer port, plug your printer into LPT1, the first printer port.

- ✔ LPT is an IBM term. It stands for Line PrinTer.

✔ A single computer is capable of handling two printers, but you must have a terribly big ego to be that possessive.

✔ If you're using a printer on a network, then the printer doesn't need to be plugged into your PC at all. You access that printer through your PC's network hose. More on network printing later in this chapter.

Loading it with paper

Your printer needs to be loaded with paper. The days of printing on thin air and reusable fiberglass paper are still in the future.

Both ink and laser printers load up using sheets of paper, similar to photocopier paper. (The old impact printers used continuous fanfold paper.)

For ink printers, load up the paper in the tray, either near the printer's bottom or sticking out the top.

Laser printers require you to fill a cartridge with paper, similar to the way a copy machine works. Slide the cartridge all the way into the printer after it's loaded up.

✔ Always make sure that you have enough printer paper.

✔ You can buy standard photocopier paper for your laser printer.

✔ Some ink printers require a special paper to get the best image. This paper is horribly expensive, so buy it in bulk. Avoid thin weight (under 20 lb.) paper since the ink bleeds through it like an uncapped pen in a shirt pocket.

✔ For about $1.40 a sheet you can get photographic quality paper for your ink printer. Some of the output looks very, very nice, but the paper is expensive.

✔ Avoid using erasable bond and other fancy "dusted" papers in your laser printer. Those papers have talcum powder coatings that come off in your laser printer and gum up the works.

✔ *Fanfold paper* is a continuous piece of paper that snakes into an impact printer. This paper must be manually separated after you print on it: You tear off each sheet at the perforation, as well as the "holes" on the sides of the paper. You can't put fanfold paper into a laser printer, but you can sit around all day and argue about what the little holes are called.

Loading it with ink (or the ink substance)

Your printer is like a banker. The banker takes your money and sticks it in a vault (or dumps it into shoddy real estate deals with powerful politicos). Your printer takes ink from some sort of storage device and transfers it onto the paper's real estate.

Inkjet printers use little ink cartridges, which are surprisingly easy to change. Just be careful with the old, used canisters, which may be inky on the bottom. I put mine in a sealable plastic baggie and dispose of them according to proper EPA hazardous ink waste disposal procedures.

Laser printers require drop-in toner cartridges. These are easy to install and come with their own handy instructions. Just don't inhale deeply near the toner or you'll die. Some manufacturers sell their cartridges with return envelopes so that you can send the old cartridge back to the factory for recycling or proper disposal.

✔ I suggest buying rubber gloves (or those cheap plastic gloves that make you look like a superhero cartoon character) and using them when changing a ribbon or toner cartridge.

✔ The old impact printers required ribbons. Gadzooks! I remember getting my hands all inky changing a printer's ribbon — even when it came in a cartridge. Thank goodness those days are over.

✔ Another option for an old toner cartridge is recharging. You can take it to a special place that will clean the old cartridge and refill it with toner. This actually works and is often cheaper than buying a whole new cartridge.

✔ In this book's previous edition, I remarked that you should only recharge a used laser toner cartridge once. However, a reader who runs such a company has reassured me that today's modern toner recharging methods allow one cartridge to be reused several times. I hope that he's right. At $120 for a new cartridge, recharging is a handy and inexpensive option.

Telling Windows about Your Printer

Windows may be smart when it comes to adding Plug-n-Play expansion cards or a USB thingamabob, but the Plug-n-Play printer is still a few light-years away. You must set up a printer deliberately.

Most likely, you configured Windows to work with your printer when you first brought your Windows PC home. One of the setup questions you answered was, "Which printer are you using?" and you, or someone else, followed the steps and chose the proper printer. No sweat.

If you just bought a new printer, however, you need to set that one up manually. Connect your printer to the PC (if you haven't already). Make sure that your printer is on, loaded with paper, and ready to print. Then tell Windows all about your printer by heeding these steps:

1. **Double-click the My Computer icon on your desktop to display a window chock-full of your PC's disk drives, plus a few weird folders.**

   One of those weird folders is named Printers.

Printers

2. **Double-click the Printers folder icon.**

   A window appears listing all the printers you already have connected to your PC, network printers, plus a special Add Printer icon.

Add Printer

3. **Double-click the Add Printer icon.**

   Look, Ma! It's the Add Printer Wizard!

4. **Click the Next button.**

5. **If you're not setting up a network printer, click the Next button.**

   If you are setting up a network printer, click Network printer, and then click the Next button.

6. **Describe your printer's make and model to Windows.**

   Using the dialog box (shown in Figure 16-1), click on your printer's manufacturer and then pluck out the model number.

Figure 16-1:
Choose
your
printer's
make and
model from
this dialog
box.

Add Printer Wizard

Click the manufacturer and model of your printer. If your printer came with an installation disk, click Have Disk. If your printer is not listed, consult your printer documentation for a compatible printer.

Manufacturers:
| Hermes |
| HP |
| IBM/Lexmark |
| Kodak |
| Kyocera |
| Linotronic |
| Mannesmann |

Printers:
| HP LaserJet 4Si |
| HP LaserJet 4Si MX |
| HP LaserJet 4Si/4SiMX PS |
| HP LaserJet 4V |
| HP LaserJet 4MV |
| HP LaserJet 4V/4MV PostScript |
| HP LaserJet 5P |

Have Disk...

< Back   Next >   Cancel

If your printer isn't listed, you need a special installation disk that (hopefully) came with the printer. If so, click the Have Disk button and browse for the disk using the Open dialog box techniques described in Chapter 8.

7. Click the Next button.

8. Pick the printer port from the list.

It will probably be LPT1, your first printer port.

9. Click the Next button.

10. Click the Next button again.

11. Click Finish.

You're done.

You can print a test page on your printer if you like. Personally, I'm shocked that the test page isn't a catalog and order form for Microsoft products. But the test ensures that your printer is connected properly and everything is up to snuff.

> ✔ Unlike DOS, where you had to install your printer for every stinkin' application, you only need go through these steps once in Windows. I know this means nothing to you, so just close your eyes for a moment and say a little prayer, "Thank you, O Most High, for saving me from the horrors of setting up a printer in DOS. Amen."
>
> ✔ Network printer? Let someone else set that thing up.

Basic Printer Operation

Here are the steps required to turn your printer on:

1. Flip the switch.

And now for a few more insights:

> ✔ Always make sure that your printer is on before you start printing. Like, duh.
>
> ✔ Your laser printer doesn't need to be on all the time. Inkjets, leave 'em on all the time since they don't use much power. But laser printers suck down power like a black hole absorbs light. Only turn on your laser printer while you're printing. When you're done, you can turn the printer off.

✔ An exception to the on-while-printing rule is for Energy Star laser printers. Energy Star means that the printer will run in a low-power mode while it's not working. You can leave those suckers on all the time if you like. I do.

Printing something, anything

Under Windows, printing is a snap. All applications support the same print command: Choose File➪Print from the menu, click OK in the Print dialog box, and — zit-zit-zit — you soon have hard copy. This is why Chairman Bill (as in Gates) bestowed Windows upon the masses.

✔ The common keyboard shortcut for the print command is Ctrl+P. This is true for all Windows 95-specific programs; some older Windows programs may use a different key combination.

✔ Always save your stuff before you print. Not that anything bad may happen; it's just a good idea to save.

✔ Many applications sport a Print toolbar icon. If so, you can click on that button to quickly print your document.

✔ It's usually a good idea to preview your printing before you condemn even more of our North American forests to death. Many Windows programs have a File➪Print Preview command that lets you pour over the page before it's splattered all over a tree slice. Save an owl. (Or something like that.)

Changing the printed page to sideways

Printing on a sheet of paper long-ways is called printing in the *landscape* mode. Almost all Windows programs are capable of this.

From the Print dialog box, click on the Properties button. Click the Paper tab in your printer's Properties dialog box (see Figure 16-2). Click the Landscape option. Click OK to close the dialog box and then click OK in the Print dialog box to print in the landscape mode.

Some programs may not use the Paper tab in the Printer Properties dialog box. For example, in Microsoft Word, it's the File➪Page Setup command, Paper Size tab. Whatever.

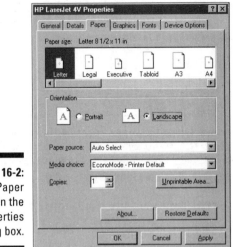

Figure 16-2:
The Paper
panel in the
Properties
dialog box.

Printing the screen

Even though a button on the keyboard is named Print Screen, it doesn't send
a copy of the screen to the printer. At least not directly. If you really need a
printed copy of Windows desktop or some window on the screen, follow
these steps:

1. **Arrange the screen so that it looks the way you want it printed.**

2. **If you want a snapshot of the whole screen, press the Print Screen key.**

   If you want a snapshot of only the top window on the screen, press
   Alt+Print Screen.

3. **From the Start menu, choose Programs⇨Accessories⇨Paint.**

   The Paint program appears on the screen.

4. **Choose Edit⇨Paste.**

   This pastes the image into the Paint program.

   If a warning dialog box tells you the image is too big, click the Yes
   button.

5. **Choose File⇨Print.**

   The Print dialog box appears. Click OK to start printing.

If the image is large, you may want to take advantage of the File⇨Print Preview command. It can show you how the final image will look, as well as how many pages it will print on (if it's incredibly huge).

Feeding an envelope

Most modern printers have a special slot into which you can feed an envelope. This is one of the things old-timers dreamed of in the early '80s. Back then, there was no way to squeeze an envelope into a computer printer. The result, sad and often, required the old-timer to take his printer apart to retrieve the mangled envelope.

To stick an envelope into a modern printer, just shove it into the special slot. Often times, you must open a hatch on the front of the computer to reveal the slot. A special illustration on the hatch tells you which way to place the envelope: face up or down and top-right or top-left. Then you tell your software to print the envelope and — *thwoop!* — there it goes and comes back again, complete with a nifty address.

- ✔ Obviously, feeding an envelope to a printer will be different for each type of printer.

- ✔ Also obviously: Each program is going to have a different command for printing envelopes. Typically, you have to tell the program how the envelope goes into your printer so that it knows in which direction to print the address.

- ✔ Some printers require you to press the On-line or Select button to print the envelope. For example, on my printer I set everything up and stick the envelope in the hatch, and then I print with my software. After a few seconds, the printer's display says "Me feed!" which I properly interpret to mean "Press my On-line button, doofus!" which I do and then the thing prints.

- ✔ If your printer doesn't have an illustration of how the envelope goes in, draw a picture on a piece of paper and tape it to the front of your printer. Something like the choices shown in Figure 16-3 should do nicely.

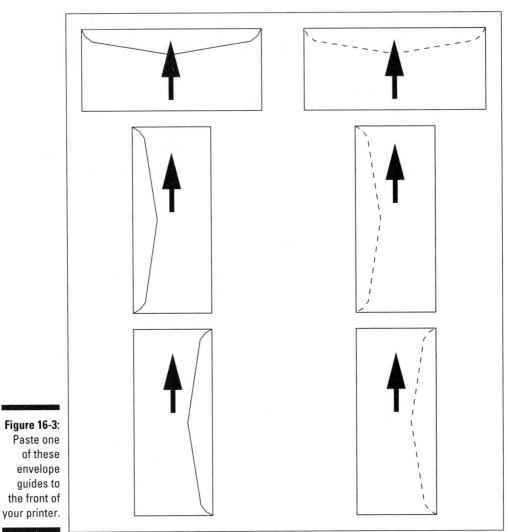

Figure 16-3:
Paste one
of these
envelope
guides to
the front of
your printer.

Important Printer Things to Remember

Printers don't come with cables! You must buy the cable separate from the printer.

The printer cable can be no more than 20 feet long. That's ridiculous, of course, since the best place for your printer is within arm's reach.

Printers don't come with paper. Always buy the proper paper for your printer. And stock up on it too; go to one of those discount paper warehouse places and buy a few boxes.

Never let your printer toner get low or ink cartridges go dry. You may think it saves money to squeeze every last drop of ink, but it's not good for the printer.

For laser printers, there is a "toner low" light or warning message. When you first see it, you can take the toner out of the printer and rock it from side-to-side. This redistributes the toner and gets more mileage from it. But it can only be done once! Replace the old toner as soon as you see the "toner low" light again.

Inkjet printers generally warn you that the ink cartridge is low, either on their panels or on your computer's screen.

Most printers have little pictures on them that tell you how the paper goes into the printer. Here is how those symbols translate into English:

- ✔ The paper goes in face down, top side up.
- ✔ The paper goes in face down, top side down.
- ✔ The paper goes in face up, top side up.
- ✔ The paper goes in face up, top side down.

If there is an arrow on one side of the paper, it usually indicates whether the top side is up or down. Then again, this could all be wrong, and what they're telling us is that we need to start using stone tablets all over again.

Chapter 17

The Modem Chapter

*C*ommunicating with a modem is one area of computing that has taken off faster than a lawn chair with 50 weather balloons attached. Personally, I'm shocked. In days of yore, having a modem and dialing up another computer was complex and laden with jargon. Then, after you were connected to another computer, you had nothing but diehard, rude nerds to talk to. It wasn't very encouraging.

Things change, however. Presently, having a modem and becoming part of the online universe — cyberspace, the Internet, what have you — is reason enough for owning a computer. The jargon is still there. And it's technical. And all the nerds I remember from 1982 are still out there, on the Net, playing God, and insulting everyone. Still, it's worth a quick dip, even if you're only mildly interested. This chapter shows you the ropes (or cables).

✔ Fair warning: Telecommunications is not simple, and nothing I can do in writing will make it simpler.

✔ In the olden days, you had to use communications software if you wanted to use a modem. The communications software would connect you to another computer or a national online service. Today, most people use modems to connect to the Internet.

✔ Using the Internet is covered in Part VI of this book.

✔ Modems can be messy, and computer communications causes a lot of headaches. Rather than spoil this uplifting chapter with that information, I've shoved it all off until Chapter 27, which discusses computer agony in depth.

What Does a Modem Do?

A modem is a device that takes the digital information from your computer and translates it into audio signals that can be sent over common phone lines. Figure 17-1 shows a typical modem, although the digital-to-audio translation part of the modem cannot be discerned by examining the figure.

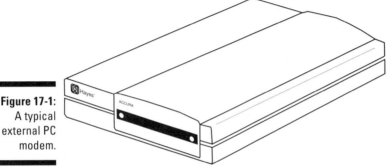

Figure 17-1:
A typical external PC modem.

In a way, the computer sends painful bits and bytes to the modem, which then converts them into sounds and sings them over the phone line (and I'm not talking opera here). Using a modem, you can send information to another computer by calling its modem on the phone.

You control a modem, and therefore talk with another computer, by using communications software. It controls the modem, dials up other computers, sends information, and does everything in a complex and confusing manner.

✔ The most common device to plug in to a serial port is a modem. In fact, the serial port is sometimes referred to as a *modem port*. Refer to Chapter 11 for the lowdown on ports.

✔ The word *modem* is a contraction of the words modulator-demodulator. But instead of calling it a lator-lator, they chose mo-dem. Also, there are more modem jokes in the computer world than anything else, typically "How many *modem* do you want?"

Types of Modems

There are a bazillion different types of modems. There are internal and external models, models with different speeds and features, different brand names, and prices from super cheap to down-payment-on-a-house expensive. It's modem madness!

Does it live inside or outside the computer?

Modems come in two breeds: *Internal,* which fits inside your computer console, and *external,* which lives in its own box that sits outside your computer console.

Both types work in exactly the same way; the external modem just has a little plastic box housing the mechanism, plus an extra power cord and cable connecting it to a serial port.

- ✔ Internal modems are cheaper. They plug into an expansion slot inside your computer. The back of the card is visible at the back of your computer; that's where its phone lines plug in and hang out.

- ✔ External modems cost more because you have to pay for its plastic box. You'll also have to buy a serial cable to connect it to your PC's serial port.

Although external modems cost a little more and take up shelf space near your computer, they have the following advantages:

- ✔ External modems have a little row of lights along the front that correspond to the online action. A light goes on when the modem is connected to another computer, for example. Other lights convey similar informational tidbits.

- ✔ Most external modems have better speakers. You can listen when the modem dials, and you can hear if you have a busy signal. (This feature comes in handy when using the modem on rapid redial to win radio station giveaways.)

- ✔ Because the external modem sits on a shelf, it's easier to reach its volume control knob. The internal modem's knob — if it even has a volume knob — is around back.

- ✔ External modems are transportable. They're easier to take to the repair shop. You can also use them with other computers or take them to a friend's house. (This is a serious step toward computer nerddom.)

- ✔ Since external modems plug into one of your PC's serial (COM) ports, there are no device drivers or interrupts to worry about. (Internal modems tend to be a real pain to install and set up properly.)

- ✔ Finally, anyone can install an external modem: Take it out of the box and peel back the Styrofoam and wrapping. Set it on your desktop. Plug the power cord into the wall. Plug the phone cord into the wall (and optionally plug the phone that was plugged into the wall into the modem). Plug one end of a modem cable into the modem. Plug the other end into your PC. *Plug, plug, plug your modem, gently into the wall; merrily, merrily, merrily, merrily, comm is such a ball!*

Internal modems have the following advantages:

- ✔ They don't junk up your desktop. Unlike the outboard modem, internal models have only one cable: the one that goes to the wall (and maybe a second cable goes to your phone). They don't have a power cord or serial cable.

- ✔ Internal modems are always ready. You have to remember to turn on an external modem; internal modems are on all the time.

- ✔ Internal modems usually come with cool software, such as a communications program, faxing software, and maybe even some Internet stuff.

I feel the need for speed

Just as some computers are faster than others, some modems are faster than others. But all modems are relatively compatible: The fastest modems can still talk to the slower ones.

Modem speed is measured in bits per second (bps), or how many bits they can toss across the phone line in one second. I've thrown all that nonsense into Table 17-1, where it's easy to skip over.

- ✔ Which modem speed is best? Why, the fastest, of course. Today, a 28.8 modem is considered average, with the 57.6 Kbps modems being about the fastest you can buy.

- ✔ Actually, the fastest modem you can buy is a cable modem. This modem plugs into the TV cable system and it's the fastest way to go — providing you have cable and that your cable company offers cable modem service and that you can afford it.

- ✔ There was a wild flirtation with the 33.6 speed modem. Those have mostly disappeared now, being replaced by the faster 57.6 (also called 56K) models.

- ✔ Don't bother with anything less than a 9,600 Kbps modem.

- ✔ Some people use the word *baud* to describe modem speed. That's inaccurate. The correct term is bps. Correct them enthusiastically if you want to sound like a true computer geek.

Table 17-1	Modem Speeds
Speed	*Possibly Helpful Information*
300 bps	Almost all modems can communicate at this snail's pace; almost none of them do. Why would you want to?
1200 bps	Although this speed is four times as fast as 300 bps modem speed, it's still regarded as too slow by today's standards.

Speed	Possibly Helpful Information
2400 bps	Most major online services still connect at this slow speed, but they're no joy to use that way.
9600 bps	This speed was the champ for a long time. I remember paying $1,000 for my first 9600 bps modem back in 1987. I still have it.
14.4 Kbps	At one time computer magazines (big respectful ones) claimed this was as fast as a modem could go. Any faster, and the phone lines would melt. Uh-huh.
19.6 Kbps	An older standard available at a price back in the mid-80s, but which never caught on among consumers.
28.8 Kbps	A minimum for the Internet. The champ after 9600 bps and before 57.6 Kbps took over.
33.6 Kbps	An oddball non-standard, flirted with briefly in the mid-90s.
57.6 Kbps	The fastest modems can currently go. If you're not connecting to the Internet at 57.6 Kbps, you might as well not own a computer.

"What is this fax modem thing?"

Modem developers noticed the similarity between modem technology and fax machine technology several years back. It was easy for them to combine the two and the result was called a *fax modem*.

With the proper software, a fax modem can not only communicate with other PCs and modems, but with fax machines as well. It was a glorious day for the computing masses back then.

Today, nearly all modems have the ability to send or receive a fax. It's like having an automatic transmission in your car; it's just not a big enough deal to brag over any more.

To use your modem like a fax machine you need special fax software. Windows 95 comes with this ability, although Windows 98 does not. Fortunately, your modem probably came with special fax software that's (I'll bet a billion dollars) is much, much easier to understand and use than anything Microsoft could dream up.

The Joys of Using a Modem

Using a modem itself is cinchy. It's the communications software that will drive you up the wall.

What do you do with your modem?

Most people use their modems for two things: calling the Internet and calling the Internet. In the olden days, calling local bulletin boards was popular. Though those systems still carry a local flavor you can't find anywhere else, the gargantuan Internet is antiquating them.

An online service is a huge computer that's hooked up to a whole bunch of modems. From your end, an online service looks like any other software program. But, although most programs make you feed them information, the online service sends you information. Like magazines, online services are subscribed to. Expect to pay anywhere from $5 per month to $20 per hour for the joy of using one. An example is America Online, which has gobbled up most of its competition and any other examples I've mentioned in previous editions of this book.

If you're using a laptop at a remote location, you can also use your modem to connect to your company's network. Even if your company doesn't have a network, you can still use your laptop's modem to call your desktop PC's modem, and the two computers can chat. Of course, getting the thing to work is more difficult than talking about it.

Internet: See Part VI of this book.

BBS: Short for bulletin board system, a BBS can be considered a tiny online service. It's usually a PC some hobbyist has connected to a modem in his or her living room. Most BBSs offer forums, just like the commercial online services, but they typically don't charge anything for access.

Setting up a modem is so easy a 65-year-old retired male doctor could do it. The following sections tell you how.

✔ The best way to use a modem is with its own phone line. Just about every house or apartment has the ability to have a second line added without paying for extra wiring. If so, have the phone company hook that line up and use it for your modem. Why? Because. . . .

✔ You can't use your phone while your modem is talking. In fact, if somebody picks up another extension on that line, it will garble the signal, possibly losing your connection — not to mention that they hear a horrid screeching in their ear.

Hooking up an internal modem

Let someone else plug the internal modem into one of your PC's expansion slots; or maybe it just came that way from the factory. Your job is to connect only one thing: a phone cable from the modem into the phone wall socket or *phone jack*.

Figure 17-2 shows what the back of the internal modem may look like. Two phone jacks are there. Plug one end of the phone cable into the Line hole. Plug the other end of the phone cable into the wall jack.

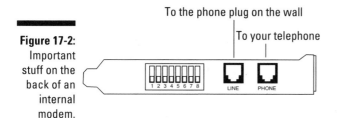

To the phone plug on the wall

To your telephone

Figure 17-2:
Important
stuff on the
back of an
internal
modem.

Phone connectors have a little release lever on them. When properly connected, they click into place. Ain't no way that sucker's falling out of there.

It doesn't matter which of the phone cord end goes into the wall or modem; plugging in a modem is just like plugging in a phone. If a phone is already plugged into the wall, unplug it. Then plug it into the Phone hole in the back of your modem.

Table 17-2 offers a quick summary of what plugs into what. Symbols may also be used instead of names for the various connectors on your modem's rump.

Table 17-2	Plugging What into What for Your Modem
Hole Name	*How It Goes*
Line	Plug a phone cable from this hole on your modem into the phone jack on the wall.
Line in	Same as the Line jack.
Phone	Plug your telephone into this jack on the modem.
Line out	Same as the Phone jack.
DTE	Plug a serial cable into this connector on the back of your modem; plug the other end into a serial port on the back of your PC. (External modems.)
Power	Plug the power cord into this hole on the external modem; the other end plugs into a power strip or wall socket. (External modems.)

Hooking up an external modem

Unlike an internal modem, anyone can connect an external modem. It doesn't even require a screwdriver. You do have more cables to connect, but that's not a true bother. Besides, after it's all hooked up, you'll never have to mess with it again.

There are four things to connect to the back of an external modem. Figure 17-3 shows them all, though they may appear differently on the back of your modem.

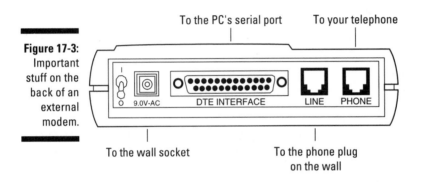

Figure 17-3: Important stuff on the back of an external modem.

Start by plugging one end of a serial cable into the rear of your PC. Plug it into either COM1 or COM2. Plug the other end of the cable into the back of your modem. The cables only go one way. You can't screw it up.

Next, plug the modem into the phone jack on the wall. Stick one end of the phone cord into the wall jack; stick the other end into the Line hole on the back of the modem. Notice that the connector snaps into place so it won't accidentally fall out.

If you had a phone connected to the wall jack, plug it into the modem's Phone hole. Otherwise, if you're just using the modem on that line, nothing needs to be plugged into the Phone hole.

Make sure that the modem is turned off. (The switch is either on the side or back.) Plug the power cord into the modem and then plug the power cord into a wall socket or power strip.

✔ Refer to Table 17-2 for a quick summary of what plugs into what.

✔ Notice that the serial port on the rear of your PC uses 9 wires, but the plug on the rear of the modem uses 25. (Don't bother counting them; I did that for you.) The modem only needs 9 wires. It has a 25-wire connector due to tradition.

✔ Some modems use symbols instead of names for the connector holes.

✔ Sometimes you may find the names or symbols on the bottom of the modem instead of the back.

✔ Familiarize yourself with the modem's on-off switch. Look for the volume control, which may be behind the modem or under one of the sides.

✔ It's okay to leave your external modem on all the time. You can turn it off to save power, but remember to turn it back on before you use it. If you don't, your communications software will become bewildered.

Installing your modem with Windows

After setting up your modem, you must tell Windows about it. This task isn't as painful as it used to be, thanks to the Windows hardware installation wizard.

The subject of the hardware installation wizard is covered in Chapter 18. Skip to there for more information on what to do next.

Some Modem Hints

Anyone who ever tells you that they don't have any problems with their modem is either lying or trying to sell you one (or both). There's probably a specific psychological term called *modem woe*. I'm certain of it.

Being a modem user since way, *way* back, I've collected a list of helpful hints and suggestions to make your modeming life easier. Better to read about this stuff here than suffer the consequences of being stuck in a hotel room in outer Wambooli, unable to deal with a phone jack that looks like a coin return on a slot machine.

Check out Chapter 27 for information on dealing with modem problems.

Making the modem appear even when Windows doesn't see it

For some annoying reason, Windows tends to lose track of the modem after you reset the computer. For example, you just reset the computer or turned the PC on and you try to connect to another computer or the Internet. Windows bemoans that it cannot find the modem. Yeah. Right.

The solution? Just try again and it should work.

- ✔ Don't blame yourself when this happens.
- ✔ If you have an external modem, double-check to make sure that it's turned on before you dial. (Sometimes this "modem's not there" problem happens when you turn an external modem off and on again.)

Dealing with "local" long distance

The phone companies seem to delight in forcing us to dial our own area code for "local long distance." This goofs up some modem programs, which assume that, since it's in your area code, it's not long distance!

To get Windows to believe local long distance isn't local, you need to fool it into thinking that you're dialing from someplace other than your local area code. To do so, pretend your computer is a laptop and create a new calling location for it. See the section "Changing your location for a laptop" later.

It dials too fast!

Modems dial phone numbers all by themselves. They can dial slowly. They can dial fast. But that's not a problem. What can be a problem is when you need to dial a 9 or an 8 before the phone number to get an outside line. That means Mr. Modem should wait after the 9 or 8 before dialing the number or you end up connecting with the nice lady who tells you that if you can't use a phone you might as well run away from civilization and start herding yaks.

To slow down your modem after it dials an 8 or 9 to get an outside line, add a comma after the 8 or 9 in the number you dial. For example:

```
8,11-202-555-7892
```

Above, you see the number I would dial to connect with the Pentagon's war room. But since my hotel in Budapest has a slow connection, I stuck a comma after the 8.

Changing your location for a laptop

If you use a laptop PC on the road, you'll need to tell Windows about your new location so that it can dial the modem properly from wherever you are.

1. Open the Control Panel

Choose <u>S</u>ettings⇨<u>C</u>ontrol Panel from the Start menu.

2. **Open the Modems icon.**

Modems

Double-click the Modems icon to open it, which displays the Modems Properties dialog box. But don't tarry there.

3. **Click the Dialing Properties button.**

The Dialing Properties dialog box appears, shown in Figure 17-4.

4. **Click the New button. The Create New Location dialog box appears.**

5. **In the Create New Location dialog box, type in a name for wherever you are.**

For example, when I visit San Diego I have a separate entry for the Hilton (out by the beach) and my mom's house (in El Cajon).

6. **Type the area code, the country, and other vital stats for your remote location.**

Here you're telling Windows just how to dial different phone numbers from that new location. (Windows is smart and knows about long distance and the like.)

7. **Click OK to save the information.**

The next time you use the Connect To dialog box, you can choose any of your locations from the DIALING FROM drop-down list. That way you don't have to re-enter information every time you're on the road.

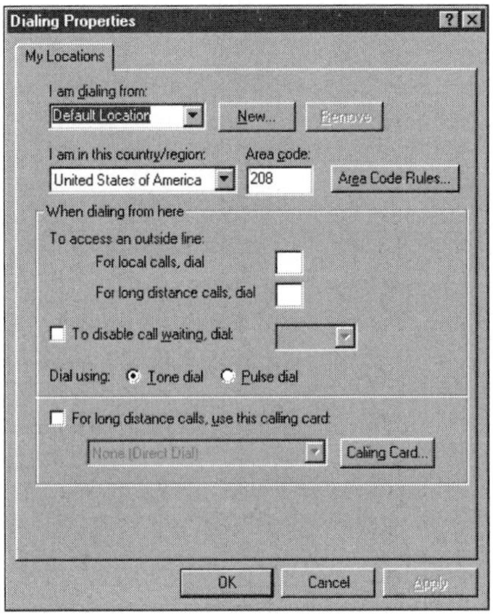

Figure 17-4:
The Dialing
Properties
window.

✔ If you don't have a laptop, and say you're living in one of those lovely areas where you have to dial the area code to call the 7-11 across the street, then after Step 3 in the preceding list click the Area Code Rules button. A special dialog box appears where you can tell Windows when and how to dial area codes for where you live. This works whether or not you're on the road.

✔ You use the Connect To dialog box whenever you use Windows to dial the modem. This can be for an Internet connection or a local system.

✔ By telling Windows the area code and location from which you're calling (plus the other information), you save yourself from having to re-input that information each time you visit that location.

✔ Save the "Default location" item for wherever your laptop is most of the time.

Chapter 18

Just Hanging Around (Peripherals)

. . . .

. . . .

The major parts of an IBM-compatible computer are fairly boring: the monitor, the console box, the keyboard. The interesting parts are the *peripherals:* Gizmos you can add to your computer to make it more useful or more fun — and certainly more expensive.

If you play your expansion cards right, your PC can become a fax machine, jukebox, video arcade system, or all three (even at the same time). This chapter takes a look at some of the more popular peripherals that attach to a PC.

Even though anything outside of the console box would be considered a peripheral, this chapter covers only those peripherals not mentioned in the previous chapters.

It's Just Extra Stuff for Your Computer

Peripheral refers to anything outside of the main. For example, the *peripheral nervous system* is all the nerves in your body outside of your brain (which is called the *central nervous system*). *Peripheral vision* includes things you can see without looking directly at them. And *peripheral nervous vision* is what first-time computer buyers get when they enter the store. With a computer, however, a *peripheral* is any accessory or auxiliary equipment you may buy and connect to the computer.

Peripherals enable you to expand your computer system without having to buy a totally new computer. You can add these extra hardware devices yourself or have a guru, computer consultant, or some other overpaid individual do it for you.

The variety of peripherals you can buy for your computer is endless. Common peripheral items include the computer's printer, although this peripheral is more or less considered part of any standard computer; a *modem,* for calling up other computers or the Pentagon by using a standard telephone; a *scanner,* for reading text or graphics images; a device for making the computer play music; and numerous other fancy — and pricey — items.

- ✔ If you were a computer, your arms and legs would be considered peripherals. However, you're restricted by design to only two arms and legs each, so your upgrade options are limited.

- ✔ All peripherals are hardware.

- ✔ Although the word peripheral refers to things outside of a computer, you can also add peripherals internally — inside the PC's console. (In a way, peripheral refers to anything beyond what comes standard in the computer.)

Telling Windows about All This Stuff (The Miracle of Plug and Play)

Wiggling in an expansion card sounds easy. Plugging in a desktop scanner is a snap. And — don't tell — it really is easy. You just turn off the PC, unscrew this and that, plug in the peripheral like a Tinker Toy, and wham — there it is.

Unfortunately, only the physical part is a no-brainer. The software part is far more difficult. That's where you have to instruct your expansion card to get along with other expansion cards in your computer, as well as your software. That process is a truly brain-numbing exercise.

In order to remove some of the pain from adding expansion cards to a PC, the industry has devised yet another standard. This one is called *plug and play.* The idea is that you should be able to plug in an expansion card and it, or your software, should be able to figure everything out and set itself up automatically.

When you think about it, shouldn't a computer do this automatically anyway?

Well, whatever, the day of plug and play is supposedly upon us. More and more expansion cards and options are being advertised as plug and play, and Windows offers plug and play as a feature.

Anytime you add any new piece of hardware to Windows, Windows instantly recognizes it the moment you turn your PC on. That hardware is then configured using a program called the hardware wizard.

Add New
Hardware

In some rare cases, you may have to run the hardware wizard yourself. For example, when you add an external modem, you must have Windows hunt for it. In that case, you open the Control Panel by choosing Settings➪Control Panel from the Start menu. Then double-click the Add New Hardware icon to run the hardware wizard. In mere moments, your new hardware should be up and running, and everything is groovy.

And to think computers were around only 40 years before the engineers thought of this!

✔ Keep your eye out for plug-and-play happy peripherals. Most new computers are plug-and-play friendly, and in a few years just about every hardware doohickey you buy will be the same way.

✔ If your PC sports a USB port, always check for a USB version of whatever peripheral you're buying: speakers, joystick, scanner, whatever. USB hardware is hands-down the best and easiest to install. Period.

✔ According to Microsoft, Windows can identify and properly configure 90 percent of the expansion cards and peripherals out there. It can guess at another 9 percent. And only 1 percent leaves Windows baffled.

✔ Yes, you'll probably end up being in that 1 percent.

✔ Plug and play isn't foolproof. For that reason, many in the industry have dubbed it "plug and pray."

Scan, Scan, Scan, Said the Scanner (The Unprinter)

If you're into messing around with graphics, a nifty peripheral that you may want to add to your PC is a scanner. Scanners work like photocopiers, but instead of producing a duplicate of a sheet of paper, the scanner converts the images to bits and bytes and stores them in your computer.

Scanners have two very useful purposes. The first is to scan graphic images for inclusion in documents and for desktop publishing or for posting on the Internet. The second is that software can *read* the documents you scan, converting the image into text for input in the computer. This is truly amazing stuff.

Scanners come in two basic styles, hand-held and desktop.

A *hand-held scanner* looks like a miniature vacuum cleaner. You slide the scanner across a picture, and the picture appears on your computer screen. After the picture is on the screen, the image can be dropped into party flyers, faxes, newsletters, books, or any other printed material.

Larger scanners, known as *flatbed* or *desktop scanners,* work more like copiers. You place the paper on top of the scanner, close the lid, and push a button. The image appears on your screen, ready to be saved to disk.

- ✔ Hand-held scanners work best for importing small images: logos, signatures, or postage stamps.

- ✔ If you don't move your hand smoothly while sliding the scanner over the image, the resulting picture looks like one of those curvy mirrors they have at the circus.

- ✔ Desktop scanners import images more clearly and much more expensively than hand-held scanners.

- ✔ Scanners typically plug into a SCSI port, a USB port, or their own proprietary port. Bribe a guru to do the dirty installation work.

Reading in text to your computer with a scanner isn't as easy as it sounds. Scanners understand only the image they scan. To convert that image into text, you need special software called *Optical Character Recognition* (OCR) software, and it reads only certain types of characters. Although OCR software is getting better — it's even tossed in with most fax software to read text from incoming faxes — be sure to run your spell checker after you've used it.

Making Your PC Sing

Do, re, mi, fa, so, la, ti, DOS!

For the longest time, IBM and compatible computers treated sound as something to be avoided. Sure, they could beep, but the PC's tiny speaker can barely be heard; there's not even a way to adjust the volume. Luckily, a few companies began creating *sound cards,* mostly so game players could hear music and antediluvian space grunts.

Today, sound cards are no longer an option — they're included! Even IBM's computers have fantastic built-in sound. Of course, people say they're buying them for *business presentations* and *educational uses,* but that really means they want to hear the *THWOK!* as the club makes perfect contact with the ball in the famous Microsoft Golf game.

In addition to the sound card, you need speakers to hear the sound. Most PCs that come with sound cards included also come with a set of el cheap-o speakers. Some home and multimedia (game-player) systems come with very nice speakers and a sub-woofer. Hey! Spend the extra $160 and wake up the neighbors!

Of course, while speakers may be more-or-less standard, a microphone is still optional. Most PCs come with a token $3 microphone. It's okay, but if you plan on using any serious recording software, get a better mike.

- ✔ Most sound cards synthesize music, as well. When a sound card plays music, it's usually using its own built-in synthesizer, just as if it were an electric organ. Instead of playing back actual digital sounds, the sound card just generates musical tones on the fly.

- ✔ The standard that dominates the sound card market is Sound Blaster, though most games recognize all the popular sound cards.

- ✔ If you put speakers on your desk, remember that they contain magnets. If any stray floppy disks come too close, they may lose their data.

- ✔ Digital sound takes up huge amounts of room on a disk. That's why most digitized sounds are limited to short bursts like golf swings and grunts.

How can I tell if my PC has a sound card?

Too many people write to me with questions about whether their computer can bleep and squawk with a sound card. How can you tell if your sound card is installed? Easy: look 'round back.

Your PC should have three connectors on its rump if it has a sound card properly installed. You should be able to find three tiny jacks — called mini-din, they accept a tiny ¹/₈-inch audio plug. The jacks are labeled Mic, Line in, Line out, or Speakers.

If your PC has the jacks, then it can produce sound. Whether the sound is working or not at that point is a software problem. (You should check with your computer dealer if you still can't hear the sound.)

Having fun with sound in Windows

If you have time to waste, you can turn your smart business computer into a goofy business computer by adding sounds to Windows. I'm not going into any detail here, because this is an area wide-open for play. But I will show you the playground:

1. Open the Control Panel.

From the Start menu choose Settings⇨Control Panel.

2. Open the Sounds icon.

Sounds

Double-click on the Sounds icon to open it. The Sounds Properties dialog box is revealed (Figure 18-1).

3. Mess around.

In the Events list are various things Windows and some of your applications do. To each one of these things you can apply a specific sound. So, for example, when Windows opens a window, you can have the sound of something unzipping (or a balloon popping or a rubber band snapping) play on your PC's speaker.

Ah, yes. Fun.

You choose sounds by using the Sounds area in the dialog box. This area is rich for fiddling.

You can pluck out a sound scheme in the Schemes area. Schemes are collections of sounds that came with Windows or the Plus! package. I enjoy the Robotz Sound Scheme, but I mix in a little Musica and Utopia for my own pleasure.

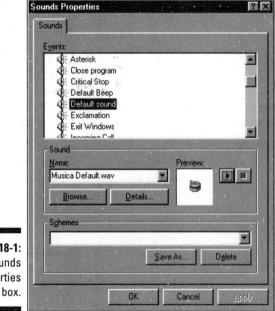

Figure 18-1:
The Sounds
Properties
dialog box.

4. Click OK **to get back to work.**

You can create your own sounds using a microphone and a sound card. If you want to record stuff from a sound effects CD or your stereo, use the sound card's line-in jack, not the microphone jack.

Oh, there's tons of sound software to mess with. It would take another book to cover it all. *PC Sound For Dummies*? Maybe.

- ✔ Don't feel like a goof when you call tech support for some reason, and they tell you to open this or that window and Mary Poppins says "Spit-spot" each time you do.

- ✔ Never, under any circumstances, play the Microsoft Sound sound. It will make you gag.

Tape Backups

Remember the old computers from the '60s? I bet you envision a room full of refrigerator-sized devices, each with two huge tape reels on it, spinning back and forth in tight jerks. Blinking lights everywhere. Men and women in lab coats. Ah, those were the days. . . .

Sorry to burst your bubble, but those refrigerator-sized devices with the tape reels were not computers. Those were really the disk drives. Back then, computers stored all their information on magnetic recording tape — a slow and cumbersome process, like getting a 4-year-old to eat salad.

Floppy disks eventually replaced tape, but you still find tape used for one purpose: backup copies of data. A tape backup unit plugs into your computer and copies the information from your hard drive to tape.

Why? For security. If anything ever happens to the hard drive — such as someone shoots it or Fred's nephew erases all the files — you can rescue your stuff from the tape backup copy. A sound idea, rarely practiced in real life.

- ✔ Tape backup drives are an optional extra on all PCs. Most don't require their own expansion card; these drives use your PC's floppy disk expansion card instead.

- ✔ Some tape drives are external, and some are internal. The external ones are more expensive, but have the advantage of being able to move them from PC to PC for backing up all the computers in an office.

✔ Beginning with Windows 98, the only realistic way to back up your PC is with a tape backup drive or ZIP or Jaz drive. You can no longer back up to floppy disks. (And it would be a silly thing to do if you did want to back up to floppies; in the days of the 2GB hard drive, it would take more floppy disks than you have room for, and all those disks would cost a lot more than the top-of-the-line tape backup unit.)

✔ Speaking of Windows and backing up, I recommend using your tape backup's software and not Windows own software for backing up your hard drive. Windows backup software stinks. Your tape backup drive probably comes with something better anyway.

✔ Most of the time, you find a tape backup on a network file server. This way, all the company's files can be backed up on one system, as opposed to a tape backup unit for each PC.

"I Have Some Money, and I Want to Upgrade My Hardware"

Most people don't trade in their cars each year. TVs, VCRs, blenders, and clock radios usually stay put until they break, and then you buy a new one. It's the Bic lighter theory: Why repair something cheap when you can just buy a new one? The same thing applies to most pets. For example, why incur a $35 vet bill on a $1.59 mouse? Toss it out and buy the kid a new one! But I digress . . .

The computer world, being bizarre and different as we know it, offers updates and upgrades on a monthly basis, if not weekly. It's technology! There's something new and better! And you still have a $1,500 credit on your VISA!

Peripheralitis: Pray you never contract it

A disease many computer owners get is peripheralitis. That's the overwhelming desire to spend more and more money on your computer, typically by buying peripherals.

PC beginners are relatively immune to this disease; most prefer to just use the darn thing and then quickly shut it off. Still, it's amazing what computers can do, provided that users have the cash or VISA credit line to pay for it all.

What to buy first

Instead of buying a new computer, it may be easier to upgrade the old one. Or, rather, have somebody else upgrade your old computer for you. But where do you spend your money first? Too many enticing things can get in the way of a sane decision. Let me help:

Memory: Your first upgrading priority should be memory. It's not that expensive and installation isn't a major headache. Just about all your software will enjoy having more memory available.

- ✔ Increased memory can make these programs work faster and handle larger chunks of information. It also lets the computer handle more graphics and sound.
- ✔ More memory is the best thing you can buy for your PC.
- ✔ For more information about memory stuff, read Chapter 12.

Hard drive: Buy a second hard drive. Make it a big one. Most PCs can handle two hard drives. And by the time you need another one, you'll know exactly how many more megabytes of storage you need.

- ✔ If you don't have room in your PC for a hard drive, you can always buy an external hard drive or replace one of your current drives. This is a complex process because you must copy all the files off the old hard drive and onto the new one. Personally, I'd rather do the following:
  - • If you have a SCSI hard drive system, you can have up to six hard drives total in a PC (up to two inside and four outside the box).
  - • By the way, larger hard drives don't take up any extra room in the computer's case, so don't worry about needing a bigger case.

Monitor: Buy a big monitor, like a 21-inch jobbie. These things are *great*. You can really see a lot of windows on the screen at once without feeling crowded. Oftentimes, it's easy to just replace the old monitor. In fact, you can do the whole operation yourself, but have someone with an expendable back hoist the thing up for you.

- ✔ For more information on monitors, see Chapter 13.

Microprocessor: Upgrading the microprocessor is something I don't recommend. Generally speaking, it's just better to buy a whole new computer. That way you get *all* new components at a cost cheaper than buying a new PC one bit at a time.

My opinion is that you're better off adding more memory to your system or a bigger hard drive. Those two upgrades give you instant results whereas a faster microprocessor may or may not be noticeable right away. Of course, this is my opinion and if you're dead-set on doing an upgrade, go for it.

When to buy a new computer

Plan on this: Every four or five years, replace your PC. By then, the cost of a new system will be cheaper than any upgrading you do.

Your PC is essentially out of date the moment you purchase it. Somewhere right now in Silicon Valley, they're devising new microprocessors and better motherboards that will cost less money. Maybe not the *minute* you purchased your PC, but sooner or later your leading-edge technology will be yesterday's kitty litter box.

But do you really need to buy a new computer? Maybe not. Look at the reasons you bought it in the first place. Can the computer still handle those needs? If yes, you're doing fine. Upgrade only when you desperately need to. No sense in spending more money on the monster.

- ✔ Computer technology grows faster than fly specks on a clean windshield. But, unless your computing needs have changed drastically, your computer can still handle the tasks you bought it for.

- ✔ Most people buy newer computers for the increase in speed. Yet speed doesn't always mean increased productivity. For instance, most word processing time is spent pondering the right choice of words. A faster computer can't help there. Faster computers do help those applications that need the extra horsepower: graphics, animation, desktop publishing, and programs of that ilk.

- ✔ Compare the price of a new computer with the amount of time you'll save at a faster processing speed. If you spend a lot of time waiting for your computer to catch up with you, an upgrade may be in order.

- ✔ Avoid the lure and seduction of those techy computer magazines that urge you to Buy! Buy! Buy! the latest PC. Remember who most of their advertisers are.

Buying and Selling Used Gear

When people upgrade their computers piece by piece, the old stuff turns up in the classified ads. This is where you can find some bargains, but only if you really, really know what you're doing. After all, the old stuff isn't as good as the new stuff. And, quite often, the new stuff is cheaper than what they're asking for the old stuff.

Should you buy used gear? Only if they're selling *exactly* what you need. For example, suppose you've used the Zot 101 printer for years and yours broke. If there's a Zot 101 for sale somewhere — and it still works to your satisfaction — then buy it used.

- ✔ Test drive before you buy. This approach is like kicking the tires, but it ensures that whatever you're taking home works. (Well, it worked at least once.)

- ✔ A big problem with used equipment you're not familiar with is that you may not get any manuals, and there is no technical support or warranty from the selling party. Although it's important to test drive old equipment, don't expect any of the service or support you find with new stuff.

- ✔ Never buy a used computer as your first computer purchase. It's just much better to pay a store for the service and support you need. (And don't shop for the cheapest price, either! Service and support are important and worth paying a bit extra for.)

- ✔ PCs have no resale value, so wipe away those visions of selling your used system for anything more than 10 percent of its purchase price. The new stuff is just better and cheaper.

- ✔ Remember, new PCs are quickly approaching the $500 mark. Even if you paid $1,500 for your three-year old beast, don't plan on selling it unless you're asking $200 or less. I'm serious! Who wants a used computer when they can buy a new one for only a few hundred dollars more?

- ✔ A better option than selling old stuff is to donate used equipment to a charity or a local school. The tax write-off is far greater than the resale value ever will be. I donate all my old stuff to our community theater, which gives them a chance to gripe about the equipment just like I used to.

- ✔ If you're selling used computer parts, try to keep all the manuals together, along with support software — the same stuff you got new with the product. Also, accept only cash. For major items, ask for a cashier's check.

- ✔ Some stuff you never get rid of. Start a collection! Make jewelry from it! I must have enough junk in my back office to make six or more computers. I actually did cobble together a PC for my son. It's the only system in the house that doesn't have a case, and rubber bands hold the hard drive in. There should be a prize for such creativity.

Part V
The Non-Nerd's Guide to Computer Software

The 5th Wave   By Rich Tennant

"HOLD ON, THAT'S NOT A PROGRAM ERROR, IT'S JUST A BOOGER ON THE SCREEN."

In this part . . .

Okay, so if software is so important, why is this part of the book *after* the part on hardware? Easy: Because you need one before you need the other. Why buy a music CD if you don't have a CD player, duh? Software needs hardware like a symphony needs an orchestra. After all, what's the point of bassoons and oboes without a foot-high stack of music for them to play?

This part of the book is about PC software. You can't avoid it. You need it. Your computer needs it. Heck, the environment needs it too, what with all the air they put into those software boxes.

Chapter 19

All about Software
(The Real Brains)

- -

In This Chapter

▶ Word processors

▶ Spreadsheets

▶ Databases

▶ Graphics software

▶ Games and education (multimedia)

▶ Utilities

▶ Office software

▶ Shareware and public domain software

- -

Computers need software like the Frankenstein monster needs an electrical storm. It gives life to the big, hulking, beast of a computer! *Life!* Without it, the computer would just be a collection of, er, *parts.*

This chapter describes the variety and flavors of software available. After all, there's more than one way to bring the creature alive.

✔ Software needs the computer as much as the computer needs it. It's kind of a yin-yang thing, though I promise not to delve too deeply into Eastern philosophy at this point in the book.

✔ The plural of software is *software.* If you say "softwares," you sound like a foreigner.

✔ Mary Shelley wrote *Frankenstein* when she was 19 years old. It was her first book.

The Wordy Stuff

Just about everybody wants to use his or her computer to write something. Whether it's a thank-you note to Aunt Sally, a letter to the wacko liberal editor of your local paper, or a 500,000-word sweeping romance novel about two entomologists in Paraguay, computers make the writing process much easier.

- ✔ Word processing is writing.
- ✔ There are three types of word-processing software: text editors, word processors, and desktop publishing software.
- ✔ If this book were *USA Today,* a little boxed-in note nearby would say 70 percent of all computers are used for word processing.
- ✔ The best part about writing on a computer is that you can change what you've written without messing up the printed page. Editing "on the screen" means that each printed page will be perfect. Or as near perfect as you and the computer can make it.

Text editors

A *text editor* is a bare-bones word processor. It probably won't let you set the margins, and forget about formatting the text or using different fonts. So why bother with a text editor?

Text editors are so simple that they're fast and easy to use. Instead of writing a gargantuan novel on the history of the paper clip, you can use a text editor to create or edit a plain text (or ASCII) file on disk. Sound dumb? Well, it turns out that *lots* of plain text files are on your disk, quite a few of which you'll end up editing from time to time.

Figure 19-1 shows the text editor in Windows, Notepad, in action. In this case, Notepad is editing an HTML file, which will eventually appear on the Internet as a Web page. (There are other tools for creating Web pages, but it can be done using a plain text editor like Notepad — if you're insane.)

- ✔ A text editor is basically a no-frills word processor.
- ✔ Text editors save their documents as plain text or ASCII files. No fancy-schmancy stuff.
- ✔ Actually, any word processor can be a text editor. The secret is to save the file as a *plain text* or *text only* type of file. Refer to Chapter 8 for more information on saving files of a certain type.
- ✔ Why should Freon cost anything?

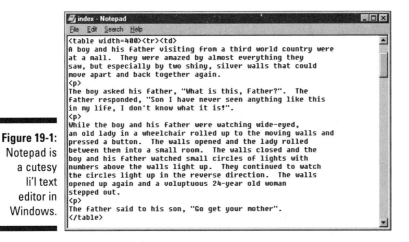

```
index - Notepad
File  Edit  Search  Help
<table width=400><tr><td>
A boy and his father visiting from a third world country were
at a mall.  They were amazed by almost everything they
saw, but especially by two shiny, silver walls that could
move apart and back together again.
<p>
The boy asked his father, "What is this, Father?".  The
father responded, "Son I have never seen anything like this
in my life, I don't know what it is!".
<p>
While the boy and his father were watching wide-eyed,
an old lady in a wheelchair rolled up to the moving walls and
pressed a button.  The walls opened and the lady rolled
between them into a small room.  The walls closed and the
boy and his father watched small circles of lights with
numbers above the walls light up.  They continued to watch
the circles light up in the reverse direction.  The walls
opened up again and a voluptuous 24-year old woman
stepped out.
<p>
The father said to his son, "Go get your mother".
</table>
```

Figure 19-1:
Notepad is
a cutesy
li'l text
editor in
Windows.

Word processors

The word processor is the natural evolution of the typewriter. No more are words written directly on paper. Instead, they're *words electric,* which you can toss around and fiddle with on the screen to your heart's content. Editing, fixing stuff up, spell-checking, formatting — computers were made for this kind of fun. It's no wonder IBM sold off its typewriter division.

✔ Word processors work with text just like text editors do, but they add formatting, styles, proofing, and a whole grab-bag full of features that no one ever takes the time to learn.

✔ The files that word processors save are commonly called *documents.*

✔ In the early part of this century, Vladimir Nabokov wrote by hand while standing up. In the latter part of this century, he probably would have used a word processor — but standing up anyway.

✔ Windows has a word processor called WordPad. It's like an early version of Microsoft Word. In fact, WordPad has features that people would have drooled over ten years ago. Today, it's considered ho-hum. (But it's free with Windows and, besides, people don't drool as much as they used to.)

Desktop publishing packages

The second phase of the word processor revolution was the addition of pictures and graphics. New word processors could arrange text in columns and add headers and footnotes and all sorts of typographical nonsense. Soon, these high-end word processors became their own, new software category: *desktop publishing.*

Today, desktop publishing programs create the fancy pages you see in newspapers, magazines, and helpful newsletters that come with the electric company bills. The fruits of these applications are ubiquitous.

✔ If you're cool, you say "DTP" instead of "desktop publishing."

✔ Typically, you create your text in a word processor and then *place* it into the desktop publishing program. Desktop publishing is primarily used to arrange words and graphics. Composing the words (as well as the graphics) is done beforehand using other software.

✔ Today's more expensive word-processing software includes many of the features of desktop publishing programs. Unless you're in the publishing business, your word processor can probably handle your desktop publishing needs.

✔ This book was created using PC software. The original text was composed in Microsoft Word. Graphics were captured from the screen by a program called HiJaak 95. Adobe Illustrator was used to create some of the graphics. Finally, everything was put together in a desktop publishing program called PageMaker.

✔ Beverages consumed while creating this book: water, coffee, diet Coke, Barq's Old-Fashioned Root Beer, coffee, more water, coffee, and Tab.

✔ Ubiquitous = everywhere.

"You can use a computer to balance your checkbook"

The old reasons for getting a computer were quaint and impractical: You could balance your checkbook, keep track of your recipes, and create a Christmas mailing list. Sheesh. They should have said: You can meet the mate of your dreams, dial up the Pentagon and launch a weapon, or kill a million space monkeys without getting blood on your tunic.

Even so, one of the more popular software packages of all time is called Quicken. It's essentially a home (and business) accounting package that makes keeping track of your money easy and fun — yes, fun, in that most people actually sit down and balance their checkbooks because it's so dern easy.

Many home and business accounting applications are available. I'm not trying to push Quicken over the others (whose names I forget at the moment). And no, I don't own any Quicken stock or anything, but I do use the software and find that everyone else I show it to seems to say the same thing: "Jeez, Dan, your car payments are outrageous!"

The Numbery Stuff

Because word processors mangle words, other special software is required to mangle numbers. That software is generically referred to as *spreadsheet* software.

A spreadsheet uses a large grid of box-like *cells* on the screen (see Figure 19-2). Into those cells you can put text, numbers, or formulas. The formula part is what makes the spreadsheet so powerful: You can add various cells, compare values, and perform any number of odd or quirky mathematical operations. The whole thing is instantly updated, too; change one value and see how it reflects everything. Millions of dollars have been embezzled this way.

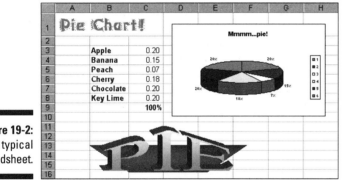

Figure 19-2:
A typical
spreadsheet.

Since their inception in the early 1980s, spreadsheets have changed dramatically. No, the math part is still the same. But as you can see from Figure 19-2, spreadsheets now have capabilities rivaling graphics and presentation programs. You can change the style of information in a spreadsheet, sprucing things up with fancy fonts, graphics, charts, and other impressive bells and whistles. All that stuff is a cinch to make. For example, the "pie" chart in Figure 19-2 took maybe 20 seconds to create after answering some simple yes-or-no questions. Amazing stuff. Good pie, too.

- ✔ The files saved by spreadsheets are called *worksheets*. A worksheet is created by a spreadsheet. Even so, many people refer to worksheets as spreadsheets. Ain't no crime in that.

- ✔ Most spreadsheets can convert numbers into graphs and charts, making it easier to visualize how much money the CEO is *really* making.

- ✔ All worksheets you create are blank, ready for you to fill them in. Some worksheets are not blank. They're called *templates,* and they're already customized to do specific tasks.

✔ Other uses for spreadsheets besides number crunching: organizing data of any type, creating charts and graphs, making illustrations, games (a popular 1-2-3 template at one time was called the Template of Doom), and creating anything that involves a grid (I know a woman who does quilt design in her spreadsheet).

✔ Number crunching = using a computer to work mathematical problems.

The databasey stuff

Because the word- and number-processing chores are snapped up by word processors and spreadsheets, database programs are required to mangle every other type of data out there.

Databases do two things: sort and report. They handle any type of information, whether it is words, numbers, or little-known bits of trivia (the *Lawrence Welk Show* was originally called the *Dodge Dancing Party* or the scientific name for a gorilla is *Gorilla, gorilla, gorilla*).

✔ Like spreadsheets, databases can be customized to match specific needs. Rather than toil on your own, you can hire a programmer to create a database perfectly suited to your line of work.

✔ Oh, heck, just put the programmer on the payroll; those guys never finish their work.

✔ Databases and spreadsheets can sometimes replace each other's jobs. If the fields in a database contain mostly numbers, a spreadsheet may work better. If a spreadsheet contains more labels and text, a database may be in order.

Database programs come in three unimportant types

Just as there are different programs to write text, there are different programs to store data. Three different types, in fact:

Free-form database: Perhaps the simplest database, it works best when you're organizing a big file that is full of random information. When you type the word *eggs,* the database retrieves every paragraph mentioning eggs, whether it is a grocery reminder, a favorite recipe, or the stock quote for a software store.

Flat-file database: A flat-file database helps retrieve information that's been organized into fields, records, and files. You can type a request or query, and the database then retrieves information about people named Thomas who drive Yugos and vote Democratic. It's more powerful than a free-form database, but it requires the information to be relatively organized to begin with.

Relational database: The most powerful database, which I don't know much about, but they tell me that it's expensive.

There are also different types of databases depending on what kind of user you are. For example, some database programs have all the forms ready and you need only fill in the blanks. Other databases require you to make the forms and design how everything looks. More complex databases have you do *everything,* including write the program that runs the database.

Essence of a database

Most database programs store information by dividing it into smaller and smaller pieces. For example, that database itself — containing all the information — is a file on disk. The file is divided into *records,* like those multicolored folders you used to see in doctors' offices. *(They claim that doctors' offices will be the very last thing to ever be computerized.)* The records are divided into *fields.* A *field* is a single piece of data: a person's last name on a form, for instance.

- ✔ In most database programs, you press Tab when you want to move from field to field in a database. (Hold down the Shift and press Tab if you want to move backward.) Use the Enter key only when you're saving a record to disk.

- ✔ Of all computer software, databases are about the slowest. Especially if you have particularly huge files, it takes a lot of time to fetch information from the database.

The Drawing and Painting Stuff

As any parent of a preschooler knows, nothing makes a mess faster than artwork in progress. With a PC, however, all the mess stays on the computer screen — no Crayola marks or paint drippings. Hundreds of graphics warriors, in fact, have already swapped their oils and acrylics for a computer. Graphics programs come in varying degrees of sophistication, each with a different target audience in mind:

Simple paint programs: These are on the level of the Paint program that comes with Windows. You can draw interesting and often useful pictures, but there is limited control and variety of the things the program can do or paint.

Drawing programs: These programs create images as objects, so you can create a box object, circle object, and text object. The objects can be edited and changed, unlike in a paint program, where you're essentially spraying pixels on the screen.

Advanced painting programs: These painting programs have a wide variety of painting tools to create all sorts of interesting effects. Figure 19-3 shows you what some effects look like.

Figure 19-3:
This graphic was created by an advanced painting program.

Illustration programs: These programs combine the tools of drawing and advanced painting programs. They're used primarily by graphics artists to create illustrations — like the ones you see in *USA Today* or on wine bottles or posters advertising art shows. You know the type. Figure 15-1 (back in Chapter 15, of course) of the 101-key keyboard was created by using a program of this type.

CAD: This software handles extremely detailed or technical drawings. CAD lets engineers do such scientific things as design new three-tray micro-wavable containers for frozen New Orleans-style chicken and broccoli.

✔ Windows comes with a simple paint program cleverly called Paint (look on the Accessories submenu). It's a basic graphical paint program, but it's powerful enough to create some of the images you see in this book.

✔ The advanced painting program used to create Figure 19-3 is Fractal Design Painter 4. It's a very complex program to master, but when you do, it's a snap to create stunning images.

✔ My favorite illustration program is Adobe Illustrator. Especially with Version 8.0, Adobe really created a handy tool for the kind of art that litters this book's pages. Also popular: CorelDRAW!

✔ CAD is a unique animal. The software is expensive, though cheap versions exist if you just want to experiment. The granddaddy here is AutoCAD. A monster of a program, but just about anyone who needs CAD software has it.

✔ Most of the best drawing and painting programs come on the Macintosh, which is why the beret-heads prefer that computer. The software is also available on Windows and works just as well.

Games and Entertainment (Multimedia)

They used to call this category "multimedia." Because multimedia describes any sort of flashy graphics mixed with sound, that catchall term generally covers programs designed to either entertain or educate you. It's a big area, one you need to cautiously tread.

✔ *Multimedia* incorporates two "mediums" — in the computer world, a computer plays sound while it displays something flashy on-screen.

✔ Multimedia applications require a powerful computer, a top-quality monitor, a large hard disk, a sound card, a 3-D graphics card, and typically a CD-ROM drive (see Chapter 7).

✔ Since every PC comes with a large hard disk, sound card, and CD-ROM drive, a "multimedia PC" isn't an exception today. No, it's the *mono-media* PC that's the exception.

✔ Most "multimedia" PCs sold today are called "entertainment" PCs. Still, it's questionable who is getting entertained — you or your computer.

Would you like to play a game?

Nintendo, Sega, and Sony shouldn't be afraid of each other dominating the home-based video gaming market. The battle is over. The PC won! Since all PCs sold today are multimedia machines as well as powerful computers, they are the best vehicle to lead the race down the arcade superhighway. PCs are *great* game machines.

You can play several categories of games on your PC:

Arcade: These are the classic games, the shoot-em-ups, puzzles, or maze games similar to the ones you used to drop quarters into back in the early 1980s. It's my favorite category, but also the smallest.

Simulation: The most popular type of game in this category is the flight simulator. Just like flying a big jet (pilot to Figure 19-4), you take off, climb to cruising altitude, navigate, see the sights, and then plow into a shopping mall as you attempt to land. Other popular simulators involve golf (do 18 holes on your butt!), war and battle simulations, sporting games (which used to be in the arcade category), and the ever-popular SimCity-like simulations, where you create and manage an artificial world, watching it grow.

Figure 19-4:
Microsoft Flight Simulator is about to take off into the Hancock building.

Virtual Reality: Once these were the "little man" games. You know: You'd navigate a little man across the screen, traversing various obstacles, picking things up, and, eventually, reaching some goal. With today's powerful PCs, now *you* are the little man. You see what he sees, you walk through his world, you suffer from his enemies and graphically see them destroyed. Games like Doom, Duke Nukem, Descent, Quake, and Myst are popular in this area. Be warned: These games can get violent! (See the following sidebar, "Rating the games.")

✔ In addition to the CD-ROM and sound card, you may also need a joystick to play most PC games. It's not a necessity, however; most games can also be played using the keyboard or mouse. But unless you have a joystick with at least 45 knobs, dials, and buttons on it, you're just a tyro.

✔ My favorite games are the arcades. I just love blasting the little aliens away — especially after being on the phone with my publisher.

✔ Another popular way to play games is online. You can find plenty of sites to play interactive games online with one or more other folks.

✔ Games are disk-hogs. Read the box before you buy to see how much disk space they need. Even if you have a 2GB hard drive, expect your extra storage to dwindle fast after you install two or three games.

✔ The best microprocessors for PC computer games are any MMX Pentium, AMD MMX, and AMD 3DNow! chips. However, to get the most from that setup, you have to buy a game that supports the MMX or 3DNow! instruction sets. It will say this on the box, so don't try to disassemble the program's code to figure it out on your own.

Rating the games

Nothing can be so disappointing as buying what you think is a nice, engaging computer game for your 9-year-old, only to find him frothing at the mouth as he controls a character on the screen who's ripping the spine from its electronic opponent. To prevent such shock (to the parent, not to the electronic opponent, who really doesn't feel a thing), two rating systems have evolved to allow parents or any PC game buyer to know what to expect before buying anything.

The Entertainment Software Review Board (ESRB) uses a five-level scale similar to movie ratings for its games (I'd show you the graphics here, but they're trademarked and I'm too lazy to get permission):

✔ **EC:** Early Childhood, the game is designed for young children and would probably bore a teenager to tears.

✔ **K-A:** Kids to adult, a G-rated game.

✔ **T:** A "teen" game, with some violence and language, but nothing too offensive.

✔ **M:** Mature audiences only, preferably 17 years old or older.

✔ **AO:** Adults only, with strong sexual content or gross violence. It's the stuff they keep in the back room.

Competing with the ESRB is the Recreational Software Advisory Council (RSAC). Unlike ESRB, which reviews software submitted to it, the RSAC is a voluntary rating decided by the software developer. It has three categories: Violence, Nudity/Sex, and Language. For each category, a tiny thermometer rates the content at four levels; level four is the most offensive. (I'm personally striving for a level five in any category.)

As an example, a game I purchased recently has an RSAC Advisory label proclaiming that the game has a Violence rating of three and a Language rating of two. The explanations given on the software box are, for Violence, "Blood and gore"; for Language it's "Profanity." (Please don't draw any conclusions about what type of game I like to play based on my "research." A-hem.)

If you have Internet access, you can get more information from these Web sites:

ESRB: `www.esrb.org/`

RSAC: `www.rsac.org/`

The box can teach

Computers have always had educational software. It may not have been as flashy or as animated and noisy as it is today, but it's a grand old tradition. And don't just think that identifying shapes or learning ABCs is all educational software can do; it can teach you anything from how to type to reading music to connecting a 24,000-watt transformer to your cell phone.

Like games, educational software comes in different types. Mavis Beacon (oh, Mavis!) teaches typing through a series of drills cleverly disguised as games. Dr. Seuss's ABCs is a read-along computer "book" that educates as it entertains. My least favorite type, however, is the book-on-the-screen software. No one wants to sit there and read text on a computer screen. It's just not fun.

✔ The best way to find good educational software is to ask around. Discover what others are using. Ask what the schools and preschools recommend. Family magazines, both computer and non-computer, have reviews and recommendations as well.

✔ Try to avoid game software that masks as educational. A hefty chunk of software designed for young children is really silly games with some educational bits tossed in as an afterthought. Your kid may have fun, but he won't be learning as well as he would otherwise.

✔ If you ever find yourself justifying a computer game with the catch-phrase "hand-eye coordination," be aware that something better is probably available. In fact, the best hand-eye coordination you can have your kids do is play catch or hit a ball with a bat.

✔ Another type of software in the educational category is the reference. The best example I can think of is the Microsoft Encarta encyclopedia. It's like a regular encyclopedia, but with animated references, sounds, and links to related topics. It's a great way to waste time and learn something all at once.

The Utility Stuff

Most software is designed to help you get to work. Utility programs help your *computer* get to work. Basically, a utility helps a computer accomplish a chore, whether it's organizing its hard drive or figuring out why it's not working right. In fact, most utilities are disk utilities.

Windows comes with many of the utilities you need. To see its portfolio of disk utilities, right-click on a disk drive and choose Properties from the pop-up menu. Click on the Tools tab, and you see three disk utilities you can (and should) run from time to time. Figure 19-5 shows the Tools tab on the disk drive Properties menu.

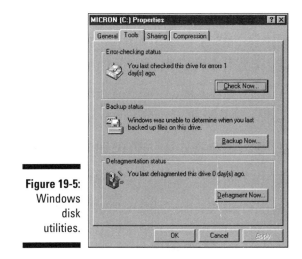

Figure 19-5:
Windows
disk
utilities.

✔ Windows comes with a few handy utilities, but that doesn't mean you shouldn't buy any more. Many third-party utilities are tons better than the stuff Windows has.

✔ One utility that Windows doesn't come with is a virus checker. These utilities scan your hard drive for any evil programs and wipe them out before the viruses try some nasty trick. Virus checkers are vitally important if you download lots of files from the Internet (refer to Chapter 24).

✔ Although Windows comes with a backup program (for making safety copies of the files on your hard drive), it's kind of lame. I recommend buying a separate backup program. If you buy a tape drive for your PC, backup software comes with it. Good stuff.

✔ Even though Windows can, supposedly, uninstall software, you might consider buying an uninstall program. This type of program does a much better job than Windows by itself, often saving you lots of disk space in the process. I recommend CleanSweep, from Quarterdeck Systems, as an excellent uninstall program.

Those Office-Type Programs

To make even more money, the software developers have come up with so-called Office Suite types of programs. These are actually several packages all sold as a single unit. You can buy them cheaper that way, plus the software company makes oodles of money selling you upgrades from time to time. (More on upgrading in Chapter 20.)

Office packages are great when you're starting out. But you might not consider one if you're buying it for just one piece of pie. For example, if you're buying Microsoft Office just to run Excel or Word, consider buying them separately. There's no point in junking up your hard drive with stuff you'll never use.

✔ Most people buy Microsoft Office to run Word. That's it! They pay for the other programs, but never use them.

✔ I might also mention that it's a waste of disk space to install programs you don't plan to use.

✔ Most office programs allow you to select which of their applications you want to install when you set them up. You always have the option of adding the other applications later, so just select what you need to start out.

✔ A good office program should offer: a word processor, spreadsheet, database, graphics or presentation program, and — most important — the capability to integrate each of those items. Everything should work together smoothly.

What about Shareware and Public Domain Software (Freeware)?

Frustrated by the system, some programmers give away their programs for free. Seriously! But there's a catch: They ask you to send them money on the honor system if you like their program. Because they're bypassing the traditional, expensive way to sell software, they don't ask for much; most charge from $5 to $45 for their *shareware*. When you mail in the check, the programmer mails back the latest version of the software and a manual.

Other programmers give away their programs but don't ask for money in return. They figure that they're making a humble contribution toward making the world a better place to compute. This free software is called *public domain* software or *freeware*.

Ask your computer guru for more details on shareware and public domain programs. Or check with any local computer user groups. Or, if you're feeling particularly adventurous, buy a modem and join an online service or cruise the Internet for software. (See Part VI.)

Chapter 20

Getting Used to Software

. . . .

. . . .

*U*sing software means using your computer. You may punch the Enter key on the keyboard, but it's some piece of software which gives that action significance, either running a word processor, launching an intercontinental ballistic missile, or erasing every last file on your hard drive. Yea, verily, software hath the power.

Tons of tomes have been written on how to make software work for you. It would be silly for me to document all that here. Instead, this chapter focuses on the getting-started aspect of software: how to buy it, set it up, get used to it, and uninstall it if you hate it.

A journey of ten thousand steps starts off with a good supply of bunion pads.
— Lao Tsu

A Few Words on Buying Software

Buying software is part of the computer-buying process. You pick out your software *first,* and then pick the hardware to match. But so many software packages are out there that it's easy to feel like you're making a dopey decision.

To prevent that foreboding and dread, you can always comparison-shop for software. Better still, I recommend seeing what other people are using. What do they use at the office? What do your computer-literate friends enjoy using or recommend? Make sure that you get what's right for you, not just what's cheap and popular.

- ✔ Try before you buy software.
- ✔ Have someone at the store demonstrate the software for you.
- ✔ Always check out a store's return policy on software.
- ✔ Check the software's requirements. They should match your computer's hardware inventory.

What's This Stuff in the Box?

Surprisingly, many large software boxes contain air or cardboard padding to make the boxes look bigger and more impressive in the store. I suppose that the idea is to push the competition off the shelf. It also gives you a sense of worth, because paying $279 for a computer CD and flimsy booklet seems more important if it's in a hefty box.

The most vital things inside the software box are the disks. The box will have either one computer CD in there or — if your PC doesn't have a CD-ROM drive — the version with anywhere from 2 to 36,000 floppy disks. You'll probably find a manual and a few other goodies, too. Here's the rundown:

Disks: Never toss these out! I always keep them in the box they came in, especially after installation.

The Horrid Manual: Most programs toss in a printed manual, typically the size of a political pamphlet. You may have more than one manual. Look for the "Getting Started," "Installation," or "Setup" section of the manual first.

Registration card: Resembling a boring postcard, this card usually sits right on top. You fill out your name and address and answer a few questions about the software, and then you mail the card back to the company. The company then (supposedly) notifies you of any defects, including nonfunctional commands or air bag problems. Some companies require you to fill out the registration card before they'll offer technical support over the phone.

Why are computer manuals so horrid?

Computer manuals have a bad rap. Things are better today than they were 15 years ago. Back then, everyone was a nerd. Most manuals just began, "Flip these switches to enter base hexadecimal address pairs for IPL." And *that* was considered user-friendly.

Why are the manuals so bad? Many reasons. Primarily, the manual is written as an afterthought. The software developer spends more time and attention on building the product. The manual is given to someone reluctant to create it, often the product manager or programmer. They're far too familiar with the product to compose a useful manual, and they don't care about getting it done properly.

Manuals must also be completed long before the product is done. It takes longer to print 10,000 manuals than it takes to copy 10,000 disks. Therefore, the manual is often inaccurate or vague.

Size is an issue. Most manuals are slim because their weight adds to the product's shipping cost. Some places don't even bother with a manual, instead putting everything on disk in "read me" or "help" files. (Obviously, it's not the developer's intention to ensure that you enjoy and use the product to its full capabilities.)

People who write computer manuals are usually paid by the hour or on salary. No one in that position is going to put his or her heart into creating the best possible work. That's why books on the subject are far better than manuals: The author is trying to make money by writing a successful book. The writers at the software company pick their noses and watch the clock.

Quick-reference card: The manual works fine for explaining everything in great detail, but you'll find yourself continually repeating some commands. A quick-reference card contains those useful commands; it can be propped up next to the keyboard for quick sideways glances. Not all software comes with these cards, however.

Quick-installation card: Computer users thrive on instant gratification: Push a button and watch your work be performed instantly. Nobody wants to bother with slow, thick manuals, especially when they're installing the software. A quick-installation card contains an abbreviated version of the manual's installation instructions. By typing in the commands on the card, you can install the software without cracking open the manual. Victory!

License agreement: This extensive batch of fine print takes an average of 3,346 words of legalese to say four things: 1) Don't give away any copies of this program to friends — make them buy their own program. 2) If you accidentally lose any data, it's not our fault. 3) If this software doesn't work, that's not our fault, either. 4) In fact, you don't even own this software. You merely own a license to use the software. We own the software. We are evil. We will one day own the world.

Sometimes the licensing agreement is printed on a little sticker on an envelope; you have to tear apart the agreement before you can get to the disks inside. Whether this means that you agree with it is up to a battalion of attorneys to discover.

Read me first: When the company finds a mistake in its newly printed manual, it won't fix it and print a new one. It prints the corrections on a piece of paper and slaps the headline "Read Me First!" across the top. Staple that piece of paper to the inside cover of your manual for safekeeping.

✔ Sometimes you don't get a manual. You may find an installation card or pamphlet. The manual is "on the disk." Egads!

✔ Thank goodness software boxes aren't junky, like those magazine publisher sweepstakes things. You can never find the things you need to fill in, stickers to place over the TV set or on Ed's head, options to clip. What nonsense! Software boxes are much neater by comparison.

Software Installation Chores

The first step in installing software is simple:

1. **Get someone else to do it for you.**

   Maybe you have a computer guru (see Chapter 26). Maybe there's an office IS guy. If not, the following guidelines may help. All software packages handle the details a bit differently, so don't be surprised if you find yourself surprised.

   Or

1. **Read the "Read Me" blurb.**

   When you first open the box, scrounge around for a piece of paper that says "Read Me First!" and follow the first instruction: Read it. Or at least try to make some sense of it.

   Sometimes the Read Me First sheet contains a sentence or two left out of the manual's third paragraph on page 127, "Dwobbling your shordlock by three frips." If you don't understand it, don't throw it away. It may come in handy after you've started using the program.

2. **Set the manual(s) aside.**

   Say "There" when you do this step.

3. **Put the Installation disk into your disk drive.**

   Find the disk marked with the words *Installation* or *Setup* or *Disk One*, and place that disk in the disk drive where it fits.

Hopefully it's a computer CD. If not, it's a 3¹/₂-inch disk. Like cockroaches, it's the first of many.

TIP

If you're installing from floppy disks, put them in a neat stack, in order, first disk on top. That way, you can easily feed them, one after the other, into the disk drive without having to rummage for the next disk later.

4. Start the Installation program.

Open the Control Panel; choose Settings⇨Control Panel from the Start menu. (On most Windows 95 and 98 computers, if you turn on the AutoRun feature, the CD or disk info automatically pops up.)

Add/Remove
Programs

Double-click on the Add/Remove Programs icon. The Add/Remove Program Properties dialog box is displayed (see Figure 20-1).

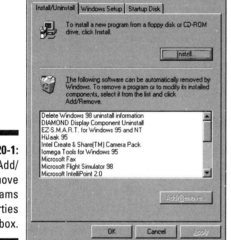

Figure 20-1:
The Add/
Remove
Programs
Properties
dialog box.

Click on the Install button.

Windows goes out to your disk drives and searches for the proper installation disk. It then runs the Install or Setup program.

That's all the Add/Remove Programs icon does. It merely looks for the Install or Setup program that truly installs your software. After that, it's your new program's installation program that takes over.

5. Read the screen carefully; click the Next button as necessary.

The installation program starts placing instructions on the screen.

Watch the instructions carefully; sometimes they slip something important in there. My friend Jerry (his real name) just kept clicking the Next button instead of reading the screen. He missed an important notice which said that an older version of the program would be erased. Uh-oh! Poor Jerry never got his program back.

6. **Choose various options.**

The software asks for your name and company name, and maybe for a serial number. Type all that stuff in.

Don't freak if the program already knows who you are. Windows is kinda clairvoyant in that respect.

When you're asked to make a decision, the option already selected (the *default*) is typically the best option. Only if you know what's going on and *truly care* about it should you change anything.

The serial number can be found inside the manual, on the CD-ROM case, the first disk in the stack of $3^1/_2$-inch disks, or on a separate card you probably threw away even though I told you to keep everything in the original box.

7. **Files are copied.**

Eventually, the installation program copies the files from the disks or CD-ROM drive to your hard drive for full-time residence.

If you're unlucky enough to be installing from floppy disks, keep feeding them, one after the other, into the floppy drive. Make sure that you get them in the proper order (they're numbered). Make sure that you remove one disk and replace it with the next disk.

8. **It's done.**

The installation program ends. The computer may reset at this point. That's required sometimes when you're installing special programs Windows needs to know about. (Windows is pretty dumb after it starts.)

Start using the program!

✔ These steps are vague and general. Hopefully, your new software comes with more specific instructions.

✔ It's also possible to get software from the World Wide Web on the Internet. See Chapter 23 for brief instructions.

✔ Keep the quick-reference card next to your computer immediately after installing the program; the card is more helpful than the manual.

A few paranoid words about sending in the registration card

You won't find this in any software manual: Be wary of sending in a registration card! I'm not recommending against it entirely; I just don't think it's absolutely necessary. Call me paranoid, but I find it odd that after I send a registration card to some outfit, I get a lot of junk mail related to the product I just registered. Also, even though I get promises to be notified of a new version, I never do. I registered six copies of one program at my office and got nothing in the mail about the latest version. My suspicions grow.

I do recommend registering any product that comes with a unique serial number. All of Adobe's software (PageMaker, Illustrator, and so on) requires this number. It won't give you support or special deals on software upgrades unless you register. For Adobe, plus a few other companies that really do notify you of new software releases, registration is a must. For most everyone else, it's iffy.

Here are some thoughts and suggestions:

✔ If you don't register your software, keep the registration card and any serial numbers handy. You may need them in the future.

✔ Never tell one software company about the programs you own from another company. For example, if you just bought a utility program, don't list all the other utility programs you use on the registration card. That's a marketing ploy; if you follow through, you will be bombarded with competitive upgrade offers.

✔ Be careful when you use your modem to register. Any program that registers you by modem may go through your computer, gathering information on all the software you own, and send that information away. Microsoft is notorious for doing that. That information in your computer is your *personal* business. No other organization should know about it. You can deselect programs you don't want the manufacturer to know about, if you're concerned about this issue.

✔ It's okay to register by fax, but print the fax on your printer so that you can edit it before sending. Use a marker to blot out any information that's none of their business.

✔ Consider filling out the registration card by using a unique middle initial or first name. For example, I registered a utility program using the name *Dan U. Gookin*. Now I know where junk mail for *Dan U. Gookin* comes from.

Uninstalling Software

To remove any newly installed program, you use an uninstall program. This is not a feature of Windows, though Windows makes it easier. Apparently, your program must have its own uninstall feature for it to work. Otherwise, you're stuck with it.

Do not attempt to uninstall *any* software by deleting it from your hard drive. You should never delete any file you did not create yourself. (You can, however, delete any shortcuts you create.)

Uninstalling software is done the same way you installed it: Open the Control Panel's Add/Remove Programs icon. This step displays the Add/Remove Programs Properties dialog box, as shown back in Figure 20-1.

The list of programs Windows knows about and can uninstall is listed at the bottom of the dialog box. Click on one of those programs, the one you want to uninstall. This step selects the program for action. Then click the Add/Remove button.

A warning dialog box is displayed before Windows yanks the cord on your program. Click Yes to zap it to Kingdom Come.

- ✔ Need I say anything about being careful with this stuff?

- ✔ Third-party uninstall programs do a better job than Windows does. For one, you may notice that not all your programs are listed in the Add/Remove Programs Properties dialog box. Those third-party uninstallers can hunt down rogue files and safely eliminate all their bits and pieces.

- ✔ The Add/Remove button can also be used to add individual components to your programs. For example, you could click on Microsoft Office to add a new component or piece of that software, something you didn't choose to install way back when.

- ✔ For adding components missing from Windows, choose the Windows Setup panel in the Add/Remove Programs Properties dialog box.

Upgrading or Updating Your Software

When a novel's written, it's finished. Subsequent reprints correct a few misspellings, but that's about it. But software's never finished. It's too easy to change. Most software packages are updated about once a year.

Why update? Sometimes the company fixes a few problems, or bugs. Most often, the software contains new features so that it can compete with the other guy's software. That's why new versions appear. The upgrade gives you access to the newer, bug-free software and its features. It also lets software companies grow rich by charging you all over again for something you already own.

My advice: Order the update only if it has features or makes modifications you desperately need. Otherwise, if the current version is doing the job, don't bother.

✔ Consider each upgrade offer on its individual merits: Will you ever use the new features? Do you need a word processor that can print upside-down headlines and bar charts that show your word count? Can you really get any mileage from the "intranet version" when you're a sole user sitting at home?

✔ Something else to keep in mind: If you're still using DoodleWriter 4.2 and everybody else is using DoodleWriter 6.1, you'll have difficulty exchanging documents. After a while, newer versions of programs become incompatible with older models.

✔ In an office setting, everybody should be using the same software version. (Everybody doesn't have to be using the *latest* version, just the *same* version.)

✔ If the book industry worked like the software industry, Tom Clancy would have gotten a phone call several years back: "Hey, Tom, babe, you know the old Soviet Union has collapsed? Time to rewrite *The Hunt for Red October!* Maybe change the bad guys to Iraqis or something. Get with the times!"

What about upgrading Windows?

Yeah, Windows is software, just like other programs on your computer. And Windows gets updated every so often. Only, when it does, it's a *big deal*. Why? Because everything else in your computer relies on Windows. Therefore, it's a major change, something to think long and deep about.

Often the newer version of Windows has many more features than the older version. Do you need those features? If not, don't bother with the update.

One problem you may have if you decide to upgrade is that your software may not work properly. None of my Adobe applications worked with Windows 95 when it first came out. I had to wait months and pay lots of money for upgrades before things got back to normal.

When Windows 98 came out, I opted not to upgrade so that I wouldn't have to go through the same hassle.

After a time, you may notice newer software packages coming to roost on the newest version of Windows. The new stuff will be better than your current stuff, meaning that you need to upgrade if you want to take advantage of it.

So where does this leave you? Don't bother updating Windows. Just wait until you buy a new computer, and then the newest version of Windows will come on that PC, all pre-installed and set up nicely. The old version will always work as long as you use it. Bill Gates himself is (or was) fond of saying, "Software never gets obsolete." I might add: as long as you're using it.

Some Tips for Learning a Program

Using software involves learning its quirks. That takes time. My first suggestion for learning any new software is to give yourself plenty of time. Sadly, in today's rush-rush way of doing everything, time isn't that easy to come by. It's a big pain when the boss sends you down to the software store expecting you to come back and create something wonderful before the end of the day. In the real world, that's just not possible (not even if you're an "expert").

Most software comes with a workbook or a tutorial for you to follow. It's a series of self-guided lessons on how to use the product. It also tells you about the program's basic features and how they work. I highly recommend going through the tutorials. Follow the directions on the screen. If you notice anything interesting, write it down in the tutorial booklet and flag that page.

Some tutorials are really dumb, granted. Don't hesitate to bail out of one if you're bored or confused. You can also take classes on using software, though they may bore you as well. Most people do, however, understand the program much better after the tutorial.

After doing the tutorial, play with the software. Make something. Try saving something to disk. Try printing. Then quit. Those are the basic few steps you should take when you're using any software program. Get to know it, and then expand your knowledge from there as required.

- Some businesses may have their own training classes that show you the basics of using the in-house software. Take copious notes. Keep a little book for yourself with instructions for how to do what. Take notes whenever someone shows you something. Don't try to learn anything; just note what's done so that you don't have to make a call if the situation arises again.

- Never toss out your manual. In fact, I recommend going back and trying to read the manual again several weeks after you start to learn a program. You may actually understand things. (Consider that the fellow who wrote the manual knew the product about as well when he first sat down to write about it.)

- Computer books are also a good source to learn about programs. They come in two types: references and tutorials. The tutorial is great for learning; references are best when you know what you want to do but forgot how.

- This book is a reference. All ...*For Dummies* books are references.

Chapter 21

The Wonderful World of Fonts

● ●

In This Chapter

▶ Peeking in the Fonts folder

▶ Previewing your fonts

▶ Listing your fonts (or not)

▶ Adding new fonts

▶ Using fonts in your applications

▶ Changing Windows desktop fonts

● ●

Something Windows requires you to think about are fonts. What type of text style are you going to use to create that shopping list? Which font would look most effective for your resignation? And will the newspaper editor take me seriously if I use the Bembo font? It's a big decision — something DOS users never had to mess with. In the PC's text mode, all programs look the same — ugly. But with Windows and all its graphical fun and mayhem, you have fonts to fuss over.

This silly chapter is all about fonts. Why? Because during my travels, I've noticed that no other book ever bothers to go into the subject. Maybe those authors think it's boring. But there are enough questions and issues on the topic of fonts to make it worthwhile reading.

Where the Fonts Are

In a rare display of logic, Windows stores all your fonts in the Fonts folder. There are two ways to get there:

▶ From the Control Panel: Pop up the Start menu with Ctrl+Esc, and then choose Settings⇨Control Panel to open the Control Panel window. Open the Fonts folder by double-clicking it.

▶ If you're using My Computer or Explorer, you can find the Fonts folder in your Windows folder: Open My Computer. Open drive C, open Windows, and open the Fonts folder. Ta-da.

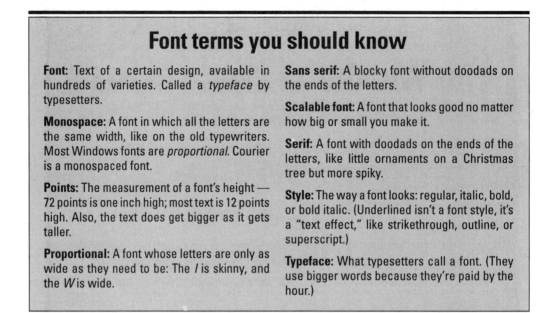

Font terms you should know

Font: Text of a certain design, available in hundreds of varieties. Called a *typeface* by typesetters.

Monospace: A font in which all the letters are the same width, like on the old typewriters. Most Windows fonts are *proportional*. Courier is a monospaced font.

Points: The measurement of a font's height — 72 points is one inch high; most text is 12 points high. Also, the text does get bigger as it gets taller.

Proportional: A font whose letters are only as wide as they need to be: The *I* is skinny, and the *W* is wide.

Sans serif: A blocky font without doodads on the ends of the letters.

Scalable font: A font that looks good no matter how big or small you make it.

Serif: A font with doodads on the ends of the letters, like little ornaments on a Christmas tree but more spiky.

Style: The way a font looks: regular, italic, bold, or bold italic. (Underlined isn't a font style, it's a "text effect," like strikethrough, outline, or superscript.)

Typeface: What typesetters call a font. (They use bigger words because they're paid by the hour.)

Figure 21-1 shows a typical Fonts window. There are way more fonts than can be shown in the window at once. Try using the View➪List command to see more at once. (Figure 21-1 shows the View➪Large Icons display.)

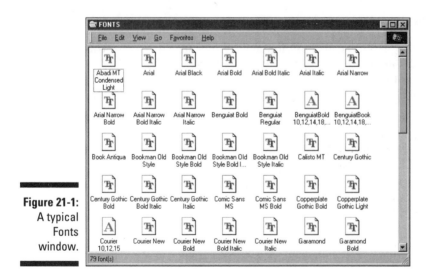

Figure 21-1:
A typical
Fonts
window.

✔ PostScript fonts and printer fonts may not be installed in the Windows Fonts folder. If you're using PostScript fonts with the Adobe Type Manager (ATM), you can use the ATM program to view your various fonts.

✔ Just because a font isn't visible doesn't mean that you don't have access to it. Check your application's Font command to confirm whether you have the font.

✔ Conversely, you may see some fonts in the Font window that don't show up on a font menu. Typically, those are screen fonts the application doesn't want you using anyway.

Previewing one of your fonts

The Fonts folder window shows you only the font's name and an icon indicating whether the font is a TrueType (TT) or Screen (A) font. To see what the font looks like, open the font icon.

Double-clicking a font icon displays a preview window, similar to the one shown in Figure 21-2. You see the font's name and other boring technical stuff, a preview of all the basic characters in the font, and then a looksee at the font in different sizes.

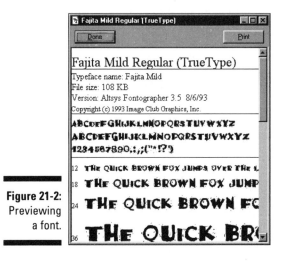

Figure 21-2:
Previewing
a font.

Close the font preview window when you're done a-gawkin'.

  ✔ Print the font preview by clicking the Print button.

  ✔ Close the preview window by clicking the Done button or clicking the window's X (close) button.

Listing all of your PC's fonts

Windows offers no way to display its entire cavalcade of fonts for you. Actually, I consider it a major concession that it even lets you preview fonts as discussed in the preceding section. Anyhoo, you have several methods for creating a list of your fonts, none of which is as easy as making toast.

First, you could buy a font manager program that organizes your fonts for you. Alas, I have no recommendations in this area, other than to say that there doesn't appear to be much demand for such software outside the graphic arts community.

Second, you can go through every dang-doodle font in the Fonts window, open it up for a preview, click the Print button, close the font, and repeat for, oh, say, 200 or so fonts.

Third (the one you're waiting for), you can create a sample text file containing all the PC's fonts. You can do it by using your word processor or WordPad.

Type every symbol, number, and letter (upper- and lowercase) for a font, organizing it all as shown in the following example. Title each font selected with the name of the font. Then select that chunk of text, and format it with that font. Here's a sample of what I mean:

Book Antiqua
Abcdefghijklmnopqrstuvwxyz
ABCDEFGHIJKLMNOPQRSTUVWXYZ
1234567890!@#$%^&*

Repeat that for every font you have, and then save the file to disk for printing and later updates. This saves oodles of time over using the font preview window. (Yeah, it still *takes* time, but this problem has no simple solution.)

  ✔ If you do opt to get a font manager utility, make sure that it's for Windows 95 or Windows 98 (whichever you have)! Most of the font managers I've run across are for the Macintosh. Better double-check that box to make sure that you're getting the right thing.

✔ If you opt to print all your fonts, go grab some three-ring hole-punched paper. Set your left margin so that it indents 2 inches. Then print each font. That way, you can bind the pages in a three-ring binder.

✔ Adobe has a free booklet, *Image Club Typeface Reference,* which includes all the fonts it sells plus a few dozen standard fonts. If you ever order anything from Image Club, ask them to send you the booklet for free. On the Web, you can visit Image Club at `http://www.imageclub.com/fonts/`.

Using Fonts

Windows comes with a few dozen fonts, and you can always add more (keep reading). Within Windows itself, and on the various font menus, you actually find two different types of fonts: TrueType and printer fonts.

The *TrueType* font is Windows' favorite. It's flagged on a font menu by the double T-T. This type of font looks good on the screen as well as on the printer. And it can be changed to any size, big or small, and still look like a font and not something a 3-year-old would build out of Legos.

A *printer font* is a font your printer is capable of creating, but one that Windows may not know about. These fonts are flagged by a tiny printer on the font menu. That tells you that the font will print properly but may not look right on the screen; Windows substitutes an equivalent font to display. What makes up for that is the fact that printer fonts print faster than other types of fonts.

A third type of font is the *screen font,* used by Windows for displaying information. These fonts are available in fixed sizes: 8, 10, 12, 14, 18, and 24 points. Most programs don't let you use these fonts, and if you do, they look good only in the sizes listed here. Otherwise, they're ugly as sin.

Installing a new and exciting font

You can buy a font at the software store, order it from a catalog, or download it from the Internet without paying a cent. Also, new fonts tend to come with new applications. Microsoft Office installs a dozen or so fonts. When I installed the latest version of Adobe Illustrator, it gave me more than 340 fonts. And your printer probably has fonts you can install. So getting new fonts isn't the problem. The problem is (and always has been) installing them.

If you got your new font with a new application, the application has probably set up everything for you. Otherwise, put your new font disk into your sweaty little hand and follow these steps:

1. **Open the Fonts folder window.**

   Refer to the instructions at the start of this chapter for information on displaying the Fonts folder window.

2. **Stick the font disk in your drive.**

   For a 3¹/₂-inch disk, put it in your floppy drive A. For a CD-ROM, drop the disc in your CD-ROM drive. (See Chapter 7 for more information on using disks and discs.)

3. **Choose File⇨Install New Font from the menu.**

   The Add Fonts dialog box appears, looking a lot like Figure 21-3.

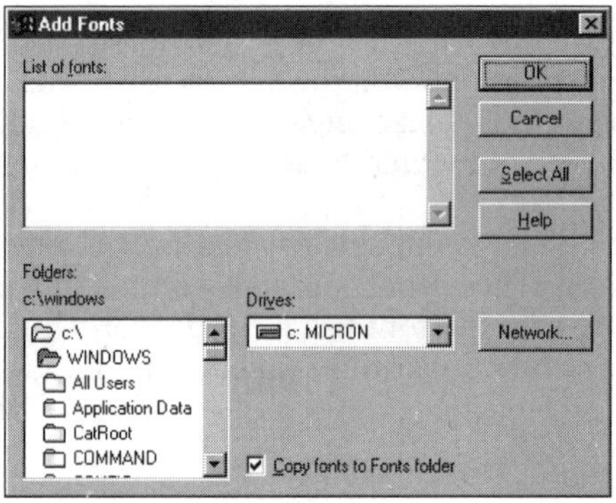

Figure 21-3:
The Add
Fonts dialog
box.

4. **Use the Drives drop-down list to locate your font disk.**

   If the fonts are in drive A, choose drive A; if they're in your CD-ROM drive, choose that drive letter. (Maybe D, could be E.)

   After choosing the proper drive, you see a list of fonts on that disk shown in the Add Fonts dialog box in the **List of Fonts** area.

   If no fonts are on the disk, you see some light text explaining, "No fonts found."

5. **Choose the fonts you want to install.**

   Click on a font to select it. Ctrl+click to select multiple fonts.

6. **Click OK.**

   The fonts are copied from the disk to the Fonts folder. You're done.

7. **Close the Fonts window (if you need to).**

✔ Remember to remove the font disk from your disk drive, especially if it's in drive A. Put the disk away in a safe place where you can get to it later if need be.

✔ Fonts can also be copied directly. You can open a window for the disk containing the fonts and then select and drag them over to the Fonts folder if you like. Personally, I find the Add Fonts dialog box easier.

✔ Install PostScript fonts by using the ATM utility. PostScript fonts may not necessarily be installed in the Fonts folder.

✔ Actually, when you buy a font, you typically get both PostScript and TrueType versions. To keep yourself sane, install only the TrueType version. You really need PostScript only if you have a PostScript printer.

Various and sundry font commands

Most programs in Windows have standardized font commands. You can change the font from a common Font dialog box or by using various buttons on a formatting toolbar.

Figure 21-4 shows a typical Font dialog box. Some may be more bleak; others, more fancy.

A Font dialog box works from left to right and from top to bottom. First, you select a font, then the style, and then the size. A preview or sample window shows you approximately what you're getting. Other text effects are added in the bottom of the dialog box.

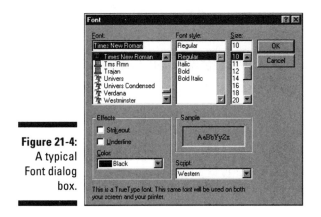

Figure 21-4:
A typical
Font dialog
box.

Outside the Font dialog box, you find various buttons and such on a toolbar.

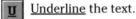

Use a font drop-down list to select a new font from a scrolling list. In some applications, your most recently used fonts appear at the top of the list. Otherwise, the fonts are shown alphabetically.

A size drop-down list is used to set the size of the font.

Make the text **bold**.

Make the text *italicized*.

Underline the text.

Set the text color.

Also set the text color (in WordPad).

Other buttons exist in various applications, some of which may work the same as these but use different pictures. Other buttons may offer more text-mangling features.

- Changes to a font affect any selected text. If text isn't selected, the new font changes affect text you type after closing the Font dialog box.

- Windows allows you to change the color of your fonts to something wild. Keep in mind that you can print in color only if you have a color printer.

- Windows is actually rather smart when it comes to fonts. You may notice various font "families" in your Fonts folder: Arial, Arial Bold, Arial Bold Italic, and Arial Italic, for example. When you're choosing a font, Windows lets you choose only Arial. If you select the Bold option, Windows automatically substitutes the Arial Bold font for you.

Changing Windows Desktop Fonts

Font play isn't limited to just your applications. You can also dink with the way Windows uses fonts. It's all perfectly legal and not a big hassle, as long as you follow these steps:

1. Summon the Control Panel.

From the Start menu, choose Settings⇨Control Panel. The Control Panel's window appears.

Display

2. **Open the Display icon.**

   Click-click. The Display Properties dialog box shows up (see Figure 21-5).

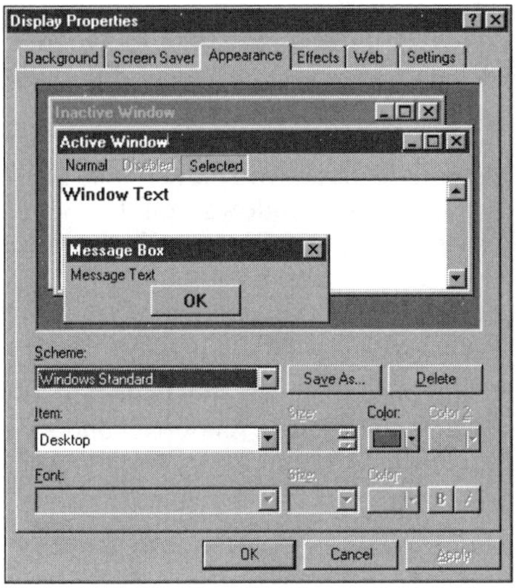

Figure 21-5:
The Display
Properties
dialog box.

3. **Bring forth the Appearance tab.**

   Click the Appearance tab to bring that page into the foreground. What you see should look almost like Figure 21-4. This is the place where you can change some of Windows' ugly features, primarily the colors and fonts.

4. **Set the font for one of the following: Active Title Bar, Inactive Title Bar, Menu (text), Message Box (text).**

   Choose one of these items from the Item drop-down list, or click the text you want to change in the preview window. After choosing the proper item, the Font drop-down list becomes active, allowing you to set a new font for one of Windows' many goodies.

5. **Optionally choose a size, color, or style for your font.**

   Select a point size for the font from the Size drop-down list.

   Choose a color for your font from the pop-up Color palette.

   The B button is used to make the font bold. It's an On-Off button; click once for bold; click again to make the text normal.

   The / button isn't a slash at all. That's an *I* for italics. Click once to make your text italicized; click again to turn it off.

   You can have both bold and italic text at the same time — if you're greedy.

6. Preview your new settings.

Click the Apply button to see how it looks "for real." That way, you can make minor adjustments easily from the dialog box. (If you click OK, the dialog box goes away after your changes are made.)

If you don't like what you've done, meaning that you've just wasted another good chunk of time in the name of "research," click the Cancel button.

If you really *hate* any changes you've made, you can choose one of the Windows preset appearance schemes in Windows from the Scheme drop-down list. The Windows Standard scheme is the one Windows came with.

✔ Several of the schemes available from the Scheme drop-down list also use interesting and different fonts. Check them out for some inspiration.

✔ Just as there are preset schemes, you can save your font and color selections as a scheme. Click on the Save As button and save your selections. They show up in the Scheme drop-down list with all the Windows presets.

Part VI
The Non-Nerd's Guide to the Internet

The 5th Wave   By Rich Tennant

©RICH TENNANT

Y'KNOW, I DON'T MIND LIVING IN A COMPUTERIZED 'SMART HOUSE,' BUT I DO MIND BEING CALLED AN IDIOT BY THE TOASTER.

In this part . . .

*W*hat was once a playground for UNIX boys and girls is now a major factor in using your PC. It's the Internet. It's big. It's vast. It's unexplainable. And it's fun and, maybe, a little useful. The former playground of UNIX is now the information garden for all PCs all over the world.

The Internet is about communications. It's sending and receiving information, either in the form of e-mail or in a magazine-like format on the World Wide Web (plus other ways and means too numerous to mention). This part of the book gives you a crash course in the Internet: connecting, using the Web, and reading e-mail. It's enough to get your feet wet and whet your appetite for more. Now go play!

Chapter 22

Doing the Internet Thing

• •

In This Chapter

▶ What the Internet is all about

▶ Five things you need to get on the Internet

▶ Finding an Internet Service Provider

▶ Setting up Windows for the Internet

▶ Connecting to the Internet

▶ Saying bah-bye to the Internet

• •

*W*ant to impress someone? Then go out and buy your own private island. Hobnobbing with Hollywood and Washington types at Martha's Vineyard every year might impress *some* people. But when it comes to computers, the only way you can impress someone is to say how much you use the Internet.

The Internet is, was, and shall be the Next Big Thing in computing. But don't believe the hype. Buried in the hoopla is a loose connection of government, educational, and high-tech industry computers that all chat with each other. There are millions of things to do and see on the Internet, plus you may actually get to meet some of the most obnoxious people in all of humanity. No wonder everyone is nuts about it!

> ✔ This chapter covers getting on the Internet and some Internet basics.
>
> ✔ Chapter 23 covers the World Wide Web, which is the most fun part of the Internet.
>
> ✔ Chapter 24 deals with e-mail, which to most people is really the best (and most productive) part of the Internet.
>
> ✔ The final chapter in this Internet discussion (Chapter 25, if you're keeping count) covers sending and receiving files on the Internet and through your e-mail.
>
> ✔ This is by no means an end-all discussion of the Internet and everything you can do there. If you find this stuff appealing, I urge you to go out and buy a book about the Internet or the World Wide Web. The shelves are full of 'em.

The 29¢ Description of the Internet

I'm often asked to describe the Internet. Here is the speech I give in reply, greatly condensed for the typical inattentive television viewer:

The Internet is not a piece of software. It's not a computer. Instead, the Internet is thousands and thousands of computers all over the world. The computers send information. They receive information. And, most importantly, they store information. That's the Internet.

Q: You mean, the Internet isn't a big computer somewhere?

A: No, Bob, I'm sorry. It's not. Bill Gates would like it to be his computer, but it just isn't.

- ✔ The idea behind using the Internet is to get at that information.
- ✔ The best way to get at the information stored on the Internet is by using a piece of software called a Web browser. This subject is covered in the next chapter.

The Five Things You Need to Get on the Internet

To access the Internet from your very own computer, you need five things. Chances are that you already have four of the five.

You need a computer. Any computer will do. Because the Internet comes through your PC's modem, it doesn't matter how fast your PC is.

You need a modem. Speed counts here. Get the fastest modem you can afford. A 28.8 Kbps modem was great a few years ago. Today, get a 57.6 Kbps modem. (See Chapter 17 for more modem mayhem.)

You need Internet software. Windows comes with Internet Explorer, a Web browser you can use to get on the Internet. Or you can use Netscape Navigator, which is a superior product, but it doesn't work well with Windows 98. (More ranting on this topic in Chapter 23.)

You need money. Access to the Internet costs you, just like cable TV. Expect to pay anywhere from $5 to $50 a month to get on the Internet, depending on what your Internet Service Provider has to offer.

You need an Internet Service Provider (ISP). This one is the only item you probably don't have. Obtaining an ISP is covered in the next section.

✔ Though the Internet isn't a program, you need special software to access the Internet and to send or retrieve information.

✔ In addition to an ISP, you can also access the Internet through an online service like America Online, CompuServe, MSN, or Prodigy. The Internet connection is made through those services' specialized software. That's okay if you're just checking things out, but if you really want to use the Internet, it's best to get an ISP and avoid the overhead of an online service.

✔ This book does not cover accessing the Internet through America Online, CompuServe, MSN, Prodigy, or any other major online service.

✔ If you work for a large company, it may already give you Internet access through the network at your office. Ditto for universities and some government installations. The best part: Access is usually free! The worst part: You can be easily tempted to do non-work stuff on the Internet, even when researching or using the Internet is part of your job or schoolwork.

The Internet Service Provider (ISP)

The best way to get on the Internet is through an ISP. It gives you a direct connection to the Internet, plus it may offer 24-hour help or classes to get you started. Most communities have several ISPs offering access to the Internet. You can find them in the yellow pages under "Internet." Some of them even advertise on TV, usually late at night along with the 1-900 psychic babe hotlines.

The ISP provides you with phone access to the Internet, various goodies on the Internet, and — since the S in ISP stands for *service* — help and support if you need it. You pay your ISP a sign-up fee plus a given amount each month, and you should receive something back for that. For the sign-up fee, you should get a little booklet or "getting started" pamphlet plus a disk with some basic Internet software on it.

In addition to a "getting started" booklet and disk, your ISP should provide you with most, if not all, of the following:

✔ **Unlimited access time:** Some ISPs charge by the hour. Avoid them. If they charge by the block of time, get a plan where you can have 100 or more hours a month. Only the very sturdy can be on the Internet for more than 100 hours in a month.

✔ **A local phone number to dial.**

✔ **Information on how to connect to the Internet:** Techy stuff like a DNS server number, gateway address, mail server name, news server name, and other names and numbers.

✔ **A login name and password:** You want a SLIP or PPP (or the newer PPTP) account.

Don't get a "shell" account unless you enjoy using UNIX.

✔ **An e-mail account or mailbox:** The name you'll be using to send and receive e-mail over the Internet. (See Chapter 24.) It's best if you get to pick your e-mail name. I hate it when they just assign you a number or some gobbledygook for a name.

Be aware that some e-mail names may already be taken. For example, both "stud" and "nerdboy" were already taken by other users at my ISP.

✔ **Access to newsgroups:** The more the merrier. Tens of thousands of newsgroups are available, about a third of which are in English. Avoid an ISP that censors newsgroups; you are your own best censor.

✔ **"Web space" or disk storage space:** A small amount of the provider's disk storage you can use for whatever. If the ISP offers it, the space can be used so that you may create your own Web page there at some point in the future.

✔ **Bonus goodies:** These apply only if you're creating your own Web page: FTP access; Real Audio/Video capabilities; CGI programming; Web page statistics; and a grab bag of other goodies that are way too complex to get into now but not bad things to find out about when you're starting.

If your area has more than one ISP, shop around. Find the one giving you the best deal. Often times the cheapest ISP lacks a lot of features other ISPs offer (but they don't tell you that unless you know what you're missing). Also, it's cheaper to pay quarterly or annually (if you can afford it). These places can wheel and deal with you — providing that you know a bit about what you want.

Don't be afraid to change ISPs if yours doesn't work out. I did that. My first ISP was snoozing and never told me about any of its new features. Heck, it didn't even offer newsgroups. Changing to a new ISP was no problem.

✔ Your Internet login ID and password will be different from the user ID and password you use to get into Windows. You need a different ID and password for each system you access.

✔ Your ISP may give you two IDs and passwords: One may be required when you first connect to the service, and another is for when you access your e-mail. Write them both down. (Put the paper away in a safe place.)

✔ The best ISP by far is the one that gives you a little booklet and a "getting started" disk. That really makes it easy.

✔ I might add that ISPs with 24-hour service rank high on my list. If your e-mail dies at 11:00 p.m. and you need to get online, it's nice to have someone there who can help you.

✔ If the ISP does give you a disk, make sure that it's for your version of Windows. The older Windows 3.1 Internet stuff should not be used on newer Windows 95 and Windows 98 PCs.

✔ The typical ISP charges around $20 for monthly Internet access.

✔ Unlimited access is best.

Configuring Windows for the Internet

Setting up your PC to do the Internet is not all that hard, providing you have the following three items:

✔ A silver bowl

✔ A ceremonial knife, preferably bejeweled

✔ An unblemished goat

No. Wait. You needed those things in the *old days,* back before Windows came with an Internet Connection Wizard. Now all you need is some information from your Internet Service Provider:

✔ The phone number to call.

✔ Your ISP's domain name — the `blorf.com` or `yaddi.org` thing.

✔ Your Internet login ID and password.

✔ The number for your provider's DNS (Domain Name Server). It's a four-part number separated by periods, like this: `123.456.789.0`

✔ The name of your ISP's e-mail server, which involves the acronyms POP3 or SMTP.

✔ Your Internet e-mail name, address, and password.

✔ The name of your ISP's news (NNTP) server.

Fortunately, your ISP should have provided you with *all* this information when you signed up. It should be handy on a sheet of paper for you, or located inside a booklet. All you need to do is tell the Internet Connection Wizard about the numbers. It does the rest.

1. **Start the Internet Connection Wizard.**

   From the Start menu (press Ctrl+Esc), choose Programs⇨Internet Explorer⇨Connection Wizard. (In Windows 95, choose Programs⇨Internet⇨Get on the Internet.)

   You may not have that menu item. In fact, if you're using Netscape, just install Netscape from the CD-ROM or floppy disk as you would any software. (See Chapter 20 for installation instructions.) Netscape's setup wizard carries on from there. (And you're done reading here.)

2. **Choose the option that tells Windows you already have an Internet account.**

   It should be the middle option, as shown in Figure 22-1. This option tells the Wizard that you've already found your ISP and have all the information you need for an account.

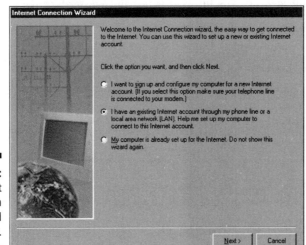

Figure 22-1:
The Internet
Connection
Wizard
window.

Don't choose the first option! If you do, Windows dials into a computer that lists various ISPs around the country. Even though my hometown has seven such ISPs, the Wizard was unable to locate them.

3. **Click the Next button.**

4. **Choose the first option because you have an ISP.**

5. **Continue to click Next and answer questions.**

   You need to know a few things as you continue through the Wizard. Most of them should be in that booklet your ISP should have given you. Others, you may need help with. Remember that it's not considered a sign of weakness to ask for help.

Generally speaking, whichever option is already selected is probably best. For example, Windows may ask whether you connect using your modem or a Local Area Network. You're probably using a modem, and notice how that item is already selected for you. If you're on a Local Area Network, your computer does need to have a network card installed.

Read the screens! Never just click the Next button and assume that everything is okay.

6. **Click the Finish button eventually.**

That means you're done.

When everything is done, you have a new folder in the My Computer window: Dial-Up Networking. This folder contains the icon you can use to connect to the Internet. However, if you're running Windows 98 and using Microsoft Internet Explorer, the connection is automatic.

✔ Connecting to the Internet is covered in the next section.

✔ You need to do this only once. Well, if you change ISPs, you need to do it again. And if you switch over to Netscape, you need to do it again.

✔ I just checked, and now *nine* ISPs are in my local area, none of which is known to the Internet Connection Wizard. (Nine ISPs isn't bad for a community of 23,000. Well, 89,000 in the whole county.)

✔ Don't toss out the booklet or sheet of information your ISP gave you! You may need those numbers later.

✔ 111,111,111 x 111,111,111 = 12,345,678,987,654,321.

Dialing Up the Internet

To access the Internet, you must force Windows to dial up your ISP or somehow connect to a computer that's already on the Internet. After you make the connection, you start using your Internet software.

You can use one of two ways to connect to the Internet in Windows. First, you can run any of your Internet software: the Web browser, e-mail, newsgroup reader, whatever. These programs should check to see whether you're already on the Internet. If not, they fire up the Connect To dialog box all by themselves.

The second way to connect to the Internet is to summon the Connect To dialog box manually. I demonstrate that now because this chapter is coming in three pages short.

Start by opening the Dial-Up Networking folder: Open the My Computer icon on the desktop and then the Dial-Up Networking folder. What you see should look something like Figure 22-2. Behold the icons you use to connect to the Internet!

Figure 22-2:
The Dial-Up Networking window.

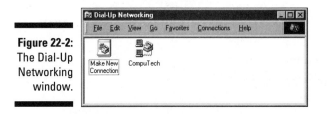

Open the icon you want to use. (Typically, there is only one.) It's the same icon you created when you originally configured Windows to talk with the Internet. You see the Connect To dialog box, as shown in Figure 22-3.

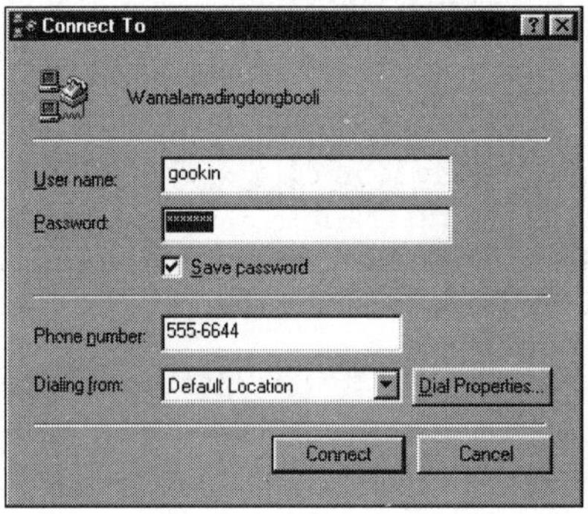

Figure 22-3:
The Connect To dialog box.

Fill in the dialog box with the following information:

✔ The username or ID you need to log in to your ISP. This ID may be different from your e-mail name.

✔ The password you need to log in to your ISP.

✔ The ISP's phone number.

Click on the Save password box so that you don't have to re-enter your password every time you try to connect.

Click the Connect button to direct your modem to dial.

Boop-beep-doop-dap-dee-dee-dee.

Hopefully, you're connected and logged in to your ISP, ready to do the Internet. If not, try again. (Refer to Chapter 17 if you're having trouble dialing.)

After you're connected, you see the Connection Established dialog box, as shown in Figure 22-4. You're there! Welcome to the Internet. Read the dialog box. Choose the `Do not show this dialog box in the future` item if you want. Then click Close.

Figure 22-4: The Connected To Whatever dialog box.

Connection Established	? X

You are connected to CompuTech.

To disconnect or to view status information, double-click the dial-up icon in the status area of the taskbar.

12:45 PM

You can also double-click the connection icon in the Dial-Up Networking folder.

☐ Do not show this dialog box in the future.

| Close | More Information... |

After closing the Connection Established dialog box (or even if it doesn't appear), you should notice a new teensy icon on the system tray (on the right end of the taskbar), looking like the graphic in the margin. That's your Connected To Whatever teensy icon indicator, telling you that you're online with the Internet and ready to run your Internet software.

Continue reading in the next section.

✔ Remember to turn on your external modem before you dial.

✔ There is a rare circumstance in which Windows does not recognize your modem, especially after just turning the computer (or the modem) on. If you see such an error message, ignore it. Try dialing again, and it should work.

✔ The original version of Windows 95 (called "version A") works subtly different from the steps described. Specifically, the dialog box in Figure 22-4 doesn't appear and instead a Connected to *Whatever* dialog, box appears (see Figure 22-5).

Figure 22-5:
Click the
Disconnect
button to
bid farewell
to the
Internet.

Connected to Wambooli	_ □ ☒
Connected at 26400 bps	Disconnect
Duration: 000:00:02	Details >>

Doing Something on the Internet (Using Internet Software)

After you've made the connection to your ISP, you're ready to run any or all of your Internet software. Fire up your Web browser, e-mail package, newsgroup reader, telnet, or any of a number of applications designed for fun and folly on the Internet.

✔ As long as you have the Internet connection, you can run any program that accesses information on the Internet.

✔ Internet programs are just like any other programs on your PC; the only difference is that you must be connected to the Internet before they can be run.

✔ Yes, you can run more than one Internet program at a time. I typically have three or four of them going at once. (Because the Internet is slow, I can read one window while waiting for something to appear in another window.)

✔ You can also stay on the Internet while using an application program like Word or Excel. Just don't forget that you're online.

✔ Close your Internet programs when you're done with them.

✔ Nothing extra is required to run Internet software, other than being connected to the Internet. After you're online, you merely run, use, and close Internet applications like any other application on your PC.

Sayonara, Internet

You use one of two ways to wave bye-bye to the Internet, depending on whether you have a more recent or older version of Windows. Well, there's a third way, but having your spouse rip the modem from the wall isn't technically the best way to disconnect.

Before you disconnect, first make sure that you've quit all your Internet software; just close all those windows and you're done.

For older versions of Windows, summon the Connected To Whatever dialog box (refer to Figure 22-5). The window may be minimized, so click its button on the taskbar to bring it up and center. Click the Disconnect button. You're done.

 For everyone one else, Windows may ask you whether you want to disconnect from the Internet when you close your Internet applications. If not, double-click on the Connected To Whatever teensy icon indicator on the system tray. A window appears, looking like Figure 22-6. Click the Disconnect button. You're done.

Figure 22-6:
Click the
Disconnect
button to
bid farewell
to the
Internet.

Connected to CompuTech	? X
Connected at 14,400 bps	OK
Duration: 000:01:24	Disconnect
Bytes received: 661	Details >>
Bytes sent: 550	

✔ Always remember to disconnect from the Internet. Sometimes you may think that you've disconnected when you close your Web browser. That may not always be the case. You should tell Windows to hang up the modem and end the Internet connection.

✔ Big hint that you're no longer connected to the Internet: The little Connected To Whatever teensy icon indicator disappears from the system tray on the taskbar.

✔ You can keep track of how much time you've spent online by viewing the Connected To Whatever dialog box. This thing is important, as you'll discover, as you eventually grow to spend several more hours on the Internet than you originally intended.

✔ Some systems may disconnect you from the Internet if you don't type anything for a while, like when you die while waiting for Web pages about special events to load, like NASA's Pathfinder or the World Cup soccer championship.

✔ If your ISP is charging you by the hour, you had better remember to hang up; otherwise, you get a monster bill. If you're using Dial-Up Networking, a little connection icon may appear on your status bar so that you can double-check to make sure that you've hung up.

✔ Another reason I prefer external modems: Their lights always indicate whether you're on the Internet, making it very obvious when you haven't yet hung up.

Chapter 23

It's a World Wide Web We Weave

● ●

In This Chapter

▶ Introducing your Web browser

▶ Going somewhere on the Web

▶ Typing a Web page address

▶ Clicking a hyperlink

▶ Using the navigation buttons

▶ Visiting your home page

▶ Finding things on the Web

● ●

*T*he Internet is a mess. Sure, lots of information is out there. But it's like a library that's been hit by a cyclone. The information is all over the place, it's uncataloged, and the librarians are scattered in the trees. Over the years, various tools were devised to get at that information more easily: Archie, WAIS, Gopher, and a whole team of interesting and obscure programs with silly names. Then along came the Web.

The Web, which is short for World Wide Web (WWW), is the best way to get at all the information on the Internet. Just as TV stations fire any news anchor over 35 years old, slowly all the old ways of getting and displaying information are fading from the Internet. The Web, with its text, graphics, and links, is quickly becoming *the* thing to do on a computer. It's the Internet software with nice hair.

✔ The Web is merely one part of the Internet.

✔ Remember that the Internet is a bunch of computers, sending, receiving, and storing information. The Web is a method for getting at that information.

✔ To do the Web, you need a special piece of software called a *Web browser.*

Say Hello to Your Web Browser

Prepare to dip yourself into the cool waters of the Internet. First you connect to the Internet (covered in Chapter 22), and then you run your Internet software.

There are two major programs just about everyone uses when they're connected to the Internet: a Web browser and an e-mail program. E-mail is for reading personal messages. The browser is for just about everything else.

Go on to Chapter 24 if e-mail is your bag.

Browser wars: Microsoft Internet Explorer versus Netscape Navigator

The first Web browser, developed by the teachers and students who created the Web, was called Mosaic. Eventually, some of those teachers and students broke away from the university and formed their own company, Netscape. For years, Netscape made the best Web browser, Navigator, used by more than 80 percent of Internet-using people. This fact did not go unnoticed by the steely eyes and pointy nose of Bill Gates and Microsoft.

A few years back, Microsoft came out with Internet Explorer. Now I'm not going to comment on the legal implications of what happened between Microsoft and Netscape, but suffice it to say that Internet Explorer is now just as popular a Web browser as Netscape Navigator.

Which is best? Why, Netscape of course. Anyone on the Internet will tell you that. However, if you're using Windows 98, you're pretty much compelled to use Internet Explorer instead. The mechanics of Windows 98 and Internet Explorer are just too tightly wound for any other browser to work just right. Although you can run Netscape, you'll find that its performance suffers (wonder why?) and that, occasionally, Windows fires up Internet Explorer instead of Netscape anyway.

✔ Because this 6th Edition of *PCs For Dummies* is designed to cover Windows 98 specifically, I'm mentioning only Internet Explorer here. True, I have Netscape Navigator and use it as my primary browser (on my Windows 95 PC and on my Macintosh G3). But if you have Windows 98, you should be using Internet Explorer, and that's what's covered here.

✔ You can still follow along here if you're using Netscape Navigator. The instructions in this chapter are generic enough that they apply to both Internet Explorer and Netscape Navigator.

Starting Internet Explorer

Internet Explorer

You can start Microsoft Internet Explorer by opening its icon on the Windows desktop. Double-click it and the Internet Explorer window appears (see Figure 23-1). Unless you've already messed with the Web, you probably see Microsoft's "home page" displayed in the Web browser's window. (More on that in a moment.)

You should notice a few things:

Button bar. Below the menu bar is a series of buttons. You use these buttons to visit various places on the Web and do basic things with your Web browser.

Busy thing. The far right end of the button bar has what I call the *busy thing.* The busy thing becomes animated when the Web browser is doing something, which usually means that it's waiting for information to be sent from the far parts of the Internet. That's your signal to sit, wait, and be patient; the Web is busy.

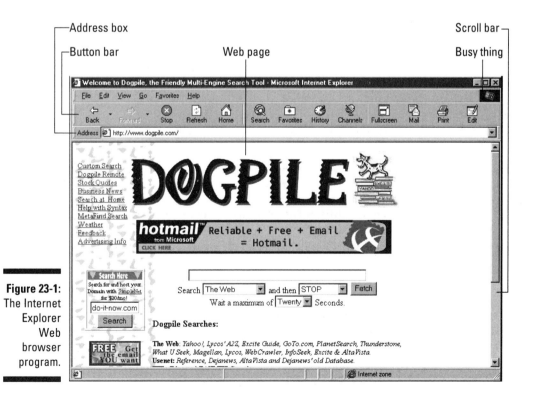

Figure 23-1: The Internet Explorer Web browser program.

Address box. As in the days of DOS, you can type various commands to make the browser visit certain places on the Web. These places are officially known as *URLs,* though I call them Web page addresses. Either way, what you type is cryptic, but you can get used to it.

Web page. The contents of the Web browser (what it displays) is a page of information on the Web. In Figure 23-1, you see the home page for Dogpile, a place to find things on the Web.

Scroll bars. What you see on the Web may often be larger than your browser's window. So you don't miss out, scroll bars allow you to move the Web page's contents hither and thither.

Links. Those odd-colored underlined words or icons or graphics on the Web page. When you click them, they take you somewhere else.

The Web browser shows you how simple it is to view information on the Internet. What you see are graphics and text — almost like a magazine. In addition, some Web pages may have animations on them. Many Web pages also play music while you're viewing them (which can be annoying). Also, most of your input is done with the mouse. Only rarely do you have to type anything. I suppose that's why it's called "browsing" and not "hunting and pecking."

> ✔ The busy thing will be busy a lot. It's often said that the World Wide Web should be four Ws: The fourth stands for Wait.

> ✔ You pronounce URL letters-only: You Are El. It's an acronym for Uniform Resource Locator. Essentially it's a command you give the Web browser to go out and find something on the Internet.

> ✔ Most URLs you type start with `http://`. That cryptic doodad is actually an Internet command. The text that follows `http://` is the address of that information — its location on some computer somewhere in the world. Think of it as the "location" of a file on the Internet, much like the location of a file on your hard drive — it's just someone else's hard drive.

> ✔ Only rarely do you type a Web page address. Normally, most navigation on the Web is done by clicking your mouse on various *links* located on a Web page or by choosing a Web page from your list of bookmarks or favorites. More on that in a sec.

> ✔ Web pages can be wider and very often longer than what you see displayed in your Window browser's window. Don't forget to use the scroll bars!

Visiting Somewhere Webbish

An estimated 100 million pages of information are on the World Wide Web. Why not visit them all?

To visit a Web page, you have two choices. First, you can manually type the address of some page somewhere on the planet — you know, all those `http://www-slash-dot-com-dot-slash-dash` things you see all over the place. Second, and more easily, you can click the mouse on a *link,* which is a piece of text or graphic on one Web page that takes you to another Web page.

Manually typing an address (the painful part)

To visit any Web page in the known universe, you can type its address. Often that's necessary when you're visiting a new place. Bear with me, and follow these steps:

1. **Click the mouse in the address part of the Web browser window.**

   This step should select whatever text is already there. If not, select the text manually by dragging over it with the mouse.

   If you don't see the address part of the Web browser window, choose View⇨Toolbar⇨Address Bar from the menu. (For Netscape, choose Options⇨Show Location.)

2. **Press the Backspace or Delete key to erase whatever text is already there.**

3. **Type a new address.**

   As an example, type the following line:

   ```
   http://www.cnn.com
   ```

   Type **http**, a colon, two forward slashes, three *w*s, a period, **cnn**, another period, **com.** There is no need to type a final period at the end of that address. Just type it like it looks, weird stuff and all.

4. **Press Enter.**

   Immediately, the Web browser searches out the CNN Web page on the Internet. It should load, displaying text, graphics, and the latest news from around the world.

✔ The keyboard shortcut for getting to the address box is Ctrl+L. When you press that key combination, a dialog box appears, in which you can type a Web page address.

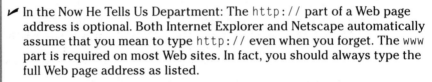

✔ Web page addresses usually start with the cryptoglyph `http://` and then something that looks very Netish with dots and slashes and occasionally ending with `html`. Essentially it's just another Net address, one that contains a Web page document. Look it up in a real Internet book if you want to know what all the jargon means.

✔ You can use your mouse and any of the Windows editing keys to edit the text in the address box.

✔ In the Now He Tells Us Department: The `http://` part of a Web page address is optional. Both Internet Explorer and Netscape automatically assume that you mean to type `http://` even when you forget. The `www` part is required on most Web sites. In fact, you should always type the full Web page address as listed.

✔ On the other hand, if a Web page address starts with `ftp://` or `gopher://`, you're required to type those commands.

Clicking on a link (the simple part)

It's called a "web" because nearly every page has a link to other pages. For example, a Web page discussion on science fiction films may have links to pages discussing *Star Wars* or *Metropolis* or *Battle Beyond the Stars* or *The X-Files*. Click on the link to see more information.

Most links on Web pages are text. The text appears underlined and usually in a different color from other text on the screen.

Links can also be graphical; some pictures are links. The only way to know for certain is to hover the mouse pointer over a link. If the pointer changes to a pointing hand, you know that you have a link you can click to see something else.

✔ Be careful when you're clicking on a graphical link that looks like Hannibal Lecter. He may bite off the mouse cursor's pointing finger.

✔ Links take you to another Web page, just like typing in a new address but without typing in a new address.

✔ Links display related information.

✔ Quite a few Web pages are simply collections of links.

✔ Any good, informative Web page will have links related to other topics. Most links are found at the bottom of the Web page, though some Web pages have the links laced throughout the text.

✔ Link is short for *hyperlink* — yet another bit of trivia to occupy a few dozen neurons.

Going back, way back, forward, and stopping

Following links can be fun. That's the way most people waste time on the Web. For example, I found a Web page recently that explained all the lyrics to Don McLean's *American Pie*. I don't know how I got there; I just ended up there after clicking a few dozen links. Unlike Hansel and Gretel, I neglected to leave bread crumbs along the information superhighway. Fortunately, the Web browser does that for you.

To return to the Web page you were just ogling, use your Web browser's navigation buttons: Click the back button. You can continue clicking the Back button to revisit each Web page you've gawked, all the way back to the first page you saw 18 hours ago.

If you really need to dig deep, use your browser's Recently Visited List or History. Click on the down-arrow at the end of the Address box. That displays the list of the last several Web pages you've visited. (In Netscape, you can also use the Go menu to see the past few pages.)

Internet Explorer 4 has a Back/Forward drop-down list feature that enables you to skip the previous nine or so pages and go back ten pages without having to hit the Back button ten times.

Often you find some place you love and want to visit again. If so, drop a bookmark on that page. That way, you can visit it at any time by choosing the bookmark from a list.

Here is where Internet Explorer is different from every other Web browser on earth: In Internet Explorer, bookmarks are not called bookmarks. They're called *Favorites*. Click on the Favorites button to either add a Web page to your list or choose a favorite Web page from the list.

In Netscape, use the Bookmarks⇨Add Bookmark command (or Ctrl+D) to set a bookmark. Then view the bookmarks on the Bookmarks menu. You can also display a window full of bookmarks with the Bookmarks⇨Go to Bookmarks command (or Ctrl+B).

The *American Pie* link:

```
http://www.urbanlegends.com/songs american_pie_
                   interpretations.html
```

Take me home!

The *home page* is the first page you see when you use the Web. It's either Microsoft's (or Netscape's or your ISP's) Web page or a Web page you pick yourself. Whatever, a home page is simply the first page you see when you start your Web browser.

For example, to use the CNN Web page as your home page, follow these steps:

1. **Choose <u>V</u>iew⇨Internet <u>O</u>ptions.**

   The command is <u>V</u>iew⇨ <u>O</u>ptions for earlier versions of Internet Explorer.

2. **Click the General tab in the Internet Options dialog box.**

   The General tab is the first tab, so it should show up first, as shown in Figure 23-2. The top area of the dialog box is where you set the Internet Explorer home page.

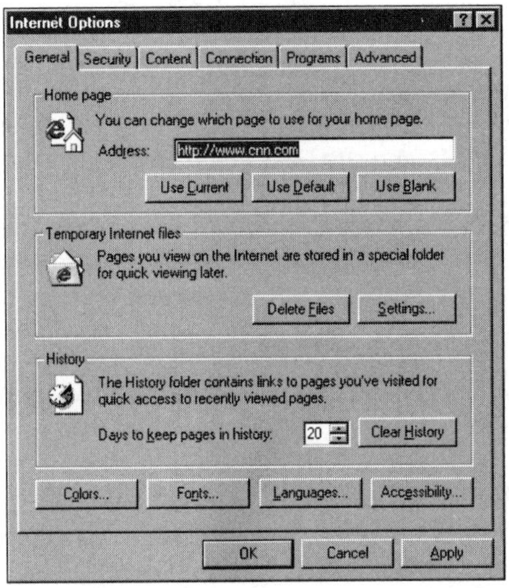

Figure 23-2:
The Internet
Options
dialog box.

3. **Type the new home page in the Address box.**

   For example, type `http://www.cnn.com`, or whatever home page you like.

4. **Click OK.**

At any time, you can return to the home page by clicking the Home button on the toolbar.

✔ It's *your* home page, so you should set it to anything you like.

✔ Home page can really mean two things. First, it's the Web page you see when you first start your Web browser. Second, it could be your personal Web page on the Internet, if you have one.

Finding Stuff

The Web is like a library without a librarian. It has no card catalog, either. And forget about finding something on the shelves: Web pages aren't organized in any fashion, nor is the information in them guaranteed to be complete or accurate. Since anyone can put anything up on the Web, well, anyone does.

Finding something on the Web isn't as hard as it used to be. There are several ways to locate information, each depending on how you want to look for things.

Yahoo!

Perhaps the most complete catalog of Web pages on the Internet can be found in the massive Yahoo! catalog. Like a card catalog in a library, Yahoo! lists Web pages topically. You can search through the catalog to find what you're looking for, or you can browse the categories by clicking on various links.

Visit Yahoo! at

```
http://www.yahoo.com/
```

WebCrawler

WebCrawler is what's known as a Web *robot*. It searches the entire World Wide Web (it "crawls," actually), looking for bits and pieces of text. If you search for Lincoln, for example, it finds any and all Web pages with that word. The first Web pages in the list have the word most often.

Although WebCrawler is wonderful for finding stuff, the stuff it finds may not be what you want. For example, Yahoo! may list Lincoln in topics such as Abe Lincoln; Lincoln, Nebraska; and Lincoln High School. WebCrawler will find you a Web page with the word *Lincoln* written on it 10,000 times. Still, WebCrawler can find stuff Yahoo! doesn't list, simply because it's a Web robot and not a catalog.

Visit WebCrawler at

```
http://www.webcrawler.com
```

Excite

When you need to look up something on the Web topically, use Excite. It works like WebCrawler in that it lists Web pages by their content. But, unlike WebCrawler, Excite lets you fine-tune your searches based on the Web page's content. If it displays a Web site kind of like the one you want, you can click on the "more like this" link to refine your search.

Visit Excite at

```
http://www.excite.com
```

Search.com

CNET's Search.com (which I pronounce "search-dot-com") is a catalog of Web catalogs. Any and every way to search the Web can be found there:

```
http://www.search.com
```

Dogpile

Finally, the ultimate search engine is Dogpile (as shown in Figure 23-1). It searches *everywhere* for *anything*.

```
http://www.dogpile.com
```

Quitting Your Web Browser

When you're done browsing the World Wide Web — meaning that it's 4:00 a.m. and you need to get up in 90 minutes to get ready for work — you should quit Internet Explorer. It's easy: Choose File⇨Close from the menu.

A dialog box may appear, asking whether you want to close the connection (meaning "hang up"), as shown in Figure 23-3. Click Yes. Go to bed. Get some sleep.

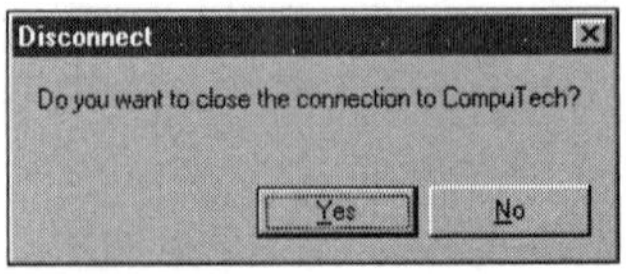

Figure 23-3:
The
Disconnect
dialog box.

Disconnect

Do you want to close the connection to CompuTech?

Yes   No

Chapter 24

Mail Call! (And Other Things)

● ●

In This Chapter

▶ Using Outlook Express

▶ Reading e-mail

▶ Sending e-mail

▶ Perusing the newsgroups

▶ Reviewing other Internet stuff

● ●

Gopher and Telnet and Archie, F-T-P,
I-R-C, H-T-M-L, and H-T-T-P,
USENET, e-mail, and Web P-P-P,
In'rnet acronyms are all right by me.
Java and XML, DHTML, POP-3,
SGML and C-G-I, and S-T-M-P,
Browsing and browsing you're up 'til past 3,
Internet acronyms are all right by me.

The main focus of the media is on the Web, but the Internet is so much more.

Beyond e-mail is a whole clutch of things you can do on the Web. This chapter concentrates on e-mail, but I've also tossed in a few tidbits on other Web things, primarily newsgroups, FTP, and Telnet — not that you'll ever use those things, but I have to cover them anyway.

Letters, Oh, We Get Letters!

One of the many things your Internet Service Provider should provide you with is an e-mail account. That way, you can become one of the millions of people all over the galaxy who send messages back and forth every day.

Say hello to Outlook Express

Several e-mail programs are available for use on the Internet. All of them have their pluses and minuses. The three biggies: Eudora, Netscape and Outlook Express.

No, this book does not cover using e-mail on America Online. Sorry.

Because this is a Windows 98 book, I'm going to concentrate on using Outlook Express for this chapter. The other e-mail programs work similarly, so you can follow along here. However when it comes to sending and receiving e-mail attachments, I do cover all three programs. (The subject of e-mail attachments is covered in Chapter 25.)

Start Outlook Express by opening the Outlook Express icon on the desktop (shown in the margin). Double-click the icon to open it. That action runs Outlook Express and optionally connects you to the Internet if you're not connected already.

Figure 24-1 shows the Outlook Express window. It contains three parts. To the left is the list of mail boxes, where sent, received, and trashed mail goes. On the top is a list of messages, with unread messages appearing in bold type. On the bottom is the text of a received message.

- ✔ If you don't see the screen shown in Figure 24-1 when you start Outlook Express, click the Read Mail icon.

- ✔ You probably won't have any mail waiting for you right away. Oh, you may see a "welcome" message from Microsoft. Like they care. . . . The best way to get mail is to send it — just like in real life.

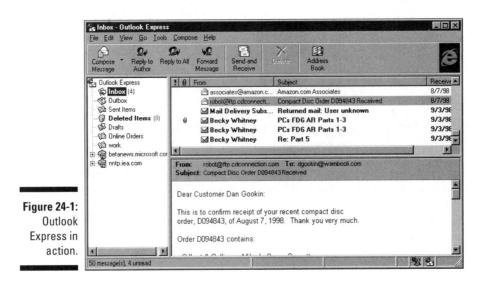

Figure 24-1:
Outlook
Express in
action.

Reading your mail

New messages appear in the Outlook Express window (refer to Figure 24-1) in bold type. To read a message, click on it. The message text appears in the bottom of the window. To see the entire message and get attachments, you have to open the message.

After you read a message, you can do one of the following things:

✔ Reply to the message (send an answer or follow-up).

✔ Forward the message to someone else.

✔ Move the message to a specific mailbox folder.

✔ Delete the message.

✔ Ignore the message and just read the next one.

✔ Print your message.

 To reply to a message, click the Reply to Author button. A message composition window appears. The sender's e-mail address (to whom you're replying) and message subject are filled in for you, as is a copy of the original message. Your job is to type the reply and click the Send button. (See the following section for more information.)

 To forward a message, click the Forward Message button. Unlike replying to a message, you need to fill in the To field for the person to whom you want to send the message on to. For example, I get silly letters from Chris all the time. When something is really funny, I forward it to my wife.

 You move a message by dragging it from the top window in Outlook Express to a mailbox folder on the left side of the window. You grab the message by the envelope icon.

 To delete the message, click the Delete button. Poof! It's gone. Or, more accurately, it's moved into the Deleted Items folder on the left side of the Outlook Express window.

To ignore a message, leaving it in your inbox for all eternity, just click the next message down in the list of unread messages.

✔ You can create folders for mail from various people or on certain subjects. For example, my copy of Outlook Express has folders for projects I work on, mail from friends, and fan mail from people who write me in foreign languages.

✔ To create a folder, choose File➪Folder➪New Folder. A Create Folder dialog box appears. You can select the folder in which you want your new folder created, type a folder name, and click OK.

  ✔ Mail you delete isn't really deleted. No, it sits in the Deleted Items folder until you manually flush everything out. To clean the Delete Items folder, right-click the folder with your mouse and choose Empty Folder from the pop-up menu.

  ✔ Sorry I can't be any more specific. Unless you have an actual e-mail sitting there ready to read, it's hard to run an example.

Sending a letter to someone you love (or hate)

To compose an e-mail epistle, you need to know the e-mail address of some other person on the Internet. That's something your friends and co-workers can give you, and it's extremely trendy to put your e-mail address on your business card and résumé.

In Outlook Express, click the Compose Message button. This step displays a new message window, as shown in Figure 24-2. Now your job is to fill in the blanks with the proper information.

Figure 24-2:
Creating a
new
message in
Outlook
Express.

Who are you sending the message to? Type their e-mail address in the To field.

If you want to send carbon copies of the message to other people, put their e-mail addresses in the CC field.

SPAM, SPAM, SPAM, SPAM

Junk e-mail is known as *spam*. The meaning behind that term is an obscure Monty Python routine — I've never gotten the connection myself. Anyway, the name spam has stuck, regardless of protests from the Hormel company (which makes SPAM the meat product).

Everyone gets spam. Get-rich quick schemes, chain letters, advertisements for questionable Web pages, and on and on. The solution? Delete it. Just don't read it. Never respond to spam, either. Sometimes responding results in even more spam being sent. (And spammers are tricky; they tell you to respond if you want to be taken off the list. Don't!)

Type a subject in the Subject field. You must type a subject. It also helps if the subject is somehow related to the message (because the recipient sees the subject in their inbox, just like you do).

The last thing to fill in is the messages itself, the contents.

```
Dear Mildred, sorry about your cat. . . .
```

Finally, you send the message. Click the Send button and it's off on the Internet, delivered more cheaply and more accurately than any post office on earth.

- ✔ An e-mail message is sent instantly. I sent a message to a reader in Australia one evening and got a reply back from him in less than ten minutes.

- ✔ Alas, you can't always expect a quick reply from e-mail, especially from folks in the computer industry (which is ironic).

- ✔ By the way, if you want to send me e-mail, my address is dang@idgbooks.com. Unlike some people, I always return e-mail.

- ✔ If you want to cancel a message, just close the message-composition window. You may be asked whether you want to save the message. Click No.

- ✔ You can send e-mail to several people at once: Just put each name in the To: field, separated by semicolons in Outlook Express or commas in every other e-mail program.

- ✔ The Cc: field is used to send a carbon-copy message to people. That's when you want to clue someone into what's going on but not write to them directly.

✔ The sneaky `Bcc:` field is used to send a blind carbon copy message to people. Those folks in the `Bcc:` field don't appear on the list when people in the `To:` or `Cc:` fields read the letter.

✔ Sending mail is only half the picture. The better half is getting e-mail. It's so important that many swell heads on the Net boast of how many e-mail messages they get a day. Wow. They must be important or something.

✔ You can also send files, pictures, and sounds using e-mail. It's known as sending an e-mail attachment. For instance, every chapter in this book was sent to my earnest editor as an attachment to an e-mail message. This subject is covered in Chapter 25.

Internet News, Newsgroups, or USENET

News on the Internet should be put in quotes: "News." What constitutes news is really up to the people who publish it. On the Internet, that's anyone and everyone. So if you're expecting Walter Cronkite in all corners of the internet, forget it.

Legitimate news organizations and sites are on the Internet. For example, *The Wall Street Journal, San Francisco Examiner, San Jose Mercury, USA Today, Washington Post, Newsweek,* the *New York Times,* and many more all publish electronic versions of their print publications. In fact, reading news online, especially on the CNN-type sites, is one of the top five things people do on the Internet. You can view all these sites with IE, Navigator, or any other Web browser.

What you sometimes get when you want "news" on the Internet is really a collection of public forums on varying topics. For example, groups out there discuss politics, science fiction, off-color jokes, genealogy, history, and a wide variety of interests.

In one way, this kind of "news" is more of a subculture of cyberspace. You can see "news" tidbits (called *postings*) from anyone. It could be an expert in the field, or it could be the most dreadful of all Net beasts: the college freshman with his brand-new Net account. *Run for the hills!* Although you can use "news" to post a message and get responses from knowledgeable people all over the world, you can also use it to argue the subtleties of the Klingon language with people who have way too much time on their hands.

As with using e-mail, you can use Outlook Express to view newsgroups on the Internet. Figure 24-3 shows what it looks like.

To read news, you need to select a news server, listed at the bottom of the left window in Outlook Express. Any newsgroups you're already subscribed to appear in the list, as shown in Figure 24-3.

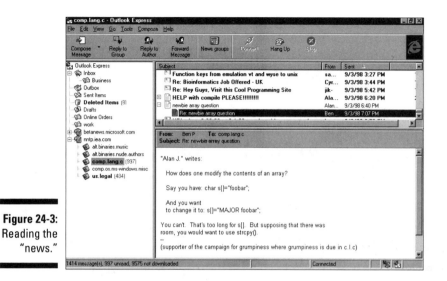

Figure 24-3:
Reading the
"news."

To add a newsgroup, right-click the news server and choose Newsgroups from the shortcut menu. A window appears, listing all the newsgroups available from your ISP. Choose one or more (or search for them) and click the Subscribe button for those whose messages you want to read.

To read a group, click on it in the list, such as the `comp.lang.c` group chosen in Figure 24-3. Reading messages works like reading e-mail New and unread messages are shown in bold type.

Posting a message to a newsgroup is done like sending e-mail. You can either reply to a post or create a new post. Use the Reply to Group button to post a reply on the newsgroup; use the Reply to Author button to send an e-mail to the message's author. To create a new post, use the Compose Message button. Remember that whatever you post to a newsgroup is read by everyone in the newsgroup.

✔ Posting a message in a newsgroup always results in a new round of spam mail for you. The e-mail spammers scan newsgroups, looking for posters. Then they send lots of junk e-mail (spam) to your mailbox. Watch out!

✔ Yes, the way to avoid SPAM is to use another name when you cruise the newsgroups and post messages. I know people who do this, but I don't. Yes, I suffer from SPAM, but I enjoy bragging about how much e-mail I get.

✔ Internet newsgroups are also known as USENET ("*yooz-net*"), which is an older term for the same thing.

✔ "News" is divided into various newsgroups. For example, `rec.arts.startrek` is where you can actually find people who devote large parts of their brain to figuring out how fast Warp 9 really is. Other groups devoted to specific subjects are given equally terse, period-peppered names.

✔ News grows. Internet newsgroups sometimes have hundreds of new postings a day. It's next to impossible to keep up (unless you have a cushy job where you can read news all the doo-da-day). On the pleasant side, you don't really have to read everything because the "news" is rather capricious (and experience will prove this to you).

Online attitude

Online telecommunications is a new and exciting way to communicate. Just as with learning a foreign language, however, you should be aware of some rules about online communications before you take the plunge. Don't get me wrong; this can be fun. I do it all the time and have made quite a few enemies of my friends.

✔ You can't "see" anyone you "meet" online, so don't assume anything about them. Modem people are old and young and come from diverse backgrounds, though studies show that they're typically male, upper income, and Republican. Still, don't hold that against them.

✔ Please don't type in ALL CAPS. Type your letters and comments in mixed case — like you do when you're writing a letter. To most online people, all caps reads LIKE YOU'RE SHOUTING AT THEM!

✔ Don't "beg" for people to send you e-mail. Participate in news discussions or just be obnoxious, and you'll always have a full mailbox.

✔ The art of written communication is lost on the TV generation. People use the phone to communicate, where you hear inflection and gather extra meaning. Unfortunately, an online message lacks such nuances. And because we don't all have the written vocabularies we should, a joke, a side remark, or kidding can easily be taken seriously (way too seriously). Remember to keep it light. Adding "ha, ha" occasionally lets people know that you're having fun instead of being an online jerk. Speaking of which. . . .

✔ There are many online jerks (ha, ha). The best policy to take with them is to ignore them. No matter how much they steam you, no matter how ludicrous their ideas or remarks — golly, even if they're a Libertarian — don't get into a "flamethrower" war with them.

✔ In an online debate, ignore anyone who quotes "the dictionary" as a source. I hate to break it to you, but there is no National Institute of English that defines what words mean. Dictionaries are written by people as ignorant as you and I. Heck, I could write and publish a dictionary if I wanted to and make up entirely new definitions for words. Nope, the dictionary is not a source to be quoted.

✔ Buy the *Illustrated Computer Dictionary For Dummies,* available from IDG Books Worldwide, Inc. and written by yours truly.

✔ An online debate isn't over until someone compares someone else to Adolf Hitler. Calling the person a Nazi or the generic "fascist" also counts.

✔ Never criticize someone over spelling. English is a beautiful and rich language, utterly lacking in logic or spelling rules. Phonics, ha! *It* starts with a P, for Pete's sake! There's no sense in drilling people on their spelling (unless it's truly awful, in which case you're probably dealing with a 12-year-old).

Other Stuff to Do on the Internet

Aside from browsing the Web, reading e-mail, and reading the news, you can find other things to do on the Internet. It's a grab bag of stuff, mostly holdovers from the old days when the Internet was more closely linked to UNIX computers and the researchers who used them.

For all these other things, you may need special software. Some of this stuff comes with Windows, some of it doesn't. But don't fret! Anything you want but don't have can be downloaded from the Web. Chapter 25 tells you where and how to do that.

Chitty-chatting

One of the more wild aspects of the Internet is the live chat rooms. These are places where you can sit and type back and forth (in "real time") with other Internet users.

```
Snooty is here! {[((((HUGS!!!))))]}
```

Pardon me while I retch. . . .

Various chat rooms exist for certain topics and special events. Quite a lot of them, however, are dedicated to cybersex. That's basically where people type dirty things to each other, like `All those 900 numbers are busy this time of the night`. Stuff like that.

- ✔ Windows 98 doesn't come with any specific Chat software. You have to find it out on the Internet (see Chapter 23).

- ✔ To visit a chat room, you need special Chat software. Netscape has a special Netscape Chat program you can get. You can also search Shareware.com on the Web to look for Chat client software.

- ✔ Chat is also known as IRC, or Internet Relay Chat.

- ✔ If you're a parent, it's probably best to keep your young children out of the Internet chat rooms.

- ✔ Not all chat rooms are dirty. Quite a few host special events where you can type back and forth with famous people or people who think that they're famous.

- ✔ A *chat room* is merely a place where a group of people type at each other. When you visit an IRC site, you're shown a list of these rooms along with their topics and have the option to join one in progress or sit in an empty room and type to yourself.

- ✔ Chat rooms quickly make you realize how poorly everyone types and spells.

Telnet

I don't know why I'm bringing telnet up, other than that Windows comes with a Telnet program.

Basically, Telnet allows you to connect with a UNIX computer on the Internet. Do you know UNIX? If so, you'll probably use Telnet and don't need me to tell you how it works. If not, that ends the discussion.

FTP

FTP is one of those ugly verb-noun things. As a verb it means to send files back and forth on the Internet. As a noun, *FTP* stands for File Transfer Protocol, which is the name of the system used on UNIX computers to send files back and forth over the Internet.

As with Telnet, Windows 98 comes with an FTP program called (surprisingly) FTP. But — get this — it's a DOS program. Ugh.

Actually, there is a shareware FTP program called (and I'm not making this up) CuteFTP. You can use instructions in Chapter 23 to learn how to find and download the latest version.

Why do you need an FTP program? Well, you don't! Only if you're sending files to a UNIX computer is it necessary. But, again, I'm referring to the part of Chapter 23 that goes into other Internet things you can do, so I had to mention it here.

- ✔ Your Web browser can be used as an FTP program, though it can only receive files and not send them. Whenever you type an URL beginning with `ftp://`, you're using the browser's FTP mode.

- ✔ Personally, I find that using an FTP program transfers files more quickly than using a Web browser, though I don't have any hard evidence to back that up.

Chapter 25

Files to Here, Files from There (And E-Mail Attachments)

● ●

In This Chapter

▶ Downloading software from the Internet

▶ Receiving a file with your e-mail

▶ Sending a file with your e-mail

● ●

*S*ending files back and forth is one of the Internet's first functions, dating back to the old UNIX days. A program called UUCP (*UNIX*-to-*UNIX copy*) was used to copy files from one UNIX computer to another. You were considered quite the lad if you knew the UUCP command back in those days.

Today, sending files is done primarily on the Web, where you can pick up — or "download" — a file as easy as clicking a link and using the Save As dialog box. Files can also be received and sent in an e-mail message. They're known as e-mail *attachments*. Everything about e-mail attachments, as well as picking up files from the Web, is described in this handy little chapter.

> ✔ This chapter does not cover sending or receiving e-mail attachments with America Online. If you have any e-mail trouble using AOL, please contact its help desk. I do not use AOL and do not know how its e-mail system works.
>
> ✔ Refer to Chapter 25 for more basic information on e-mail.
>
> ✔ The term *download* means to copy, or transfer, a file from another computer (on the Internet) to your PC. *Upload* means to send a file from your PC to another computer. Weird terms, I agree.
>
> ✔ You can only download files from the Web. To send files, you have to use either an e-mail attachment or an FTP program. (FTP programs are not covered in this book; see a real Internet book for more information.)

Grabbing Software from the Internet

Programs galore are all over the Internet, and the Web provides a handy way to find and grab almost all of them. Downloading software is as easy as clicking a link. Cinchy, in fact.

My favorite way to find software is through the CNET Web page: It's at Shareware.com. It lets you search the Web for software in specific categories for specific operating systems. And there's no charge! (Well, if you download shareware, you're expected to pay for it, but there's no charge to download it.)

Suppose that you want to find a new Windows card game. Here's how you would search for one:

1. **Visit Shareware.com.**

   Type this address into your Web browser:

   shareware.com

   In a few moments, the Shareware.com Web page appears on your screen. Figure 25-1 shows what it looked like when I wrote this book; it will probably change looks in the future.

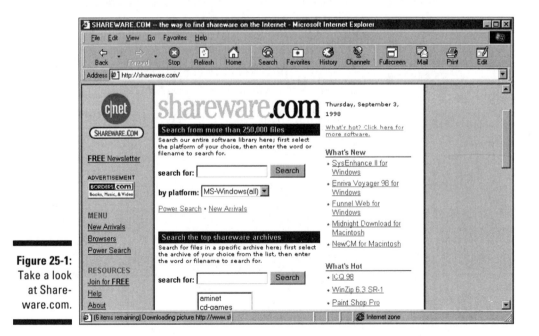

Figure 25-1:
Take a look at Share-
ware.com.

2. Locate the first Search For text box.

3. Click the mouse in that box.

It's an input box, similar to the ones you find all over Windows.

4. Type card game.

5. Choose your operating system from the drop-down list.

Choose MS-Windows (All) to search for all Windows programs (which should run on Windows 95 or Windows 98).

6. Click Search.

The busy thing goes nuts. It may take a few seconds for Shareware.com to find matches.

Eventually you see the Search Results page. You find a list of programs you can take (download) along with a brief description. Read them all!

Pay special attention to the file size. That clues you in to how long it will take the Internet to send you the file. At 28.8 Kbps, a 500K file takes about 5 minutes to download, more or less.

If more matches are found, you see a link at the bottom of the page that says NEXT 25 (or something). Click it to see even more matches.

7. Click on the file you want to download.

For example, there's that Whist game I've always wanted.

The Download page is displayed. You see lists of the files on various computers on the Internet.

Choose a link from the Try These Sites First section. Those are typically sites near you or reliable sites. You also see a Reliability Guide, which tells you the likelihood of connecting to various sites.

If you get an FTP error or the site is busy, try another site.

8. A warning dialog box appears.

The browser may ask you what to do with the file the other computer is sending. Tell it to save the file to disk.

From here on you save the file as you would normally in any application.

Do not disconnect from the Internet until the file has been completely sent! If you do disconnect, you won't have the entire file!

Don't just sit and watch the screen, either. You can visit other Web pages and do other things on the Internet or work in other applications, like Word, while the file is being received.

9. Run the file.

After you get the file, run it: Open its icon. Most of the files are ZIP files that unzip themselves. (If not, you need the WinZIP program to unzip the files.)

After the file has unzipped, look for the README or SETUP icon. Open it up, and you're on your way.

- ✔ *Shareware* is software you try before you buy. If you use the software, you're expected to register it by sending the poor programmer a check. Do it. You'll be rewarded in the afterlife.

- ✔ Most shareware you download is encased in a ZIP file. Hey! Visit the WinZIP Web page and download an evaluation version of its program:

  ```
  www.winzip.com/
  ```

  If you like WinZIP, you can order a copy right there from the Web page. I did. And no one stole my credit card number, either.

- ✔ I'm shocked! I was able to write this section without putting in a nasty unzip pun.

Look, Ma! It's an E-Mail Attachment!

Getting an e-mail attachment is fun — unless you don't know what to do with it. Fortunately, the three major e-mail programs (Outlook Express, Eudora, and Netscape) all handle attachments quite easily. You just need to know a few basic tricks to get the attachment out of the e-mail and on your PC's hard drive.

The following points apply to all e-mail programs and attachments:

- ✔ Someone may send you a file your PC cannot digest, a file of an unknown format. If so, and if it's from someone you know, respond to their e-mail and tell them you cannot open the file. They should resend it in another format.

- ✔ Beware of attachments from people you don't know! You cannot get a computer virus from regular e-mail, but if someone sends you a program and you run that program, it could infect your PC. Accept attachments only from people you know. Otherwise, just delete the e-mail message and you'll be safe.

- ✔ Personally, I do not accept program files over e-mail.

TECHNICAL STUFF

ZIP-a-dee-do-da, UNZIP-a-dee-ay

Most files you download are *archives*. These single files hold even more files — like a single beehive holds hundreds of angry bees. Before you can get at the files and really do something, you must crack the archive nut.

Fortunately, most archive files are "self-extracting." For example, you may have downloaded the game NINJA.EXE. When you run it, the self-extractor takes over automatically, unpacking and "exploding" the various files in the archive, like you'd unpack after moving. Whereas you had one file before, you have several (dozens, sometimes) other files, each of which makes up the Ninja-whatever you downloaded. Only then can you start playing the game.

Why archives? Well, considering that this is a techy sidebar and I am allowed to spout off here, the history is rich and tradition-filled. In the old days, it used to take several hours to download just one file. The solution was to compact a file into a smaller size for easy downloading. Then, as computer programs grew more advanced, the compacting programs allowed more than one file to be packed and shrunk at the same time. The result was the archive.

The term *ZIP* comes from one of the programs that makes archives. ZIP archive files end in ZIP, and you need the UNZIP program to unpack them. However, if the archive ends in EXE, it unpacks itself.

If you need a ZIP archive program, I recommend WinZIP. You can download an evaluation copy from the WinZIP Web page, at www.winzip.com/. Refer to Chapter 24 for more information on downloading software from a Web page.

Grabbing an attachment from Outlook Express

The key to getting attachments in Outlook Express is the paper clip icon. It appears next to the message subject in the top part of the Outlook Express window. That paper clip indicates that the e-mail message has one or more files attached to it.

When you read the message, you see a second paper clip appear in the upper-right corner of the message's window, as shown in the margin. You can click on that paper clip to see a list of files attached to the message — but that's boring. What you really want to do is save the attachment to your hard drive.

To save the attachment, choose File⇨Save Attachments. A submenu appears, listing the files attached to the message. Choose the file you want to save (typically, you have only one). A Save As dialog box appears, allowing you to save the file to disk.

Ta-da! The attachment is saved. Now you can reply to or delete the message as you normally would.

- ✔ I save my attachments in the My Documents folder. After looking at them or examining their contents, I then shuffle them off to the proper folder.

- ✔ Outlook Express displays graphics files attached to messages as images right at the end of the message text. Neat-o.

Opening an attachment in Eudora

Eudora is my personal favorite e-mail program. When you get an attachment in Eudora, it appears at the bottom of the message as a Windows icon. To open the attachment, double-click. This works great for receiving graphics files, documents, or ZIP files.

The only drawback to receiving an attachment in Eudora is that it doesn't provide an easy way for you to move the file elsewhere on your hard drive. Eudora keeps all its attachments in a directory you specify. So, in a way, it's nicer than Outlook Express in that the attachments are automatically saved to disk (in addition to appearing as an icon at the end of the message).

To discover in which directory Eudora places its file attachments, choose Tools⇨Options from the menu. In the Options dialog box, scroll down to find the Attachments category. Click on that item and you see the attachment directory listed as a button, as shown in Figure 25-2. Click the button to set a new attachments directory.

In Figure 25-2, you see that the attachments directory is set to the My Documents folder on drive C. That's as good a place as any, and it means that all file attachments received by Eudora are automatically saved as files in that folder.

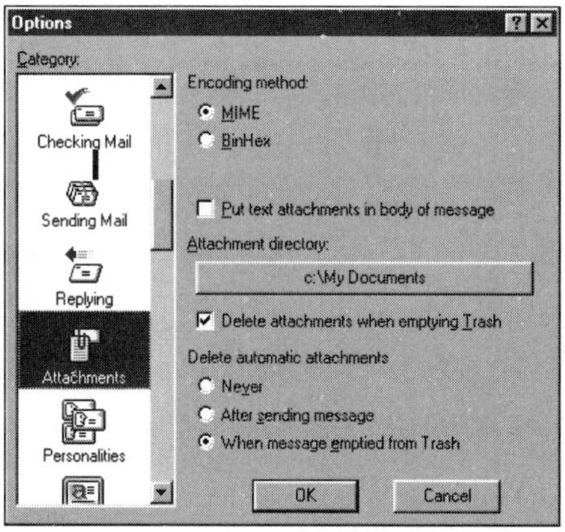

Figure 25-2:
The Options
dialog box
in Eudora
Pro.

Getting an attached file in Netscape Navigator

When you get a file attachment in Netscape, it shows up at the bottom of the message looking like a Web page link. That can be puzzling. The best thing you can do is to save the link to disk.

To save the attached file in Netscape, right-click the link with your mouse. A pop-up menu appears, as shown in Figure 25-3. Choose Save Link As. A Save As dialog box appears, which you can then use to save the attachment.

✔ Remember to look at the filename, which appears by the link at the bottom of your e-mail message. Watch out for program files being sent from people you don't know.

✔ If you click the link, you run whatever program created the file being sent: Word, Excel, whatever. But don't click the link if a program file was sent!

✔ If the attachment is a graphics file, clicking the link displays the image in Netscape.

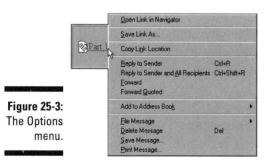

Figure 25-3:
The Options
menu.

How files are *really* attached

Actually, you never really send a file with an e-mail message. Instead, what you send is a secret code — which looks like a lot of nonsense if you don't have the proper e-mail program to decipher the code.

An e-mail message is all text. A file, on the other hand, could be anything: text, data, binary information, whatever. To send a file, your e-mail program translates the file into a text-only format that can be sent as an e-mail message. The format is known as MIME or Binhex or UUE or whatever — it's unimportant! What is important is that your e-mail program translates the file into text so that it can be sent along with your message.

When a file is received, your e-mail program translates the encoded text back into a file. With Eudora, that happens automatically. With Outlook Express and Netscape, you must save the file to disk, which decodes it.

Sending a File to Someone through E-Mail

For some reason, sending an e-mail attachment is easier than receiving one. I dunno. I suppose that it's because sending the file is like saying, "Here, this is your problem!" But I digress.

As you would expect, sending an e-mail attachment varies depending on which e-mail program you're using. This section covers the three major e-mail programs: Outlook Express, Eudora and Netscape.

- ✔ Instead of sending several small files, consider using the WinZIP program to archive your files into one handy ZIP file.

- ✔ If you don't have WinZIP, you can send more than one file at a time. Just keep using your e-mail program's File Attach command to keep ganging up files on the message.

- ✔ Do not send file shortcuts; send only the originals. If you send a shortcut, the person receiving the file won't get the original.

- ✔ Try not to move or delete any files you attach to e-mail messages until *after* you send the message. I know this sounds dumb, but too often I'll be waiting for e-mail to send and (while I'm not busy) I'll start cleaning files. Oops!

- ✔ It's best to confer with whomever you're sending files to ensure that they can receive an e-mail attachment. Furthermore, check with them to make sure that they have software to open whatever file you're sending. It's just proper.

Sending an attachment in Outlook Express

Attaching a file in Outlook Express is done by — can you guess? — clicking the paper clip button in the message-composition window.

Start by creating a new message or replying to a message. When you're· ready to attach a file, click the paper clip button (shown in the margin) or choose Insert⇨File Attachment from the menu.

Use the Insert Attachment dialog box, which works exactly like an Open or Browse dialog box, to find the file you want to attach. Select the file. Click Attach.

The file you attach appears as an icon at the bottom of the message you're sending. To send the message and the file, click the Send button. And it's off on its way.

Attaching something to your e-mail in Eudora

To attach any file to an e-mail message in Eudora, use the Ctrl+H command. I don't know why they chose Ctrl+H. Here's a file! Hey! I'm attached! I don't get it.

After pressing Ctrl+H, you see an Attach dialog box, which works exactly like an Open dialog box. Browse to find the file you want to attach, select it, and then click Open. The file's pathname appears in the message header, in the Attached field.

Sending the message sends the file.

Using Netscape's e-mail to send a file

Attaching a file in Netscape's e-mail is done by clicking the paper clip/Attach button on the button bar. This action displays a menu, from which you should choose the File command. Or you can choose File⇨Attach⇨File from the menu. The Enter to Attach dialog box appears.

Use the Enter to Attach dialog box like an Open dialog box to browse for a file you want to attach. When you find the file, select it by clicking on it once, and then click the Open button.

The attached file appears in the message header as a full pathname. Sending the message sends the file.

Part VII
Something's Wrong!

The 5th Wave   By Rich Tennant

"YO-I THINK WE'VE GOT A NEW KIND OF VIRUS HERE!"

In this part . . .

There I was, just sitting there, minding my own business, when all of a sudden — for no reason whatsoever — the computer up and died. What did I do wrong?"

Computer owners are too quick to blame themselves for the folly of their PCs. People always assume that it's their fault, that they have somehow offended the delicate sensibilities of the PC. Wrong! Computers foul up on the slightest whim. Don't mistake their flakiness for anything you've done. Instead, refer to the chapters in this part for remedies. Make this part of the book your place to turn to when the computer up and dies — or just crosses its eyes and says "Blean!"

Chapter 26

When to Scream for Help

● ●

In This Chapter

▶ Finding yourself a PC guru

▶ Getting computer help from others

▶ How to tell whether something is really wrong

▶ Properly explaining the problem

● ●

*Y*ou may be a major executive, a teacher, a mad scientist, or any smart, talented, gifted individual. But this computer thing makes you feel like a dummy. No problem. That's why this book was written. I'm not going to argue against computer literacy; everyone should know how to use an automated teller machine, and not being afraid of a computer is important. But should you memorize everything about a computer? Naaaaa. There's no need to. Plenty of other people have already done that. Your task is to use those people's skills, thank them profusely, and then get on with your work.

This chapter discusses how to get help from PC-knowledgeable friends and office comrades. Regardless of whom you decide to ask for help, call that person your *PC guru*. This chapter also discusses the differences between major problems that require assistance and things you can remedy yourself.

Who Is Your PC Guru?

Your personal computer guru is someone — anyone — who loves computers and knows enough about them to offer help when you need it. Your guru is an important person to know and respect. Everyone has one — even the gurus themselves! If you don't have one, you need one.

At the office, the guru is probably the computer manager, but ask around to see whether anyone else can do the job. Quite a few computer zanies may be lurking around the office. If you find one, he or she may be able to offer help and advice more quickly than the computer manager (who goes by a schedule). Especially for help with particular types of software, turn to people who use the programs regularly; they may know tricks they can pass along.

What about them thar computer consultants?

A *computer consultant* is someone who likes computers and charges you a fee because of it. Consultants help you get out of trouble, offer suggestions, buy things for you, set up your system, train you about software, and create custom programs — all for a fee. Having a consultant might be worth the cost. I should warn you, however, that most of these gurus for hire do no more than the free, bribable gurus, and you typically pay them by the hour, one hour minimum. That's a lot of money to have someone plug in a phone cord.

For the home, finding a guru can be more difficult. Usually a neighbor, friend, or relative knows enough about computers to help you install hardware or software, or at least give you advice about some program.

Whatever your situation, identify your guru and keep that person in mind for troubled times or for extracting advice and tips. It's like having a good mechanic handy or knowing a friendly doctor. You may not use your guru all the time, but knowing that he or she is available makes computing easier.

✔ Remember that a certain amount of finesse is involved in using your computer guru's talents; a line must be drawn between getting occasional help and taxing your guru's patience.

✔ Computer gurus can handle remarkable geekistical operations but only if they know what you're talking about. If you ask them to "check the kyoowooi for you," they shrug and move off to floss their RS-232 ports. Learn the basics of pronunciation; a *queue* is pronounced *Q,* for example. When in doubt, write it on a card and wave it over your head.

Other Places You Can Look for Help

Computer gurus aren't everywhere. Suppose that you live on Pitcairn Island and your PC just came by mail order from PCs Limited (along with your absentee ballot for the 1988 presidential election). Who's going to be your guru? Definitely not the lady who makes festive potholders out of palm fronds.

When you don't have a real guru handy, you have alternatives. Here's a bunch I can think of right off the top of my head:

✔ Some computer stores may offer classes or have coffee groups where you can ask questions. But keep in mind that this is a limited source of information.

- Local computer clubs dot the nation. Don't be afraid to show up at one and ask a few questions. You may even adopt a guru there or learn about special sessions for beginners. Many computer clubs or special interest groups (SIGs) are designed specifically for questions and answers. Check your local paper or computer flier at the store.

- Community colleges offer introductory courses on computers and some software programs. Come armed with your questions.

- Don't forget the gurus you already paid for: the technical-support people at your computer store or the telephone support you get with every piece of software you buy. Everything comes with support; it's part of the purchase price (or so they claim). Especially for software, call the support department if you're having trouble. (Don't abuse phone support; it's not an excuse for not reading the manual.)

- If these traditional avenues fail, consider the unconventional. If you're a member of the Prodigy online service, try there for help. Or try one of the other numerous online services, such as MSN, America Online, or CompuServe. (Of course, this advice assumes that you know how to wrestle with a modem in the first place.) The Internet also has various forums and places for new users to ask questions.

Some really great questions to ask your guru

Darn, I'm in a good mood today. Here are some questions you can ask a computer guru that will turn the tables. At once, you'll have the feeling of superiority as the so-called guru stands there baffled, not knowing what you're talking about. Use them sparingly:

- I keep losing my document through an intermittent data fistula. Can you patch it up?

- My PC has a coolant leak. Do you know how to remove liquid nitrogen stains?

- The frangellico dirigible osmosis is hosed.

- The biotransfer filter on my keyboard is popping out. Can I stuff it back in using a flat-edged screwdriver?

- Something in the error induction coils is transducing my document while it's being printed.

- Where is the "Frane" key?

- The Canis Familiaris virus gormandized my homework.

- I hear that new encephalophage virus is carried in common cerumen.

- My pixels are converging due to negative ion density. Is that a software or a hardware problem?

- The manual says to "depress the Enter key." Which putdowns work best?

Is Something Really Wrong?

You need to call someone else for help in two circumstances. The first circumstance is when you want to do something and need to know how it's done. For example, you want to use columns in WordPerfect but don't have a clue how to do it. That's when you need a true guru — someone who has mastered the PC or its software and, if he or she doesn't know the answer, can sift through the manuals and discover it quickly.

The second circumstance is when something runs amok in a computer. This situation happens all the time, even to the gurus. Computers are like garden hoses in a way; they can tie themselves into twisty tangled knots with little or no effort on your behalf. I call it the "It worked yesterday" syndrome. Because learning about a PC or knowing the innards of Windows or some piece of software is beyond a normal person's abilities, it's time to call for help when you need this kind of expertise.

✔ Before calling your guru for assistance, try working through the problem again. For example, if you're trying to print and it just doesn't work, try again after a few moments. Working out a problem ahead of time lets your gurus know that you're not abusing their help.

✔ Use your application's online help. You may find suggestions, advice, and hints about using the program. The big-selling programs offer more help than no-name (or *el cheapo*) programs. Try this method of getting help first before calling someone else. If this method doesn't work, you could try the manual. (Yeah, right.)

✔ Press the key labeled F1 to get help.

✔ Don't be too quick to blame yourself if you can't do something. If you've done it the way the manual says and it still doesn't work, either the manual or the computer program is wrong. What you have is a genuine bug, and your guru — or the software manufacturer — should be made aware of it.

✔ Some computer gurus operate for free. Never take advantage of their generosity.

How to Scream for Help

Approaching your guru with a problem requires skill. You don't just say "It doesn't work" and toss up your hands. Unless you're a soap opera star or royalty, don't expect much help from that approach. Instead, try the following:

1. Relax.

Everyone has things to do and deadlines to meet. Don't dump your stress on the computer guru. If that's a problem for you, arrange to have your guru look at the PC when you're not there. No guru will help a rude user. (Who would want to?)

2. Document what's going on.

When something doesn't work, write it down or be very detailed when you recite the problem. For example, don't just say, "I tried to start my computer, and it won't boot." Instead, write down any messages you see, such as "Not a system disk." Or, if the computer beeps, write that down. If the printer doesn't print yet the light is flashing, make a note. This information helps the guru determine the problem — and it also shows that you care.

3. Demonstrate the problem.

If you happen to be with your guru, show what the computer does. Your guru may want to sit in your chair. That's okay. Just tell your guru what you wanted to do and demonstrate how it didn't work. For example, print your spreadsheet and show your guru the odd characters that appear.

If the guru can't be there in person, try to be near your computer when you're on the phone. Type commands as the guru instructs you. Try to be accurate about describing your situation or what appears on-screen.

4. Offer a suggestion.

This step is optional. Obviously, you don't know how to fix the problem. But, by offering a suggestion, you're showing the guru that you care. If you can't think of anything to say, make something up: "The disk drive needs a new steering wheel" or "The printer is in Italian mode" or "I think it needs to be plugged into a 220-volt socket." The best suggestion to make is "Something needs replacing."

✔ Nobody will help you if you ask the same questions over and over again. After telling you three times how to print your spreadsheet sideways, your guru may become understandably rude and uncooperative. Rather than let that happen, write down the answer and keep a log book handy if you need to.

✔ You don't really want to learn anything about a computer. Even so, some gurus may try to teach you something. If so, grab the old yellow pad and write down everything your guru says. True, you may never use those instructions. But writing them down makes the guru happy.

Chapter 27

(Trouble) Shooting Your PC

*W*hy is it that computers run amok? If cars had the same troubles, no one would drive. Heck, no one would walk, sit, or play anywhere near a road. As humans, we count on things to be reliable and consistent. Life is supposed to be that way. Heaven must be that way. Hell? It's probably wall-to-wall computers down there.

There can be millions of reasons that computers go insane and turn on their owners. (Calling Stephen King! Are you dry on ideas?) I can't list them all here. But I can list several common ones, plus a few steps to take for regaining control of the beast. That's all listed here, as much as I could squeeze into this book (which they tell me is already getting too fat).

> ✔ The problems listed in this chapter are all easily fixable by either you or your PC guru.

> ✔ Before you consider taking your computer into the repair shop, see Chapter 28.

General, Up Front, Panicky Advice

When your computer screws up, STOP WORKING ON IT!

If you're having disk troubles and getting disk reading or writing errors, do not attempt to save new files to disk. Do not attempt to load old files. Just stop everything.

If you have another disk you can use, Drive D, a removable disk, or a floppy drive, try to save to that disk instead. That will work. But do not continue to use the bad disk. Try to fix the disk first.

There. I got it out of my system.

The "It Was Working Yesterday" Syndrome

Computers should make funny noises before they go south. The car? It makes noises. The squeak turns into a whine and then a thumping noise, and then something metal and dripping with hot oil punches up through the hood. That's the car's subtle way of letting you know that something is awry.

With a computer, it just stops working. You do the same things you did yesterday, the day before, all week, month, and year long and then — maybe it's the phase of the moon? — the computer becomes uncooperative. It's maddening.

Just resetting

Whenever something *weird* happens, just reset. Follow the instructions in Chapter 4 for resetting your PC. Do it. When the computer comes alive again, the problem might just be automagically fixed.

✔ Why does this trick work? I have no idea. I think, maybe, the computer just gets tired. It needs to be reset every so often to keep itself awake.

✔ I actually heard a "guru" on the radio once tell a listener that their PC had "tired RAM." Gimme a break.

✔ *Tired* is not the proper term, of course. Typically, what happens is that the PC's memory gets mangled. It never happens on purpose; over time, programs with subtle faults induce memory errors. These errors grow until you need to reset to fix them.

✔ Some programs are memory hogs and prevent other programs from working properly — even though you may have many megabytes of RAM. The ugly finger of blame gets pointed squarely at Microsoft Word here. It's a big memory hog. If you notice that other programs don't seem to function when you're using a memory hog like Word, quit the memory hog program and start it up again later. When you get the message that Word cannot open a document because the PC is "out of memory," you probably have to close everything and restart your computer.

Think about the past

Sometimes the "It was working yesterday" syndrome has a cause, only you just forgot it. Ask yourself these questions:

✔ Did I add any new PC hardware recently?

✔ Did I add any new software?

✔ Have I changed any software?

✔ Have I reset any of the Windows options?

✔ Did I uninstall anything?

Oftentimes you remember what happened: "Oh, yeah, I set the printer to print sideways yesterday. No wonder all my correspondence came out looking so funky."

Killing off a program run amok

Programs can up and die. They don't even wave good-bye or make that "Eugh!" sound kids make when they play army. They just go. Sometimes one program can bring down the entire PC. I experienced this a lot when I was learning to program in the C language. Even some well-meaning programs may collapse the system if they're pushed too hard. To see whether you still have control, try moving the mouse around. If it still works, that's a good sign.

Next, try popping up the Start menu in Windows: Press Ctrl+Esc to do so, which ensures that your keyboard is still functioning. (Press the Esc key to make the Start menu go away.) You may have to wait for Windows to re-spond; sometimes a misbehaving program numbs your PC's operating system for a time.

After that, press the Alt+Tab key combination to switch to another program or window. If that works, chances are that you can safely kill off a program that ran amok. Here's how:

1. Press Ctrl+Alt+Delete.

This step brings up the Close Program window (see Figure 27-1).

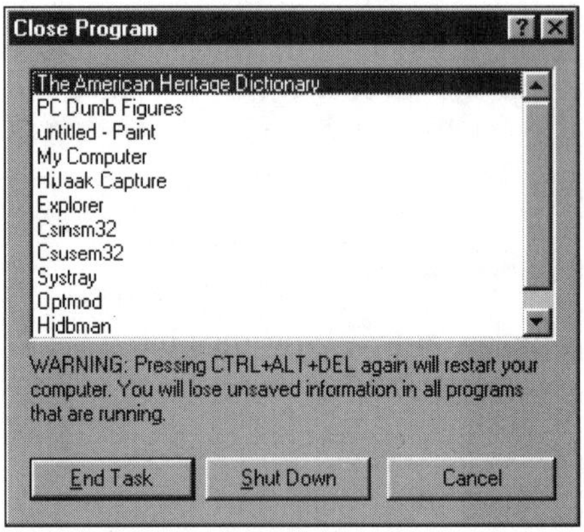

Figure 27-1:
The Close
Program
window.

2. Sniff out any recently deceased programs.

You see the words *not responding* in parentheses after the dead program's name in the list. For example:

```
Sheriff (not responding)
```

Click that program's name in the list.

If more than one program is not responding, repeat all these steps to rid yourself of each of them.

3. Click the End Task button.

The program is killed off.

✔ If you ever do kill off a program with the Close Program window, it may be a good idea to go ahead and restart Windows, just to be safe. Usually a dead program isn't fully killed, and pieces of it get lodged in Windows' teeth and start to rot. (That's kind of a metaphor.)

✔ Be careful not to choose the Shut Down button rather than End Task. Sometimes that makes sense — when you want to "shut down" the AWOL program, for example. But the Shut Down button actually shuts down Windows — and without warning. So don't choose it casually!

✔ If you can't use the mouse or your keyboard, you have to manually reset your computer. Refer to Chapter 4.

"Does My PC Have a Virus?"

A common question that zips through the mind of a bewildered user facing a silly PC is, "Could this be a virus?" I hate to say it, but yes it could — especially if you can answer yes to any of the following:

✔ I download files from the Internet or a local BBS.

✔ I ran a program someone I don't know or trust sent me through e-mail.

✔ I started a game on my PC from a boot disk in drive A.

✔ I use stolen software my friends and co-workers give me.

✔ Other people use my PC.

The answer may be yes in all those situations, and you may not have a virus. But the odds are pretty good that you do have one if you follow those nasty habits. Sadly, Windows doesn't come with any antivirus software. You need to run down to the Software-o-Rama to buy some. Antivirus software removes viruses from your PC and assists you in spotting such nasty programs before they invade again.

✔ Most PC viruses display nasty messages on the screen. The one I got said `Arf! Arf!` and that was it — right after it erased my hard drive.

✔ Some users are too quick to blame the virus. Don't be. The media loves to hype PC virus stories because folks in the media are paranoid about computers anyway (and feel that you are more so).

✔ Believe your antivirus software when it tells you that no viruses are in your PC.

✔ Antivirus software does a particularly good job of detecting and removing the pesky viruses known as *macro* viruses (especially common with Word and Excel), which are sent by e-mail.

✔ Windows doesn't come with virus-protection software, which is ironic because DOS came with a nice virus scanner. In addition to going to the Software-o-Rama for antivirus software, you can also download such utilities from the Web. One of the best places to visit is McAfee. Here's its Web page address:

```
http://www.mcafee.com
```

✔ The Windows 98 Plus! package comes with an antivirus program. Unfortunately, I don't cover the Plus! package in this book. Sorry!

✔ No, you can't give your PC a virus by sneezing on the monitor. But you should have a box of Kleenex handy for when that does happen.

"I Can't See Anything on the Screen!"

Sometimes, the monitor appears blank. Other hints may tell you that the computer is on — it's making noise, its lights are on, and so on — but the monitor appears to be broken. If so, follow these steps:

1. **Make sure that the monitor is plugged in.**

2. **Make sure that the monitor is turned on.**

   Some monitors have On-Off switches separate from the computer's main On-Off switch.

3. **Touch a key.**

   Hey! Did your screen saver come on? Touching a key — either a Shift key or the spacebar — restores the image.

4. **Check the brightness knob.**

   Someone may have turned it down, in which case adjusting the brightness (or contrast) knob brings back the image.

   Another problem may be the software you're running. Some software is dumb. It doesn't let you know if you don't have the proper graphics adapter. Instead, you see a blank screen. If you try the steps I just mentioned and they don't seem to work, reset your computer by following the instructions in Chapter 4.

"Where the @$% Is the Mouse?"

Most likely, the mouse is still on your desktop or clutched in your palm as you roll it about wildly. Unfortunately, the mouse *pointer* on the screen is either missing or frozen in time. Because Windows is a mouse-intensive operation (like Disney), you're probably stuck with nothing to do.

First, move the mouse to the left and right and up and down in large strokes. It may be hiding on the screen.

Second, if you really can't see the mouse pointer or it's invisible in some windows but visible in others, reset the computer! See the section "Just resetting," earlier in this chapter.

If the mouse pointer is frozen on the screen, chances are that your computer has locked up. Dead mouse pointers are dreadful. Try to press Ctrl+Esc to pop up the Start menu and use the Shutdown command. If that doesn't work, wait a few minutes and try again. Then reset the computer (refer to Chapter 4).

In some cases, all you have to do is clean the mouse. Sometimes dust under the ball causes the cursor to stick. Turn your mouse over, snap off or unscrew the little plastic cover, take the little ball out, blow out the dust, and put everything back together.

Printer Trouble

Nothing induces woe like the printer. First, there are so many types of them. Second, printers are very mechanical, which leads to programs mangling and paper jamming. Third, you may use a printer only once in a blue moon, and you can forget how it works. Fourth, your cables may be loose so that the printer and computer can't communicate with each other. All this and more can lead to printer trouble.

Weird characters at the start of the document

Occasionally, you may see some odd characters at the top of every page or just the first page you print. For example, you may see a ^ or &0 *or* E@, or any number of ugly-looking characters that you didn't want there and that don't show up on your screen. It requires a major "Hmmm."

Hmmm.

Those characters are secret printer-control codes. Normally, the printer swallows the characters as it prepares itself to print. The problem is that the software on the computer is sending your printer the wrong codes. Because your printer doesn't understand the codes, it just prints them as is. Hence, you see ugly characters. The solution is to select the proper printer driver for Windows. You want a printer driver that knows your printer and how to send it the proper codes. This stuff is best done by the person who (supposedly) installed your software on the computer. It can be changed in most cases. But better make someone else do that for you.

If you are printing on a network, try printing your document again.

A common problem may be choosing a wrong printer in the Print dialog box (refer to Chapter 16). If your PC uses more than one printer, make sure that you pick the proper one from the list *before* you print. You don't want to send a draft of your résumé and cover letter to your boss, do you?

"The page didn't come out of my laser printer!"

Laser printers are unlike their more primitive impact-printer cousins. With an impact printer, aside from getting mediocre text quality, you get to see what you print as it's printed (even hear it, too!). Laser printers are quiet. But they don't print until one of two situations occurs:

1. **The laser printer prints if you printed a whole page full of text, and not before.**

   Unlike with the dot-matrix printer, nothing is really put down on paper until you fill up a sheet.

2. **You can always force a laser printer to print what's been sent to it so far by giving it a form feed.**

   Press the printer's online or select button to take it offline (the Ready light turns off). Then click the Form Feed or Page Advance button. Remember to put the printer back online when you're done.

In a jam?

Paper flows through your printer like film through a projector; each sheet is magically ejected from a laser printer like the wind blowing leaves on an autumn day. Poppycock! Paper likes to weave its way through the inner guts of your printer like a three-year-old poking his fingers into your VCR. When this happens, your printer can become jammed.

For impact printers, you can unjam most paper by rewinding the knob. But turn off the printer first! This action disengages the advancing mechanism's death grip on the paper platen, which means that it makes it easier to back out the jammed paper. If the paper is really in there tight, you may need to remove the platen. When that happens, you need to take the printer apart to get at the problem; call someone else for help unless you want to take it apart yourself.

For laser printers, a light flashes on the printer when the paper gets jammed. If the printer has a message readout, you may see the message `Paper jam` displayed in any of a variety of languages and subtongues. Make your first attempt at unjamming by removing the paper tray. If you see the end of the paper sticking out, grab it and firmly pull toward you. The paper should slip right out. If you can't see the paper, pop open the printer's lid and look for the jammed sheet. Carefully pull it out either forward or backward. You don't have to turn the printer off first, but watch out for hot parts in the printing mechanism.

Sometimes printers jam because the paper you're using is too thick. If that's the case, removing the paper and trying it again probably won't help; use thinner paper. Otherwise, paper jams for a number of reasons, so just try again and it will work.

Most copy paper comes with recommended sides up. Check the package to see which side should be up.

Another bugaboo: Moisture in the air can lead to paper jams. For some reason, if the paper is not crisp, it just doesn't feed into the printer very well.

"It Won't Even Boot!"

Generally speaking, when your PC won't boot, it's time to call in a pro. There may be nothing you can do, but it helps if you pay attention to a few things.

For example, how far does the computer get? Do you see a startup text message? Does the computer beep? Does Windows show up and then the screen freezes? These observations help whoever fixes the PC to narrow down the problem.

- ✔ If you have a non-booting computer, turn on your monitor before you turn on the console. That way, the monitor is warmed up and ready, allowing you to see any startup messages.

- ✔ If the computer tells you that the setup or CMOS is wrong, you probably have a PC that needs a new battery.

- ✔ If Windows is being stubborn, you can start it in Safe mode. Press the F8 key after you see the Starting Windows message. A menu appears, from which you should choose Safe mode. That starts Windows without any of its fancier features. If Windows does boot (and it looks ugly), you can change some basic options or uninstall software that may be causing the computer to go nuts.

- ✔ Honestly, a non-booting computer can be fixed only by an expert. I sincerely wish that I had an easy fix for you — whacking the monitor — there just isn't such a thing.

Chapter 28

Servicing Your PC

● ●

In This Chapter

▶ Determining whether the problem is hardware or software

▶ Checking cable connections

▶ Checking various power sources

▶ Listening for strange noises

▶ Checking your disk drives

● ●

*T*he best way to handle trouble is to let someone else deal with it. Often, there is no one else. In fact, most computer trouble happens at the absolute worst time: the weekend. Why is it that most computer stores close on Sundays? Maybe it explains why everything is so hectic on Monday mornings. Anyway, you shouldn't be working on the weekends — not when it's sunny outside and especially not when they're having that Russ Meyer Film Festival at the Revival House.

Figure Out Whether It's a Hardware or Software Problem

Your guru, or even you, may be able to fix hardware problems, but most times they require taking the computer to the shop. Software problems, on the other hand, can generally be cured by your guru or by a phone call to the developer's technical-support hot line (or wait-on-hold line). But which is which? It's important to know because computer doctors get irked when you hand them a PC with a software problem. Here are the clues:

1. **Does the problem happen consistently, no matter which program you're running?**

   For example, do Word, Excel, and your accounting package all refuse to send stuff to the printer? If so, it's a hardware problem. Take it to the doctor.

2. Did the problem just crop up?

For example, did the page preview mode work last week but not today? If so, it could be a hardware problem, network problem, or software driver problem — provided that nothing has been changed on your computer and no new software added since the last time the program worked properly. Take it to the doctor.

3. Does the problem happen with only one application?

For example, does the computer always reset when you try to print using Notes? If so, it's a software problem. Call the developer.

Generally speaking, if the problem happens in only one program, it's software. If it's consistent across all your applications or it happens at random times, it's hardware.

Check Cable Connections Yourself

Loose cables can be the bane of existence — and not just in elevators. If your keyboard goes dead, your mouse freezes, or the monitor blinks out, it may be a loose cable. Here's what you should do to check:

1. Turn the computer off.

Shut everything down — *everything*. Refer to Chapter 4 for proper shutdown procedures.

2. Check all the cables behind the computer.

Wiggle each one to make sure that it's in the connector nice and snug.

3. If something is loose, gently plug it back into its socket.

If the cable is stretched, move whatever it is that's stretching it so that you can plug it back into the socket.

Some cables attach to the computer's console with handy thumb screws. Some use tiny annoying screws that require a tiny, annoying screwdriver to tighten them. Others may just plug in limply. The network hose might twist as it plugs in. Printer cables have two wingdings and slide into clips on the printer.

4. After everything is checked out, turn on the computer again and check for the same problem.

If it persists, take the computer to the doctor.

"How much of my PC do I take into the shop?"

If you really can't nail down the problem, should you box up every last jot and tittle by your computer, all the cables and whatnot, and send it all off to the shop? Probably not. But then again, they may ask you to.

I once had a printer problem, and they wanted me to bring the console, printer cable, and printer down to the shop. I didn't have to bring my monitor, keyboard, or mouse because they had those already and didn't suspect them to be guilty of any mayhem.

Always ask what you need to bring and what should stay home. If you do bring several things to the shop, double-check to ensure that they have those items written down on your receipt. You want to get each of them back. It also pays to write your name and driver's license number or some other ID on the *inside* of the console case, under the keyboard, beneath the printer, and so on.

Some Things to Try When the Sucker Just Won't Turn On

Nothing fills thy heart with dread like flipping the PC's On-Off switch and hearing "click." "Hey! The mouse is supposed to go "click!" The PC is supposed to warble to life and entertain me!"

The following sections offer some wholesome suggestions for things to try yourself before phoning the repair shop in a dead panic.

Plug the computer into a different outlet

Sometimes wall sockets go dead. If the computer won't turn on, consider plugging it or your power strip into a different wall socket.

A doohickey you can buy at Radio Shack tests wall sockets. It sells for about $5. You just plug it into a wall socket, and little lights will come on if the socket is supplying juice. Tell the Radio Shack people what it is that you want, and they'll cheerfully steer you over to it.

Bypass the power strip

If you think that the power strip (your computer command center) is broken, try plugging the computer directly into the wall. If it works, the problem is with your power strip. Buy a new one.

Check the circuit breaker

Of course, the only time you really need to check the circuit breaker is when nothing else in the room comes on either. If the lamp is on and your PC sits there dumb, it's probably a wall-socket or power-strip problem. Otherwise, saunter down to the power box and look for one of the switches that's halfway on. Turn it off and then all the way on.

The reason that your circuit breaker *trips* is that something on the line overloaded the circuit. This overload could be caused by faulty equipment or, more likely, too much of a power drain. If you're in an older building, your computer (or laser printer) may be pulling too much power from the line. Solution: Consider buying a new house.

Help Out the PC Doc by Listening for Noises

Computers make a cacophony of sounds: The hard drive whirs, and its chipmunks squeal when you access data; the power supply's fan constantly hums; monitors make a high-pitched noise that only those under 30 can hear; and the keyboard goes clackity-clack as you type on it. If something goes wrong, can you still hear the noises you're supposed to? Is any noise missing? Or are there new and frightening noises?

Although you can't do anything to cure the noise problem, you should make a note of it and tell the computer technician. Unlike car noises, computer noises generally don't go away when you get to the shop.

One noise that increases over time is the hard-drive hum. At first, the sound can barely be noticed. But, as you use the computer, the hum gets louder and louder. This increase is caused by wear on the hard drive's bearings, and there's nothing you can do about it. When the noise becomes unbearable, back it up to another hard drive, the network, a tape backup, ZIP disk, or even floppy disk, if you have to. Then you should consider buying a new hard drive (although the loud noise doesn't always indicate impending doom).

Determine whether a Disk Is Damaged

Like wine, disks age. Unlike wine, older disks lose their flavor and quickly turn to vinegar. Also, disks become damaged with wear and tear. When they wear out, you can't use them again. Ask your guru whether he or she can resuscitate the disk (sometimes that's possible).

You can check any disk yourself by using one of the marvelous disk tools in Windows. Follow these steps:

1. **Open My Computer.**

   Double-click on the My Computer icon to open it and reveal that window full-o-disk drives.

2. **Click on a suspect disk drive in the list.**

3. **Choose File⇨Properties.**

   The drive's Properties dialog box appears.

4. **Click on the Tools tab to bring that panel forward.**

5. **Click the Check Now button.**

   This step starts the ScanDisk program, which checks the health of your disk drive like a doctor listens to your ticker. Figure 28-1 shows the ScanDisk dialog box.

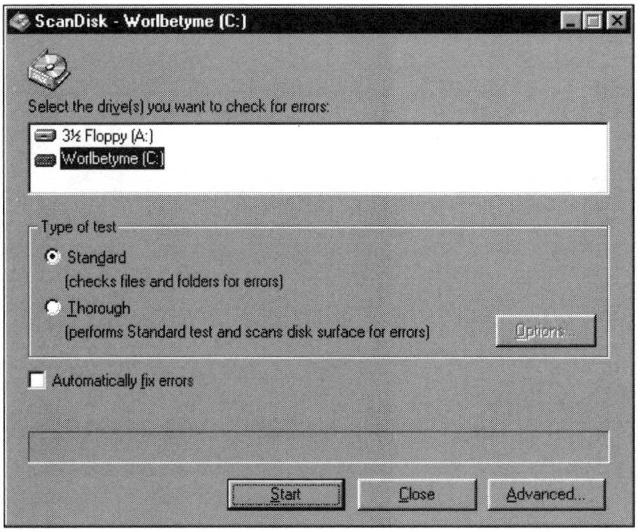

Figure 28-1:
ScanDisk
listens to
your disk's
ticker.

6a. If you haven't been having major disk disasters, check the Standard radio button.

6b. If "disk disasters" is your PC's middle name, check the Thorough button.

7. Click the Start button.

ScanDisk checks your drive and, hopefully, will find nothing wrong.

The scanning takes longer if you check the Thorough button.

After scanning is completed, you see a summary dialog box chock-full of meaningless statistics. Hopefully, no errors were found.

If errors were found, ScanDisk offers to fix them. Direct it to do so. Don't bother with the safety or recovery disk in drive A; it's a waste of time. ScanDisk fixes your hard drive up as best it can under the circumstances.

8. Click the Close button (twice).

You're done. (Click OK once.)

If ScanDisk reports a number of disk errors, it may be a sign that your hard drive's days are up. Do a full backup of all the files on the hard drive, and buy a replacement immediately.

Part VIII
The Part of Tens

The 5th Wave   By Rich Tennant

"OH YEAH, AND TRY NOT TO ENTER THE WRONG PASSWORD."

In this part . . .

They say that Anne Boleyn had 6 fingers. No, she wasn't missing 4; she had 6 fingers on each hand — 12 total. Stand back at the piano recital!

I have just 5 fingers on each hand, thank you very much. And because of that, I decided to end this book with a big part containing lists of tens — important information, rules, do's and don'ts, and other trivia I could conveniently stick into various lists. Poor Anne would have had to do lists of 12.

Yes, I know that there aren't always ten items in each chapter. Sometimes there are more, and sometimes there are less. Still, all the information is good and organized to help you find it quickly. Now get your mind off Henry's wife and back to computers.

Chapter 29

Ten Common Beginner Mistakes

In This Chapter

▶ Buying too much software

▶ Buying incompatible hardware

▶ Not buying enough supplies

▶ Not saving your work

▶ Using a floppy disk instead of the hard drive

▶ Not backing up files

▶ Keeping the monitor up too bright

▶ Turning the computer rapidly on and off again

▶ Not labeling your floppy disks

Sure, there are a million mistakes you can make with a computer, whether it's deleting the wrong word or dropping the monitor on your toe. But I've narrowed the list down to ten (okay, there are nine of 'em). Now, these aren't the classic boners, but they're closely related. These are the day-to-day operating mistakes that people tend to repeat until they're told not to.

Buying Too Much Software

Why would I advise against buying too much software? I'd be a hypocrite if I did because I have hundreds of pieces of software. (Of course, I'm a nerd, so it's all right.)

What I'm really advising against here is buying too much software at the same time. Buying software is much different from buying CDs at the music store. You can listen to a stack of CDs in three days. They're enjoyable the first time, and they age well.

But software is gruesome on the first day, and the enjoyment curve rises slowly after that. It can take months to learn the basics of a single piece of software. Even after a year, you still find features, shortcuts, and new tricks.

So have mercy on yourself at the checkout counter and buy software at a moderate rate. You learn it faster and don't have the headache of installing five programs in one night, finding out that your computer no longer works, and then having to narrow down a list of five suspects at the scene of the crime.

Buying Incompatible Hardware

A computer must be put together like a happy family from a 1950s TV show. All the parts must live together in a dreamy, happy way. A computer's separate pieces all affect each other, and if one of them is belligerent, the whole show can go off the air.

For example, when you're buying a new monitor, you must make sure that the monitor matches your video adapter card (the thing inside your computer that sends the information to the monitor). Likewise, you can't use an old XT keyboard with a newer computer. It just won't work. Sometimes, even the simplest things go wrong: You've bought low-capacity disks, and you have only a high-capacity drive.

There are two ways to avoid these types of errors. First, always have someone else upgrade your hardware. Second, pay attention to everything you buy. Never buy anything — especially floppy disks — in haste.

Not Buying Enough Supplies

People buy toilet paper in big eight-roll packages because they know that they will use it. The same goes with floppy disks and printer paper. Sooner or later, they're all used up.

You don't have to sit down and format an entire case of floppy disks. But when you open a box, format all the disks in that particular box. That way, you always have a formatted disk handy when you need to copy something in a hurry.

Paper's cheaper by the case, too, and it ages well as long as it's kept away from wet garage corners and moist, humid basements.

Not Saving Your Work

The first time you lose something on your computer, it's frustrating but expected. After all, you're a beginner. About the third or fourth time, however, it moves from frustration to aggravation. Eventually, it reaches the despair level.

Whenever you write a blazingly original thought, choose the Save command and save your document to the hard disk. Whenever you write something dumb that you're going to patch up later, choose the Save command, too. The idea here is to choose Save whenever you think about it — hopefully, every four minutes or sooner.

You never know when your computer will meander off to watch Larry King while you're hoping to finish the last few paragraphs of that report. Save your work as often as possible. And always save it whenever you get up from your computer — even if it's just to grab a Fig Newton from the other room.

Using a Floppy Disk Instead of the Hard Drive

Floppy disks have worth. You use them to move files from one PC to another. You need floppies for backups. And floppies are used to distribute software. But one thing you don't need a floppy for is saving your work; always save your work to the hard drive.

I got a letter from a reader once who was frustrated that he couldn't save a large graphics file he created on his floppy disk. It turned out that he had never used his hard drive — not even once since he bought the computer. He was afraid that it would overflow or something. So he used only floppy disks instead. It drove him bonkers.

Please, use your hard drive. Fill it up. Buy another if it gets too full. Use your floppy disks only for backups. Speaking of which. . . .

Not Backing Up Files

Saving work on a computer is a many-tiered process. First, save the work to your hard drive while you're creating it. Then, at the end of the day, back up your work to floppy or ZIP disks. Always keep a safety copy somewhere because you never know.

Backup programs are a pain, but backing up to a tape drive can be painless. Around my office, the computers are scheduled to begin backing up files daily at 2:00 a.m. This process happens automatically to a backup tape stuck in the mouth of every PC.

Keeping the Monitor Too Bright

I don't have much explaining to do here. Keeping the monitor turned up too bright is bad for the eyes, and it wears out the monitor more quickly.

To adjust the monitor to pink perfection, turn the brightness (the knob by the little sun) all the way up and adjust the contrast (the knob next to the half moon) until the display looks pleasing. Then turn the brightness down until the little square outside the picture's edges disappears. That's it!

Turning the Computer Rapidly On and Off

People who turn the computer on and off again rapidly, flicking the switch like a kindergartner at a shopping-mall kiosk, can actually damage their computer. If you must turn off the PC, give it at least a 20-second rest before switching it back on again.

Sometimes, you may not be responsible for turning the PC off and on again quickly. A half-second power outage at my office one day cost me the life of my hard drive. It cost $1,000 to replace (back in 1989). An uninterruptible power supply (UPS) now guards all my PCs in case of another violent attack.

Not Labeling Your Floppy Disks

Floppy disks require a proper label for identification. Even if the label just says "Stuff," it's great (unless you label all your disks "Stuff"). And use the disk labels, not a stick-on note. I once had to grab a disk at the office for a home assignment. The disk had a sticky label on it that fell off. So I had a stack of 20-or-so disks. I took 'em all home because I'd rather waste time there looking for the right disk than examining each disk at an office PC.

When you stick the label on the floppy, be careful not to cover any moving parts: that little window where the disk shows through, that little sliding metal cover, or anything else that looks important.

Chapter 30
Ten Things to Avoid

*Y*our mother loves you very much. Okay, she may not treat you like you're the Lord Almighty, but she loves you. That's important. Before you left the house, Mom typically gave you some rules: Don't run around, don't step in any puddles, don't pick up anything dead, don't eat dirt, stay away from the junkyard, don't throw rocks at crazy Mrs. O'Malley's house, and don't play with that awful Thompson kid. And, of course, you'd promise everything and then rush off to Billy Thompson's house for a trip to the junkyard via old Mrs. O'Malley's.

This chapter contains a list of things to avoid doing, looking at, or stepping in while using your PC. Your mother would probably tell you the same things had she written this book.

Resetting to Quit a Program

Never reset your PC to quit a program. This method was popular in the old days and may still be done in back offices across the land: You were done word processing, so you'd punch the Reset button. That was the way the person before you did it, and the person before them, and before them, and all the way back to Moses.

Always properly quit any program you're running. Never use the Reset button for anything other than a cold, sweaty computer panic.

Booting from an Alien Disk

The number-one way to get a computer virus is to start your computer from a strange floppy disk. I'm not talking about starting the PC by using a boot disk you create or one that comes in a hermetically sealed software box. I'm talking about that — wink, wink — *game* Vern slipped you last week. You know the one. (Heh, heh.) Boot from that disk and you're inviting who-knows-what into your PC. Don't.

Forcing a Floppy Disk into the Disk Drive

Floppy disks fit into your floppy drive in only *one way.* If the disk won't go in, you have one of two problems:

Problem 1: You're putting the disk into the drive the wrong way.

Solution 1: Reorient the disk and try again.

Problem 2: A disk is already in the drive.

Solution 2: Remove the disk from the drive before you put a new disk in the drive.

Freebie Software (For the Most Part)

That's why they have uninstall programs: A lot of the freebie stuff you may get in the mail is junk. Don't waste hard drive space with it.

Plugging the Keyboard into the PC While It's On

```
The sizzling sound you just heard is your motherboard's
last gasp. You need to buy a new one. Or you need to re-
place your keyboard.
Always turn the PC off before you plug anything into it.
You've been warned.
-- Your Computer
```

Opening Things You're Not Supposed To

Not everything inside or around your PC has the words "Don't open" on it. Some stuff is meant to open. New console cases actually have flip-top lids for easy access. The old cases had six screws on them. Why the improvement? Because lots of people open up their PCs for upgrading.

Your monitor? Don't open it. It says so right by the screws. Same goes for some items inside the console, such as the power supply. Don't open them.

Don't open your printer ribbon and especially a laser printer's toner cartridge.

There is no need to open a modem or any other external device on the PC.

If you are bold enough to open your console for upgrading or just poking around, *always* turn off and unplug your PC first. It's good for you and good for your electronics.

Opening or Deleting Random Icons

Unless you created the icon, don't delete it. Unless it's a program you know about, don't run it. Windows has dozens of files and programs, most of which it uses for its own, internal, secretive purposes. Don't randomly click an icon just to see what it does. And don't delete *anything* you didn't create yourself.

Not Properly Quitting Windows

When you're done with Windows, shut it down. Choose the Shut Down command from the Start menu, click OK, and wait until the screen says that it's safe to turn off your PC.

Don't just flip the power switch when you're done. Heavens! That's worse than throwing a rock and breaking old Mrs. O'Malley's window. Sheesh.

Chapter 31

Ten Things That May or May Not Be a PC

● ●

In This Chapter

▶ Desktop PC

▶ Laptop

▶ Notebook

▶ Macintosh

▶ NC (or Windows Terminal)

▶ Network PC

▶ Palm-size PCs

▶ Tower PC

▶ WebTV

▶ Workstation

● ●

*T*his thing, this *computer*. The one over here. The teeny one with a flip-up lid that runs off AA batteries. Is that a PC? What about this laptop? PC or not? And does this tiny box you connect to your TV count as a PC? How about the stuff IBM sells?

Since PC means personal computer, it could theoretically be any device a person uses that somehow computes something. At this stage in the game, that could mean almost anything. The traditional description this book offers is pretty solid for most of what counts as personal computers sold in the world today. The rest may or may not be listed in this chapter.

Desktop PC

Yes, of course. A desktop is a PC. It's a computer that fits on top of your desk, and it used to be the most common model. They call it a "desktop" model because that's where it lives: flat on your desktop.

Laptop

A *laptop* is a portable PC. It has nearly all the features of a desktop PC, but it's smaller, lighter, and lots more expensive. Laptops run off batteries or can be plugged into electrical outlets with an adapter and can typically be opened and set on your lap. They lack the expansion options of a desktop PC, but can be used as desktop models when plugged into a docking station unit. The docking station allows the laptop to use a traditional PC's monitor and keyboard, plus add a few expansion options.

Macintosh

Nope. Not a PC. No way.

Yeah, I know. Technically, a Macintosh is a person's computer. But because the PC is so tied into IBM-DOS-Windows-Microsoft, the Mac people hate it when you call their personal computers PCs. A stubborn lot, but they're switching like lemmings to Windows. So there!

NC (Or Windows Terminal)

NC is a Network Computer, not a Network PC (see the next definition). It's essentially a dumb terminal — just a keyboard and monitor. The rest of the computer is located elsewhere on a network.

A *Windows Terminal* is the same thing as an *NC,* except that it runs specifically Windows — actually, Windows NT.

Network PC

A Network PC is closer to a real PC than an NC. Even so, a *Network PC* is essentially a gutless computer designed to be a slave on a network. It has a hard drive, but no floppy drives or CD-ROM. It would be a bad choice for an individual, but great for big companies that want to enslave all their computer users.

Notebook

Same as a laptop.

Palm-size PCs

Palm-size PCs are a group of computers that work like a teensy laptop. They have little expansion capabilities, but they may have a keyboard and screen and, typically, built-in software. Some even come with a tiny version of Windows called Windows CE. Others, like the 3-Com Palm Pilot, have their own operating system, called the Palm OS. Generally speaking, however, these types of computers are often limited to certain tasks. They make nice road computers if you find a traditional laptop too bulky.

Tower PC

A *tower* PC is like a desktop PC that sits "on its side" on the floor, under your desk, though some "mini-towers" can sit right on your desk. It's a great type of PC to have if you need lots of expansion. I personally prefer them. I put the tower to one side of the monitor and the keyboard below the monitor. That way, the keyboard doesn't block the disk drives, as it does on most desktop systems.

WebTV

WebTV is yet another attempt by the computer industry to use a TV set as a computer monitor to use the Internet to make the TV interactive, and to give those who want to surf the Net the choice to not buy a PC. You'd think that they'd have learned from the early 1980s that it doesn't work, but no. Essentially, *WebTV* is an NC (dumb terminal) hooked up to the Internet through a modem or a cable, with the results displayed on your screen. Some people love 'em, especially if they just want to surf the Web with their remote control after a long day of typing at their real job. If you want an expandable, upgradable, and productive computer, you need a real PC.

Workstation

Your PC could be a workstation. They may call it that at the office. But, traditionally, a workstation is a high-end computer, such as the Silicon Graphics computers that create animations for television and the motion picture industry. Sun Computers makes UNIX workstations. And if you have a PC with all the latest gizmos and hardware installed, it could be used as a workstation, but it's still really only a PC.

Chapter 32

Ten Things Worth Buying for Your PC

. . . .

In This Chapter

▶ Software

▶ Mouse pad

▶ Wrist pad

▶ Antiglare screen

▶ Keyboard cover

▶ More memory

▶ Larger, faster hard drive (when you need it)

▶ Modem

▶ Adjustable, swiveling monitor stand

▶ Power strip

. . . .

I'm not trying to sell you anything, and I'm pretty sure that you're not ready to burst out and spend, spend, spend on something like a computer (unless it's someone else's money). But you may want to consider buying some nifty little things for Mr. Computer. Like ten things worth buying for a dog (leash, cat-shaped squeeze toys, pooper scooper, and so on), these ten things make working with the beast more enjoyable.

Software

Never neglect software. Jillions of different types of software programs are available, each of them designed to perform a specific task for a certain type of user. If you ever find yourself frustrated by the way the computer does something, consider looking for a piece of software that does it better.

Mouse Pad

Rolling your mouse on your tabletop may work okay, but the best surface is a mouse pad, a screen-size piece of foam rubber with a textured top ideal for rolling mice around. Avoid mouse pads with a smooth finish. You pay more for pads with cute pictures or the new mood pads that react to temperature. The best mouse pad is one with your zodiac sign on it, a picture of various cheeses (which makes the mouse happy), or some clever sayings in Assyrian.

Wrist Pad

Like a mouse pad, the wrist pad fits right below your keyboard. It enables you to comfortably rest your wrists while you type.

"Sloppy, sloppy," you hear your typing teacher, Mrs. Goodrich, scream from across the room. "Good typists raise their wrists, striking each key with a deliberate stab!" Before she waddles on over to whack the undersides of your palms with a ruler, tell her this: "Stop, you hulking bruja! Your archaic typing methods aren't needed for the delicate computer keyboard. I can lay my wrists sloppily on a colorful wrist pad and type with reckless abandon. Go make thy husband suffer!"

If you have an ergonomic keyboard, you probably don't need a keyboard wrist pad. The ergonomic keyboard is shaped in such a way that typing on it isn't stressful to your wrists.

Antiglare Screen

Tawdry as it may sound, an antiglare screen is nothing more than a nylon stocking stretched over the front of your monitor. Okay, these are professional nylons in fancy holders that adhere themselves to your screen. The net result is no garish glare from the lights in the room or outside. It's such a good idea that some monitors come with built-in antiglare screens.

Glare is the number-one cause of eyestrain while you're using a computer. Lights usually reflect in the glass, either from above or from a window. The antiglare screen cuts down on the reflections and makes the stuff on the monitor easier to see.

Some antiglare screens also incorporate antiradiation shielding. I'm serious: They provide protection from the harmful electromagnetic rays emitted from your monitor. Are they necessary? No. A lot of alarmists claim that monitors induce nuclear madness. Because this premise can't be disproved, they keep at it. Buy a nuclear-proof shield if it makes you feel better or if you notice your hair falling out in fist-sized clumps.

Keyboard Cover

Buy a protective cover for your keyboard. If you're klutzy with a coffee cup or have small children with smudged fingers using the keyboard, the keyboard cover is a great idea. You may have seen them used in department stores: They cover the keyboard snugly but still enable you to type. A great idea because without it, all this disgusting gunk falls between the keys. Yech!

In the same vein, you can also buy a generic dust cover for your computer. This item preserves its appearance but has no other true value. Use a computer cover only when the computer is turned off (and I don't recommend turning it off). If you put the cover on the PC while it's on, you create a mini-greenhouse, and the computer does — sometimes — melt. Nasty. This result doesn't happen to the keyboard, which is a cool character anyway.

More Memory

Any PC works happier with more memory installed. Memory has an upper limit of anywhere from 128 to 512 megabytes or so, which is ridiculous — well, presently. Still, upgrading your system to 32 or 64 or 128 megabytes of RAM is a good idea. Almost immediately you notice the improvement in Windows and various graphics applications and games. Make someone else do the upgrading for you; you just buy the memory.

Larger, Faster Hard Drive (When You Need It)

Hard drives fill up quickly. The first time it's because you've kept a lot of junk on your hard drive: games, things people give you, old files, and old programs you don't use anymore. You can delete those or copy them to floppy disks for long-term storage. Then, after a time, your hard drive fills up again. The second time, it has stuff you really use. Argh! What can you delete?

The answer is to buy a larger hard drive. If you can, install a second hard drive and start filling it up. Otherwise, replace your first hard drive with a larger, faster model. Buying a faster model is a great way to improve the performance of older PCs without throwing them out entirely.

Modem

A modem is a fun and interesting thing to have on a computer. Although it's not really necessary in most cases, you open up a whole new world when you buy a modem. Suddenly, your single computer becomes one of many. You can use the modem and your phone to dial up other computers, chat with other modem users, and call national networks like America Online, MSN, CompuServe, and Prodigy. Maybe even the Internet. It can be fun and addicting.

One other thing you need if you have a modem is an extra phone line for it. This purchase has the same logic as when you get a separate phone line for your teenager: Modems are notorious phone hogs. When you're on the modem, no one can call in or dial out. It's just best to get an extra line specifically for the modem. The phone company doesn't charge extra for using a modem, and the calls are billed like any other phone call.

Adjustable, Swiveling Monitor Stand

Some monitors have built-in swivel stands. They enable you to adjust the way the monitor points, primarily so that the monitor points right at your face — not at your chest or over your shoulder. If your monitor is static, don't stick a manual under one edge to line it up; get a swiveling stand.

Some monitor stands are actually mechanical arms. They lift the monitor up off the desk and enable you to position it in the air in front of you. Mechanical arms are great but expensive.

Power Strip

Computers use more power plugs than anything you find in the garage or kitchen. You need at least three plugs for the basic computer setup: one for the console, one for the monitor, and another for the printer. Everything else you add — a modem, a scanner, speakers, a desk lamp, or your clock — requires another power socket. To handle them all, buy yourself one of those six-socket power strips.

Some power strips are more expensive than others. They usually offer protection against some electrical nasties that can flow through the power lines. If that happens often in your area, consider the heavy-duty power strip as an investment. For just about everyone, however, the basic $15 model will do.

Chapter 33

Ten Things You Should Always Remember

*W*hat! More things to remember? Stuff to remember besides pressing the F1 key for help? Pressing the spacebar as the "Any" key? Hitting the printer on the side when it jams?

Yeah, but these things aren't as hard to remember. And they're more fun. Keep these ideas floating in the back of your memory for an easier, more trouble-free session while computing.

You Control the Computer

You bought the computer. You clean up after its messes. You feed it floppy disks when it asks for them. You control the computer, simple as that. Don't let that computer try to boss you around with its bizarre conversations and funny idiosyncrasies. It's really pretty dopey; it's an idiot.

If somebody shoved a flattened can of motor oil in your mouth, would you try to taste it? Of course not. But stick a flattened can of motor oil into a disk drive, and the computer will try to read information from it, thinking that it's a floppy disk.

You control that mindless computer just like you control an infant. You must treat them the same way, with respect and caring attention. Don't feel like the computer's bossing you around any more than you feel like a baby's bossing you around during 3 a.m. feedings.

They're both helpless creatures, subject to your every whim. Be gentle.

Upgrading Software Isn't an Absolute Necessity

Just as the models on the cover of *Vogue* change their clothes each season (or maybe that should be change their *fashions* each season), software companies issue perpetual upgrades. Should you automatically buy the upgrade?

Of course not! If you're comfortable with your old clothes, you don't buy new ones just because the season changes. And if you're comfortable with your old software, there's no reason to buy the new version (unless you're a nerd).

The software upgrade probably has a few new features in it (although you still haven't had a chance to check out all the features in the current version). The upgrade probably has some new bugs in it, too, making it crash in new and different ways. Feel free to look at the box, just as you stare at the ladies on the cover of *Vogue*. But don't feel obliged to buy something you don't need. (And I apologize for all the parentheticals.)

If You've Backed Up Your Files, You've Lost Only a Day's Work

Backing up files is about as exciting as vacuuming under the couch. You know it should be done, but it's boring, and chances are that it won't really matter whether you do it.

But accidents happen. Cats can drag dead roaches from beneath the couch when Grandma's over. And your software can crash, leaving you with nothing but a blank screen.

Back up your files every time you're through working with your computer. If you back up your files every day, at the very worst you have lost only one day's worth of work. And train the cat to not only drag out the roaches but also to toss them in the trash before Grandma arrives.

Most Computer Nerds Love to Help Beginners

It's sad, but almost all computer nerds spend most of their waking hours in front of a computer. They know that that's kind of a geeky thing to do, but they can't help it.

It's their guilty consciences that usually make them happy to help beginners. By passing on knowledge, they can legitimize the hours they whiled away on their computer stools. Plus, it gives them a chance to brush up on a social skill that's slowly slipping away: the art of actually talking to a person.

But, remember, computer nerds are more accustomed to computers, not to people. Whenever a nerd gives a command to a computer, the computer acts on it. So whenever a computer nerd has answered your question, write the answer on a stick-on note. Keep the answer handy so that you don't have to bother the computer nerd again with the same question. Don't try to keep nerds away from their computers for too long.

Life Is Too Important to Be Taken Seriously

Hey, simmer down. Computers aren't part of life. They're nothing more than mineral deposits and drab plastics. Close your eyes and take a few deep breaths. Listen to the ocean spray against the deck on the patio; listen to the gurgle of the marble Jacuzzi in the master bedroom.

Pretend that you're driving the convertible through a grove of sequoias on a sunny day, with the wind whipping through your hair and curling over your ears. Pretend that you're lying on the deck under the sun as the Pacific Princess chugs south toward the islands with friendly, wide-eyed monkeys that eat coconut chunks from the palm of your hand.

You're up in a hot-air balloon, swirling the first sip of champagne and feeling the bubbles explode atop your tongue. Ahead, to the far left, the castle's spire rises through the clouds, and you can smell Chef Meisterbrau's waiting banquet.

Then slowly open your eyes. It's just a dumb computer. Really. Don't take it too seriously.

Index

(continued)

(continued)

(continued)

(continued)

(continued)

Notes

WWW.DUMMIES.COM

Discover Dummies Online!

The Dummies Web Site is your fun and friendly online resource for the latest information about ...*For Dummies*® books and your favorite topics. The Web site is the place to communicate with us, exchange ideas with other ...*For Dummies* readers, chat with authors, and have fun!

Ten Fun and Useful Things You Can Do at www.dummies.com

1. Win free ...*For Dummies* books and more!
2. Register your book and be entered in a prize drawing.
3. Meet your favorite authors through the IDG Books Author Chat Series.
4. Exchange helpful information with other ...*For Dummies* readers.
5. Discover other great ...*For Dummies* books you must have!
6. Purchase Dummieswear™ exclusively from our Web site.
7. Buy ...*For Dummies* books online.
8. Talk to us. Make comments, ask questions, get answers!
9. Download free software.
10. Find additional useful resources from authors.

Link directly to these ten fun and useful things at
http://www.dummies.com/10useful

For other technology titles from IDG Books Worldwide, go to
www.idgbooks.com

Not on the Web yet? It's easy to get started with *Dummies 101*®: *The Internet For Windows*®*98* or *The Internet For Dummies*®, 5th Edition, at local retailers everywhere.

Find other ...*For Dummies* books on these topics:
Business • Career • Databases • Food & Beverage • Games • Gardening • Graphics • Hardware
Health & Fitness • Internet and the World Wide Web • Networking • Office Suites
Operating Systems • Personal Finance • Pets • Programming • Recreation • Sports
Spreadsheets • Teacher Resources • Test Prep • Word Processing

IDG BOOKS WORLDWIDE BOOK REGISTRATION

Register This Book and Win!

We want to hear from you!

Visit **http://my2cents.dummies.com** to register this book and tell us how you liked it!

- ✔ Get entered in our monthly prize giveaway.

- ✔ Give us feedback about this book — tell us what you like best, what you like least, or maybe what you'd like to ask the author and us to change!

- ✔ Let us know any other *...For Dummies*® topics that interest you.

Your feedback helps us determine what books to publish, tells us what coverage to add as we revise our books, and lets us know whether we're meeting your needs as a *...For Dummies* reader. You're our most valuable resource, and what you have to say is important to us!

Not on the Web yet? It's easy to get started with *Dummies 101*®: *The Internet For Windows*® *98* or *The Internet For Dummies*®, 5th Edition, at local retailers everywhere.

Or let us know what you think by sending us a letter at the following address:

...For Dummies Book Registration
Dummies Press
7260 Shadeland Station, Suite 100
Indianapolis, IN 46256-3945
Fax 317-596-5498

...FOR DUMMIES™

BESTSELLING BOOK SERIES FROM IDG